In the Skies of Europe

Air forces allied to the Luftwaffe
1939–1945

In the Skies of Europe

Air forces allied to the Luftwaffe
1939–1945

Hans Werner Neulen

Translated by Alex Vanags-Baginskis

THE CROWOOD PRESS

© 1998 by Universitas Verlag
in der F.A. Herbig Verlagsbuchhandlung GmbH, München

First published in Great Britain in 2000 by
The Crowood Press Ltd
Ramsbury, Marlborough
Wiltshire SN8 2HR

English translation © The Crowood Press 2000

British Library Cataloguing in Publication Data
A catalogue record for this book is available from the British Library.

ISBN 1 86126 326 0

Typeset by Phoenix Typesetting
Ilkley, West Yorkshire

Printed and bound in Great Britain by Biddles, Guildford

Contents

Acknowledgements

The author is extremely grateful that, during the research for this book, he could rely on the invaluable support of various archives, museums and private individuals, who provided documents, data, information and photographs without which it would have been impossible to compile this study. No fewer than fifteen colleagues in the writing fraternity who specialize in the subject of contemporary history and the history of aviation unselfishly allowed the author access to their archives as well as the results of their own research work, thus helping to resolve many uncertain points.

In Italy helpful assistance was provided by my long-standing colleagues and friends, Dr Marino Vigano and Dr Nicola Cospito, as well as Nino Arena and the journalist and publisher Giorgio Apostolo; in Belgium Jean-Louis Roba, Eric Mombeek and the late aviation expert Gaston Botquin, who sadly died on 28 March 1997, have my gratitude. The co-operation from Scandinavia was indispensable, and was provided in exemplary fashion by my good friends Tapio Huttunen in Finland, Lennart Westberg in Sweden, and Jörn Junker in Denmark. Collaboration with the Hungarian aviation historian Dénes Bernád, who is now living in Canada, proved extremely fruitful, as was that with Mitja Maruško in Slovenia, Hendrik Arro in Estonia and Alex Vanags-Baginskis in Great Britain. Without the help of Todor Valkov in Sofia it would not have been possible for the author to acquire an accurate synopsis of the history of the Bulgarian air force. Other invaluable assistance was furnished by Frédéric Liège in France and Carlos Caballero in Spain. In Germany, it was mainly such experts as Gebhard Aders, Georg Schlaug and Hans Ring who assisted the author with material, suggestions, hints and their own extensive specialist knowledge. Not to be forgotten are Ian E. Hougen, who undertook the time-consuming task of translating the extensive and unpublished manuscripts of his brother Harald from Norwegian into German, or Sighart Dinkel from the Traditionsverband JG 27 traditional formation.

ACKNOWLEDGEMENTS

Of the different archives and museums that readily gave the author various particulars, information and photographs, special mention should be made of the Krigsarkivet in Stockholm, the Bundesarchiv/Zentralnachweisstelle in Aachen, the Archiv der Deutschen Lufthansa AG in Cologne under the current management of Werner Bittner, the Heeresgeschichtliche Museum/Militärhistorische Institute in Vienna, the Centre d'Études et de Documentation Guerres et Sociétés Contemporaines (CEGES) in Brussels, as well as the Keski-Soumen Ilmailumuseo at Tikkakoski in Finland, whose director, Hannu Valtonen, supported the author in exemplary manner.

Special thanks are due to the eye witnesses from eight countries who obligingly and patiently answered all questions put to them by the author, and, by their valuable statements, contributed to a better understanding of the contemporary time and aviation history of that epoch. They are Luigi Gorrini in Italy, Henri Dannemark and Joseph Justin in Belgium, Remi Milk in Sweden, 'Joppe' Karhunen in Finland, Alf Lie and Harald Hougen in Norway, the former wartime airmen Hendrik Arro, Kalju Reitel, Dr Benno Abram, Kalju Alaküla, Valdo Raag and Arvo Putmaker in Estonia, Arnolds Mencis in Latvia, and 'Edu' Neumann, Heinrich Heuser, Indulis Ozols, Charles F. Kern and Artur Gärtner in Germany.

Cologne, October 1997

8

They should have had more
squadrons to hang in the sky
than they actually had planes.
Gerd Gaisler, *Die Sterbende Jagd*
(The Dying Chase)

Introduction

Until now no cohesive history of the air forces of Italy,
Romania, Hungary, Bulgaria, Croatia, Slovakia, Finland, and
Vichy-France, or of the foreign members of the German
Luftwaffe in the Second World War, has been available.[1]
Indeed, it could probably only be compiled now, after the fall
of the Iron Curtain, when the aviation historians in Eastern
Europe could tackle the subject without making any ideological
'amendments' and the survivors in the former Communist
countries are able to express themselves about the past without
fear of reprisal.

The air forces of what are, for the most part, Eastern European
countries and Italy played a bigger role during the war years
than has been hitherto conceded by research of the contemporary history. To be sure, they never achieved the
personnel strength and material size of the German Luftwaffe but, for a while, a quarter of all aircraft facing the Soviet
Union were flown by either allied or foreign pilots of the
Luftwaffe.

In 1941 Romania, Hungary, Finland, Italy, Slovakia and
Croatia contributed nearly 980 aircraft, of various types and
varying quality, to the conflict against the Soviet Union. Apart
from the participation of Romania and Finland, which was
expressly desired by Berlin, National Socialist interest in the
participation of other countries in the attack on the Soviet
Union was initially limited, and the air forces of these countries
were viewed with some scepticism. All this was to change during
the course of the war because, to make good personnel and
material losses, 'the Luftwaffe increasingly fell back on the
smaller air forces of its Eastern allies,'[2] which then played a

9

decisive role, especially on the southern flank of the Eastern Front.

However, the industrial capacity of Germany's allies, as well as that of Finland and Vichy-France, which was dependent on Germany, did not suffice to compete with the leading Allied powers. All the countries allied to Germany could produce only 22,000 aircraft during the war years (*see* Appendix 2), while at the same time the German aviation industry built 117,881 aircraft, the British 131,549, the Soviet Union 158,218 and the United States no fewer than 324,750 units. This material and quantitative inferiority, which, in a war of technical attrition, could hardly be made good by quality, soon became generally noticeable, and sarcastic ditties about the supposed invincibility of the Axis began to circulate in the Reich. For instance, in the Berlin air raid shelters some wag would always be ready to recite the verse *'Wer im Keller hat durchwacht die Nächte, Der kennt die Kraft der Achsenmächte'* ('Those who have laid awake all night in cellars, know the strength of the Axis powers').

Germany, who initially only hesitantly supplied aircraft to its allies and vassals – often consisting of used machines that were of unsatisfactory quality and technically obsolescent – was soon induced to deliver modern aircraft as well, to enable Hungary, Romania, Bulgaria and Finland to create at least modest aerial umbrellas over their homelands and their most important towns and industrial centres. The inclination to pass on inferior aircraft to one's allies was incidentally not a German prerogative: the Americans, for example, channelled large quantities of their somewhat wanting Bell P-39 Airacobra to the Soviets, as well as to the Free French air force and the southern Italian Co-Belligerent air force.[3]

The Messerschmitt fighters delivered abroad were mostly flown by first-class pilots. While it is decidedly questionable that the German allies (including the Finns) actually shot down 16,000 Soviet aircraft on the Eastern Front as claimed,[4] it cannot be overlooked that, until 1944, despite inadequate training and shortage of aviation fuel, the Finns, Hungarians and Italians produced fighter formations comparable to the international elite. Furthermore, as far as the Hungarians and Italians were concerned, they did not give in but fought on even when there could no longer be any doubt about the outcome of the war.

From 1943 onwards at the latest, fighters were the most important weapon of the Axis air forces for the defence of their homeland. The Italian Regia Aeronautica, the Romanian FARR and the Hungarian Honvéd air force did not possess impressive bomber components, nor forces that would have been in a position to carry out strategic operations. It was left to the Italians, who also had torpedo-bomber formations manned by highly motivated crews, to fly at least a few isolated long-range operations that showed signs of strategic purpose but which only served psychological propaganda ends.

Nobody asked the pilots in Budapest, Bucharest, Helsinki, Rome, Bratislava, Sofia or Zagreb if they wanted to take part in a war against the Western allies. Anti-Communism was probably one of the very few common structural elements that brought them into an alliance. Some of them, such as the Finns and the Romanians, harboured a legitimate resentment against the Soviet Union for annexing parts of their respective territories; others followed the orders of their governments without any great enthusiasm. The fight for a German colonial empire in the East was neither their concern nor their desire. If they had pronounced political opinions they were mainly concerned with the creation of a Greater Romania, Greater Hungary or, in the case of Croats, the liberation from the Serbian subordination – but not a racially organized Europe in which the National Socialists would set the tone.

As a rule the performance and operational readiness of the air forces of the countries allied to Germany reached their highest level when their homelands were in immediate danger, and they had to protect their populations against blows from the skies.[5] One fighter pilot, Romanian Alexandru Serbanescu, offered the following explanation, just a few days before his death in action in August 1944, of what motivated pilots to carry on fighting even in the most desperate situations: 'As long as I live, I am not going to allow aircraft to bomb Romanian soil and kill Romanian fellow citizens unpunished.'[6]

The post-war fates of the members of the air forces allied to Germany and the foreign members of the German Luftwaffe differed, and were largely determined by the respective political systems in their homelands. The Finns returned to normal everyday life, the Spaniards achieved elevated positions as general officers, while those Italians who had not followed their king in autumn 1943 were ostracized for years to come. The Slovaks and Romanians were silenced, the Hungarians – if they were mentioned at all – were described as criminals and traitors. The worst fate awaited the Croat and Bulgarian pilots, many of whom had to suffer torture and death, and long, grue- some imprisonment. The Estonians and Latvians were forced to work as Stalin's slaves in the Gulag camps. Whenever possible, many of the remaining pilots made their way to the West, while Italian members of the Republican air force emigrated to Argentina.

In conclusion, the author feels it to be of some importance to clear up the situation regarding the described aerial victories. The practice of attributing individual victories to fighter pilots goes back to 1914, and, as a rule, is not seriously questioned by aviation historians. However, one has to take care not to treat these victories as some kind of 'sporting achievements'. Aerial combat had long since lost its chivalrous and sporting character, and the idea of a fair duel became extinct in massed warfare and ideological conflict, although some still tried to retain an element of chivalry. What counted was the destruction of enemy aircraft; the death of the enemy crew was either considered inci- dental or deliberately intended. The German author and former fighter pilot Gerd Gaisler is surely right when he describes the enemy pilots as hostile cousins who would spit 'iron into each other's cockpit', whose only ambition was to 'stamp each other out'; but they did not actually mean 'each other', 'but the insignia that were on their aircraft'.[7]

That attitude, too, was to change during the course of the war, because with extended duration of the conflict, the 'hostile cousins' became merciless opponents. A clear indication of this was the increasing number of cases of pilots, who having baled out of their stricken aircraft and hanging completely helpless beneath their parachutes, were deliberately shot at and killed by enemy fighter pilots.[8] This revealed not only increased radicalization and brutality, but was an indication that the victorious pilot who perpetrated this deed was afraid that his defeated enemy might – if not eliminated – climb into another aircraft and appear in action again.

Introduction to the English Edition

The author is pleased to take the opportunity offered by this English edition to correct a few errors found in the original German edition, adjust the list of the most successful Italian fighter pilots in accordance with the latest research data, and include some additional material. This relates to Russian airmen serving in the German Luftwaffe and the Dutch pilots, whose almost unknown story is described in a short new chapter.

At the same time the author would also like to thank all those who have perused the German edition and in a sympathetic manner offered constructive criticism, suggestions and information that has contributed to this improved narrative. Of these, F. Gerdessen and Edo van der Laan from the Netherlands, and an Italian colleague, Giovanni Massimelo, deserve special mention.

The translator, Alex Vanags-Baginskis, too, deserves special praise. Despite all kinds of difficulties, he has managed to complete his task with patience, commitment and a high degree of competence. It is seldom that an author has the privilege of having a translator who is not only an expert but, simultaneously, someone who was closely affected by the events and can thus add the necessary feeling for the historical context of this narrative.

Hans Werner Neulen
Cologne, summer 1999

I
The Allies

Italy

Regia Aeronautica

Sufficit animus – Boldness is enough – was the motto coined for the Italian torpedo bombers at the end of the First World War by the Italian aviator and poet Gabriele d'Annuncio (12 March 1863–1 March 1938). It could also have been the motto for the entire Regia Aeronautica. To those pilots, who often had to face almost overwhelming odds with underpowered, under-armed and obsolete machines, only boldness remained as a means of compensating for the technical inferiority. For all that, in the early 1930s the Royal Italian Air Force was considered an efficient, highly motivated and combat-efficient service. Conflicts in Ethiopia and Spain seemed to confirm this view. But the Regia Aeronautica failed to live up to expectations. Too many wrong decisions and failed developments of combat aircraft prevented it from becoming an equally matched partner for the German Luftwaffe or opponent to the British. The story of the Italian air force became a tragedy.

The Regia Aeronautica was founded on 28 March 1923. An independent Air Ministry came into being two years later, in August 1925. Mussolini, who had a civil pilot's licence since May 1923 and obtained his military pilot's licence as well in 1933, initially took over the Air Ministry himself. Acting as his Undersecretary of State for Air was Artillery General Alberto Bonzani. The army and navy watched jealously that this new competition, the Armata Azzurra (Blue Armada), did not develop at their expense. Like many other problems in the Fascist Italy, the question of the auxiliary air forces of the army and navy were solved by a compromise. The statute of 4 May 1925 envisaged that the Armata Aerea (air power) as the actual air force would have 78 squadrons. The other branches of the armed forces nominally had more aircraft: the army had 57 squadrons, the navy 35, and another 12 squadrons were based in the Italian colonies.[1] However, all these units remained an

17

integral part of the Regia Aeronautica, which was thus made up of four contingents.

After the first consolidation phase of the air force, Mussolini replaced General Alberto Bonzani with Italo Balbo in November 1926. With this move one of the most interesting protagonists of Italian Fascism stepped on to the stage of aviation politics.[2] Balbo, born on 6 June 1896 in Quartesana, was one of the most popular *gerarchi* (dignitaries) of the regime. His youthful charm, his boldness, dynamism and organizational talent impressed both friends and opponents. Balbo, who had served as an officer in the First World War, joined Mussolini's fighting formations at Ferrara early in 1921. The Squadristi, built up and guided by Balbo, carried out a campaign that was virtually a civil war against the Socialists, smashing their offices and organizational installations in the lower Po province. In October 1922 Balbo was one of the four Quadrumviri who led and co-ordinated the Fascist 'March on Rome'. Two years later, in November 1924, due to moral involvement in the murder of a political opponent, Balbo had to relinquish his post as commander of the militia. This did not, however, mean the end of his career. In April 1925 he founded the provincial newspaper *Corriere Padano*, which distinguished itself with its intelligent commentary and independent views, and in many aspects took a controversial stand against the official line dictated from Rome. In November 1925 Mussolini appointed Balbo as Undersecretary in the Ministry of National Economy; a year later Balbo moved into the Air Ministry.

In 1926 the Italian aviation industry produced hardly more aircraft than in 1915[3] and Balbo too was unable to increase noticeably the State financial allocation for the Regia Aeronautica. The Italian air force received only one seventh of the defence budget; the bulk was shared by the army and the navy.[4] From 1927 until 1933 Balbo never received more than 770 million lire (approximately 40 million dollars) a year to build up and modernize the Armata Azzurra. Nevertheless, even with such meagre means, he succeeded in building up an independent, efficient and disciplined force, and gained for it world-wide recognition. As indicated by the rather modest financial support, it was never the spoiled child of the regime, but, at least on one level, it justified the reputation of the *arma fascistissima*, the Fascist arm of the service. Mussolini's ideology as well as that of the air force propagated the glorification of technology and modernity and appealed to heroic individualism.

One of Balbo's undisputed achievements was the build-up of Italian civil aviation. The first regular airline service was started in April 1926, with a flight from Turin to Trieste; by the end of the year 4,000 passengers had taken the opportunity to travel by air in Italy. By 1930 the number had increased tenfold, and Italy had become the third largest air travel nation in Europe after Germany and France. The national airline company, Ala Litoria, was founded in 1934, with 79 aircraft and 30 air traffic routes, and included the Fiat-owned Avia Linee-Italiana, which serviced four routes with 12 aircraft. Finally, in 1939, the Linea Aerea Transcontinentali Italiane (LATI) with Savoia-Marchetti SM.83 aircraft, started a regular air mail service to Brazil, which extended to Argentina in July 1941; this was to be operated until December of that year when the Italians had to suspend their flights to South America.[5]

Balbo and the Regia Aeronautica became famous for their record-breaking 'round trips' with seaplanes. Between 1 April 1927 and 1 November 1939 Italian airmen established no fewer than 110 records, winning world championships in round trips, long-range flights, high speed flights and altitude flights.[6] Possibly their most brilliant success was the world speed record of 664km/h (412.6mph) achieved by the Macchi-Castoldi MC.72 floatplane in March 1933. In October 1934 the Italian pilot Francesco Agello increased the world speed record to 709km/h (440.6mph).[7] Prerequisites for such victories were appropriate technical preparations and training of personnel involved. To prepare this essential foundation Balbo created the necessary schools and training centres. In 1927 a study and experimental centre was founded at Montecello, followed in 1928 by the famous High-Speed Flight School in Desenzano on Lake Garda, and, in 1933, the Ocean Air Traffic Training School at Ortebello, near Rome.

The Italians amazed the world especially with their round

trips.[8] Between May 1928 and August 1933 Italian airmen carried out four long-range formation flights with seaplanes. Of these, the first flight to South America in 1930, and the flight to the USA and back to Italy again in 1933, a total of 19,000km (11,800 miles), were real pioneering achievements and appreciated as such. Balbo had prepared the USA flight thoroughly. No fewer than 11 ships for weather observation and reporting were stationed along the flight route. The Americans in Chicago and New York prepared an enthusiastic reception for the crews of the S.55X flying boats. Balbo, who led the flight himself, was received by President Roosevelt, and a street in Chicago was named after him.

The flight had indeed been a 'wonder of organization, harmony and discipline'.[9] With this collective bold venture, Balbo had accomplished one of the last pioneering deeds in aviation. The reasons for these spectacular formation flights were obvious. For one thing, they trained the flying personnel in massed flights; for another, they served to raise funds for the Italian aviation industry. Nor should their political propaganda value be underestimated: these *crociere* (round trips) were also intended to increase the prestige of Italy and Fascism in the world.

Mussolini did not stint his gratitude and appreciation for his chief of aviation. In August 1928 Balbo was made a General of Aviation, in September 1929 he took over the Air Ministry and, after the Chicago flight, was promoted to the rank of Marshal. However, in November 1933, the Duce relieved Balbo of his duties and made him the governor of Libya. Mussolini himself took over the Air Ministry, with General Giuseppe Valle as Undersecretary of State.

This periodic exchange of ministers and higher functionaries was part of Mussolini's style of leadership. In transferring Balbo, another factor may also have played a role: the Duce may have wanted to remove the opportunity for any further spectacular successes by an extremely popular rival. It had also not escaped Mussolini's attention that the record massed flight conception favoured by Balbo had in fact not significantly improved the efficiency of the Regia Aeronautica.[10] This had

Formation Flights by Italian Seaplanes 1928–33

Period	Aircraft Used	Route	Distance	Commander/ Leader
25.5.1928– 2.6.1928	51 S.59 8 S.55 1 Cant 22	Ortebello–Western Mediterranean– Sardinia–Mallorca– Spain–France– Ortebello	2,800km (1,740 miles) in 6 stages	General De Pinedo
5–19.6.1929	37 S.55 2 S.59 2 Cant 22	Ortebello–Eastern Mediterranean– Athens–Black Sea– Varna–Odessa– Ortebello	4,700km (2,920 miles) in 9 stages	Col Pellegrini
17.12.1930– 15.1.1931	14 S.55A (of which 3 were lost)	Ortebello–Africa– South Atlantic– Rio de Janeiro	10,400km (6,462 miles) in 6 stages	Italo Balbo
1.7.1933– 12.8.1933	25 S.55X (of which 2 were lost)	Ortebello– Great Britain– Iceland–Atlantic– Chicago–New York– Atlantic–Portugal– Rome	19,000km (11,800 miles)	Italo Balbo

already been clearly pointed out by General Francesco de Pineda, a rival of Balbo, in a memo prepared as early as August 1929: 'With a great expenditure of energy it is possible to form a wing of seaplanes into a formation or 15 squadrons for a training exercise of air power, and so bolster the reputation of the air force, but the striking power of the air force is another matter entirely…'[11]

As a matter of fact, Balbo had considerably raised the effectiveness of the Italian armed forces. His concept of modernization encompassed marked strengthening of the navy and air force at the expense of the army. The army was to be limited to just 20 divisions, but these would be highly mobile and, in the manner of an expedition corps, could be ready for action anywhere at short notice. The size of the air force was to be quadrupled. However, neither the financial situation of the Italian kingdom nor its foreign policy made such rearmament measures feasible; furthermore, such forced rearmament also endangered the domestic power balance.[12] Yet one thing one could hold against Balbo was his failure to establish an original air doctrine. He adopted the stance of General Giulio Douhet (1869–1930) – who called for an independent, strong bomber arm, which, by ruthless destruction of the enemy's towns and industry, would force it to its knees – only in so far as the importance and the complete independence of the air force were concerned. Thus, by a statute of 6 January 1931, the auxiliary air forces of the army and navy were considerably reduced, without, however, regulating the co-operation between the three branches of the armed services.

General Valle, Balbo's successor, hardly brought anything new to the Regia Aeronautica, barring one – rather mad than otherwise – idea he developed during the Ethiopian campaign: if Britain should go to war against the Italian colonial venture he wanted to organize special suicide squadrons that would dive on the British fleet. The general, 'a rather grey character, in a field abounding in talented personalities'[13] had taken over an air force that abounded with self-confidence, in a society where the pilot had become a symbol of daring, bravery and technical proficiency. The recent indisputable successes of the Regia Aeronautica waterborne aircraft had led to self-deception and a sense of complacency in Valle as much as anyone. Yet it was precisely in the field of aircraft engines that considerable deficiencies lay, because Italian industry was not in a position to develop an efficient low-drag liquid-cooled engine that would produce an output of 1,000–1,500hp.

The first test for the air force came in October 1935, when Mussolini ordered an attack on the Ethiopian kingdom. During the final stages of the war, the number of aircraft deployed on the Italian side rose to 386 machines,[14] which operated from Eritrea and Somalia. The airmen of the Regia Aeronautica did not have to face any opposition in the air because the Ethiopian 'air force' consisted of only 15 aircraft at the start of the hostilities, only nine of which were serviceable.[15] None of these aircraft carried out any operational sorties, their activity being limited to transport and liaison flights.

The absolute aerial superiority of the Italians was one of the prerequisites for their victory over an inferior enemy. But the Regia Aeronautica also lost its good name in this colonial war because it used poison gas bombs against the Ethiopian defenders.[16] This not only violated the basic principles of humanity and international law but was also a decidedly cynical act for a nation that had tried to justify its campaign by claiming, among other things, that slavery still ruled in Ethiopia. This conflict cost the Italian air force 72 aircraft and the death of 122 aircrew members.[17] The fighting was by no means over after the official end of hostilities on 5 May 1936, however, because, for the next 13 months, the Armada Azzurra had to assist Italian forces in fighting against the Ethiopian guerrillas. By that time, Mussolini's sons and the Fascist functionaries who had taken part in the campaign were already back home in Italy. The best known among them had served in the 15th Bomber squadron 'La Disperata'. These included Bruno and Vittorio Mussolini, the Minister of Propaganda and later Foreign Affairs Galeazzo Ciano, the former Secretary of the Fascist Party, Roberto Farinacci, the journalist and Party functionary Alessandro Pavolini, as well as Ettore Muti, the future secretary of the Fascist Party.

After the official conclusion of fighting in Ethiopia, General Valle presented his concept for the re-equipment and modernization of the air force, the 'R' Programme.[18] This envisaged an expansion of the air force to 3,000 aircraft by December 1940. No less than 45 per cent of the aircraft strength was to comprise bombers, 30 per cent was to be fighters, 19 per cent reconnaissance aircraft, 5 per cent close support and assault aircraft, and 1 per cent transport aircraft. This programme could not, at first, be realized. For one thing, there was no consistent political-strategic foundation on which to base it. For another thing, the interests of those affected by this programme – the army, navy and industry – were too different. Within the Regia Aeronautica, too, two schools of thought were in conflict for ascendancy. On the one side were the 'Douhettiani', supporters of the strategic bomber; on the other, the adepts of Amedeo Mecozzi (1892–1971), who argued that Italian industry was too weak to realize the Douhet concept and therefore vigorously advocated the tactical fighter-bomber and assault aircraft. Moreover, Italian participation in the Spanish Civil War absorbed aircraft, personnel and industrial capacity, hampering a purposeful modernization of the air force. In 1939, after three years delay, the 'R' Programme finally entered its realization phase, with a change in emphasis to fighters. This new programme was to comprise 782 bombers, 857 fighters, 484 reconnaissance aircraft, 365 training aircraft and 6,053 aero engines.[19] Even taking into consideration the cost in aircraft of the Spanish Civil War, this was a rather modest programme.

On 17 July 1936 General Francisco Franco had begun an uprising against the People's Front government in Spain. On the evening of 24 July the Duce decided to help the insurgent Nationalists prevent Spain from coming within French or Soviet zones of influence. On 29 July the vessel *Morandi* left La Spezia for Melilla in Spanish Morocco, loaded with ammunition, bombs, aviation fuel and aircraft spares. A day later Lt Col Ruggero Bonomi – commander of the Ocean Air Traffic Training School founded by Balbo in Ortebello and former participant in the formation flight over the Western Mediterranean in 1928 – received an order to take off for Melilla with 12 Savoia-Marchetti SM.81 bombers.[20] To avoid international complications the crews were then to join the Spanish Foreign Legion. Among the Italian airmen was Ettore Muti, the Consul of Militia and a highly decorated participant of the Ethiopian campaign who later was to become Secretary of the Fascist Party. Officially he was a bomber pilot, unofficially an observer for the Foreign Minister, Count Ciano. All nationality and recognition markings were removed from the SM.81 bombers, and the crews, all of whom had volunteered, had to dress in nondescript flying overalls.

The 12 Savoia-Marchetti aircraft took off from Elmos in Sardinia at the crack of dawn on 30 July. Normally these bombers, armed with five 7.7mm machine guns, had a maximum speed of 340km/h (211mph) and a range of 1,800 km (1,118 miles), so should have covered the 1,300km (808 mile) route to Melilla without any problems. In the event an extremely strong headwind made a shambles of the calculations. Apart from that, the pilots were instructed to fly in formation and in sight of each other, and this enforced flight regime also used its share of the fuel reserves. The estimated flight time was 4½ hours, but after 5 hours the aircraft had still only reached the latitude of Oran. One of the bombers crashed into the sea and the crew drowned. Eventually only nine machines landed at Nador (Melilla). Two others, short of fuel, were forced to make emergency landings in Algiers. A routine flight had cost this detachment a third of its strength and the lives of nine airmen.

The Italian aircrew joined the aviation formation of the Spanish Foreign Legion (Aviacion del Tercio) and began flying operations for the Franco forces. The Italians supported the Nationalists to a far greater extent than National-Socialist Germany did. Altogether Mussolini sent to Spain more than 70,000 ground troops and 6,000 aviation personnel, as well as about 720 aircraft, including 100 three-engined SM.79 bombers and 380–400 Fiat CR.32 fighters.[21] Soon the Italian airmen were combined into the Aviazione Legionaria and their Fiat CR.32 fighters clearly dominated in the air, proving superior to the Soviet Polikarpov I-15 biplanes and I-16 monoplanes of the Republican air force. Indeed the Italian aircraft earned for itself, according to Italian propaganda, the reputation of being 'the best fighter biplane of all time'.[22] All told, the Aviazione Legionaria claimed to have shot down 903 Republican aircraft between 1936 and 1939, a figure that in all probability was greatly exaggerated; a more realistic number seems to be about 500 aerial victories.[23] For their part, the Italians lost 86 aircraft in combat and another 100 as a result of other causes, in addition to nearly 200 flying personnel.[24]

But these successes did not directly benefit the Regia Aeronautica, and the machines sent to Spain remained in Nationalist hands after Franco's victory. This effectively reduced the establishment of the Italian air force. The Spanish adventure had cost the Regia Aeronautica almost 10 per cent of total Italian aircraft production between 1935 and 1939, which amounted to 7,573 aircraft.[25] To be sure, only a few of these were up-to-date models, such as the SM.79. Much more important than the material losses was the fact that the Italian air force command drew the wrong conclusions from the air war over Spain. The Air Ministry, blinded by the success of the CR.32, persisted in its belief that the biplane was a fighter *par excellence*, and in 1938 ordered a large series production of the more advanced Fiat CR.42 biplane. This aircraft was already dated when it made its first flight, but nevertheless was to remain in production until the summer of 1944!

Another wrong decision concerned aircraft armament. Allegedly in the Spanish Civil War the aircraft cannon, due to its lower rate of fire, had proved less effective than the machine gun[26] and consequently no cannon armament was intended for Italian aircraft. As a result, in the following years, Italian fighter pilots had to make do with the modest armament of a pair of 12.7mm machine guns.

The Undersecretary of State responsible for this, Gen Valle, made another grave error in 1937 when he deferred research work on aerial torpedoes because it had caused squabbles between the navy and the air force. It was to be almost three years later, in July 1940, that his successor established an experimental torpedo-bomber squadron in Gorizia.

There were also considerable shortcomings in the training of pilots. Aerobatics dominated everything, as did also belief in personal heroism and the idealistic concept of aerial combat as a sporting duel.[27] These chivalrous ideals were extremely unsuited to modern warfare, but the virus of bold action had infected Italian pilots since Balbo's days. Moreover, their training period was far too short. According to the instructions issued by the General Staff of the Italian air force, a prospective fighter pilot had to undergo 150 hours of flight training, a prospective bomber pilot 250 hours. In reality many pilot trainees joined their operational units after just 80–85 hours of flying.[28] It was therefore not surprising that, at the beginning of the war, Italian aircrews were not as a rule conversant with instrument flying or trained in blind flying! Also, for some inexplicable reason, the blind flying school (Scuola di volo senza visibilita) at Littoria (Latina) – which was only intended for bomber pilots in any case – was closed down in June 1940. Finally there were simply not enough trained pilots: already in 1940 there was a shortage of 1,500.

The greatest drawback, however, was the Italian air industry, which not only suffered from a shortage of raw materials but also had 'organizational defects, functional faults, inefficiency, technical and moral inadequacies of a supervisory nature and a predominance of personal interests'.[29] The industry lacked innovative spirit and, initially, was unable to close the technological gap that had opened between it and the industries of the Germans, British and French. The Italian companies were noteworthy for their undisciplined production of prototypes rather than for their efficiency in constructing suitable aircraft models for the air force. Many of the aircraft built were scarcely fit for service use. Such strikingly inadequate aircraft included the twin-engined Cant Z.1101, Caproni Ca 135, Ca 135bis, Piaggio P.32 and Breda 88 bombers, the unsuccessful SM.85 dive bomber and the three-engined SM.84 bomber, almost all of which had to be withdrawn from operational service.[30] This meant that the air units were left painfully short of effective machines.

This unenviable situation was exacerbated by an irresponsible waste of resources. Aero engine manufacturers, such as Piaggio, Fiat, Alfa Romeo and Isotta Frascini, had 'specialized' in air-cooled engines and had failed to produce reliable power plants developing more than 1,000hp. For this reason, Alfa Romeo acquired production rights in 1939 for the German DB 601 inverted-V liquid-cooled 1,175hp engine. When it came to actual manufacture, however, the Italian plant found itself unable to complete the pre-production series of the Daimler-Benz engine, known as the RA 1000 RC 41L, before 1941.[31] The Italian air force was consequently forced to import DB 601 engines from Germany to improve the performance of its fighters. Had Italian industry obtained the Daimler-Benz engine in 1938 the Macchi MC.202 fighter would have been available at the outbreak of hostilities and could have played a dominant role both over the Mediterranean and in North Africa.

27

A particularly flagrant example of the inefficiency of Italian aviation industry – which, after all, had exported aircraft to no fewer than 39 countries between 1937 and 1943 – concerned the cockpit hoods of the Fiat G.50 and Macchi-Castoldi MC.200 fighters. The initial series were delivered with enclosed cockpits, which by then was the international norm. In service use, however, it soon became evident that at certain speeds the cockpit hoods could no longer be opened, so the pilot was therefore trapped inside his cockpit. Instead of finding a technical solution to this problem, aircraft in the following series were simply built with open cockpits.

The concepts of rationalization and concentration also remained alien to the Italian aviation industry. If the Messerschmitt works, for example, needed 4,500 working hours to build one Bf 109, the Aeronautica Macchi required 21,000 working hours to complete one MC.200.[32] Mussolini, whose system rested on a power balance between the Fascist Party on one side and the royal family, middle class and industry on the other, and was, in fact, far removed from being totalitarian, probably knew about the quantitative and qualitative shortcomings of the Italian industry but apparently lacked the power to implement the necessary fundamental changes. It was only in December 1942 that he tried to introduce a German-Italian commission for the reorganization of Italian aircraft production, but the intended President, Vittorio Cini, refused to accept the post.[33] A Ministry for War Production that was intended to co-ordinate and concentrate the industrial potential was finally created in February 1943 – far too late to have any effect.

The blame for the circumstances that would lead to the downfall of the Regia Aeronautica did not lie with the manufacturers alone. The air force command also carried a large share of the responsibility for this situation. Not only was it too submissive to industry, it lacked clarity in its technical thinking. Balbo's decision to separate the scientific-experimental development of aviation from the office that selected the aircraft types for procurement proved disastrous. The procuring office had no technicians and, although it received recommendations and reviews from the Department of Aviation Development, was not obliged to act upon them and often made decisions that were completely irresponsible from the technical point of view. For example, in 1938, Gen Valle decided in favour of the series production of the Fiat CR.42, Fiat G.50 and Macchi MC.200 fighters, despite the fact that the research department had adjudged the competing Caproni group product as superior.[34]

This was to be one of the last erroneous decisions to be taken by Valle. On 31 October 1939 Mussolini replaced him with Gen Francesco Pricolo. Among other things, he inherited what seemed to be a very impressive balance sheet from Valle, according to which the Regia Aeronautica possessed 8,528 aircraft, although 3,184 of these were still under construction. But Valle's figures had to be taken with caution. The Foreign Minister, Count Ciano, had suspected as early as April 1939 that Valle's figures were inaccurate, and had mentioned this to Mussolini: 'Fantasies are being woven around the air force. He (the Duce) possesses figures given to him by Valle which show ludicrous optimism. I have advised an investigation by the Prefects: they are to count the aircraft in the hangars and get at an accurate figure, which should not be an impossible undertaking. Up to today we have not succeeded in getting at the truth.'[35] Pricolo succeeded. After patient and painstaking research, he established that the number of modern combat aircraft capable of wartime operational service was no more than 858: 647 bombers and 191 fighters![36] One of the first tasks Pricolo had to perform after taking office was to order the scrapping of 1,842 obsolete aircraft.

On 28 April 1939 Italo Balbo had stated in the Italian Parliament: 'Only a well-equipped aerial army that operates independently and with determination, is sure of itself and is competently led, can guarantee the freedom of the skies over Italy, the defence of its cities and the safety of its industrial centres.'[37] The Regia Aeronautica was not up to these tasks in 1939/40. In so far as the public was concerned, the Italian air force was still seen as the splendid air arm that, in July 1939, held no fewer than 33 world records, far more than Germany (15), France (12), USA (11), Soviet Union (7), Japan (3), Great Britain (2) and Czechoslovakia (1). But this lustre was deceptive:

Pricolo had to admit that behind this 'glittering facade there was no solid structure, only a fragile framework'.[38]

When Italy entered the war on 10 June 1940 the Regia Aeronautica had a 'paper strength' of 3,296 machines, of which only some 2,000 were serviceable and fit for operations. The Italian fighter arm possessed only 166 modern aircraft: 89 Fiat G.50s and 77 MC.200s, all of them slower than such potential opponents as the Hawker Hurricane, the Supermarine Spitfire and the Dewoitine D.520. Furthermore, the Italian air force had no long-range fighters to escort its bombers, and no night fighters.

One might have expected that the Italian armed forces would now concentrate all available means on neutralizing and occupying Malta, later to become such a thorn in the flesh of the Axis powers. At that time the island was practically defenceless, but nothing of the sort happened. Mussolini also ordered the forces on the front with France to adopt a strictly defensive stance. Italian aircraft were not only forbidden to overfly the French territory, they were not allowed to fly closer than 10km (6 miles) to the border. Behind these instructions lay the fear of French air raids on the practically undefended northern Italian industrial centres. This defensive Italian stance was abandoned after RAF aircraft bombed Turin (Torino) on 12 June. Subsequently Regia Aeronautica planes began increasingly to attack targets in southern France, Corsica and north Africa. The lack of co-operation between the air force and the navy was first exposed on 15 June, when a strong French naval flotilla shelled the Ligurian coast and the Italians proved unable either to prevent this action or to attack the enemy ships effectively.

Other deficiencies of the Italian air force were also unsparingly revealed during the first days of hostilities. The Fiat CR.42 biplanes proved hopelessly inferior to the French Dewoitine D.520, while other aircraft types had to be taken out of operational service because of their complete unsuitability. The Breda 88 light bombers, with which the 7° Gruppo Autonomo Bombardimento and 19° Gruppo based at Alghero were equipped, turned out to be technically completely unreliable after only a few operational sorties. When, on 21 June,

Italian Air Raids on Gibraltar 1940–4

Date	Aircraft Used	Results
17/18.7.1940	3 SM.82 (Reparto Sperimentale)	4 dead, including 3 civilians
25/26.7.1940	3 SM.82 (Reparto Sperimentale)	1 SM.82 damaged by AA fire
20/21.8.1940	2 SM.82	1 SM.82 shot down by AA fire
6.6.1941	2 SM.82	1 SM.82 had to return to base, the other missed its target
13.6.1941	1 SM.82	La Linea in Spain bombed in error; 4 Spaniards killed
11.7.1941	1 SM.82	?
13.7.1941	1 SM.82	?
14.7.1941	1 SM.82	?
1.4.1942	3 SM.82 (47a Squadriglia 'T')	No damage
28/29.6.1942	5 P.108B (274a Squadriglia BGR)	4 P.108B reached their target, 3 forced to land in Spain due to fuel shortage
3.7.1942	1 P.108B (274a Squadriglia BGR)	P.108B (MM.22601) crashed near the Balearic Islands
24.9.1942	2 P.108B (274 Squadriglia BGR)	No damage
20.10.1942	4 P.108B (274a Squadriglia BGR)	1 P.108 lost in forced landing
21.10.1942	3 P.108B (274a Squadriglia BGR)	1 P.108 (MM.22602) lost in forced landing
4/5.6.1944	10 SM.79bis (Gruppo Autonomo Aerosiluranti 'Buscaglia', ANR)	2 SM.79bis attacked the target; 1 had to make a forced landing in France, 3 in Spain
19.6.1943	9 SM.79	5 aircraft had to return due to engine problems

the Italians went on to the offensive on the Alpine front, the bombers were ordered to attack and neutralize the French mountain fortifications, pillboxes and caves. Their success was zero because the Italians lacked a dive bomber that could perform pinpoint attacks.

During the short war against France the Italian air force lost 10 aircraft and 24 aircrew personnel. The enemy losses were estimated at 10 aircraft shot down in aerial combat and 50 destroyed on the ground.[39]

In July 1940 the Regia Aeronautica began its attacks on the British crown colony of Gibraltar and its important naval base.[40] In the course of the war, until June 1944, Italian aircraft bombed 'the Rock' 16 times. It proved to be a waste of energy and resources, as the number of bombers used was too insignificant even for nuisance raids. The 14 mini-raids carried out by a total of 32 aircraft up to October 1942 could have had hardly any effect on the enemy. The two retaliation raids on Gibraltar flown by the Vichy-French Armée de l'Air de l'Armistice on 24 and 25 September 1940 were carried out with more aircraft than the Italians could raise against Gibraltar during the entire war.

From the autumn of 1940 a new target for the Regia Aeronautica was Great Britain. The Italian air force command, well aware of the inadequacy of its aircraft material, was opposed to this move, but the Foreign Ministry at Palazzo Chigi wanted to make a 'political gesture' because the collapse of Britain seemed only a question of time. Accordingly, an independent air corps for operations against Britain, the Corpo Aereo Italiano (CAI) under Gen Rino Corso Fougier, was established on 10 September, comprising the units listed in the table opposite.[41]

Altogether the Corps had 170 aircraft, although many of these were unsuitable for operations against the United Kingdom under any circumstances. The twin-engined Fiat BR.20 bomber lacked de-icing equipment and, with a bomb load of 800kg (1,764lb), had a range of only 800km (497 miles); its cruising speed did not exceed 315km/h (196mph). The Fiat G.50 fighter had a maximum speed of 470km/h (292mph) at an altitude of

Corpo Aereo Italiano (CAI)

- 13° Stormo B.T. (Bombardamento Terrestre)
  with Fiat BR.20Ms
  11° Gruppo
    11a Squadriglia
    4a Squadriglia
  43° Gruppo
    3a Squadriglia
    5a Squadriglia

- 43° Stormo B.T. with Fiat BR.20Ms
  98° Gruppo
    240a Squadriglia
    241a Squadriglia
  99° Gruppo
    242a Squadriglia
    243a Squadriglia

- 56° Stormo C.T. (Caccia Terrestre)
  18° Gruppo with Fiat CR.42s
    83a Squadriglia
    85a Squadriglia
    95a Squadriglia
  20° Gruppo with Fiat G.50s
    351a Squadriglia
    352a Squadriglia
    353a Squadriglia

- 172a Squadriglia Autonoma RST (Ricognizione Strategica Terrestre) with
  Cant Z.1007bis

5,000m (16,400ft) – but the model in service at that time had no armour protection for the pilot's seat or protected fuel tanks. Besides, the G.50 radius of action was only 445km (276 miles). The Fiat CR.42 biplane with its fixed undercarriage and a maximum speed of only 430km/h (267mph) was also technically obsolescent by that time. Moreover, all Italian aircraft had weak and unreliable radio equipment.

As for flying personnel, the aircrew had only limited operational experience and their training in instrument and blind flying was insufficient. Under these circumstances the Corpo

Operations of the CAI Bomber Formations across the English Channel

Date	Unit	Target	Results
24.10.1940	12 BR.20M of 13° Stormo 5 BR.20M of 43° Stormo	Ramsgate	3 BR.20M destroyed, 1 crew killed; 1 BR.20M damaged
27.10.1940	15 BR.20M of 43° Stormo	Ramsgate	Attack called off
29.10.1940	15 BR.20M of 43° Stormo	Ramsgate	1 BR.20M destroyed, crew wounded
5.11.1940	8 BR.20M of 13° Stormo	Ipswich and Harwich	1 BR.20M damaged
9.11.1940	5 BR.20M of 43° Stormo	Ramsgate	Attack called off due to bad weather
10.11.1940	8 BR.20M of 13° Stormo	Ipswich	Attack called off due to bad weather
11.11.1940	10 BR.20M of 43° Stormo 5 Cant Z.1007	Harwich and London (feint)	3 BR.20M shot down, 3 BR.20M badly damaged
17.11.1940	6 BR.20M of 43° Stormo	Harwich	Attack carried out without losses
20.11.1940	1 BR.20M of 13° Stormo	Norwich	Attack called off
21.11.1940	12 BR.20M of 13° Stormo	Ipswich and Harwich	1 BR.20M missing, 1 BR.20M forced to return before attack due to icing up
28.11.1940	6 BR.20M of 13° Stormo	Ipswich, Harwich, Great Yarmouth and Lowestoft	Due to bad weather none of the aircraft reached their targets

29.11.1940	10 BR.20M of 13° Stormo	Ipswich, Harwich, Great Yarmouth and Lowestoft	1 BR.20M destroyed on landing
5.12.1940	12 BR.20M of 13° Stormo	Ipswich	Attack called off due to bad weather
14.12.1940	7 BR.20M of 13° Stormo 4 BR.20M of 43° Stormo	Harwich	3 aircraft unable to carry out the raid due to technical problems
21.12.1940	4 BR.20M of 13° Stormo 2 BR.20M of 43° Stormo	Harwich	Attack carried out
22.12.1940	6 BR.20M of 43° Stormo	Harwich	1 BR.20M lost
2.01.1941	4 BR.20M of 13° Stormo	Ipswich	Due to technical problems 2 BR.20M unable to carry out the attack

Aereo Italiano had no hope of success in its operations against Great Britain.

The technical shortcomings of the new Corps led to painful and unnecessary losses already during its transfer to Belgium, which began on 27 September and was completed by 19 October. Altogether, two Fiat G.50 fighters and 20 Fiat BR.20 bombers were lost in forced landings and crashes, and three airmen lost their lives.[42] In Belgium the CAI units were deployed on the following airfields: 13° Stormo B.T. was accommodated at Melsbroek, as was the 172° Reconnaissance squadron; 43° Stormo B.T. operated from Ursel and 22° Gruppo C.T., with 50 serviceable Fiat CR.42 fighters, was based at Maldeghem. All these airfields were relatively far from the British Isles so that the Italian fighters, with their short range, could only operate for about 10 minutes over southern England.

Operationally the CAI was subordinated to the German Luftflotte 2. During their patrols and escort sorties, the Fiat

G.50 fighters were never involved in any air combat with British aircraft, but it was a different story with the Fiat CR.42 biplanes of 18° Gruppo. On 11 November 40 Fiat CR.42 fighters escorted 10 Fiat BR.20 bombers of 43° Stormo B.T. on a raid to Harwich. The formation was intercepted by RAF Spitfires and Hurricanes and lost three bombers and two fighters. A third Fiat CR.42 had to make a forced landing in Suffolk.[43] At this point, there was nothing to indicate that a Fiat CR.42 pilot serving with 85° Squadriglia, Luigi Gorrini, would one day be one of the most successful Italian aces.

The 17 bombing raids carried out by the Italians in total did not cause much material damage, but they did annoy Winston Churchill. When he received the report about the successful defensive action on 11 November, his mood rose noticeably: 'The Prime Minister shouted with joy...'[44]

Bad weather and inadequate aircraft hindered effective action by the CAI. Already in mid-December 1940 the General Staff of the Italian air force decided to withdraw the corps and return it to Italy. The decisive factors in this were strategic. Aircraft were urgently needed both at the Greek front, where an Italian offensive had just failed, as well as in Cyrenaica, where a successful British counter-offensive had started on 9 December. The withdrawal of aircraft and aircrews began on 10 January 1941, although for the time being (until April 1941) two squadrons of 20° Gruppo remained at the Channel front. Their pilots were retrained on the Bf 109E at Cazaux, but, to their great disappointment, did not receive any Messerschmitts after the completion of their conversion training. Thus ended the disappointing military operations of the CAI. The Italians had lost 36 aircraft (including 26 in accidents) and 43 aircrew members, but had not succeeded in shooting down a single British aircraft![45]

On the Greek-Albanian front things were also going badly for the Italians. Rome had begun the offensive on 28 October 1940. Mussolini's decision to attack Greece was driven by the fear that the Germans, who had sent a 'training squad' to Romania, wanted to secure the entire Balkan region as a zone of influence. On 28 October the Italians had the following flying units in Albania: nine squadrons of fighters with 40 Fiat G.50s, 46 Fiat CR.42s and 14 obsolete Fiat CR.32 biplanes. The offensive force consisted of eight squadrons with 24 SM.81 and 35 SM.79 bombers.[46] Other formations were deployed in Apulia. Altogether the Italians had 193 aircraft at their disposal for use against Greece. Among them were also two squadrons of dive bombers of 96° Gruppo Autonomo B.a.T (Bombardieri a Tuffo), equipped with 20 Ju 87B Stukas. These were based at Lecce.

Rather optimistically the Regia Aeronautica had originally thought that it had found the ideal dive bomber in the Savoia-Marchetti SM.85. Unfortunately this single-seat shoulder-wing cantilever monoplane revealed numerous shortcomings. To lower the dive brakes the pilot had to decelerate to 200km/h (124mph)! At this speed the aircraft was not only easy prey for enemy fighters, but in danger of stalling! In June 1940 96° Gruppo Autonomo B.a.T., consisting of 236a and 237a Squadriglia equipped with 19 SM.85 dive bombers, was deployed to the island of Pantelleria. The formation was unable to make any operational sorties, and only a month later had to be withdrawn to the mainland. In June 1940 Gen Pricolo approached his German allies with a request for 50 Ju 87 dive bombers. The German OKW turned this down, but Göring approved.[47] The new agreement envisaged the delivery of 15 Ju 87Bs in July, another 15 in August and the remainder in September. The first group of Italian pilots started its four-week conversion training at Stukaschule 2 in Graz-Thalersdorf in July, and the first Italian-crewed Ju 87 dive bombers arrived in Italy in late August.

The Italians certainly had a numerical superiority over the Greek air force (Elliniki Vassili Aeroporia), which was composed of a motley collection of partly obsolete aircraft of widely different origins.[48] The nucleus of the Greek fighter force consisted of six Czech Avia B.534 biplanes, two British Gloster Gladiators (a present from a rich Greek businessman) and nine French Bloch MB.151 monoplanes; the remainder was made up of 36 Polish PZL P.24 high-wing monoplanes. The three bomber squadrons had 25 Potex 633s, Bristol Blenheim IVs and

Fairey Battle Is, as well as six Hawker Horsley torpedo-bombers. Another 130 aircraft of various types were used for training and for land and naval reconnaissance.

The Italians proved incapable of making effective use of their superiority for several reasons. The poor infrastructure in Albania hindered communications between the flying units as well as their movements. Only two airfields – Tirana and Valona – had Macadam runways. Thus the autumn and winter weather made all fighter operations much more difficult. Another problem was the Regia Aeronautica's failure to concentrate its bomber forces in Apulia for use against Greece, these instead remaining dispersed between Apulia, Sicily and Sardinia. There was also the usual lack of co-operation between the three branches of the armed services, and the Regia Aeronautica failed to support the infantry effectively. Finally, only a few days after the start of their offensive, the Italian pilots were confronted by the RAF, which had sent Nos 30, 211 and 84 Squadrons with Bristol Blenheim bombers, No 80 Sqn with Gloster Gladiator biplane fighters and No 70 Sqn with Vickers Wellington bombers. In January and February 1941 the British reinforced their presence with another three squadrons, one of which was equipped with Hawker Hurricane fighters.[49]

The Regia Aeronautica, too, reinforced the strength it deployed against the Greeks, but it was only the start of the German offensive against Yugoslavia on 6 April 1941 that brought a turning point for the Italians. For the brief campaign of only 11 days against Yugoslavia, the Italians deployed more than 600 aircraft. They shot down five aircraft for the loss of five of their own, and destroyed 100 Yugoslav machines on the ground. Fighting against Greece was more costly: the Italians lost 79 aircraft, of which 65 were shot down. More than 400 Italian aircraft were damaged.[50] The personnel losses amounted to 223 killed and missing and 65 wounded. On the success side, the Italians claimed 218 Greek and British aircraft shot down, as well as the possible destruction of another 55 aircraft in aerial combat.

When, late in April 1941, the survivors of the British Expeditionary Corps in Greece began evacuating to Crete, the

Italian position in East Africa was seriously threatened. Italian East Africa (Africa Orientale Italiano, AOI) formed of Ethiopia and the colonies of Eritrea and Somalia, was about to fall. The long distance from the Motherland and the poor connections with it made it impossible for the Italians to effectively protect the colonies of 1,725,330sq. km (666,150sq. miles) in area with a population of 12,165,000. Initially the Italian forces in East Africa, commanded by the Viceroy Prince Amedeo d'Aosta, consisted of about 75,000 men (not counting the police and Guardia di Finanza), plus 182,000 colonial troops. The Regia Aeronautica had 195 fighters, bombers and reconnaissance aircraft, as well as 25 transport aircraft in East Africa.[51] The fighters were exclusively Fiat CR.42 and CR.32 biplanes. The bomber force had a large number of three-engined Savoia-Marchetti SM.81 Pipistrello (Bat) machines, which had a modest maximum speed of just 340km/h (211mph) and were already obsolescent by the beginning of the war. Of the more modern SM.79 bombers there were only 12 examples in East Africa. Most of the aircraft park – more than 80 machines – was made up of the Caproni Ca 133 three-engined high-wing monoplanes. These aircraft were especially designed for colonial use, but due to their low speed and large size provided easy targets for British fighters.

The Italian flying forces were distributed in three sectors :

- Northern (Eritrea) with 26°, 27°, 28° and 29° Gruppi as well as Gruppo Gasbarrini and one HQ squadron
- Western (Ethiopia) with 4°, 44° and 49° Gruppi as well as one HQ squadron
- Southern (Italian Somalia) with 25° Gruppo and one HQ squadron

Most of the Italian airfields were on the periphery of their colonial territories.

The British were supported by their air force units based in Sudan and Aden. In addition, the Southern Rhodesian air force and the SAAF also sent aircraft to Kenya, including 18 Junkers Ju 86s of the SAAF, former airliners that had been converted for bombing and reconnaissance tasks. There were also some 20 aircraft in French Somalia, which, however, were hardly to make an appearance. Apart from a handful of Hawker Hurricanes, the aircraft of the Empire formations were just as obsolete as those of the Italians.

The Regia Aeronautica opened hostilities with aerial attacks on Sudan and Aden. On 13 June 1940 four SM.81 bombers from 4° Gruppo took off for an air raid on Aden. None returned to base: one was shot down and the other three had to make forced landings during the return flight (one of these aircraft fell into British hands). Subsequently both sides began lively aerial reconnaissance and bombing activity. Scenes reminiscent of the First World War were played out in the desert skies when Fiat CR.32 and CR.42 biplanes clashed with British Gloster Gladiators or South African Hartebeeste biplanes. Occasionally skilled Italian pilots managed to shoot down the far superior Hurricane. On 4 July five squadrons of the Regia Aeronautica supported an Italian attack with 8,000 troops on the Fort Gallabrat and the traffic junction at Kassala, in Sudan.

A month later, on 5 August 1940, the Italian offensive against British Somalia began. This operation was effectively supported by 27 bombers, 23 fighters and seven reconnaissance aircraft. The British began the evacuation of Berbera on 16 August, completing it just three days later. An Italian flag now flew over British Somalia, but the British were not daunted. On 18 August five Vickers Wellesley bombers from No 223 Sqn raided Addis Ababa and destroyed one SM.75, one SM.79 and three Ca 133s on the ground. This did not change the fact that, for the time being, the Italians had aerial superiority. Within the first three months of hostilities in East Africa they had lost 84 aircraft; a total of 143 aircrew personnel had been killed and another 71 wounded.[52] At that time these losses had no adverse effect on the activities of the Regia Aeronautica. On 16 October one SM.79 and nine Fiat CR.42s from 412a Squadriglia of 29° Gruppo attacked the Gedaref airfield in Sudan and destroyed all eight Vickers Wellesley bombers of No 47 Sqn that were based there. Two days later four overloaded SM.82s took off from Rhodes on a strategic raid. This small formation was led by Maj Ettore Muti, Fascist Party functionary and a bomber pilot (and a participant in the ill-fated flight to Melilla in July 1936). The aircraft overflew Syria, Jordan and then Iraq to reach their target, the oil refineries of Bahrain. They bombed this vital target, but without causing much damage. All four SM.82s then turned towards Eritrea, where they landed after a non-stop flight of 15½ hours that had covered a distance of over 4,200km (2,608 miles). Even if this flight was not a military success, it was still an outstanding achievement.[53] On their return flight, via Benghasi to Rome, the four SM.81s of 41° Gruppo also bombed Port Sudan.

This remarkable long-distance flight could not hide the fact that the Regia Aeronautica in East Africa was in crisis. At the end of October, the supply situation of the Italian air force units based there had become critical and aviation fuel had to be rationed. On the opposing side, the supply system functioned the way it should, and the flying formations of the British Empire consistently received material and replacements. The SAAF alone was reinforced with 16 new Hurricane fighters in October, and there was no fuel shortage.

After sufficient reserves had been built up, the British forces began their offensive against Ethiopia on 6 November 1940, thrusting in the direction of Fort Gallabrat in Sudan, which the Italians had occupied. The fort was in British hands again the same evening, but the Regia Aeronautica hit back hard and effectively. Already in the first hour of the British offensive the Fiat CR.42 fighters of the high-scoring 412a Squadriglia led by Capt Antonio Raffi shot down five Gloster Gladiators without loss. Over the battlefield the Italians had undisputed aerial superiority, and the British were forced to evacuate Fort Gallabrat once more. On 12 December pilots from the same 412a Squadriglia made a surprise attack on the British landing field at Gaz Regeb in Sudan and managed to destroy five aircraft on the ground.

Time was working against the Italians, however. On 15 December the British launched a new offensive from Kenya. On 1 January 1941 the Regia Aeronautica in East Africa still had 19 transport and 132 combat aircraft, including 27 SM.79s, 52 Ca 133s and 22 Fiat CR.42s.[54] An additional 125 aircraft were under repair. Although the Italian pilots had fought splendidly they could not prevent the loss of 137 aircraft or improve their overall situation. On 14 January 1941 the British started another new offensive from Kenya with the aim of recapturing British Somalia. A few days later British Empire troops thrust from Sudan towards Eritrea. On 24 January, during an attempt to hold up the British advance, the Italians lost six aircraft to ground fire, with three others badly damaged. The Viceroy reported to Rome that the British Empire air forces were about to gain the quantitative and qualitative upper hand. In another report, on 1 February, he stated that his air force had only 82 serviceable aircraft left and that, if they were to maintain operations at the current level, their strength would be exhausted within 15 days.[55]

This touched on the dramatic supply situation. The following reinforcements reached Italian East Africa up to 3 February 1941: 39 SM.79s, one SM.82 and 32 Fiat CR.42s. However, the loss of Cyrenaica in February 1941 put an end to any further flights of the three-engined Italian aircraft from Benghazi to Addis Ababa, and the fighters could only be transported packed dismantled into the large transport aircraft. Until March 1941, the end of the 'air bridge', the dependable SM.82 Marsupiales carried a total of 51 Fiat CR.42 fighters to the beleaguered Italian colonies.

Air transport tasks were the responsibility of the Servizi Aerei Speciali (SAS), formed in June 1940, which incorporated airliners drafted from the three Italian airline companies, Ala Littoria, LATI and Avio Linee Italiane. In 1939 these airlines served a route network of 60,385km (37,500 miles). The SAS, which had a total of 132 civil aircraft of all types[56] (including 31 SM.75s, four Ju 52/3ms and one Douglas DC-2) either carried out transport tasks for the Reparti Transporto (transport formations) or, under the umbrella of the Nuclei Comunicazioni (communications centres), flew along the essential civil air traffic routes, for example to Berlin, Madrid or Lisbon. At that time the personnel strength of the SAS was at least 550 pilots and mechanics as well as 3,300 employees divided into 13 squadrons and four groups:

145th Independent Group with 604 and 620 Squadrons at Tobruk

147th Independent Group with 601, 602 and 603 Squadrons at Littoria (Latina)

148th Independent Group with 605 and 606 Squadrons at Reggio Calabria

149th Independent Group with 607, 608 and 609 Squadrons at Naples-Capodichino; 611 Squadron at Tirana (Albania); 615 Squadron at Guidonia; and 616 Squadron at Rome-Littorio

as well as the Groups

Ala Littoria at Littoria
Ala Littoria (seaplanes) at Ostia
Avio Linee at Milan
LATI at Rome-Littorio

During the Greek campaign SAS aircraft carried thousands of soldiers and hundreds of tonnes of supplies and food to Albania. These militarized civilian airliners gained a special significance while supplying the Dodecanese from North Africa and Italian East Africa. They carried torpedoes and other weapons to Rhodes; fuel, military equipment and troops to Libya and, in 1942/43, also Tunisia, as well as medical supplies and spare parts to Italian East Africa. On their return flights these planes not only evacuated the wounded, but also civilians. Altogether, in 1940/41, the SAS made 330 flights to Ethiopia, Eritrea and Italian Somalia. These supply flights helped Prince Amedeo d'Aosta to prolong resistance, but they were insufficient for him to achieve victory.

February 1941 was not a very cheerful month for the Italians. On 25 February they lost Mogadishu, capital of Italian Somalia. They also lost two of the most successful fighter pilots in that region: Staff Sgt Enzo Omiccioli (five victories) was shot down and killed on 5 February, and Capt Mario Visintini (16 victories) of 412a Squadriglia, who was fatally wounded in a crash on 11 February. He was posthumously decorated with the Medaglia d'Oro, the highest Italian award for bravery.

By the end of February the Regia Aeronautica had only 42 aircraft left in East Africa, and the British were now clearly superior. On 27 March the British Empire forces captured the strong natural fortress of Keren in Eritrea; 40,000 Italian troops laid down their arms. By the end of March surplus personnel of the Italian air force units had to fight as infantry. The lack of air cover also contributed to the tragic end of the desperate and, in the event, suicidal sortie by Italian destroyers from the barricaded Port Said. No return to base was planned, and all five destroyers – *Pantera*, *Tigre*, *Battisti*, *Manin* and *Sauro* – were lost.[57]

By this time the capital of Ethiopia, Addis Ababa, was only a few days away from capitulation. Max Peroli, an SAS pilot, had no wish to be captured and ordered three aged SM.73 monoplanes (I-NOVI, I-ARCO and I-VADO), found on the local airfield, to prepare for take-off. These civilian machines could each take 18 passengers and flew at a modest 325km/h (202mph). Although these aircraft did not have the necessary range to reach Italian-controlled territory, Peroli took off on 3 April, two days before the fall of Addis Ababa, and got away with 42 members of the Regia Aeronautica who preferred risk the flight rather than become British POWs. Their journey over the next few weeks was a true odyssey, as they faced engine problems, sandstorms, emergency landings in the desert and internment in Saudi Arabia. On the night of 13 May 1941, after covering a total flight distance of 6,270km (3,894 miles), the three SM.73s finally regained Italian territory.[58]

By the end of April 1941 the Italians had only 13 serviceable aircraft remaining in East Africa. In May these were ordered to concentrate at Gondar (Ethiopia), where the last remaining Italian forces were assembling. The exceptional pilot Max Peroli made sure Gondar was supplied with essential supplies to tie down the British forces, which otherwise would have been deployed to North Africa.[59] He made another four flights with his unarmed SM.75 (I-LUNO) carrying Red Cross markings, covering the 12,000km (7,452-mile) route Rome–Benghazi–Gondar–Djibouti (French Somalia)–Benghazi–Rome. His first flight, which began on 20 June 1941, took 82 hours, including 48 hours flying time. During the fifth flight, on 5 October, a South African fighter pilot shot I-LUNO into flames on the Djibouti airfield. All resistance in Gondar terminated on the evening of 27 November 1941.

Italian East Africa was lost, but Italian aircraft appeared twice more over that region during operations that ranked high as flying achievements, but served political-propaganda rather than military purposes. In May 1942 a single three-engined SM.75 made the dangerous flight over Egypt, Sudan and Ethiopia to drop leaflets over Asmara (Eritrea) for the local Italian population. The proven three-engined SM.75 was also chosen for the second and last operation. Fitted with additional fuel tanks, this aircraft had a greater range and was designated SM.75GA (Grande Autonomia). In March 1943 Maj Giulio Cesare Villa, the ADC of Gen Santoro, the Deputy Chief of Gen Staff of the Italian air force, was given the task of preparing to carry out a bombing raid on enemy installations in occupied Italian East Africa. For this operation, too, the primary motivation was psychological, because the Regia Aeronautica wanted to prove that it was still capable of attacking distant points effectively at this stage of the war. The selected target was the Gura base in Eritrea, which housed an important American air force station. The distance from Rhodes to Gura was 3,000km (1,863 miles) and the raid was carried out by two SM.75GA aircraft. Both took off from Gandurra (Rhodes) on 23 May 1943: I-TAMO (MM.60543) captained by Maj Villa and the I-BUBA (MM.60539) with Capt Max Peroli, the 'courier of Gondar', at the controls.

On the way Peroli noticed that I-BUBA was using too much fuel and consequently he would be unable to complete the flight from Gandurra to Gura and back. He therefore turned towards the secondary target, Port Sudan, over which he released his bomb load. Maj Villa reached his target as planned and dropped his bombs over the Gura airfield installations, setting them alight. After 23 and 24 hours respectively of non-stop flight, both SM.75GA trimotors touched down on Rhodes once more.

It was not only Italian East Africa that worried the government in Rome; the strength of the Regia Aeronautica was also insufficient to protect and supply Libya. Instead of 2,000 front-line aircraft Italy needed 10,000 to consolidate its empire successfully and challenge the British.

In June 1940 the Armata Azzurra had 300 serviceable front-line aircraft in North Africa, including 88 fighters – exclusively Fiat CR.32 and CR.42 biplanes – and 125 bombers.[60] The actual 'combat readiness' of many of these machines was somewhat doubtful. For instance, 50° Stormo d'Assalto was equipped with the Breda Ba 65, which was to be replaced by the more modern twin-engined Caproni Ca 310. But the Breda could carry an offensive load of 1,000kg (2,205lb) and had a maximum speed of 400km/h (248mph), while the Caproni – which had already been rejected by the Hungarian government because of its unreliability – could only take 400kg (882lb) and had a modest maximum speed of just 350km/h (217mph). Apart from that the Ca 310 also proved extremely unreliable and soon had to be withdrawn from active service.[61] And so the cadre of 50° Stormo d'Assalto reverted once again to the Ba 65 and Fiat CR.32.

During the first phase of the war in North Africa Italian aircraft were not employed to combat the roughly comparable Western Desert Air Force, but to hunt British armoured reconnaissance vehicles that had broken through the lines and were creating some consternation in the Italian communications areas hundreds of kilometres behind the front. By doing so, the Regia Aeronautica had sunk to the level of acting as the 'flying artillery' for the army, and that in the country of Italo Balbo who had so often extolled the theories of total air war propounded by Giulio Douhet. Balbo's time was already running out, however. On 28 June 1940, while approaching Tobruk, Balbo's SM.79 was shot down by Italian naval AA guns and he was killed outright. Tobruk had just experienced a British air raid and the naval AA gun crews had mistaken Balbo's SM.79 for a British bomber. Because Balbo enjoyed immense popularity in Italy and was also known as an opponent of National Socialism and its race laws, rumours that he had been a victim of a 'murder plot' engineered by Mussolini to get rid of an unpleasant rival prevailed for a long time. In fact, Balbo died as a victim of a banal error by the Italian AA gunners.

In September, after weeks of inactivity, his successor, Marshal Rodolfo Graziani, began an offensive against Egypt, which ended with the capture of Sidi Barrani. At that stage the British counter-attacked and chased the numerically superior but poorly motorized Italian troops a long way back to the west. The Italian flying formations, combined into the 5° Squadra Aerea (air corps) commanded by Gen Felice Porro, tried their utmost to slow down the British advance, but their efforts had little effect. First Bardia, then Tobruk and finally the whole of Cyrenaica were captured by the British forces. The reinforcements sent belatedly from the Italian motherland – 18° Gruppo C.T. with Fiat CR.42 biplanes, 155° Gruppo C.T. with Fiat G.50s and ten Ju 87Bs dive bombers of 96° Gruppo Tuffatori – could no longer affect the issue. Half of the Fiat G.50 fighters had no sand filters so their engines seized after only a few sorties. By the time the British halted their offensive, on 6 February 1941, because many of their troops were transferred to Greece, the Italians had lost 400 aircraft through being shot down, destroyed on the ground or captured by the enemy.[62]

Germany now had to help out its ally and sent the first units of the newly formed Afrika Korps to Tripolitania, while X.Fliegerkorps was transferred to Sicily. On 9 January 1941 a total of 156 Luftwaffe aircraft were in Italy. The Fliegerführer Afrika, subordinated to X.Fliegerkorps, received two Gruppen of Ju 87 Stukas and a Staffel of Bf 110 long-range fighters and, in addition, an advance detachment of I./JG 27 arrived in Tripoli late in February 1941. The attitude of the German pilots towards the Italian airmen was 'at first restrained as they had a tendency to judge their Italian comrades-in-arms somewhat sceptically. Later on, the German fighter pilots of I./JG 27 were grateful for every Italian aircraft that helped them to escort the Stukas. The Italians were always ready to co-operate in a comradely way with the German fighter pilots...'[63]

By the end of February 1941, 5° Squadra Aerea had more than 120 serviceable aircraft in Tripolitania, while the Luftwaffe had only 80 (20 Bf 110s and 60 Ju 87s). With this modest air support, Gen Rommel began an offensive on 24 March, and by 13 April had recaptured all of Cyrenaica with the exception of Tobruk. The reinforcements sent to 5° Squadra Aerea were limited. In April it received 27° Gruppo B.T. bomber group and 374a Squadriglia equipped with MC.200AS fighters. The AS (Africa Settentrionale) was a tropicalized version fitted with a sand filter in the engine air intake. It was also in April that a young Italian fighter pilot, Luigi Gorrini, first caught the eye.[64] Born in Emilia on 12 July 1917, he came to North Africa as a member of 85a Squadriglia of 18° Gruppo C.T. in January 1941, and achieved his first victory, a Bristol Blenheim bomber shot down over Derna, on 16 April.

Despite every effort and the use of German and Italian Ju 87 Stukas the Axis forces could not take Tobruk. The Italian Ju 87s of 239a Squadriglia, known as Picchiatelli, flew their sorties escorted by Fiat CR.42 fighters of 18° Gruppo C.T. and Fiat G.50s. The few Italian-manned Ju 87s claimed the following successes against the Allied shipping supplying the surrounded port of Tobruk: sinking of the British sloop *Grimsby* (990 tons) and the merchant vessel *Helka* (3,471 gross tons) on 25 May 1941; the British sloop *Auckland* (1,200 tons) on 24 June, and the Australian destroyer *Waterhen* (1,100 tons) on 29 June.[65] Tobruk held out, although the British were unable to relieve this important port from the outside. Both British attempts to achieve a breakthrough at the Sollum front in May (Operation *Brevity*) and June (Operation *Battleaxe*) failed. After the fighting finished on the Sollum front 18° Gruppo C.T. was returned to Italy and replaced by 160° Gruppo C.T.

While the air components of the British Empire could rely on considerable reinforcements, such help was wanting on the Axis side. In November 1941 200 Italian and 120 serviceable German aircraft were faced by 1,311 British aircraft, of which almost 1,100 were ready for action. These included Hawker Hurricane IIs, Bristol Beaufighters and American-built Curtiss P-40s and Douglas Bostons, all of them modern combat aircraft, while the

Italians still had to make do primarily with their Fiat CR.42 biplanes.

The British forces used their superiority for a new offensive (Operation *Crusader*), which began on 19 November 1941, broke the siege of Tobruk and forced the Axis troops to temporarily relinquish Cyrenaica. On the first day of their attack the British forces occupied the Sidi el Rezeg airfield, where they captured 16 Fiat G.50 fighters. Another 13 Italian aircraft were destroyed on the ground at Ain el Gazala. During the retreat three new Italian fighter formations were deployed in the area: 17° Gruppo (71a, 72a and 80a Squadrigli), transferred to Martuba airfield on 25 November, 6° Gruppo (79a, 81a and 88a Squadrigli) and 9° Gruppo (96a and 97a Squadrigli). All these units were equipped with the new Macchi MC.202 Folgore (Lightning) fighter, which, powered by a licence-built German DB 601 engine, achieved a maximum speed of 599km/h (372mph). This high performance was, in part, negated by weak armament of just two 12.7mm SAFAT machine guns, which proved inadequate in combat. Only from production Series VII (April 1942) on was the MC.202 armed with two additional 7.7mm machine guns in the wings.

The delayed transfer of the new Macchi fighters to North Africa allowed the British Western Desert Air Force to retain its aerial superiority, but that could not prevent the occasional Axis successes. For example, during their baptism of fire on 26 November the MC.202s of 9° Gruppo met a formation of Curtiss P-40 fighters and, according to Italian reports, shot down seven P-40s without loss. But the serviceability of the Italian and German aircraft declined steadily. Over the Christmas period JG 27 could count on just six serviceable Bf 109 fighters out of its original strength of 120.

Malta, with the British naval and air forces based there, proved a deadly danger to the supply lines of the Axis forces. The Italian convoys that sailed from Italy to North Africa, carrying arms, ammunition, fuel, provisions and other supplies for the Axis troops, suffered considerable and irreplaceable losses due to the attacks by Malta-based RAF and Royal Navy. In October 1941 only 78.7 per cent of the loaded tonnage reached North Africa; in November, it was down to 37.6 per cent!

Attempts to 'neutralize' Malta through countless air raids had only limited success. The task of 'eliminating' the island had been given to the 2° Squadra Aerea, based on Sicily, in June 1940. At the beginning of hostilities this formation was composed of five bomber wings, one fighter wing, one fighter group, one dive bomber group and various reconnaissance units. Initially Malta's only defence consisted of just three Gloster Sea Gladiator biplanes called *Faith*, *Hope* and *Charity*. But the Regia Aeronautica did not carry out its attacks in a determined fashion or in strength. The Italian-manned Ju 87 Stukas of 96° Gruppo ceased their operations in September 1940 after only three raids on Malta, and the general level of Italian aerial activities against the island slackened in intensity towards the end of that month. On the other hand, the defensive strength of Malta increased all the time, and it soon had a couple of squadrons of Hurricanes. But supplying the island was fraught with danger and did not always succeed. On 17 November 14 Hurricane fighters took off from the aircraft carrier *Argus*, setting their course towards Malta. The aircraft carrier was 400 miles (644km) away from the island, but only four Hurricanes reached Malta; the rest were lost.[66]

Up to the end of 1940 the Regia Aeronautica carried out 7,410 sorties against Malta, dropping 550 tonnes of bombs and losing 35 aircraft in the process. The Italians also claimed to have shot down 66 British aircraft, but these claims were considerably exaggerated. During the first five months of 1941 the aerial attacks on Malta were carried out almost exclusively by German aircraft from X.Fliegerkorps. In that time the Axis lost 71 aircraft, 59 German and 12 Italian.[67] Up to the end of that year it remained the task of the Italian air force to suppress the island effectively, but it did not succeed in doing so. All that happened was that the Italians sacrificed men and material over Malta without achieving anything.

The fight against convoys bringing supplies to Malta and the Royal Navy in the Mediterranean was also far from effective and revealed grave deficiencies in communication between the

Italian navy and air force. Thus, during the naval battle at Punta Stilo on 7 July 1940, Italian bombers attacked their own fleet in error. On 27 September 1940 nine Italian-manned Ju 87 Stukas took off from Comiso, escorted by 15 Macchi MC.200 fighters from 10° Gruppo C.T., in search of a supply convoy sailing from Gibraltar to La Valletta in Malta. The formation could not find the Allied convoy, and on the return flight ten MC.200 fighters ran out of fuel and crashed into the sea.

There were also some more promising developments, however, such as the Italian torpedo-bombers, which proved themselves excellent aerial weapons – although at the beginning of the war it did not seem likely that this arm of the air force would come into existence at all. An experimental torpedo-bomber unit, Reparto Sperimentale Aerosiluranti, was established early in 1940 in Gorizia, with four SM.79s. It was really a makeshift solution, Italy having no specialized torpedo-bombers as such. However, the three-engined SM.79, which had first taken to the air in October 1934, and was known as *il gobbo maledetto* ('the damned bloater') because of the hump on the upper part of its fuselage, was well suited to the torpedo-bomber role.[68]

The experimental formation was transferred to Libya in August 1940 and soon began to fly operations against Allied shipping. On 17 September the 'damned bloaters' damaged the British 14,200-ton cruiser *Kent* so badly that she could only just be towed to Alexandria. On 14 October the 11,350-ton cruiser *Liverpool* was hit in the bow by an aerial torpedo and suffered considerable damage. After this, the experimental formation was given the status of a squadron and became 278° Squadriglia Autonoma Aerosiluranti. It also adopted the proud motto *Pauci sed semper immites* ('Few, but always aggressive'). The first torpedo-bomber training centre was founded at Gorizia in October 1940, a second following at Naples in November, and third at Pisa in January 1942. Within a short space of time another six independent torpedo-bomber squadrons, consisting on average of five to six aircraft, were raised. The élite of the Italian air force personnel now volunteered to join the torpedo arm. The idea of a duel – aircraft against ship – exercised a great fascination for the young Italian airmen.

The Aerosiluranti attacked every type of ship carrying the British flag in the Mediterranean: merchant ships, submarines, corvettes, destroyers, cruisers, battleships and aircraft carriers. They avoided only one class of vessel – the hospital ship. Their enemies had fewer scruples in this respect: on 11 August 1941 British torpedo-bombers sank the 13,060-gross ton hospital ship *California* in the port of Syracuse, and on 9/10 September 1942 the 8,024-gross ton *Arno* north of Tobruk.

The year 1941 was one of intense activity for the Italian torpedo-bombers. During this period they definitely sank nine ships and damaged another 30, but the daring Italian pilots also paid a high price for these successes: 14 SM.79s were lost and another 46 damaged.[69] Up to 1943 the survival chances of the torpedo-bomber crews diminished steadily; on average an SM.79 would be shot down after just three operational sorties. The most significant achievements of 1941 were the torpedoing of the 11,350-ton British cruiser *Manchester* and the sinking of the destroyer *Fearless* on 23 July. Both ships were part of an escort force protecting a supply convoy of six cargo ships and one troop transport that was sailing from Gibraltar to Malta. On 27 September the pilots of 36° Stormo, taking off from Deciomannu, succeeded in damaging the 38.950-ton (full load) British battleship *Nelson* south of Sardinia, and from the same Malta-bound convoy they also sank the 12,427-ton *Imperial Star*. On 14/15 November the British lost the transports *Empire Pelican* (6,463 tons) and *Empire Defender* (5,649 tons), torpedoed by the Aerosiluranti off the Tunisian coast.

Not all these successes could be attributed to the SM.79. A few torpedo-bomber units, such as 288a Squadriglia, were equipped with the SM.84, a more modern equivalent of the proven 'bloater'. However, the SM.84 suffered so many technical problems that it became known as the 'flying coffin' and was unpopular with its crews.

Despite all Italian effort, Malta remained unbeaten: occasional successes could neither starve or 'neutralize' the island. Therefore Hitler decided, in October 1941, to transfer another, larger Luftwaffe unit to southern Italy. This formation, II.Fliegerkorps, flew no fewer than 950 sorties against the British island fortress during the first weeks of January 1942. At first the British did not seem to be impressed. Their Blenheim bombers, taking off from Luqa, attacked the Castel Vetrano airfield in Sicily and destroyed numerous Axis aircraft on the ground.[70] The intensified German air offensive against Malta began on 20 March 1942, and continued until 28 April, with only a symbolic participation by the Regia Aeronautica. It cost the Luftwaffe 177 aircraft, but brought Malta close to collapse. On 20 April the five RAF fighter squadrons based there (Nos. 126, 185, 249, 601 and 603) could field only seven serviceable aircraft between them. But the Luftwaffe did not continue its offensive; 60 per cent of II.Fliegerkorps strength was withdrawn and transferred to the Eastern Front and North Africa. The Regia Aeronautica was to carry out further attacks on Malta, but the Italian effort was nowhere near so intense as it had been previously. Already in May the number of air raids on the island fell to just 25 per cent of the quota achieved during the German aerial offensive. Malta recovered quickly, and the Axis lost its aerial superiority over the island for good. From the British point of view, the Italian airmen failed because they displayed insufficient determination in their attacks.[71] Certainly the Italian airmen had great respect for the Maltese AA artillery and the fighters based there, so much so that the flight to Malta became known as the *rotta della morte*, the 'route of death'. But when it came down to it, could the Italians, with their technologically inferior aircraft, really have held their own against an enemy that was being continually supplied with modern equipment? On 8 May alone, 64 Spitfires took off from the aircraft carrier *Eagle*, of which 61 landed on Malta; at the end of that month another 55 Spitfires reached Malta. Then 4° Stormo, with its MC.202 fighters, was transferred to North Africa, so these planes were now unavailable in the battle for Malta.

For its offensive against the island, between 1 and 14 July, the Regia Aeronautica could concentrate the following forces: 45 bombers (11 Fiat BR.20s, 25 Cant Z.1007bis and nine SM.84s), 15 Ju 87s and 78 fighters (60 MC.202s and 19 Reggiane

ITALY

Re.2001s).[72] The Re.2001 of 2° Gruppo/18° Stormo based at
Caltagirone in Sicily was a progressive development of the
Re.2000. It was powered by a licence-built DB 601 engine designated Alfa Romeo RA 1000 RC 41-I, but its maximum speed of
545km/h (338mph) was lower than that of the MC.202; on the
other hand, the pilots praised its manoeuvrability. However, at
high altitudes the Re.2001 was not equal to the Spitfire VI. The
Italian Air Ministry had originally ordered 600 machines of this
type, but Alfa Romeo pointed out the considerable difficulties
being encountered in the licence-production programme, and,
in fact, could only complete 100 engines in 16 months – an
example of the chaotic and completely inadequate utilization of
available production capacity of the Italian aviation industry.
The original order consequently had to be considerably
reduced, and in the event only 237 Re.2001 fighters had left the
assembly halls by 8 September 1943.[73]

It was impossible to subdue Malta with just 138 aircraft. The
losses suffered by the Italian North African convoys, which had
been less than 1 per cent during January and February 1942,
began to climb and reached 22.1 per cent in June. But the British,
too, had difficulties trying to supply their island fortress. The
convoys 'Harpoon' (from Gibraltar) and 'Vigorous' (from
Alexandria) suffered furious attacks from German and Italian
aircraft. Furthermore, on 14 June, the Gibraltar convoy was
attacked by 15 SM.84 torpedo-bombers of 36° Stormo taking off
from Sardinia, six SM.84s being lost. Later the convoy was
attacked by 132° Gruppo from Sicily with its 278a and 281a
Squadrigli. For this battle the Italians sent the élite of their
torpedo-bombers. The crews, captained by Faggioni, Buscaglia,
Graziani, Marino Marini, Aichner and Pfister, dropped 15
torpedoes from close range, but only one of those hit its target,
the 2,520-ton British destroyer *Bedouin*, which sank.[74]
Subsequent investigation revealed that the torpedoes used had
been faulty, possibly due to sabotage.[75] The director and the
responsible engineer of the delivery plant in Naples were
arrested.

Both the German Luftwaffe and the Italian Regia Aeronautica
assembled strong forces against the big convoy that had put to

sea as part of Operation *Pedestal* in mid-August 1942, consisting of 13 transport ships and a tanker, protected by a powerful escort.[76] A total of 189 Italian aircraft were concentrated in Sardinia: 60 M.79 torpedo-bombers, 30 SM.84 bombers and torpedo-bombers, nine Cant Z.1007bis reconnaissance aircraft, eight Fiat CR.42 fighter-bombers, and 22 MC.202, 30 Re.2001, 16 CR.42 and 14 Fiat G.50 fighters. Another 123 aircraft waited in readiness in Sicily, among them 14 SM.79 bombers and six SM.84 torpedo-bombers, 25 Fiat BR.20s and SM.84s as well as some SM.79 bombers, 11 SM.79 and Fiat CR.25 reconnaissance aircraft, 27 MC.202 and 20 Fiat CR.42 fighters. For once the co-operation between the U-boats and the German and Italian air forces was exceptionally successful, and the convoy was almost completely wiped out: nine merchant ships, one aircraft carrier, two cruisers and one destroyer were sunk. The Italians lost 25 aircraft, the Germans lost 14 and the RAF lost ten. But Malta did not give up. The third and last aerial offensive against the island took place between 10 and 20 October 1942, for which the Regia Aeronautica deployed three bomber groups (with Cant Z.1007bis), one dive bomber group (Ju 87), three fighter groups (MC.202) and one fighter-bomber group (Re.2001). However, these formations were all below their establishment strength – all four bomber groups could only field 18 Cant Z.1007bis and seven Ju 87 Stukas. Malta, whose conquest had been vetoed by Hitler, survived this last aerial offensive as well. For its operations against Malta between 1 January and 8 November 1942 the Regia Aeronautica had to write off 100 aircraft lost in action. And in December 1942 the loss rate of the Italian North Africa convoys rose to 52.6 per cent.

In North Africa Rommel had started another offensive on 21 January 1942, but was stopped short by the British 8th Army in the El Gazala area on 7 February. On 26 May Rommel tried again. This time he was supported by 670 aircraft, including 450 Italian planes. At this stage the 5a Squadra Aerea in North Africa had reached it greatest strength. The nucleus of the Italian fighter force consisted of 60 MC.202s of 1° Stormo (6° and 17° Gruppi) and 4° Stormo (9° and 10° Gruppi). Already on the morning of 6 May, the Macchis succeeded in destroying more than 20 British aircraft at Gambut. In that month, if only for a short period of time, the Messerschmitt and Macchi fighters secured aerial supremacy in North Africa. The ground support operations, however, still had to be carried out by the completely obsolete Fiat CR.42AS (Africa Settentrionale) fighters (the letters AS did not stand for some technically optimum version, but only indicated that the planes' engines had been fitted with a sand filter and the aircraft featured underwing racks for bombs up to 100kg/220lb). These biplanes, aged in design if not manufacture, equipped 50° Stormo d'Asalto (158° and 159° Gruppi), 101° Gruppo d'Assalto and part of 160° Gruppo C.T. Between 26 May and 10 June 1942 the Italian ground support units flew 480 sorties and lost, together with the fighters, 17 aircraft.

Tobruk fell on 21 June, but on 3 July the British 8th Army brought the exhausted Axis troops to a halt at El Alamein. Against Field Marshal Kesselring's determined opposition, Rommel had embarked on his campaign to capture Egypt with far too weak forces, without even eliminating the threat to his flank posed by Malta. Of special worry to Kesselring was the unequal ratio of the two sides' air strength: according to his estimates only 120–140 Axis fighters and bombers faced about 600–700 British aircraft.[77]

During the coming months the British could systematically establish their position in Egypt and strengthen their forces almost undisturbed. Meanwhile, a large part of the supplies intended for the Axis was sinking to the bottom of the Mediterranean. In August 33 per cent of the supplies carried by Axis convoys were lost; in September 20 per cent; and in October 44.2 per cent. Before the start of the British counter-offensive at El Alamein, the ratio of forces in the air was at least 2:1 in the Allies' favour. The Regia Aeronautica now had 392 machines:[78] 25 Cant Z.1007bis bombers, 34 SM.79 bombers, 90 Fiat CR.42 and G.50 fighter-bombers, 93 MC.202, 46 MC.200 and 43 Fiat G.50 fighters as well as 24 Ca 311, 17 Cant Z.501, 6 Cant Z.506 and Ghibli aircraft. The planes fitted with Fiat engines (CR.42, G.50 and MC.200) now showed signs of considerable wear and tear, so many of them had to be withdrawn from front-line service. While the Luftwaffe formations were concentrated in the El Alamein area, the Italian 5a Squadra Aerea was distributed in the west between the front and Tripoli.

The British Western Desert Air Force began its onslaught on 19 October with attacks on Axis airfields, supply posts, troop concentrations and supply bases. In four days the British flew 2,209 operational sorties, dropping 300 tonnes of bombs and losing 18 aircraft in the process. The strongest counterstroke of the Axis forces against the advancing British troops took place on 27 October. Altogether, 20 Ju 87 Stukas from St.G3 and 43 Fiat CR.42s from 50° and 101° Stormi, protected by Bf 109 and Macchi MC.202 fighters, raided targets in the Tell el Tisa sector.[79] They were intercepted by 16 Curtiss Kittyhawks and 24 Spitfires. Only four Fiat CR.42 fighter-bombers managed to reach the target area. One Ju 87 and four Fiat CR.42s were shot down, while the British lost three aircraft. But the advance of the superior British forces could not be halted. On 8 November they captured Marsa Matruh, on the 11th, Sollum and on the 13th Torbuk. In 14 days the Luftwaffe and the Regia Aeronautica had lost 250 aircraft. At the end of October, 4° Stormo had only ten MC.202 fighters left, which were passed over to 3° Stormo. Afterwards, 3° Stormo C.T. moved back to Martuba, where it received 30 new aircraft. The losses suffered by the Fiat CR.42 fighter-bombers were so high that this biplane could no longer be used in daytime. The British aerial superiority took on alarming scale. Sergio Flaccominio from 389a Squadriglia spoke of the 'sparse and gradually thinning German-Italian swarms of midges which seemed mad when they dived into a sky crowded with enemy wasps'.[80]

After the successful Anglo-American landing in French North Africa the Axis forces in Libya were in danger of being surrounded. The Italians transferred their 17° and 53° Gruppi Autonomo independent fighter groups, with a total of 47 MC.202s, to Sardinia, from where, together with the Re.2001 fighter-bombers, they began attacking targets in Tunisia. Once again the Regia Aeronautica suffered from the lack of an operational long-range bomber. In fact the Italian air force *had* a heavy bomber, the Piaggio P.108, powered by four Piaggio P.XII RC.35 radial engines of 1500hp each. It had a crew of seven and could carry a bomb load of 3,500kg (7,717lb). The conception of the aircraft, which featured remote-controlled machine gun barrettes, was quite advanced, but the chronically unreliable engines caused numerous accidents. Among others, a son of the Duce, Capt Bruno Mussolini, lost his life while test-flying a P.108. By the autumn of 1942 only one unit, 274a Squadriglia BGR (Bombardamento a Grande Raggio – long-range bombing) was equipped with the P.108B, with which it carried out a few raids on Algerian ports. The main burden of fighting had again to be carried by the 'damned bloaters' of the torpedo-bomber squadrons.[81]

In the evening of 8 November aircraft from 105° Gruppo of torpedo-bombers attacked ships in the port of Algiers, joined by 130° Gruppo. On 11 November four crews from the famed 132° Gruppo Autonomo Aerosiluranti – Buscaglia, Graziani, Faggioni and Angelucci – took off to attack Allied ships in the Bay of Bougie in Algeria. The aircraft from 278a and 281a Squadrigli were led by Maj Buscaglia, who, until then, had carried out and survived 29 torpedo-bomber attacks and was the undisputed ace of the Italian torpedo-bomber arm. Despite strong AA defences, the four SM.79s managed to torpedo and sink the troop transporters *Awatea* (13,482 tons) and *Cathay* (15,225 tons). The SM.79 captained by Angelucci was shot down and exploded while trying to make an emergency landing.[82] On 12 November 132° Gruppo made another attack with six aircraft (Buscaglia, Aichner, Bargagna, Marini, Moci and Pfister), but they could not repeat the success of the previous day. The SM.79 captained by Buscaglia was hit by AA fire, crashed into the sea and disintegrated in a ball of flame. One of the torpedo-bomber pilots, Giuseppe Cimicchi, wrote at the time: 'The best pilots of our air force die one after another. Meanwhile, the game was lost. We were fighting with fury in our hearts. Our actions were now outbreaks of rage and vengeance, desperate gestures.'[83]

The Germans and Italians succeeded in establishing a bridge-head in Tunisia, and late in December the Regia Aeronautica transferred four fighter squadrons there. The 5a Squadra Aerea, which had left Libya and retreated to the Tunisian region, had previously repatriated all aircraft unsuitable for further action to Italy. This amounted to 180 machines, including 82 Fiat CR.42s. During 1942 the 5a Squadra Aerea had lost 595 aircraft: 120 had been shot down, 215 destroyed on the ground and 260 abandoned on their airfields.

On 21 February 1943 the 5a Squadra Aerea still had the following formations in Tunisia:[84]

Northern sector: 348a Squadriglia with MC.200s in Tunis
6° Gruppo C.T. with three squadrons of MC.202s at Sfax and Gammarat
386a Squadriglia d'Assalto with Fiat G.50s at Sfax

Southern sector: 3° Stormo with six squadrons of MC.200s and MC.202s at El Hamma
remainder of 13° Gruppo d'Assalto with MC.200s at El Hamma
16° Gruppo C.T. with three squadrons of MC.200s and 12 Fiat G.50s

Although these forces were quite insufficient they nevertheless achieved quite notable successes. For example, on 17 March, 17 Macchi MC.202 fighters from 16° Stormo claimed nine Spitfires and one Lockheed P-38, losing only two of their number. But such results were the exceptions. In the air the Anglo-American forces outnumbered those of the Axis 6:1. During the months of February and March 1943, as a result of Allied attacks on Tunisian airfields, the Regia Aeronautica lost 20 MC.202s, one MC.200 and one Fiat G.50, while 64 other aircraft were damaged. Between 3 and 12 March the personnel of 384a and 386a Squadrigli, as well as that of 13° Gruppo d'Assalto, had to be recalled from northern Africa because their units had no aircraft left. They were replaced by 109a Squadriglia d'Assalto, followed by 7° Gruppo C.T. (MC.202) and 110a Squadriglia d'Assalto (MC.202). The 3° Stormo with 6° Gruppo C.T. were also recalled to Italy, both units being at the end of their strength in terms of both personnel and equipment.

An 'air bridge' had been established to supply the German-Italian bridgehead in Tunisia. With the use of all available transport capacity the Regia Aeronautica managed to fly 72,000 ground troops and 5,000 tons of war material into Tunisia. But the cost of this effort was high. The slow-flying German and Italian transport aircraft were shot down by the dozen. The pilots of the SAS, flying only a few metres above the sea hoping to reach the north African coast, suffered such losses that they could no longer be made good. The 'black day' for Axis aerial transport was 17 April, when three formations taking off one after another were intercepted by Allied fighters.[85] The first, an all-German aerial convoy, lost 15 of its 18 Ju 52/3m transports. From the second, an all-Italian formation, 12 SM.82s, three Fiat G.12s and one SM.75 failed to reach their destination, while the third formation, consisting of 18 German and Italian aircraft, lost seven of its number. The total personnel losses of the SAS on the route to Tunisia that day amounted to 67 killed and wounded. From November 1942 to May 1943 the transport formations of the Regia Aeronautica lost 82 aircraft and 220 flying personnel in their attempts to maintain the 'air bridge' to Tunisia. The supplies that reached their destination prolonged the death struggle of the Axis troops, but could not prevent their defeat. On 13 May 1943 all fighting ceased in Tunisia.

The destruction of the Regia Aeronautica in the desert had been preceded by the suffering of the Italian flying formations on the snow-covered steppes of Russia. In August 1941 the Italian air force command sent one air corps, formed of 22° Gruppo C.T. with four squadrons (ie one more than a normal Gruppo) equipped with 51 MC.200 fighters, and 61° Gruppo, consisting of three squadrons of Ca 311 twin-engined machines, to the Eastern Front. This air corps comprised 1,900 personnel, including 140 officers and 180 NCOs, and had a park of 300 motor vehicles.[86] It was actually intended for the support of the Italian Expeditionary Corps in Russia (CSIR), but was often deployed for the benefit of the German Wehrmacht.

The Italians carried out their first operations from Krivoi Rog

Flying Formations of the Italian Expeditionary Corps on the Eastern Front (CSIR) in 1941

Commander of the flying forces of the CSIR:	Col Carlo Drago
Operational bases:	Krivoi Rog, Zaporozhye, Stalino

Fighter Forces

22° Gruppo Autonomo C.T.	Maj Giovanni Borzoni
359a Squadriglia	Capt Vittorio Minguzzi
363a Squadriglia	Capt Germano La Ferla
369a Squadriglia	Capt Giorgio Iannicelli[1]
371a Squadriglia	Capt Enrico Meille

This group had 51 MC.200s, three Ca 311s and two SM.81s.

Reconnaissance

61° Gruppo Autonomo Ricognizione	Lt Col Bruno G. Ghierini
34a Squadriglia	Capt Cesare Bonino
119a Squadriglia	Capt Giovanni Disegna
128a Squadriglia	Capt Igino Mendini

The group had 32 Ca 311s and one SM.81.

Transport

245a Squadriglia with 10 SM.81	Capt Ernesto Caprioglio[2]
246a Squadriglia with 10 SM.81	Capt Nicola Fattibene[3]

[1] Capt Iannicelli was killed on 29 December 1941. He was posthumously awarded the highest Italian decoration for bravery, Medaglia d'Oro al VM.

[2] This squadron was formed on 1 September 1941 at Bucharest and took over the two SM.81 transports of 22° Gruppo.

[3] This transport squadron from Viterbo did not arrive in Russia until 25 November 1941.

Source: Malizia, Nicola, Ali Sulla Steppa (Rome, 1987), p. 211

on 27 August 1941, achieving eight aerial victories over Soviet bombers and fighters. The co-operation between the Italian air force and the German command did not function well at first, as was to be tragically demonstrated by the loss of four Italian aircraft to German flak by the end of September. This naturally subdued the initial enthusiasm of the Italian pilots. On 5 October the Undersecretary of State for Aviation and Chief of Staff of the Air Force, Gen Pricolo, paid a visit to his airmen in Krivoi Rog. At that time his SM.75 had so many technical problems that, to his annoyance, Pricolo had to use a Ju 52/3m of Ala Littoria to get to the Eastern Front.

Late in October 22° Gruppo C.T. – which, for a short while, had been subordinated to V.Fliegerkorps – was transferred to Zaporozhye, together with 128a Squadriglia of reconnaissance aircraft. In the meantime 245a Squadriglia Transporto with ten SM.81s had been formed at Bucharest on 1 September to support the Italian air corps. Additionally, 246a Squadriglia Transporto with ten SM.81s arrived from Viterbo on 25 November. The first snow had fallen already early in November, and the Italians were hard put to it to keep themselves warm with their thin overcoats, which were the same type as those worn by their comrades in Libya! Soon all flying activities were limited by the severe winter weather.

In December 371a Squadriglia C.T. was transferred to Stalino but replaced there only two days later by 359a Squadriglia C.T., with 11 MC.200s, who were joined there by 119a Squadriglia Ricognizione reconnaissance squadron. When, on Christmas Day, the Black Shirt Legion 'Tagliamento' was attacked by Soviet troops at Novo Orlovka, the Italian fighter pilots of the Air Corps helped their beleaguered comrades with effective low-level attacks on ground targets in the Burlova sector. They also shot down five Soviet aircraft. On 27 December 369a Squadriglia was also transferred to Stalino. The following day was a very successful one for the Italians: they shot down nine Soviet aircraft, including six I-16 fighters in the Timofeyevka and Polskaya area without loss. All these victories were achieved by 359a Squadriglia.

No individual aerial victories were recognized by 22° Gruppo

C.T.; all enemy aircraft shot down in combat were credited to the respective squadrons or added to the Gruppo score.[87] Moreover, the accepted norm within the entire Regia Aeronautica was that an individual aerial victory was only recognized if one pilot had achieved it. If several pilots fired at the same aircraft, which was then shot down, this victory was credited to the participating unit. This system was intended to suppress individual conceit, and, apart from a few exceptions, did indeed prevent élite fighter pilots, or 'aces' appearing from the rank and file.[88]

On 29 December 369a Squadriglia lost its commander, the 29-year old Capt Giorgio Iannicelli, who fought a lonely aerial battle against more than ten I-16s and MiG-3s. He was posthumously awarded the highest Italian decoration for bravery, the Medaglia d'Oro. The 'Christmas battle' ended on 31 December, with an Italian defensive success.

On 13 January 1942 22° Gruppo C.T. acquired a new commander, Maj Giuseppe D'Agostinis. Due to the bad weather, very little flying activity took place during January and February, but, on 4 and 5 February, Italians destroyed 21 Soviet aircraft on their airfields, and achieved five aerial victories. Up to the end of March they gained a further 21 aerial victories. In the same month the personnel of three fighter squadrons of 22° Gruppo were posted back to Italy. For a time only 371a Squadriglia remained on the Eastern Front, the personnel of which were to instruct the pilots of the 21° Gruppo Autonomo C.T., which arrived in the East in May. The 61° Gruppo Ricognizione was also recalled to Italy and replaced by the 71° Gruppo with only two squadrons – 38a and 116a Squadrigli. The 61° Gruppo Ricognizione had flown a total of 337 operational sorties and lost eight Ca 311s. The two transport squadrons were not relieved but reinforced by 247a Squadriglia.

The 21° Gruppo Autonomo C.T., commanded by Maj Ettore Foschini, brought only 18 new MC.200s to the Eastern Front, and the pilots had to make do with the somewhat worn machines of 22° Gruppo. During the battle for Kharkov the Italian pilots flew escort for the German bombers and reconnaissance aircraft. In May the Italians received praise from the commander of the German 17th Army, particularly for their daring and successful attacks in the Slavyansk area.[89]

On 27 June 1942 21° Gruppo Autonomo C.T., with its four squadrons and 33 MC.200 fighters, was transferred to the Barvenkovo airfield. On 29 June an SM.75GA (Grande autonomia, long range) landed on the airfield of the Ukrainian industrial town of Zaporozhye on the Lower Don. This aircraft had taken off from Guidonia in Italy and was on its way to Tokyo! The Italian leadership saw this long-range flight as a chance to strengthen contacts with the Japanese Empire, as well as raising Italian prestige. Apart from that, it was an opportunity to find out if an exchange of important goods by air between Europe and Asia was a realistic proposition. The SM.75GA took-off from Zaporozhye on 30 June and flew 6,200km (3,850 miles) over enemy territory, until, after 21 hours, it landed at Pao Tow Chen in China. On 3 July the aircraft finally reached its destination, the Japanese capital. The return flight, again with intermediate landings at Pao Tow Chen and Zaporozhye, was also accomplished without any major problems. However, a Japanese attempt to emulate the visit failed.

Following the German advance in summer 1942 21° Gruppo Autonomo C.T. transferred to the Makeyevka, Tazinskaya, Voroshilovgrad and Oblivskaya airfields in succession. On 25 and 26 July five MC.200s were lost in aerial combat. Increasingly, the Italians were being ordered to fly escort for German aircraft.

At long last the Italian air corps began to receive more modern aircraft: a total of 17 MC.202 fighters[90] and some Fiat BR.20s for 71° Gruppo Ricognizione. During the Don battle – the Italian fighters were then based at the Millerovo and Kantamirovka airfields – the Italian airmen fought well. On 13 August seven Italian pilots were decorated with the German Iron Cross, 2nd class. At this time the German authorities were unaware that some Italian pilots, by using all kinds of pretexts and subterfuges, were obtaining grain requisitioned by the German Wehrmacht, and supplying it to the needy Russian population living around their airfields. The relations of the Italian soldiers with the local population were as a rule excellent, and, in some cases, exceptionally cordial, and no Italian thought of treating the Russians and the Ukrainians as 'second-class' human beings, as the Germans did.[91]

By the autumn of that year hardly any of the Italian pilots still believed in the 'final victory over the Soviet Union' of Axis propaganda: 'It was a bleak and mournful autumn, which extinguished our last hopes of advancing further into the heart of the Soviet Union.'[92] The Soviet counterattack on the Don front began on 19 November, and the offensive against the Italian 8th Army was launched on 16 December. At this point the Italian air corps had 32 MC.200s, 11 MC.202s, 17 Fiat BR.20Ms, 15 Ca.311s and 12 SM.81 transports. On 18 December the Italians had to give up the Kantamirovka airfield. Pilots flying combat sorties against the advancing Soviet troops suffered frostbite – the Russian winter was overwhelming. The front began to disintegrate, and 11,000 Italians were surrounded by the Red Army at Scertkovo. The commander of the Italian air group, Gen Enrico Pezzi, came to help out in person, arriving in an SM.81 from 246a Squadriglia Transporto loaded with provisions, medical supplies and a doctor. After a successful landing in the 'pocket', the SM.81 was loaded with wounded and took off again on 29 December, but never reached Voroshilovgrad. Every trace of the SM.81 and its passengers was lost in the snow-covered Russian steppes. The well-worn Savoia-Marchetti transport aircraft were continuously in action, flying supplies to the front and returning with wounded, but five aircraft from 245a and 246a Squadrigli Transporto were lost.

The final operation of the 21° Gruppo Autonomo C.T. took place on 17 January 1943, when 25 Macchis attacked Soviet tanks and infantry in the Millerovo area to assist the hard-pressed German troops. After that the Italian air corps was pulled out of the front and transferred initially to Odessa. The German authorities refused any practical assistance, and the Italians began to experience a profusion of vexations and humiliations which reached such a pitch that the Italian air attaché in Berlin had to intervene. This was a more than bitter experience for the Italian airmen who had so often flown operations for the benefit of the German Wehrmacht and whose fighters had shot down 88 enemy aircraft on the Eastern Front.

In mid-May 1943 21° Gruppo Autonomo C.T., with 356a, 386a and 361a Squadrigli, was based at Florence and, like 22° Gruppo, another former Eastern Front formation, was engaged in home defence duties. The Italians had argued vigorously for an increase in the Axis air forces in the Mediterranean theatre since the end of December 1941. During his visit to the Führer's headquarters on 18 December 1942, the Chief of the Great General Staff, Marshal Ugo Cavallero, had requested a strengthening of the Axis air forces, especially on Sardinia and Sicily, by another 500 aircraft. In the following weeks, this figure of 500 additional aircraft became a constant subject matter of German-Italian consultations. Of course the German Reich could not deliver such a large number of planes, particularly fighters. In November 1943, during the course of an internal conference, Generalfeldmarschall Milch stated quite clearly: 'Today we just have not got the fighters, even if we produce 1,000 a month, to supply sufficiently the fronts and the Homeland.'[93] Naturally Hitler did not want to admit this to the Italians and based his refusal on the grounds that the Italian airfields were already overcrowded and overloaded, and that, apart from that, the aircraft based there were not adequately protected against attack, and the airfields themselves were also poorly organized.[94] These allegations were not unjustified, although some of the problems could have been resolved with German assistance. In any case the Regia Aeronautica urgently needed aircraft, above all modern machines, because the Italian air force was suffering a severe crisis. In a report dated 15 April 1943, Gen Rino Corso Fougier, who had replaced Gen Pricolo as Undersecretary of State and Chief of Staff of the Air Force on 15 November 1941, referred to the difficulties suffered by the Regia Aeronautica without any attempt to minimize them:[95]

> Its material resources are quantitatively inadequate owing to the overly modest capacity of the Italian aviation industry, which has demonstrated its inability to manufacture aircraft in large series; qualitatively, the aircraft material also leaves much to be desired,

which is also due to the deficiencies of the industry and its technical tardiness; the flying personnel are in part inadequately trained and insufficient in numbers.

Fougier demanded a realistic operational strength of 38 fighter groups equipped with modern aircraft that had to be equal to Anglo-American planes.[96] However, at that time the Regia Aeronautica had only 12 fighter groups equipped with aircraft that were not completely outclassed (MC.202 and Re.2001).

Insofar as the fighter arm was concerned, there were several possibilities to relieve the situation: increased use of captured French aircraft, acquisition of German Messerschmitt fighters, and accelerated production of the most modern Italian models (the 5th series).

The transfer of captured French aircraft to Italy began in January 1943, but, apart from the LeO 451 and the Dewoitine D.520, Italy had no practical use for the machines of the former Vichy-French air force. The Italian air force command had high hopes for the D.520 fighter, which was supposed to be brought into the Italian Home defence. Luigi Gorrini from 85a Squadriglia, who had served as a ferry pilot for a while, reported: 'I have collected several dozen Dewoitine D.520s from various French airfields and the Toulouse factory. At the time, when we were still flying the MC.200, it was a good, if not a very good machine. Compared to the MC.200, it was superior only in one point – its armament of a 20mm cannon.'[97] The Hispano-Suiza HS 404 cannon, firing through the propeller hub – a weapon which the Italians lacked – promised better results when used against the heavy American bombers. Thus a total of 72 D.520 fighters[98] were passed on to the Regia Aeronautica to find use in various formations, such as 22°, 50° and 161° Gruppi. For the majority of Italian pilots, however, the D.520 seemed slow, heavy and unwieldy; they preferred the MC.202.

The Messerschmitt Bf 109, supplies of which began to reach Italy in spring 1943, found more acceptance.[99] To begin with the Luftwaffe fighter units operating in Italy passed over only 50 planes to their Axis partners, but by the Armistice in September

1943 the Italians probably received 114 examples.[100] Most of these were used operationally by 150° Gruppo Autonomo C.T. (49 Bf 109Gs, mostly of the G-6 version) and 3° Gruppo Autonomo C.T. Originally it was also intended to re-equip 4° Stormo C.T. with the Bf 109G, but as it received the Macchi MC.205 Veltro (Greyhound), the unit gave up its Bf 109Gs to 3° Stormo. The vast majority of the Italian-flown Bf 109 fighters were lost in the fight for Sicily.

What remained for the Italians were the hopes vested in the fighters of the famous 5th Series, designed as a result of a competitive tender – the Macchi MC.205V, the Fiat G.55 and the Reggiane Re.2005.[101] The Reggiane Re.2005 Sagittario (Archer) had made its first flight on 30 April 1942, and was subsequently thoroughly tested and compared to the Fiat G.55 at the Centro Sperimentale Aeromobile in Guidonia. The results were not as positive as the Reggiane works had hoped: they still had to overcome some teething troubles, such as the weak undercarriage. In addition, some test aircraft had suffered structural failures and distortions in dives and high-speed turns. The Reggiane works were also reproached for their inability to maintain a continuous production tempo, which had already led to complaints in the past. Nevertheless, a total of 750 Re.2005s was ordered by 18 April 1943. Of these, hardly 50 were to be delivered before the Armistice. These machines were allocated to 22° Gruppo C.T. and proved themselves in combat.

Of the three competing fighter models built by Fiat, Reggiane and Macchi (all powered by the licence-built DB 605 engine), the consensus of experts – including Germans – adjudged the Fiat G.55 Centauro as the best aircraft. The Luftwaffe authorities in Berlin were also interested in this model and, in autumn 1943, ordered 500 Centauros, of which, in the event, only 148 were to be completed. The Italians planned production of 3,600 machines for the Regia Aeronautica, far too ambitious a goal, because the British air raids on Turin late in 1942 had destroyed the assembly halls and thus rendered quick production of this excellent fighter impossible. As a result only 32 Fiat G.55s were actually delivered to the air force before the Armistice. The

Fighters of the 5th Series

	Macchi MC.205[1]	Fiat G.55	Reggiane Re.2005
Power plant	R.A.1050 R.C.58	R.A. 1050 R.C.58	R.A.1050 R.C.58
Span	10.5m (34.44ft)	11.85m (38.87ft)	11m (36.08ft)
Wing area	16.8sq. m (180.84sq. ft)	21.11sq. m (227.23sq. ft)	20.40sq.m (219.59sq. ft)
Length	8.85m (29.03ft)	9.38m (30.77ft)	8.73m (28.72ft)
Height	3.05m (10ft)	3.77m (12.36ft)	3.15m (10.33ft)
Empty weight	2,581kg (5,691lb)	2,730kg (6,020lb)	2,600kg (5,733lb)
Max. useful load	827kg (1,823.5lb)	990kg (2,183lb)	1,010kg (2,227lb)
Total weight	3,408kg (7,515lb)	3,720kg (8,202.6lb)	3,610kg (7,960lb)
Max. speed	644km/h (400mph)	620km/h (385mph)	629km/h (390mph)
Climb to 5,000m (16,400ft)	4.47 min	6.10 min	5.56 min
Climb to 6,000m (19,680ft)	5.53 min	7.12 min	6.33 min
Climb to 7,000m (22,960ft)	7.6 min	8.24 min	8.15 min
Climb to 8,000m (26,240ft)	9.10 min	9.54 min	9.42 min
Service ceiling	11,200m (36,736ft)	12,750m (41,820ft)	11,500m (37,720ft)
Range	950km (590 miles)	1,020km (633 miles)	980km (608.6 miles)
Standard armament	2 x 12.7mm[2] 2 x 7.7 mm	4 x 12.7mm 1 x 20 mm	4 x 12.7mm 1 x 20 mm

[1]A progressive development of the MC.205V was the MC.205NI resp. N2 Orione, which had an enlarged wing span and wing area for better performance above 10,000m (32,800ft).
[2]Armament of the I. Series. The III. Series were fitted with 2 x 20mm cannon instead of 2 x 7.7mm machine guns in the wings.

Centauro was to fly with 353a Squadriglia for the first time on 5 June 1943.

The Macchi MC.205 Veltro did not really correspond to the specifications of the 5th Series tender as it was not an entirely original creation but rather an improvement of the MC.202 with a considerably more powerful engine. The weak feature of the aircraft was its high-altitude performance, which left something to be desired. Nevertheless, more MC.205s were built prior to September 1943 than Fiat G.55 and Re.2005 combined, a total of 177 machines, of which 146 reached the front-line formations. The Macchi fighter possessed some excellent qualities, and the Italian pilots made optimum use of the aircraft, which had a maximum speed of 644km/h (400mph). Among others, it was used operationally by 4°, 51° and 3° Stormi C.T. The 1° Stormo was also equipped with a few MC.205Vs. On 20 April 1943 the Italian fighter pilots proved what they were capable of when mounted on up-to-date equipment. Over the Straits of Sicily 30 MC.202s and MC.205Vs from 1° Stormo clashed with 60 Spitfires. Losing only two of their own fighters, the Italians shot down 17 Spitfires. As a special favour, Luigi Gorrini from 3° Stormo C.T., who had by February 1943 achieved four confirmed victories and one unconfirmed, was also given an MC.205V. On 27 August he succeeded in shooting down two Boeing B-17 Fortress bombers (confirmed) and one Lockheed P-38 Lightning (unconfirmed) over Latium in central Italy; up to the Armistice Luigi Gorrini claimed 18 victories, including three unconfirmed ones.[102]

These individual successes could not disguise the fact that far too few MC.205V fighters were being delivered, a result of the completely inadequate Italian production planning. In parallel with the MC.205V, the factories were still continuing to build the MC.202 and even the totally outdated MC.200. Because of this only 55 modern MC.205Vs were completed in the period September 1942 to May 1943, but in the same time 372 MC.202s and no fewer than 109 MC.200 fighters were delivered! This was an irresponsible waste of resources and production capacity. Many Italian fighter pilots still had to take off in tired and obsolete Fiat G.50s and MC.200s to face modern Anglo-American

ITALY

machines when the invasion of Italy began. Some of the pilots
were close to desperation. 'Why haven't we got better aircraft?'
a fighter pilot from 8° Gruppo C.T. asked in June 1943, just after
he had attempted in vain to shoot down an American B-17
bomber. 'I have a strange taste in my mouth, and blood runs over
my lips, I have bitten them till they bled ... and then there are
tears, which blind my goggles, burning tears, which I cannot
hold back, tears of desperate rage...'[103]

The Regia Aeronautica was insufficiently armed or prepared
to repulse an Anglo-American assault on its homeland.[104] This
was the case with all its equipment, but especially the night
fighters.[105] As no serviceable night fighting structure or suitable
aircraft were available in Italy, in January 1942 the Regia
Aeronautica turned to its German allies for assistance. In the
event, among the 200 aircraft delivered by Germany to Italy
there were only 18 night fighters, three Bf 110s and 15 Do 217Js!

For the defence of Sicily the Axis powers proffered 1,400
aircraft, including 620 Italian, distributed on airfields in Central
Italy, Apulia, Sicily and Sardinia. This impressive number
becomes relatively less so when one takes into account that only
40–60 per cent of the Italian aircraft were operational, and that
the Allies had an air fleet of 3,680 machines for the invasion of
Sicily. The Italian fighter pilot Adriano Visconti gave Maj
Johannes Steinhoff, commander of JG 77 in Italy, the following
overview of the almost hopeless situation the Italian fighters
were in:[106]

He began to talk about the miserable conditions. His primary
means of command was the telephone, with which he could only
seldom achieve contact with his commander. There were also no
contacts whatsoever with the German radar at Marsala, and he
could only observe with envy how the German fighters, warned
in time, would take off for action, because it had become clear to
him that without this ground control success could only come
by pure chance. Nobody warned him when the enemy was
approaching, and he never received any orders in the air at all.

In June 1943 the Allies began their preparations for the invasion with a concentrated aerial offensive against the airfields,

road and rail junctions in Sicily. In the first week of July the Axis pilots succeeded in shooting down 375 Anglo-American machines, but they themselves lost almost the same number of aircraft, many of them on the ground.[107] When on the night of 10 July the Allies landed on the Sicilian coast (Operation Husky), the Regia Aeronautica sent everything southwards, to Sicily and Calabria, to drive the invaders back into the sea. On 12 July 161 Italian fighters (77 ready for action), 91 close-support aircraft, 26 Italian-manned Ju 87 Stukas and 15 bombers and torpedo-bombers (12 operational) were deployed in the combat area. If these aircraft did not manage to seriously affect the battle, this was due solely to Allied aerial superiority, not to lack of courage or determination on the part of the Axis pilots: unlike some of their command, who had already made prepara-tions for a switch to the Allied camp, they had 'not yet allowed themselves to be poisoned by politics'.[108]

Two examples suffice to demonstrate the intensity of the fighting at that time. On 13 July eight Ju 87 Stukas of 121° Gruppo Tuffatori, protected by only five MC.202 and MC.205V fighters from 4° Stormo, took off from Crotone (Calabria) to attack targets near Augusta. Seven of the Italian-flown Ju 87s were shot down. Six days later, 16 Re.2002s of 5° Stormo d'Assalto, escorted by six MC.202s and 14 Bf 109s, dived on Allied ships. They were intercepted by Spitfire V fighters from No 152 Sqn, based on Malta, and five Re.2002s were shot down. Most of the Axis aircraft were destroyed on the ground, however. The following airfields were already no longer usable by 12 July: Gerbini, Sciacca, Gela and Caltagirone S. Pietro; others were only marginally operational.[109] It was the situation on these airfields that moved Hitler, on 19 July, to give Mussolini a severe lecture about the deficient organization of the Regia Aeronautica. When the Allies took Catania they found 132 damaged and destroyed Axis aircraft, and another 189 in Gerbini. In the two months of fighting around and over Sicily, the Italians lost 800 aircraft, and the Germans 586.[110] Most of the Italian public was apathetic and war-weary, and often reacted indifferently to the self-sacrifice of their own air force. Some Italian pilots even had markedly unpleasant encounters with their own civilian population. Amleto Monterumici, from 90a Squadriglia, 10° Gruppo/4° Stormo C.T., was shot down over Sicily on 9 July. For three days he wandered around the island, subsisting on apples and prickly pears. Then he chanced upon an elderly woman in a remote farmhouse: 'I politely asked her for a glass of water, and she replied with insults in the Sicilian dialect, spat in my face and threatened me with a large stick, because the war was our soldiers' fault.'[111]

Sicily fell to the Allies on 17 August after 38 days of fighting. Mussolini had already been overthrown on 25 July, but this had had no decisive effect on the morale of the Regia Aeronautica. Luigi Gorrini, from 85a Squadriglia, 18° Gruppo/3° Stormo G.T., recalled:[112]

After 25 July, despite the arrest of Mussolini, the morale of the unit and my personal readiness for action remained high. Despite all the reverses that Italy had suffered by that time, our Stormo was the only one still fully ready for combat: my section was detailed to defend Rome. The larger part of the Regia Aeronautica was uninterested in politics or parties – they were men infatuated with flying and determined to defend the land of their birth and to give their lives if necessary in the attempt to stop the bombing of Italian towns.

During the last two years of the war Allied bombing raids cost 64,000 Italian lives.[113]

In his first inspection speech Gen Renato Sandalli, Fougier's successor, left the Italian airmen in no doubt that the war would go on despite Mussolini's removal from office: 'The path we have to travel is clearly laid out: to do our duty utterly and completely, silently and with the greatest discipline.'[114] The switch to the Allied side had long been decided in Rome, however. On 3 September a then still secret armistice was agreed between the Italian Kingdom and the Anglo-Americans at Cassibile, Sicily. On the same day, the British 8th Army landed on the southern coast of Calabria. The diminishing remnants of the Regia Aeronautica at once began to attack the landing zone. A group of 15 Re.2002s from 5° Stormo d'Assalto, led by their commander, Maj Giuseppe Cenni, took off from Manduria and threw itself against the invading troops. Three pilots, including Cenni, were killed in combat. 'Nobody at the front knew that an armistice had been signed on 3 September under the olive trees of Cassibile. For those few people in Rome who knew about this, the lives of Cenni and his pilots were apparently worthless – or perhaps only of value insofar as they helped to conceal the capitulation.'[115]

In early September 1943 the Regia Aeronautica was wasting away and at the end of its strength. It had just 800 operational aircraft, but they were distributed all over Italy and in occupied foreign territory.[116]

The Regia Aeronautica in early September 1943

On the Italian Peninsula

1st Air Fleet	78 aircraft (63 fighters and 15 bombers)
2nd Air Fleet	1 bomber
3rd Air Fleet	121 aircraft (64 fighters and 57 bombers)

Outside the Italian Peninsula

Sardinia	43 aircraft (incl. 33 fighters and 8 bombers)
Aegean	33 aircraft (25 fighters and 8 bombers)
Albania	56 aircraft (16 fighters and 40 bombers)
Greece	9 fighters
Slovenia/Dalmatia	26 aircraft (13 fighters and 13 bombers)

A further 146 army aircraft, 104 naval seaplanes and 133 transport aircraft can be added to this total, as well as training and liaison aircraft, and others under repair.

The break from the Axis on 8 September 1943 found the Regia Aeronautica, with its 12,000 officers and 167,000 NCOs and other ranks, completely unprepared. It dissolved and disinte-

ITALY

grated, and a number of personal and collective dramas and tragedies were played out. Only 200 pilots obeyed the orders of their government, which had taken flight under the Allied protection, and flew their aircraft southwards. German troops occupied northern and central Italy, and seized hundreds of Italian aircraft. Referring to this, the Chief of the Wehrmacht Führungsstab (Operations Staff) declared in a statement about the military situation on 7 November 1943 that the booty amounted to 4,553 aircraft, including 2,867 front-line models.[117] However, these figures have to be taken with some caution and seem exaggerated, even if one adds the sports aircraft and sail-planes, aircraft still under construction and written-off machines. An indication of the actual size of the German booty can be found in the Flugzeugbestands- und Flugbetriebsstatistik (Aircraft Inventory and Flying Operations Statistics) of the GQM (Quartermaster-General) of the Luftwaffe for March 1944.[118] The Italian air force contingent in German service totalled 1,031 aircraft, although by that time numerous Italian aircraft had already been given back to the new Republican-Fascist air force, the ANR.

The story of the Regia Aeronautica as part of Mussolini's forces came to an end on 8 September 1943. From 10 June 1940 up to that date, the Royal Italian Air Force had lost 12,748 men, including 1,806 officers. The aircraft losses amounted to 6,483 planes, including 3,483 fighters, 2,273 bombers, torpedo-bombers and transports, as well as 227 reconnaissance aircraft. The Regia Aeronautica itself claimed the destruction of 4,293 enemy aircraft, including 1,771 reportedly destroyed on the ground.[119]

The government in southern Italy tried to build up another fighting force from the remains of the air force found in that area. This new air force not only had to look for spare parts for its aircraft on the former battlefields of North Africa, but the Allies also forbade them to operate over Italy. Instead, the reconstituted Regia Aeronautica began flying over the Balkans, carrying supplies to the Tito Communist partisans – the same partisans who now claimed Trieste and the Italian territories in Dalmatia. Many of the pilots were disillusioned, had doubts

75

about the sense of their operations and despised the politicians whose slogans no longer meant anything to them.[120] In the summer of 1944 the reconstituted Regia Aeronautica became part of the Allied Balkan Air Force and received replacement aircraft from the Allies to compensate for the high wear-and-tear rate of the Italian types then in service. These deliveries amounted to 149 Bell P-39 Airacobra and 33 Spitfire V fighters, and 33 Martin Baltimore bombers. The reconstituted Regia Aeronautica was not rated as an ally by the Anglo-Americans, but only as a co-belligerent air force, and for that reason had to be satisfied with second-hand, reconditioned aircraft.[121]

Aeronautica Nazionale Repubblicana (ANR)

In the meantime, the Repubblica Sociale Italiana (RSI) had been created in northern and central Italy under the leadership of Mussolini, who had been liberated by the Germans. The young republic began to build up new armed forces, including an air force, which was designated ANR (Aeronautica Nazionale Repubblicana). On 12 October and 31 December the legendary Lt Col Ernesto Botto, the newly appointed Undersecretary of the new Republican air force, appealed to airmen to recruit over the radio, and his plea did not go unheard: by January 1944 6,997 men[122] had enlisted in the ANR. Ernesto Botto had lost a leg while serving as a fighter pilot in Spain, but had continued to fly operationally during 1940–3. He had commanded the fighter-training school at Gorizia before joining the ANR.

Motives for joining the new air force varied. For one thing, Mussolini's educational system had stressed for years the high value of the terms 'fatherland', 'honour' and 'national dignity'. For another, the abrupt change of sides of the Badoglio regime seemed reprehensible, not only to the Fascists but to many ordinary Italians. What happened on 8 September had thrown the country into chaos and had led to the dissolution of the armed forces, while the pro-royalist caste had removed themselves to southern Italy and safety in good time. Joining the ANR was therefore often not only an expression of patriotism but also rebellion against the politics of the king and Marshal Badoglio.

Furthermore, a dislike of stabbing their long-standing allies in the back and abandoning the population of northern Italy to Allied bombing raids influenced the decision of many pilots in their reaction to Botto's appeal. Luigi Gorrini did not hesitate to rejoin combat against the Anglo-Americans:[123]

> After flying for three years side by side with the German pilots, on the English Channel, in North Africa, Greece, Egypt, Tunisia and finally over my own homeland, I had made friends with some of them, particularly from JG 27 ... I did not want to hang my coat in the wind, so to speak, and perhaps fire on my German friends. Also, I wanted to protect the northern Italian towns from indiscriminate bombing as much as possible.

Other pilots were traumatized by the events, absolutely distrusting politics. In a country convulsed by a serious moral, military and political crisis, where the values of yesterday were no longer worth anything, the squadron and trusted comrades were the only reliable reference point.

Twenty-three-year old 1st Lt Vittorio Satta, a former member of 374a Squadriglia, 153° Gruppo C.T. of the Regia Aeronautica, wrote the following lines in his diary on 23 December 1943:[124]

> Today my first flight in the new formation of the Republican air force: take-off with an MC.205 from Lagnassco airfield. A day that dispelled all the doubts that had tortured me during the last few months; a day that cleared up all uncertainties and had made me content, even if my present pleasure will always be combined with a grain of sadness ... Two forward-firing cannon in the wings have reawakened in me a clear sense of duty, and have revived in me the decision to offer the extreme sacrifice and restore the honour of our people in the eyes of the world. The little that I can do, I will.

Satta proved that his diary note was more than just a momentary sentiment. He died on 25 May 1944, in aerial combat with P-38 Lightnings 7km (4 miles) south-east of Parma.

A large part of the élite of the former Regia Aeronautica came together in the ANR: the fighter aces Adriano Visconti, Ugo

Drago, Mario Bellagambi and Tito Falconi, as well as the torpedo-bomber pilots Marino Marini (rescued from the Mediterranean by the German submarine *U-331* in February 1942), Carlo Faggioni (killed on 10 April 1944), Irnerio Bertuzzi and Ottone Sponza. One well-known Italian airman could not follow Botta's call: Col Ettore Muti was shot dead under mysterious circumstance in Fregere, near Rome, on 23 August 1943. There are indications that the principal behind this murder was Marshal Badoglio, who saw this highly decorated war hero and former Fascist functionary, with his good contacts in Germany, as a threat and wanted to eliminate him.[125]

As the Wehrmacht had seized all serviceable Italian aircraft, it took several rounds of Italian-German negotiations to acquire machines, material and personnel for the Republican air force. In October 1943 Botto reached an agreement[126] in Berlin with Generaloberst Korten, Chief of the Luftwaffe General Staff, that envisaged that the Italians would initially form one Gruppo each of fighters, torpedo-bombers, bombers, and reconnaissance and transport aircraft, as well as one Gruppo of seaplanes. The Germans promised to return the confiscated aircraft and to make available to the ANR the Italian flying personnel that had in the meantime been taken into Luftwaffe service. As a matter of fact, some Italian pilots were flying operationally with the Luftwaffe in German uniforms. The Luftwaffe night harassment group NSGr.9, formed at the end of 1943, had 14 Italian pilots in its ranks for a while, and the Italian fighter pilot Renato Gori had been taken on by 8./JG 53. Some former Regia Aeronautica pilots also served with JG 77, the II.Gruppe of which operated with requisitioned MC.205V Veltro fighters until the end of 1943.[127] One of these airmen was Feldwebel Igino Scarpa (5./JG 77) who transferred to 3a Squadriglia of 1° Gruppo of the ANR in spring 1944. A special unit was formed to return the seized Italian machines from Germany. It operated under different names, appearing as Gruppo Transporte Velivoli (GTV) on 12 May 1944. By spring 1944 the pilots of the GTV had ferried 1,300 aircraft of all types to their intended Italian airfields. Due to the poor technical state of the aircraft, however, there were numerous accidents and about 40 pilots lost their lives.[128]

ITALY

The 1° Gruppo C.T. of the ANR came into being quite spontaneously, driven by the desire of the pilots to resume the fight. It was equipped with MC.205s, and, at the end of January 1944, was based at the Campoformido airfield. Its first operations, on 3 January, began with a surprise blow right away: the Italian fighter pilots shot down four P-38 Lightnings. By 25 February 1° Gruppo C.T. had reported 26 victories for nine losses.[129] Extremely bitter aerial combats took place on 11 March. The Italians claimed 12 victories for themselves, but lost three of their own pilots, including 1st Lt Boscutti, who was killed by an American P-38 Lightning pilot after he had baled out from his stricken fighter and was hanging helpless under his parachute. This barbarity was repeated on 18 March, when 90 Axis aircraft – 30 MC.205s from 1° Gruppo C.T. and 60 Bf 109s from JG77 – joined combat with about 450 Allied bombers and their escort fighters. The ANR pilots shot down at least four enemy aircraft, but Corp Zaccaria was killed while hanging from his parachute by a P-38 Lightning pilot who deliberately fired at him from close range. Allegedly there was an RAF order that authorized the shooting of Axis pilots hanging from parachutes.[130] On 22 April 1944 1° Gruppo C.T. was transferred to Regia Emilia. They had to protect themselves against intense Allied air attacks aimed at destroying the Republican aircraft on the ground. Generally, however, aircraft losses were made good relatively quickly; for instance, late in May, 1° Gruppo C.T. received 27 Fiat G.55 Centauro fighters from 2° Gruppo.

The Republican fighter pilots who tried to stem the Allied bombing raids on northern Italian towns also had to learn that large sections of the population had only one wish – to end this war one way or another, at practically any price. For them the ANR were not defenders but people prolonging the war. The ANR pilots encountered distrust and even hatred. When 1st Lt Satta was wounded late in January 1944 and taken to a hospital, he was confronted by open hostility – 'from people who I had not believed could adopt such a hostile attitude'.[131] Yet others did give the ANR pilots the moral support they needed, for successful cash collections to acquire new aircraft were carried out in several towns.

The Republican torpedo-bomber group 'Buscaglia' joined the action in March 1944. It was still equipped with the robust but dated SM.79, of which no fewer than 61 (36 operational) had been in Regia Aeronautica service on 8 September 1943. One reason for such a high number of non-operational planes was that on aircraft powered by the Alfa Romeo 128 radial engines it was possible to increase the maximum speed to 486km/h (298mph) for a short period of time by using ethyl injection, but this also resulted in a high degree of engine wear and tear. Only 15 more SM.79s were built after 8 September 1943, and an additional five were overhauled by the Reggiane works.[132] The Republican pilots flew mostly the SM.79-III version, which had no ventral 'bathtub' position and featured strengthened armament. Counting the aircraft taken over from the Regia Aeronautica, the new deliveries and aircraft found in the depots and workshops, the ANR had a total of 73 SM.79s at its disposal. They were mostly based at Venegono, other approved bases being Merna di Gorizia and Perugia S. Egidio.

Their first target was the massed Allied shipping near the Anzio-Nettuno beachhead, where the US VI Corps had landed on 22 January 1944. On the evening of 10 March six ANR SM.79s attacked the enemy merchant ships, one SM.79 being lost. Five torpedo-bombers repeated the attack on the night of 13–14 March. The 'Buscaglia' group suffered heavy losses on 4 April. During a ferry flight by 13 aircraft from Lonate Pozzolo to Perugia the formation was intercepted by P-47 Thunderbolt fighters. Five SM.79s were shot down, and 27 members of the ANR lost their lives. Six days later the torpedo-bombers were operational again, but were again hit by disaster: only one of the four SM.79s sent out to attack the Anzio bridgehead returned. Capt Faggioni, the initiator of the Republican torpedo-bomber arm, was hit by AA fire and crashed into the sea. Capt Marino Marini took over the command of the group, which once more ventured into the lion's den, the rock fortress of Gibraltar.

This time it was a splendidly planned and prepared operation, carried out with great determination, but the group again fell victim to ill luck. On 4 June 1944 ten SM.79s took-off from Istres, in southern France, heading for Gibraltar. Nine aircraft reached the target and dropped their torpedoes over the port. On the return flight three aircraft ran short of fuel and had to land in Spain, the remaining machines, led by Marini, reaching their base in France. This attack came as a complete surprise to the British, but there is no definite information about the results of this action to this day. German observers at Algeçiras in Spain reported that four ships totalling 30,000 tons were badly damaged and two others were hit. The British dispute any Italian success and refer to the torpedo nets screening the port.[133] In any case the operation demonstrated the flying skills and high morale of the Republican torpedo airmen. It should be remembered that the Allies had taken Rome on the same day, and the territory of the Repubblica Sociale Italiana, ravaged by a brutal civil war, was shrinking rapidly.

A short while after the grim losses of April, Gruppo 'Buscaglia' was in action again. On the night of 6–7 July five SM.79s attacked the roadstead of Bari and claimed to have sunk one freighter of 8,000 tons and damaged two other ships. Afterwards several SM.79s were transferred to Eleusis/Athens to carry out anti-shipping strikes in the Eastern Mediterranean. It was hoped that this area offered better operational chances for these ageing machines. Their crews reported some successes when they returned to Lonate on 12 August. In October this ANR torpedo-bomber formation was renamed Gruppo O. M. Carlo Faggioni.[134]

In the meantime 2° Gruppo C.T. had been formed at Bresso, initially commanded by Lt Col Antonio Vizzoto, and later by Lt Col Aldo Alessandrini. The new unit received 40 Fiat G.55 fighters, but took part in only two aerial combats prior to 1 June, claiming three victories. At the end of May, this formation gave up its Fiat G.55s to the exhausted 1° Gruppo C.T., receiving German Messerschmitt Bf 109G-6/R6 fighters in exchange. These comprised 43 ex-I./JG 53 and II./JG 77 machines. This re-equipment was necessary because the Allied air raids on the Fiat works at Turin had considerably delayed Centauro production. A German order for 500 Fiat G.55 fighters also had to be revoked on 12 September, and only 148 G.55s had been completed by June 1944.[135]

Flying formations of the ANR on 1 July 1944

Unit	Base	Commander
Comando Caccia	Reggio Emilia	Lt Col Ettore Foschini
1° Gruppo C.T.[1]	Reggio Emilia	Maj G. Arrabito[2]
3a Squadriglia 'Occarso'	Reggio Emilia	Maj Cesare Marchesi
Squadriglia 'Bonet'[3]	Reggio Emilia	Capt Giulio Torresi
2° Gruppo C.T.	Cascina Vaga	Lt Col Aldo Alessandrini
1a Squadriglia 'Caneppele'	Cascina Vaga	1st Lt Ugo Drago
2a Squadriglia 'Magaldi'	Cascina Vaga	Capt Mario Bellagambi
3a Squadriglia 'Graffer'	Cascina Vaga	1st Lt Giuseppe Gianelli
Replacement fighter group[4]	Venaria	Lt Col Tito Falconi
Training squadron[5]	Cervere	Capt Fernando Malvezzi
Training school fighter sqn	Casabianca	Capt Vittorio Pezzè
Comando Aerosiluranti	Venegono	Lt Col Arduino Buri
Gruppo A.S. 'Buscaglia'	Lonate Pozzolo	Maj Marino Marini
1a Squadriglia	Lonate Pozzolo	1st Lt Gianfranco Neri
2a Squadriglia	Lonate Pozzolo	Capt Irnerio Bertuzzi
3a Squadriglia	Lonate Pozzolo	Capt Carlo Chinca
Training sqn	Venegono	Capt Dante Magagnoli
Instructional sqn	Bettola	Capt Michele Palumbo
Comando Aerotransporti	Bergamo	Lt Col Giuseppe Morino
Gruppo Transporto		
'Terracciano'[6]	Goslar	Maj Egidio Pellizzari
1a Squadriglia	Goslar	Capt Nicolò Falco
2a Squadriglia	Goslar	Capt Silvio Brighenti
3a Squadriglia	Goslar	Capt Ugo Pierotti
Gruppo Transporto		
'Trabucchi'[7]	Goslar	Maj Alfredo Zanardi
1a Squadriglia	Goslar	Capt Salvatore Cantarella
2a Squadriglia	Goslar	Capt Eugenio Geymet
3a Squadriglia	Goslar	Capt Erio Fantini
Sq Bombardamento 'E. Muti'[8]	Lonate Pozzolo	Maj Gino Giordanino
Gruppo Transporto Velivoli[9]	S. Pietro di Gorizia	Maj Pietro Zigiotti
1a Squadriglia	S. Pietro di Gorizia	Lt Adolfo Sehernet
2a Squadriglia	S. Pietro di Gorizia	1st Lt Renato Lamborghini
3a Squadriglia	S. Pietro di Gorizia	1st Lt Pompeo Nespolo
Reparto Aereo Collegamenti	Bresso	Maj B. Quattrociocchi

ITALY

The retraining of the Italian pilots on the Bf 109G proceeded without a hitch because many of them had already flown this type of plane while serving with the Regia Aeronautica in 1943. The training programme followed the German standard, with special emphasis on formation flying and radar-controlled guidance from the ground.

While 2° Gruppo C.T. was retraining 1° Gruppo was beset by a crisis, which had both psychological and political origins. After six months of hard fighting against a numerically superior enemy a number of the pilots were feeling exhausted, especially after learning that the German National Socialists were trying to reduce the RSI to the status of a protectorate, and were interfering in all its internal affairs. The well-liked Botto was forced to leave in March, not least because in his speech of 31 December he had struck a clear note and taken a stand against any subordination to the German partner: 'Those who are only servile and carry out their work for the Germans out of opportunism cannot be with me. Only honest allies and comrades of the Germans can join me.'[136]

Maj Adriano Visconti, commander of 1° Gruppo C.T., presented Gen Tessari, Botto's successor, with a catalogue of clear-cut demands that left nothing in doubt. He demanded a

---

[1] The 1st and 2nd Squadrons were effectively disbanded in mid-June 1944
[2] Maj Adriano Visconti took over the command of 1° Gruppo C.T. again on 26 July 1944
[3] Formed as Squadriglia 'Montefusco', but named after its leader Giovanni Bonet, who was killed in action on 29 May 1944. Mid-June attached to 1° Gruppo C.T.
[4] Disbanded on 15 September 1944
[5] Became 3° Gruppo C.T. on 15 August 1944
[6] German designation: Transport-Gruppe Italien 10
[7] German designation: Transport-Gruppe Italien 110
[8] Formed on 15 June and disbanded on 30 September 1944
[9] Subordinated to German Luftflotte 2 up to May 1944; disbanded on 4 August 1944

Source: Alegi, Gregory, 'La legione che non fu mai. L'Aeronautica Nazionale Repubblicana e la crisi dell' estate 1944', in *Storia contemporanea*, December 1992, pp. 1,084–5

strict segregation of politics and the armed forces, a thorough cleansing of the ANR of all incompetent elements and profiteers, a clear explanation of the relationship of the RSI to the Reich, particularly regarding the German operational zones in the Alpine foothills and the Adriatic coastal areas, which had broken free from Mussolini's sovereignty. He further demanded an immediate intervention by the Fascist government to stop confiscations and deportations by the Germans.[137]

Gen Tessari's reaction was to send Visconti 'on leave', and then dissolve 1a and 2a Squadrigli and the 'Bonet' replacement squadron attached to them. Despite this weakening, the unit continued to fly operationally.

The 2° Gruppo C.T. took off from Cascina Vaga on its first operational flight with its Bf 109 'Gustavs' on 22 June 1944. Three days later it shot down two P-47 Thunderbolts from the Gaullist French G.C.II/3. At this stage the Italians planes had increasingly to take over the role of home defence as the Luftwaffe command had progressively reduced the number of single-engined fighters assigned to this task from 380 on 1 July 1943 to just 65 by the end of June 1944. Apart from that, the ANR pilots also had to operate increasingly beyond their own borders. For example, on 25 July, 18 Bf 109Gs from 2° Gruppo were ordered to Tulln in Austria, where they were tactically subordinated to JG 53 and operated together with German fighters against a massed Allied bomber raid. Eight B-24 Liberators were shot down during this combined German-Italian action.

Neither the Allies nor serious political-psychological problems had been able to destroy the Aeronautica Nazionale Repubblicana, but the Germans now attempted to 'neutralize' the small but active air force of their Axis partner. Already at the end of 1943 the Chief of Luftflotte 2 in Italy, Generalfeldmarschall Wolfram Freiherr von Richthofen, had supported the idea of transferring highly qualified Italian air force personnel into German service, although this attempt was stymied by the agreement between Botto and Korten. Now, in summer 1944, the time seemed ripe for Richthofen to realize his plan. The ANR was to be dissolved and its personnel taken over by a 'Legione Aerea Italiana' as part of the German Luftwaffe. As usual with National Socialist decisions, this undertaking took the form of an act of force, uninfluenced by any sympathetic understanding or political considerations.[138] To begin with the ANR were refused aviation fuel. Then, on 25 August 1944, German troops surrounded the airfields used by the ANR and presented the Italian airmen with an ultimatum: join the German-controlled Legion, or be transferred to the flak arm. In response to this provocation, the pilots of 1° Gruppo C.T. set fire to their 30 MC.205V and Fiat G.55 fighters. The 2° Gruppo was approached by the commander of JG 77, Johannes Steinhoff, who passed on the message from his GFM in person. But nobody joined the Legion. Some Italian airmen, including Visconti, asked Mussolini to intervene. He sent a bitter letter to Hitler on 30 August: 'Matters have been handled as though it were Badoglio's air force at issue rather than the Republican one. The humiliation suffered by the soldiers and officers is truly grievous and incomprehensible.'[139] After this the Legion project was not pursued any further, and GFM von Richthofen went on sick leave, being replaced by Ritter von Pohl. This stupid action had paralyzed the ANR, which remained inactive for ten weeks, as the Germans had also seized all Bf 109G fighters flown by 2° Gruppo.

The dissolution of both Italian transport groups 'Trabucchi' and 'Terracciano' had also to be viewed in connection with the Richthofen plan: both units ceased to exist following an OKL order of 21 August 1944. The transport group 'Trabucchi' (German designation: Transport-Gruppe Italien 110) was never used operationally and, after being disbanded, was based at Goslar. The transport group 'Terracciano', commanded by Maj Egidio Pellizzari, was formed at Bergamo and transferred to Goslar in January 1944, where 40 SM.81 transport aircraft were waiting for the Italians. These three-engined machines were in a deplorable condition, some being unserviceable and others damaged, and they had to be restored to operational state by their future crews. Administratively the Italians were subordinated to the ANR, but operationally to the Luftwaffe, a situation that left ample scope for friction and vexation with the

Germans to develop. On 8 April 1944 the first squadron equipped with 12 SM.81s was deployed to Šiauliai in Lithuania, followed by other aircraft from the 2nd and 3rd squadrons as they where reconditioned. As in Goslar, the co-operation between the alliance partners was encumbered by the hostile and discriminatory behaviour of the German authorities. The 'Terracciano' group, known under the German designation as 'Transport Gruppe Italien 10', flew its supply and delivery operations over the Baltic States, Russia and Finland, evacuating the wounded and carrying fresh troops to the front. At the time of the Soviet breakthrough to Jelgava in Latvia late in July 1944, the unit still had 32 operational aircraft. It could have carried on flying, but the fuel shortage and lack of German interest in Italian transport led to the group being disbanded.

The reconstruction of the ANR began in September 1944, when the last German fighters were withdrawn from Italy, leaving the task of opposing some 3,500 enemy aircraft solely to the Italians. The Luftwaffe Oberst 'Edu' Neumann, who knew and valued the Italians from their joint operations in North Africa, was appointed as Jagdfliegerführer (fighter leader) Northern Italy.[140] It was a fortunate choice for both sides, and from then on things began to happen quickly. Neumann soon discovered that, despite the course of the war and the arbitrary German actions of August, the fighting morale of the Italian pilots was higher than in some fighter formations of the old Regia Aeronautica (see Appendix 4). The 2° Gruppo received new Bf 109Gs and resumed its operations against the enemy from its bases at Ghedi (Brescia) and Villafranca on 19 October 1944. In November 1° Gruppo was transferred to Holzkirchen for retraining on the Bf 109. On their return to Italy (from February 1945) the Italian pilots, based at Malpensa and Lonate Pozzolo airfields, rejoined the conflict with 52 Bf 109Gs on 10 March. In December 1944 the remaining 17 pilots of 1° Gruppo had been redeployed to Rangsdorf, in Berlin, to initiate a training course for later operations with the Me 163 Komet rocket fighter. However, this course was destined not to be completed and the pilots returned to their parent unit in February 1945.

There was also a 3° Gruppo C.T., which had been officially established on 15 August 1944, and had been posted to Holzkirchen with 76 pilots for retraining on the Bf 109. Only four Bf 109Gs from this group were to reach northern Italian airfields before the end of hostilities.

After a pause, the ten serviceable SM.79s of the torpedo-bomber group, which had operated from Ghedi in October, became active again. On 25 December they attacked a convoy near Ancona and Capt Bertuzzi reported a torpedo hit on a freighter of 7,000 tons. One day later a swarm of P-47 Thunderbolts destroyed 14 of Marini's torpedo-bombers on the Lonate Pozzolo airfield. On 5 January 1945 two SM.79s flew the last operational sortie of the group and sank a 5,000-ton ship off the Dalmatian coast. The planned re-equipment of the torpedo-bomber group with Fiat G.55s carrying an underslung 920kg (2,028lb) Whitehead torpedo could in the event not be realized.

At first the considerable losses suffered by both ANR fighter groups in February and March 1945 seemed to have little effect insofar as the operational readiness of the pilots was concerned. On 14 March alone, 1° Gruppo lost nine Bf 109Gs. On 2 April 2° Gruppo experienced a catastrophe when, during aerial combat with American fighters, 14 Bf 109Gs were shot down and seven Italian pilots lost their lives. On 19 April another two Italian pilots died in aerial combat: Lt Aurelio Morandi from 1° Gruppo and Corp Renato Patton from 2° Gruppo. Patton's death was especially tragic because he was a victim of the Italian civil war: an Italian resistance 'fighter' had sabotaged his parachute.[141]

During the hectic days of the collapse of the RSI, various plans, first aired months earlier, were again discussed by the ministers, functionaries and members of Mussolini's entourage – plans to help Mussolini escape by submarine or aircraft.[142] The 'safe havens' under consideration were Spain and Argentina, and suitable aircraft included a Cant floatplane, the proven SM.75GA that had demonstrated its capabilities during the long-distance flight to Tokyo in summer 1942, and a Piaggio aerial ambulance that could reach the Balearic or Canary Isles. In mid-April 1945 an SM.79 with a specially selected crew was standing on the Ghedi airfield, ready to fly the Duce to Spain. Even on 25 April, when Mussolini left Milan and headed in a northerly direction, he could still have saved himself by climbing aboard an aircraft standing ready for take-off at Milan-Linate. But he turned down all such rescue plans.

The wave of terror that convulsed northern Italy in spring 1945 and ended the civil war did not spare the Republican airmen. Probably the last members of the ANR to lose their lives were the commander of 1° Gruppo C.T., Maj Adriano Visconti, who, with at least 10 victories to his credit, was one of the most successful Italian fighter pilots of the war, and his ADC, Lt Valerio Stefanini, who were murdered by Communist partisans in Milan on 29 April after their unit had already surrendered.

Until recently the accepted figure of aerial victories achieved by the ANR fighter pilots between January 1944 and April 1945 has stood at 240, plus another 115 unconfirmed.[143] A recheck with British and American records shows that the actual number of victories was probably only a quarter of this figure.[144] 'It would serve no purpose to accuse the protagonists of falsifying their claims or, even worse, to underrate their moral involvement and personal bravery that was so essential to continue fighting under conditions of total inferiority ...'[145] Certainly the Swiss, on whose territory many war-weary crews and their aircraft found sanctuary, could testify to ANR dedication in that, at the end of the war, there were no fewer than 186 American heavy bombers parked on Swiss airfields, but there was only one ANR machine, an MC.205 that had landed at Lausanne on 4 March 1944.[146]

Romania

Fortele Aeriene Regale Romana

The Royal Romanian Air Force (Fortele Aeriene Regale Romana, FARR) came into being in 1913. Although Romania was an agrarian state, the FARR was eventually able to rely on the support of a national aviation industry[1] that was dominated by three firms: the Societates Pentru Exploatari Tehnice (SET), founded in Bucharest in 1923; the Industria Aeronautica Romana (IAR) founded in Brasov in 1925 and nationalized in 1938; and the Interprenderes de Constructii Aeronautice Romanesti (ICAR), established in Bucharest in 1932. In the period 1936–8 SET built 60 SET 7K observation and liaison aircraft and 80 American Fleet 10G two-seat trainers. In 1940 this aircraft plant also delivered 40 licence-built Italian Nardi FN 305 fighter-trainers and, in 1941–2, assembled 36 Polish RWS trainers from parts received from Germany. Further production series consisted of models that really should have been built by the IAR but could not be because production of the IAR 80 fighter took priority. So in 1941–2 SET built 30 IAR 39s, and, in 1943–4, 110 IAR 39A three-seat biplanes that were to be used for reconnaissance, as light bombers and as liaison aircraft. During the period 1939–2 SET also built 80 IAR 27 two-seat trainers.

ICAR was also to limit itself to the building of training and liaison/communications aircraft. During the period 1939–43 a total of 210 Fleet 10G trainers left the ICAR works; up to 23 August 1944 this concern also completed 10 Fieseler Fi 156 Storchs.

The largest aircraft producer was the Brasov-situated IAR. Between 1925 and 1933 it produced exclusively French designs, but in 1937–8 built 95 Polish PZL P.11F fighters under licence. Despite its rather modest maximum speed of 390km/h (242mph), this high-wing monoplane still equipped the Romanian 41st and 46th Fighter squadrons in 1940 and these machines were not passed on to the training units until 1942.

Other Polish fighters built under licence by the IAR were 25 PZL P.24Es in 1939, which, together with five examples bought direct from Poland, were allocated to two fighter squadrons of Grupul 6 Vanatoare (Fighter Group). But, relatively early, the IAR had begun to develop its own original models. Among these were the IAR 37, 38 and 39 biplanes, which equipped 12 liaison/communications squadrons (Esc. 11–22) between 1940 and 1944. These machines also found use as reconnaissance aircraft, light bombers, low-level attack aircraft and in the coastal defence role.

The IAR's most famous brainchild, however, was the IAR 80 single-seat fighter, which made its first flight in April 1939 and surprised the aviation experts with its maximum speed of 510km/h (317mph), service ceiling of 11,000m (36,000ft) and ability to climb to 5,000m (16,400ft) in 6 minutes. In December 1939 the government in Bucharest ordered 100 IAR 80s, succeeded by another 100 in August 1940. Further orders for batches of 50 IAR 80s followed on 5 September 1941 and 11 April 1942, then another 100 on 28 May 1942, to be followed by 35 of the IAR 8IC development in February 1943, with a further 15 in January 1944.

The first 20 IAR 80 fighters powered by the IAR 14 K II C 36 radial engine of 930hp and armed with four 7.92mm Browning machine guns were delivered in February 1941. The following 30 machines were fitted with a more powerful engine of 960hp. These aircraft were allocated to the Grupul 8 Vanatoare. An unusual feature of these aircraft was that they did not have a tail wheel but a tail skid. In the event, the IAR 80 was built in a number of versions. As the German Luftwaffe command refused to grant permission for the licence-production of the BMW 801 to improve the IAR 80 performance, the Romanian fighter could only be fitted with a 1,025hp engine and was considered outdated from 1942 onwards. Nevertheless, the well-armed IAR 81C version still achieved notable successes against low-flying American bombers. Altogether 21 Romanian fighter squadrons were equipped with the IAR 80 or one of its derivatives.

The following subtypes of the IAR 80 were built between 1941 and 1944:[2]

Model	Number	Particulars
IAR 80A	90	6 x FN 7.92mm mgs 1 x IAR 14 K 1000A radial of 1,023hp
IAR 81	50	Dive bomber; 1 x 225kg (496lb) bomb under the fuselage. Some machines had devices for an additional 50kg (110lb) bomb under each wing
IAR 80B	50	4 x FN 7.92mm mgs 2 x 13.2mm mgs Some machines had attachments for an additional under-fuselage fuel tank or a 50kg (110lb) bomb
IAR 80C	50	4 x FN 7.92 mm mgs 2 x Ikaria 20mm cannon Some machines had attachments for two additional fuel tanks or 2 x 50kg (110lb) bombs
IAR 81A	10	IAR 81 modified as a fighter
IAR 81C	150	2 x FN 7.92mm mgs 2 x Mauser MG 151/20 20mm cannon
IAR 80M	?	IAR 80A fighters brought up to IAR 80C armament standard.
IAR 81M	?	IAR 81 fighters brought up to the IAR 81C armament standard

The IAR 81C was manufactured until July 1944. Romanian plans to replace the proven but outdated IAR 80 and its developments with licence-built Messerschmitt Bf 109 were not to be realized. The Germans eventually granted the required licence in 1943, but only six Bf 109G-4 fighters were completed by the time of the Romanian subversion in August 1944. This batch was followed by 11 more built by the end of the war, with a further 58 completed afterwards, the total output thus amounting to 75 'Romanian' Bf 109G-4s.

What the IAR 80 was to the FARR fighter arm, the Italian Savoia-Marchetti SM.79B was to the bomber arm. In 1937 Romania ordered 24 twin-engined SM.79B bombers fitted with Gnôme-Rhône K 14 radials of 1,000hp. However, these aircraft proved to be underpowered, and further examples of the bomber built under licence by the IAR were fitted with two Jumo 211B inline engines of 1,200hp each. This version was designated JRS 79B (J for Jumo, R for Romania, S for Savoia). Because of inadequate Romanian industrial capacity eight Jumo-engined bombers were ordered directly from Italy in February 1940[3] but these were not delivered until 1941–2 as JIS 79 (I for Italy). A further development was the JRS 79B1, armed with a 20mm Ikaria cannon and with space for a fifth crew member. This version was used for low-level attacks on ground targets, and suffered a correspondingly high loss rate.

The capacity of the Romanian aviation industry was not sufficient to make the FARR a high-quality force, particularly after the ambitious plan that was approved in March 1940, stipulating the expansion of the air force to 84 squadrons with 834 combat and 338 reserve aircraft as well as 350 trainers.[4] For that, the aircraft matériel had to be acquired abroad. For years France had been the main supplier of aircraft to Romania, which, together with Yugoslavia and Czechoslovakia, belonged to the so-called 'Little Entente', formed to keep the losers of the First World War and revisionist states of Hungary and Bulgaria in check. The French delivered mostly Potez machines, among others 20 Potez 63 B2 twin-engined light bombers, which arrived in 1939. At the end of 1941 the FARR received ten Potez 63 C2s from Vichy-France, these being intended to offset the combat losses. The promise, given after the occupation of the previously unoccupied France by the German forces late in 1942, to supply Romania with 48 Latécoère 298 torpedo bombers was not kept by the German authorities, however. Italy, too, exported aircraft to Romania – not only SM.79B bombers, but also numerous seaplanes, including 12 Cant Z.501s in 1941.

Poland was the earliest large-scale supplier of military aircraft to Romania, delivering 50 PZL P.11b fighters in 1934 and five PZL P.24Es in 1939. After the Polish defeat in late autumn 1939, 200 Polish aircraft successfully escaped to Romania and strengthened the FARR. Thus Escadrila 49 and 50 were equipped with the PZL P.11C and bomber Esc. 76 and 77 received the PZL P.37 and 37B Los, while the PZL P.23

Karas and the RWD 13 went to Esc. 73 and 108.

Great Britain was late in supporting Romania with military aircraft, at the point where the appeasement policy was finally abandoned in favour of attempts to check German influence in the Balkans and Danube states. Between June 1939 and March 1940 a total of 40 Bristol Blenheim bombers and 12 Hawker Hurricane fighters arrived, the latter being allocated to Esc. 53.

German pre-war deliveries included 30 Heinkel He 112 fighters. This all-metal, low-wing monoplane had lost out in head-to-head tests with the Bf 109. The Luftwaffe command had adopted the Messerschmitt as its standard fighter because of its lighter and cheaper construction, and because it had advanced closer to large-scale production capacity. Therefore Ernst Heinkel had had to find other clients for his product. The Luftwaffe Chief of Procurement, General Udet, had advised Heinkel in his typical free and easy way: 'Sell off your birds dirt cheap to the Turks or Japanese or the Romanians, or anybody else you want to. They are all licking their fingers for them ...'[5] The Romanian He 112s were allocated to Esc. 10 and 11 of Grupul 5 Vanatoare. In October 1939 these squadrons were renumbered 51 and 52. In autumn 1942 Esc. 52 converted to night fighting duties. The He 112 was to prove itself in action over Odessa and the Black Sea, until the surviving aircraft were passed on to flying training schools in 1943. A total of 18 He 112s survived the war.[6]

Since the war in the West made further deliveries of French aircraft impossible, Germany helped out with 32 He 111H-3 bombers and 50 Bf 109E-3/E-4 fighters. These aircraft deliveries from the Reich led to frequent German–Romanian tensions and disagreements, as most of the German aircraft had already been used, and the Romanians naturally felt cheated when they had to pay the full price for them as if they were new aircraft.[7] Furthermore, many models, such as the He 114 seaplanes delivered early in 1942, were already obsolete. When it came to modern military aircraft, the Romanians again had to be satisfied with certain limitations. Thus, for example, the Ju 88A bombers delivered from Germany in 1943–4 were not transferred to the FARR but were only given on loan. The German leadership feared a separate Romanian–Hungarian war over Transylvania and for that reason retained the final power of disposal over the aircraft.

The Soviet annexation of Bessarabia and North Bucovina on 28 June, the loss of northern Transylvania to Hungary on 30 August (Second Vienna Arbitration) and then the surrender of the Southern Dubrudja to Bulgaria on 7 September were traumatic experiences for Romania in 1940. From then on, Romania began to lean closer to Germany. In October a strong German army and Luftwaffe mission was sent to Romania, and, on 23 November, the country joined the Tripartite Pact. The decision of the Prime Minister Ion Antonescu to participate in the German Eastern Campaign was based not only on strongly held anti-Communist views and political expediency – after all, the Axis seemed to be winning – but was also an attempt to regain Bessarabia and North Bucovina, and, by virtue of a strong Romanian contribution to the war, achieve a revision regarding the other territorial losses of 1940.

On 22 June 1941 the FARR staked 'all its combat-ready means' against the Soviet Union. According to a report by the Romanian Undersecretary of State for Aviation on 13 January 1943,[8] these consisted of the following:

  17 fighter squadrons
  14 bomber squadrons
  16 reconnaissance squadrons
   7 liaison squadrons
   1 aero-medical squadron
  43 heavy AA batteries
  34 light AA batteries
  12 AA machine gun batteries (13.2mm)
  15 searchlight batteries

However, these impressive figures had to be considered in the light of the heterogeneous aircraft arsenal possessed by the FARR, and the fact that spare parts for the British, French and Polish models were unavailable, which was inevitably to lead to a reduction of combat readiness within a short period of time.

Moreover the Romanian air force did not possess enough fighter and bomber pilots, as was made clear by the following statistics of 1 March 1940:[9]

Air Force Personnel	Authorized Strength	Actual Strength	Deficit	Excess
Reconnaissance pilots	992	1,317		325
Fighter pilots	504	243	261	
Bomber pilots	435	219	216	
Reserve pilots	1,159	838	321	
Observers	395	267	128	
Radio operators	260	218	42	
Air gunners	379	239	140	
Total	4,124	3,341	1,108	325

But Bucharest, like Berlin had set its hopes on a short war. On 22 June 1941 the Romanian Undersecretary of State for Aviation, Gen Gheorghe Jienescu, issued the following martial order of the day to swear in his pilots for the coming conflict:[10]

Airmen! The honour of carrying the tricolour Romanian Cross of victory is yours. The order of the day is: aircrew that have fired all their ammunition but have not achieved a victory during the combat, will dive on the enemy aircraft. Young airmen! The country expects the greatest sacrifices from you. The day of great deeds has come. Bring forth achievements that will become a legend. You did the same in peacetime. I am certain, I am convinced that you will handle yourselves without hesitation and deserve the trust that the King and the leaders of the country have put in you. Young airmen, let the trumpets resound, let the forests render their echo. Let the skies tremble from the roar of your engines, the song of the nation. To arms! We trust in God!

The FARR pilots did not allow themselves to be blinded by this rhetoric: not one of them threw himself with suicidal determination against the enemy. The Grupul Aerien de Lupta (GAL), formed to support the Romanian 3rd and 4th Armies deployed at the southern flank of the Eastern Front, comprised the most modern aircraft of the FARR. Included among these were the Bf 109E-3/E-4 of Esc. 56, 57 and 58 of Grupul 7 Vanatoare, and the IAR 80 of Esc. 41, 59 and 60 of Grupul 8 Vanatoare. The home defence was initially confined to the obsolete PZL P.11 fighters.

The first day of the Romanian offensive, 3 July 1941, developed most unfavourably for the GAL. It lost 11 aircraft, including four Bristol Blenheims, but claimed for itself the destruction of 48 Soviet aircraft, including eight in aerial combat. With 1,270 aircraft in that area the Soviets had a clear numerical superiority and started an offensive against Bucharest, Ploesti and the port of Constanza. However, their unescorted DB-3 bombers became easy prey for the AA guns and the Romanian and German fighters. The first Romanian aerial victories of the war were achieved by Lt Horia Agarici of Esc. 53 who, flying a damaged Hawker Hurricane that should really have been in a repair shop, shot down three Soviet bombers that had attempted to bomb the Romanian fleet. National propaganda made great play of this success and for months afterwards all Romanian radio stations broadcast a popular song about Agarici's success. The Soviets also listened in, and do not seem to have appreciated the anti-Communist text: after the change of sides in August 1944, this fighter lieutenant was arrested and confined in a penal comp.[11]

The Russian aerial offensive against Romania did not prove very successful and therefore the Soviets increasingly relied on harassing raids. Up to the end of 1944 they lost 145 aircraft over Constanza alone; of these 59 were shot down by Romanian and 69 by German fighters. The obsolete Soviet bombers were welcome prey for the Bf 109Fs from III./JG 52 that had been transferred for a short period to Mamaia near Constanza on 24 June 1941.[12]

The Romanian attack to recapture Bessarabia and the North Bucovina had come to a successful conclusion by 26 July 1941, and the FARR had made its contribution to this. From 22 June to 28 July 1941 the Corpul Aerien de Lupta had flown 2,263 sorties, including 1,004 by fighters and 813 by bombers.[13] During this brief campaign the FARR lost 20 aircraft but could count 71 confirmed and 44 probable aerial victories.

On the express wishes of Hitler the 4th Romanian Army continued its advance towards Odessa and the Romanian air force was now tasked with providing tactical support to the advancing ground troops. The GAL could only do this to a limited degree because its aircraft strength was declining catastrophically. This was due less to combat activities than the fact that the Royal Romanian Air Force lacked spare parts for its Polish, French and British aircraft types. In the period to 2 September 1941 the effective strength of the GAL dropped to only 91 operational aircraft.[14] Apart from that, the GAL also lacked the necessary resources to quickly prepare the captured airfields around the surrounded Odessa for its own use. It thus hardly came as a surprise that, between 11 and 15 September 1941, the Romanian infantry attacks against Odessa had to be carried out under conditions of local Soviet aerial superiority. The FARR also found itself unable to neutralize the port of Odessa or to hinder the Soviet evacuation by sea, which took place between 2 and 16 October, because it had neither torpedo or dive bombers. Despite its limited means, the GAL still managed to carry out 5,594 more sorties (including 3,735 by fighters and 1,179 by bombers) between 29 August and 16 October, at the cost of at least 20 Romanian aircraft. The GAL pilots claimed 144 confirmed and seven probable aerial victories, their total between 22 June and 16 October amounting to 266 victories. Undersecretary of State Jienescu estimated a total of 546 Soviet aircraft destroyed in the air, by AA guns and on the ground. Subsequent internal Romanian research led to the conclusion that the victory tallies for the Odessa area at least were somewhat too high. The Romanian air force command took notice of this and issued new and stricter conditions for the recording of aerial victories.[15] Later on Romanian pilots were to complain that these new FARR preconditions were considerably more restrictive than those applied by the German Luftwaffe!

At this stage the FARR urgently needed a break for rest and reorganization. In a letter dated 14 January 1943 to the Commander of the Luftwaffe mission and the German Air Attaché at the German Embassy, Generalmajor Gerstenberg,

Gen Jienescu stated that after the conclusion of the first phase of the Eastern campaign (16 October 1941) the Romanian air force had only 20 per cent of its initial strength remaining.[16] This was certainly an exaggeration because the aim of this letter was to persuade the Germans to provide more generous deliveries of qualitatively better aircraft, but there could be no doubt that the Romanian air force was considerably weakened.

In December 1941 only Esc. 19, 21 and 111 – all of them engaged on liaison and communications duties – were at the Eastern Front. The remaining formations had been withdrawn for restructuring and modernization. Thus, the surviving Hawker Hurricanes were retired from front-line service and passed on to training units, and the same fate befell the SM.79B bombers. The obsolete Polish PZL P.11 and P.24 fighters still remained in service with Esc. 73 and 76. New deliveries filled these gaps, with Vichy France sending 10 Potez 63 C2 reconnaissance bombers from a pre-war contract, which passed to Esc. 74 Bombardment. Assistance from the German allies, however was limited:

German Deliveries to FARR

Number	Aircraft Type	Period of Delivery	Allocation
10	He 111H-6	Jan–March 1942	Grupul 5 Bombardment
15	Bf 109E-7	Jan–March 1942	Escadrila 56
10	Do 17M	Apr–May 1942	Escadrila 2
18	Ju 52/3m	1942	Escadrila 105
10	He 114	Apr 1942	Escadrila 102
14	Fi 156C-3	Apr 1942	
3	Hurricane	Sep 1941	
3	Blenheim	Sep 1942	Escadrila 1 and 3

The Hurricanes and Blenheims came from the German booty in Yugoslavia. However, the Romanian expectations of their Axis partner were somewhat higher. When Reichsmarschall Göring and Marshal Antonescu met at Karinhall on 13 February 1943 the Romanian chief of State declared that if the FARR was to be ready for action in April, it needed two squadrons of Bf 110s, four squadrons of communications aircraft for reconnaissance tasks, and 16 Ju 52/3m transports. Further, Romania also urgently needed a licence to build the Bf 109 fighter and the DB 605 aero engine. Yet the only positive pledge the Romanian Marshal received concerned the three-engined Ju 52/3m transports.[17]

Owing to this limited German assistance, the FARR had to rely primarily on indigenous aircraft production to modernize its formations. With about 314 aircraft completed in 1942, the Romanian aviation industry reached its highest output so that the Royal Romanian air force could be re-equipped as follows:[18] Esc. 47, 48 and 52 (Grupul 9 Vanatoare), Esc. 43, 44 and 50 (Grupul 3 Vanatoare) and Esc. 41, 42 and 60 (Grupul 8 Vanatoare) received the new IAR 80A. Esc. 53 also replaced its Hurricanes with the IAR 80A, while Grupul 6 Bopi re-equipped with the IAR 81. There were also changes in the bomber fleet: four new bomber squadrons were formed (Esc. 81–4) and equipped with the IAR 37 biplane, and Grupul 1 Bombardment exchanged its Italian SM.79Bs for the JRS 79B and JIS 79B.

While the new aircraft were being delivered or completed, and new airmen trained in Romania, the activities of the FARR on the Eastern Front remained modest. Between 16 October 1941 and 1 August 1942, a period of nine and a half months, Romanians carried out 1,380 reconnaissance and observation flights, 1,038 liaison/communication flights and 1,021 fighter sorties. The latter took place mainly over the Black Sea. During these months the FARR reported only seven aerial victories. The Romanian transport airmen were more active, supplying the Romanian 3rd Army in Crimea and flying out the wounded. At the beginning of 1942, the total personnel strength of the FARR numbered about 13,000 men.[19]

After 26 July 1942, when the German Army Group A and the Romanian 3rd Army commenced an attack from the Don bridgehead towards the Caucasus, the Romanian air force also increased its activities. The GAL, with its headquarters in Rostov, now had more modern aircraft than at the beginning of the Eastern campaign, but the logistical connections to the homeland remained unsatisfactory. The combat formations of the GAL were now combined into the so-called Corpul Aerien (air corps) and subordinated to the German Luftflotte 4. The fighter forces, combined into the Flotilla 2 Vanatoare, consisted of the following formations:[20]

Romanian Air Force, June 1942

Grupul 6 Bopi	Grupul 7 Vanatoare	Grupul 8 Vanatoare
Cdr Lt Col N. Radulescu	Cdr Capt C. Grigore	Cdr Lt Col E. Pirvulescu
Escadrila 61 10 x IAR 81	Escadrila 56 12 x Bf 109E	Escadrila 41 12 x IAR 80A
Escadrila 62 10 x IAR 81	Escadrila 57 12 x Bf 109E	Escadrila 42 12 x IAR 80A
	Escadrila 58 12 x Bf 109E	Escadrila 60 12 x IAR 80A

From mid-September Grupul 7 operated from Karpovka, joined on the same airfield by Grupul 8 at the end of the month. From 28 October Grupul 6 Bopi flew its sorties from Picaj. The Romanian bomber arm formed three groups (Grupul 1, 3 and 5) with a total of seven squadrons, which, among other planes, had 15 He 111H-3s and 15 JRS.79Bs and JIS.79Bs. The reconnaissance element was formed of eight Do 17Ms and six Blenheims of Esc. 1 and 2, supported by Potez 63s from Esc. 3. In mid-August 1942 the Romanian 3rd Army was withdrawn from the German Army Group A area and regrouped before taking over a 120km (75-mile) long defensive sector at the Don river on 10 October, being deployed between the Italian 8th and the German 6th Armies. At the end of October the Romanian 4th Army was deployed south of the German 6th Army. Its defensive sector was 250km (155 miles) wide, although the Romanians had fewer than 100,000 men.[21]

The task of the Air Corps was to support of the Romanian 3rd Army. Very soon reconnaissance aircraft established that the Soviets were preparing for a large-scale attack. There was also an alarming increase in the number of aircraft bearing the Red

Star: by 20 November 1942 the Soviet air force facing the Romanian 3rd Army comprised 790 machines. To compound matters, bad weather on 19 and 20 November precluded any operational use of the FARR aircraft. And it was on that day that the Soviets launched their offensive against both Romanian armies and in a short space of time penetrated deeply into the sector held by the 3rd Army. Another Soviet blow shattered the front held by the 4th Army; the Romanians' lack of heavy weapons meant they were hardly able to defend themselves. Already on 22 November both Soviet spearheads joined hands at Kalatch, deep behind the front: the German 6th Army and two Romanian divisions were surrounded. On the disintegrating main battle line outside the 'cauldron' some Romanian formations defended themselves with desperate courage against threatened annihilation. One of these was a battle group formed of three divisions from the 3rd Army, commanded by Gen Mihail Lascar, which fought a bitter battle under hopeless circumstances.

While the Romanian Air Corps could operate against the enemy on 21 November, bad weather on the following two days prevented all Romanian efforts to check the advancing Soviet forces from the air. Nevertheless, on 22 November, five Ju 52/3m transports from Esc. 105 managed to supply ammunition, fuel and provisions to the surrounded Lascar group and fly out many wounded. By this time, the fighters of Grupul 7 Vanatoare based at Karpovka were already threatened by Soviet tanks. Alexandru Serbanescu, who was to become the most successful Romanian fighter pilot, took matters into his own hands, organizing the defence and evacuation of the airfield. The Romanian guns managed to hold up to Soviet tanks for two days. On the eve of 23 November 19 Bf 109Es of Grupul 7 Vanatoare took-off from Karpovka; 16 reached their new bases at Morozovskaya and Tazinskaya. Two days later 'bad weather conditions and superior enemy fighter forces'[22] hindered all German and Romanian aerial operations. Despite this the German XIII Fliegerkorps, to which Grupul 7 was subordinated, attempted the impossible – to stabilize the front. 'Assault aircraft, Stukas and bombers from Oblivskaya, Moro

(Morozovskaya) and Tazi (Tazinskaya) supported this battle, which would have been hopeless without their participation. We operate until the Soviet ground fire makes it impossible to use the advanced airfields.'[23]

Depending on weather conditions, the Romanians were flying up to 50 sorties a day. In December the transport squadron Esc. 105, which also included several pilots from the Romanian LARES airline, carried out supply flights to Pitomnik and evacuated from there the personnel of Grupul 7 and numerous wounded. Grupul 7, whose aircraft strength had been considerably reduced, was initially transferred to Novocherkask, but Grupul 3 Bombardment had to leave the combat area altogether, its antiquated machines posing insoluble maintenance problems.

Marshal Antonescu also faced problems that could hardly be overcome. His 3rd and 4th Armies had been destroyed and the allied German Wehrmacht either left the Romanian soldiers in the lurch or forcibly integrated them with German units. There were also executions by the Germans of alleged Romanian deserters. On 9 December 1942 Antonescu sent a bitter letter to Generalfeldmarschall Manstein in which he complained sharply and without a trace of diplomatic courtesy about the treatment of his soldiers: 'I feel obliged to draw your attention to the fact that unless this attitude and these occurrences cease forthwith, I will have to reconsider the situation of our troops with regard to your Front...'[24] Despite this serious crisis in the German–Romanian alliance, the mutual fighting and dying continued.

On 12 and 13 December the Romanian airmen supported the German counterattack from Kotelnikovo towards Stalingrad by the Panzergruppe Hoth of the Heeresgruppe Don. Grupul 6 used its IAR 81s as dive bombers, but the attack failed to break through the Soviet defences. Instead, the Red Army launched an offensive against the Italian 8th Army and tore its front-line wide open. The FARR now had to support the Italians as well as the German Armeegruppe Hollidt, which was also under Soviet attack. The situation worsened still further on Christmas Eve, when the Soviet forces reached the Tazinskaya airfield and the Romanians lost a large number of aircraft on the ground. As a result, GAL operations dropped to about 20 sorties a day. The Romanian forces – or what was left of them – were then withdrawn from the Eastern Front. When Grupul 7 deployed back to Stalino on 20 February 1943, the unit had only three operational Bf 109s left! Altogether 18 Romanian divisions had been destroyed, with the personnel losses of both annihilated armies amounting to 173,000 dead, missing or wounded – a figure still disputed to this day.[25]

The GAL operational balance sheet for the second phase of the Eastern campaign was rather modest: during the period 16 October 1942 to 15 January 1943 it had flown 3,900 sorties. Of these the bombers accounted for 1,306, dropping about 2,000 tonnes of bombs, and the fighters had recorded 1,345 sorties. A total of 61 Soviet aircraft had been shot down, of which 39 were claimed by the Romanian AA guns. The Romanian air force losses amounted to 538 dead, missing and wounded, and 79 aircraft.[26]

According to the Romanian Air Ministry, the following losses were incurred due to wastage and enemy action during the period September 1942 to 1 January 1943:[27]

   2 fighter squadrons of Bf 109s
   2 fighter squadrons of IAR 80s
   1 bomber squadron of He 111s
   1 bomber squadron of SM.79Bs
   3 light bomber squadrons
   2 long-range reconnaissance squadrons

Afterwards, the indigenous aviation industry and German deliveries helped to partly restore and modernize the FARR. At this stage, the Romanians also began to receive such German aircraft models as the Bf 109G, Ju 87, Hs 129 and Ju 88. However, for fear that the Romanians might use the German aircraft against the Hungarian allies, the aircraft delivered to Corpul 1 Aerien of the FARR were loaned rather than donated.[28] After the modernization programme of 1943 the Royal Romanian Air Force was equipped as follows:

Formation	Aircraft Type
Grupul 1 Vanatoare Esc. 63, 64	IAR 81C
Grupul 2 Vanatoare Exc.65, 66	IAR 81C
Grupul 4 Bopi Esc. 45, 46, 49	IAR 80C
Grupul 7 Vanatoare Esc. 56, 57, 58	Bf 109G
Grupul 5 Bombardment Esc. 73, 81, 85	Ju 87D-3, Ju 87D-5
Grupul 5 Bombardment Esc. 77, 79, 80	Ju 88A-4
Grupul 8 Asalt Esc. 41, 42, 60	Hs 129B

Additional German deliveries included the Ju 52/3m for Esc. 107 transport squadron and the Bf 110C for a Romanian night fighter squadron. The Romanians received 12 used Bf 110Cs at a cost of almost 7 million Reichsmarks; these aircraft were allocated to Esc. 51.[29] Later on the Romanians also received the more modern Bf 110F version. In German records Esc. 51 night fighter squadron – last designation Escadrila 1 Vanatoare de Noapte – was listed as 12.Staffel of IV./NJG 6. This unit never achieved a single nocturnal victory, due to its lack of experience and insufficient training of its crews as well as the fact that the Romanians were not supplied with the more powerful Bf 110G version with DB 605 engines.

All more modern aircraft were concentrated in the newly reconstituted Corpul 1 Aerien. This air corps began operations from Mariupol on 16 June 1943. Until that time the Romanian aerial presence after the Stalingrad disaster had been symbolic more than anything. Esc. 20 and Esc. 43, with their IAR 39s and IAR 80s, had fought over the Kuban bridgehead, and Grupul 7, led by Lt Col Radu Gheorghe, operated over the Ukraine from 28 March to 1 July 1943, together with units of the German JG 3 'Udet'.

The Romanians, among them Capt Alexandru Serbanescu

commanding Esc. 57, were very successful in this phase of the
'free hunting' – at least 14 Romanian pilots each achieved five or
more victories. Grupul 7 was particularly effective after its
subordination to Corpul 1 Aerien in mid-July. On 19 July the
German High Command report stated: 'Romanian fighters shot
down 17 Soviet aircraft.'[30] In fact, the pilots of Grupul 7
shot down 23 Soviet aircraft in just two days.

Corpul 1 Aerien was composed of 22 squadrons with 260
aircraft, including two fighter groups (Grupul 6 and 7) with six
squadrons. From late summer 1943 onwards, the Romanian 1st
Air Corps carried almost the entire burden of the air war over
the southern wing of the Eastern Front. Thus Grupul 3,
equipped with Ju 87D-3 Stukas and based on the Kertch peninsula, was the only Axis bomber formation that could support
the German and Romanian troops in the Kuban bridgehead.
Grupul 3, commanded by Lt Col Galeno Francesco and
comprising Esc. 73, 81 and 83, was an extremely successful unit,
and its operations were to bring Soviet tank and infantry attacks
to a halt time and again. This unit also laid mines in coastal
waters and attacked Soviet shipping. The doggedness of the
fighting was shown by the fact that, by 9 August, 33 out of 44
aircraft of this group had been damaged in action.

The re-equipment of Grupul 5 Bombardement with the Ju
88A-4 took place at Kirovgrad in May 1943. Grupul 5, with its
components Esc. 77, 79 and 80, was deployed for operations at
the Mius front already in June, when they were not nearly ready!
Within a few weeks the formation lost a quarter of its inadequately trained crews in action. To compensate for these
heavy losses, Grupul 6 Bombardement, also being trained on the
Ju 88A-4, had to hand over some of its aircraft and personnel to
Grupul 5.

Escadrila 2 Recunoastere reconnaissance squadron also
received modern machines – 12 Ju 88D-1 strategic reconnaissance bombers without dive brakes. That one of these machines
stands today on display in an American museum is thanks to
Romanian sergeant Nicolae Teodoru,[31] then a 28-year-old
former LARES pilot called up in April 1943 and transferred to
the above reconnaissance squadron in Mariupol on 20 June

1943. Unable to adapt himself to the military lifestyle Teodoru decided to desert after completing 11 operational sorties. His intention was to reach Beirut via Aleppo. On 22 July he climbed into the Ju 88D-1 Wk. Nr. 0880 430 650 and took off, his direction Novorossisk. However, an easterly wind drove him off course and over Turkish territory. He was later intercepted by RAF Hurricanes over Cyprus and forced to land at Limassol. His Ju 88D-1 was then taken over by the USAAF, and, after a long flight with many intermediate landings, ferried to the USA for further tests. Years later it was refurbished to exhibition standard.

A complete novelty for the FARR was the newly formed Grupul 8 Asalt close support group, comprising Esc. 41, 42 and 60.[32] It had come into being in May 1943, when Grupul 8 fighter group, based at Targsor with a personnel strength of 320 men, was reconstructed as a close-support group. On 14 May the flying personnel of this new assault group were transferred to Kirovgrad, where German instructors retrained the Romanians on the twin-engined Henschel Hs 129B-2 armoured close-support aircraft. This special plane, built in series from 1943 onwards (total production 870) was an excellent tank destroyer and weapons carrier, although its two Gnôme-Rhône 14M radial engines of 700hp each were rather prone to malfunction.[33] Under its new commander, Lt Col Vasiliu Dutsu, Grupul 8 Asalt began combat operations from the Kramatorskaya airfield in August 1943. The demand for their support was so great that the Romanian Hs 129 pilots each had to fly up to nine sorties a day, which soon wore out both aircrew and machines. Their main operational areas were over the Donetz and the Mius fronts, where they brought relief to the hard-pressed German and Romanian troops. But the operational wastage was high, a good example being Sgt Ion Enoche of Esc. 42, who was shot down three times during the first three weeks of September. Later that month, and into early October, the unit had to be moved back to Genitsesk and Kherson, but the rest period was brief. At the end of October the Romanian 24th Infantry Division was surrounded on the isthmus between Genitsesk and Perekop. Grupul 8 Asalt made

superhuman efforts helping the division to break out westwards, with the Romanian pilots each flying up to 16 sorties a
day to loosen the investing Soviet ring and save their comrades.
Lack of sleep, permanent exertion and the nervous strain associated with these led to the complete exhaustion of the pilots –
but they achieved their goal: 10,000 men from the 24th Infantry
Division managed to fight their way back to their own lines.

There were also some changes in the fighter arm. After the
American air raid on Ploesti on 1 May 1943, Grupul 7 Vanatoare
was withdrawn from the front in September and replaced by
Grupul 9, which, until then, had had little success in retraining
on the Bf 109G due to the majority of the machines being immediately passed on to Grupul 7. This unit now gave up its Bf 109G
fighters to Grupul 9 and took over home defence duties with the
IAR 80 fighters previously used by this unit. In March 1944
the unit was re-equipped with the Bf 109G-2. Incidentally, 13
pilots from Grupul 7 remained on the Eastern Front, continuing
flying operationally as part of Grupul 9.

By that time the initiative on the battlefield had been taken
over by the Soviets, and their attacks forced Grupul 1 Aerien to
make frequent changes of its operational bases. Melitopol, base
of the Romanian air force, fell into Soviet hands on 24 October.
On 1 November a Soviet breakthrough all the way to the Dniepr
estuary cut off the German 17th Army, including seven
Romanian divisions, from all land connections on the Crimea.
This crisis led to the establishment of a German–Romanian air
bridge between Odessa and the Crimea. The 18 Ju 52/3m transports of Esc. 105 and 107 proved themselves by flying in supplies
to the peninsula and taking out wounded, as did also the hastily
organized Esc. 106, allocated old twin-engined aircraft such as
the SM.79B, Bloch MB.210, Potez 65 and Potez 543. Up to the
loss of the Crimea on 12 May 1944 the German and Romanian
aircraft managed to fly out 21,937 troops, in some cases under
unimaginable conditions.

As was to be expected, the continuous demands and
operational stresses due to the hard defensive battles wore out
Corpul 1 Aerien: by 2 March 1944 the corps had only 59 combat
aircraft left. At that time it operated from Bessarabia, and, in

April, was strengthened by aircraft from Grupul 7 Vanatoare and the newly formed 6th Dive Bomber group. Gradually the fighting in the sector held by the Heeresgruppe Südukraine (South Ukraine) eased – temporarily until 20 August – and the Romanian air corps had a short breathing space for re-equipment and reorganization. During a year of continuous fighting the formation had flown 18,227 sorties and had shot down 401 enemy aircraft.[35] In summer and autumn 1943, thanks to its improved aircraft park, the FARR had reached the zenith, performance wise, and was often praised by German troop commanders for its brave and spirited intervention in ground fighting. Quite rightly, the commander of Corpul 1 Aerien, Gen Emanoil Ionescu (17 March 1893–13 July 1949) was awarded the Knights Cross of the Iron Cross on 20 May 1944.[36] However, at the end of August he was to set aside this high decoration and play a decisive role in arranging that the Commanding General of the Luftwaffe in Romania and the German Commandant of the Romanian oil well area, Gen Gerstenberg, should fall into a trap and be taken prisoner.[37]

In 1944 the aircraft losses of the FARR could hardly be made good from Romanian production and the German deliveries combined, particularly as some of the aircraft arriving from Germany were outdated, such as the He 111H-3 and Ju 86. This lack of suitable aircraft led to the abandonment of the planned Grupul 11 Asalt; the ex-Luftwaffe Hs 129Bs delivered only sufficed to form one squadron, Esc. 38. On the other hand, German supplies of the Bf 109G were such that they sufficed to replace all Romanian losses on the Eastern Front, re-equip Grupul 7 with new fighters, and have Grupul 5 partly equipped with the 'Gustav', at least on a temporary basis.

From the German side the deliveries to maintain the Romanian combat strength were as follows: 60 Bf 109Gs in July, 40 in August and 20–25 a month from September onwards. At least, that was the plan.[38] The Romanian licence production of the Bf 109G-4 never really got off the ground and came to a halt in August 1944, after just six machines had been completed.

To oppose the Soviet threat to the homeland another air corps, Corpul 2 Aerien, was formed on 14 April 1944. This formation received the more dated foreign and indigenous aircraft models and thus had only a limited combat effectiveness. However, within a month and under direct threat to their own land, the FARR began to intensify its activities. No fewer than 476 operational sorties were flown on 30 May, and another 300 on the following day. Even the old IAR 37 biplanes, equipped as light bombers, took part in this fighting. The German Luftflotte 4 had to hand over aircraft to other fronts and had only 200 machines left in July. This meant that the FARR had once again to carry the main burden of the fighting, as in summer 1943. Corpul 1 Aerien was ordered to support the Army Group Dumitrescu in its defence of Bessarabia, and Corpul 2, re-designated Corpul 3 Aerien, was to take over the defence of the coast and the Danube estuary.

But by that time the Romanian kingdom had been forced to split its forces because for some time it had also had to combat new and more dangerous enemies in the air, the RAF and the USAAF. Their attacks were directed at the oil refinery installa-tions at Ploesti in particular, as paralysis and destruction of the oil refineries and railway marshalling yards would cut off the German fuel supplies essential to waging the war. The first Allied raid on Ploesti, carried out on 12 June 1942 by 12 American B-24 Liberator bombers that had taken off from Fayid, near Cairo, was more symbolic than damaging.[39] Never-theless, the Romanian authorities were worried and requested some German night fighters to strengthen the Ploesti air defences. It was Hitler himself who temporarily turned down this request, put to him by the Romanian Vice Prime Minister Mihai Antonescu on 23 September 1942, pointing out the tech-nical difficulties associated with the setting up of a new night fighting zone.[40]

In August 1943 the Americans came again, but this time with quite different forces, the aim being to destroy the refineries. As part of Operation *Tidal Wave* a total of 178 B-24 Liberator bombers of the 9th USAAF set off to attack Ploesti, but the whole undertaking became a disaster. German Bf 109s of I./JG 4 and Romanian IAR 80Bs of Esc. 61 and 62, as well as IAR 80Cs from the newly formed Esc. 45, Bf 109Gs from Esc. 53 and even

Bf 110s from the Romanian night fighter squadron dived on the low-flying, four-engined bombers belonging to five USAAF bomber groups (the 44th, 93rd, 98th, 376th and 389th). The balance of this raid was rather painful for the Allies: '178 B-24s took off; one crashed soon afterwards, two were lost on the way out, 13 lost their bearings, 22 landed on other Allied airfields, 51 were lost in combat or on the way back, and only 89 reached their bases – of which only 31 were serviceable to fly a mission the following day.'[41] A total of 110 American airmen were taken prisoner; the Romanian pilots claimed 25 certain and probable victories for just two losses; and Romanian AA guns claimed another 15 bombers. Three of the B-24 Liberators that made forced landings were eventually put back into flying condition.

On the credit side for the Americans, there were some damaged oil refineries, although no hits landed on the vital crude oil pumping plants. According to a note from the German Foreign Ministry, dated 13 August 1944, the crude oil output before the American raid amounted to an average 450,000 tonnes a month. 'It is estimated by the German and Romanian specialists that the refineries can by the end of September be restored to such an extent that from October the crude oil yield will again be 450,000 tonnes.'[42] Despite this optimistic prognosis, Romanian oil production sank from 5.6 million tonnes in 1942 to 5.3 million tonnes in 1943, and, consequently, Romanian exports were reduced from 3.3 to 3 million tonnes, as reported by the head of the department, Clodius, to the German Foreign Ministry on 17 February 1944. It was also calculated that crude oil production would sink to 5 million tonnes in 1944.[43] Nonetheless, there were grounds for taking precautions to strengthen the defensive capabilities of Ploesti in view of expected further bombing raids. The air defences of the Ploesti area where largely transferred to the Luftwaffe, while the defence of the capital, Bucharest, was exclusively in Romanian hands. Early in 1944 Grupul 6, with its components Esc. 59, 61 and 62, had concentrated on the Popesti-Leordeni airfield, while Corpul 7, with its Esc. 53, 57 and 58, was based at Pipera. At that time the following Luftwaffe formations were protecting Ploesti:[44] III./JG 77 at Mizil; 10./JG 301 at Targosul Nou, with an operational section of four aircraft at Galati; Stab and 10./NJG 6 at Otopeni; 11./NJG 6 at Zilistea; and 2./NJG 100 dispersed on the Otopeni, Zilistea and Focsani airfields. NJG 6 also looked after the Romanian night fighter squadron. The immediate defence of Ploesti could also call upon Esc. 44 and 55 with IAR 80s and IAR 81s from the Ghimbav fighter-training school, and the IAR works squadron at Brasov.[45] The German Fighter Leader (Jagdführer or Jafü) for Romania was then Obstl 'Edu' Neumann, who has stated the following about his service post and collaboration with the Romanians:[46]

In 1943–4 there was a duty station (Dienststelle) Balkan, subordinated to which were some fighter sectors, including Jagdabschnitt Rumänien (Fighter Sector Romania) in the same location as the Jafü Balkan, north of Bucharest. In January 1944 I took over as Abschnittsführer (Sector Leader) Romania ; the Jafü Balkan was at that time Oberst Bernhard Woldenga. Subordinated to him were several other duty stations, such as the ones covering Bulgaria and Yugoslavia. The Commanding General of the Luftwaffe in Romania was not satisfied with so many fighter command sectors and tried to have only one Jafü duty station in his area, namely Jafü Romania. And he managed to achieve this: about February 1944 the Balkan HQ was transferred to Serbia, north of Belgrade, and the Fighter Section Romania became a full-scale Jafü Romania.

We could not give any orders to the Romanian fighter stations, that would not have been appropriate and could have offended the Romanian national dignity. However, in our command post, which was nearly as big as a command post in Germany, we also had Romanian officers and specialists who would telephone the relevant information to their own duty stations. All this relates to the day fighters. Our co-operation was good and also comradely.

Early in April 1944 the USAAF set its sights on Romania again. On 4 April their 449th Bomb Group raided Bucharest. A strong formation of 350 B-17 Fortress and B-24 Liberator bombers escorted by 119 P-38 Lightning fighters took off from Foggia, Italy, but due to bad weather conditions only 32 B-24 Liberators reached their target. During the ensuing encounter

111

the Romanian fighters shot down three of these four-engined bombers, while four others were lost to German fighters or AA guns. A day later 134 B-24 Liberator and 95 B-17 Fortress bombers, accompanied by a strong P-38 Lightning escort, headed for Ploesti again. This attack cost at least 13 machines, but the Luftwaffe, too, had to pay dearly that day. According to reports by the commander of Grupul 6, Dan Vizenty, his pilots shot down 63 American machines on 4 and 5 April 1944.[47] This report has to be viewed with some scepticism because the official Allied losses on those days were considerably lower.

Within the FARR, Grupul 2 Vanatoare replaced Grupul 7, which had been deployed to the Eastern Front in April. Of the six squadrons composing Grupul 2 and 6 only one was equipped with the Bf 109G (Esc. 58), so that the Romanian fighter pilots had to face the American bombers (B-24 with 10 x 12.7mm machine guns and B-17s with 13 x 12.7mm guns) with their relatively lightly armed IAR 81C. These April days were only a prelude to a four month-long battle for the Romanian oil, without which the German war machine would virtually have ground to a halt.

Between 5 April and 19 August 1944 the American day bombers carried out 19 large-scale raids in the Ploesti area, in addition to another 22 attacks on oil pipelines, rail and road traffic installations and industrial targets, such as the IAR works at Brasov. The RAF contributed 15 nocturnal raids during the same period.[48] A total of 7,693 Romanian civilians lost their lives. All this was too much for the German and Romanian AA artillery and fighter defences; they just could not stem the endless stream of Allied bombers and escort fighters, although there were occasional successes, as 'Edu' Neumann recalls:[49]

In my time as the Jafü there were far too few day fighters for the defence of the Romanian capital and the oil region, mostly just two groups of fighters from various wings. The Romanians – even with their IAR 80 fighters – were a valuable help. Once, thanks to an operational error by the American fighters, they managed to achieve a notable success. But the Romanians and Germans also had to suffer harsh losses in daytime.

It was a different matter at night. We had an entire group of night fighters and an independent squadron at our disposal. Guided from a good command post and based on accurate data supplied by the ground radar, the night-fighters could infiltrate the bomber stream, pick out the targets on their AI radar sets and shoot them down. The British Wellington bombers suffered such a high loss rate that they had to give up further operations. Attempts were also made to use the day fighter formations from the now nearer Eastern Front against the American bombers, but they were unsuccessful. The demands put on these pilots were very different and no more than one or two such attempts were ever made.

To strengthen the air defences of the crude oil producing area additional AA artillery and fighter formations were deployed there. The latter comprised I./JG 53 and single-engined of 6./JG 301 night fighters.[50] This mix of different fighters was magnified in the eyes of the hard-pressed American bomber gunners who reported being attacked by 'Fw 190', 'Fiat G.55' and 'Macchi 205' fighters over Bucharest and Ploesti. These were probably the IAR 80 and 81, then unknown to the American air crews.

This aerial offensive by the four-engined bombers against the crude oil pumping and refining installations of Ploesti, and the communication lines such as the railways and the Danube shipping, soon began to have an effect. Claims by Grupul 2 Vanatoare of having shot down 35 enemy aircraft (plus another nine probables) for only four losses during the period 21 April to 18 May 1944[51] were most certainly overly optimistic, and, in any case, made no difference.

Already after the third bombing raid on 5 May, the shortfall of mineral oil reserves reached 140,000 tonnes. For the Chief of the OKW (Supreme Command) it was 'a catastrophe'.[52] Nevertheless, German and Romanian pilots continued their fight to fend off approaching disaster. At the end of May Grupul 2 Vanatoare with two IAR 81c squadrons (Esc. 65 and 66) relieved Grupul 7 at the Eastern Front and was deployed on the Baca-Gheraesti airfield. Grupul 7, with its Esc. 53 and 57 squadrons joined by Esc. 58, now took over home defence tasks, while Grupul 6 was re-equipped with the Bf 109G-4 and G-6.

On the morning of 10 June 1944, when this reorganization was still incomplete, the Americans had the bizarre idea of attacking Ploesti with 36 P-38 Lightnings of the 82nd Fighter Group carrying one bomb each, escorted by 39 P-38 Lightnings of the 1st and 82nd FGs. The German fighters from I./JG 53 and 2./JG 77, as well as the Romanian IAR 81Cs from Grupul 6, were ready and prepared a hot reception. Dan Vizanty reported the following about this 12-minute aerial combat:[53]

> Our lightning attack came as a complete surprise to the Americans. My pilots threw themselves on the enemy aircraft one after another, diving onto the American machines ... Our attack was so quick that not one of the 100 [sic] American aircraft managed to fire a single shot at our aircraft parked on the ground. The problem with this aerial combat was the low altitude, because everything happened between ground level and about 2,000m (6,550ft), and was total confusion. I was excited and proud of my 'mills', the IAR 80s, which, thanks to their extraordinary agility, remained victorious in the air. I saw their crazy dives, quick rolls, reverse turns and inverted flying, always with just brief bursts of fire to save the ammunition. It was an incredible sight, but also a drama for the Lightning pilots, who, at this low altitude, were inferior to the ever-present, nimble IAR 80s.

The FARR had demonstrated once again what it was capable of under favourable operational conditions and with good leadership. After landing, the Romanian pilots were surrounded by their 'black men', the mechanics, who embraced them and carried them on their shoulders. Tears of joy and relief were shed – but there was to be no repeat of this spectacular defensive success. From then on the Americans took care not to send their Lightnings alone to Romania. The USAAF had lost 23 machines, the exact number claimed by Grupul 8 for themselves – although the Luftwaffe and AA guns also achieved some successes.[54] The Americans, for their part, were far more generous with their accounting: they also claimed 23 victories, although the Romanians and Germans lost only one aircraft each on 10 June.

At this time the Luftwaffe could only spare 75 fighters for the protection of Romania and the Romanians hardly more than that against the Western allies. What could these few aircraft achieve against 607 (15 July), 495 (22 July) or 339 (28 July) American heavy bombers? One has also to bear in mind that not all of these defensive fighters could be in the air at the same time because their operational readiness could never achieve 100 per cent. During his last visit to Hitler's headquarters on 5 August 1944, Marshal Antonescu rightly complained about the thin and inadequate air umbrella over Romania: 'Only 30 to 40 German and Romanian fighters can be put up against 700 intruding bombers, and the AA artillery is completely insufficient.'[55]

But even these modest German and Romanian fighter forces still managed to inflict painful losses on the 15th USAAF during the previously mentioned raids on 15, 22 and 28 July: 20, 24 and another 20 American bombers were lost. Then, on 31 July, the remaining Luftwaffe fighters were hit so seriously that hardly any made an appearance in August. On that day, 30 Bf 109Gs from I./JG 53, III./JG 77 and 6./JG 301, as well as 20 Romanian machines, most probably from Grupul 9, encountered 101 P-51 Mustangs from the 31st and 325th Fighter Groups. During this combat 23 German fighters were shot down.[56]

On 3 August Grupul 9 Vanatoare, the Romanian Eastern Front fighters, was transferred back to Popesti-Leordani, but with just 13 operational aircraft it did not pose any threat to the USAAF. Four days later, the Romanian Air Ministry issued a secret instruction ordering the discontinuation of attacks on the Western allies. The FARR fighters were to be saved for the defence against the expected major Soviet offensive. The consequences of this directive soon became apparent to the Germans. Gen Gerstenberg appealed to Capt Serbanescu, commander of Grupul 9 Vanatoare, not to leave the Luftwaffe in the lurch in its fight against the enemy bombing, and his plea was successful. When, on 18 August, the Americans sent 373 heavy bombers against Ploesti, Captain Serbansecu also took off and joined the combat, which was destined to be his last. At the time of his death, Serbanescu was the most successful Romanian fighter pilot with 45 (according to other sources, 52) aerial victories to

115

his credit. A day later the German envoy in Bucharest sent the following report to the Foreign Ministry in Berlin:[57]

> The air defence of Romania is becoming ever more inadequate. The German command and the German and Romanian fighters are doing their best, as is also the AA artillery. The operational willingness is excellent overall, but the defences can no longer cope with the enemy numerical superiority. Yesterday, only 50 fighters had to face 1,100 [sic] enemy aircraft. The fighters are simply pushed aside by the numerically far superior enemy forces, and most are shot down. If improved AA artillery and more fighters cannot be sent to Romania, the oil refinery area can no longer be held. The best Romanian fighter pilot was killed yesterday. For military and political reasons something must happen.

On the same day as the German envoy's report, 19 August, the Americans made their last raid on Ploesti, and this time there was no aerial opposition. The Allied air offensive against Ploesti was over, but the cost had been high: a total of 223 bombers had been lost in these raids in 1944 alone. When one adds the British losses, the P-38s on 10 June, and Operation Tidal Wave of 1943, the total Allied losses increase to 339 aircraft. For the Americans alone, the personnel losses amount to 2,829 men, of whom 1,123 became POWs.[58] The Romanians, who claimed for themselves 197 aerial victories plus another 76 aircraft shot down by their AA guns – figures that are most certainly somewhat inflated – admitted losing 40–50 aircraft.

The expected major Soviet offensive began on 20 August, when the 2nd and 3rd Ukrainian Fronts rose against the German-Romanian forces of the Army Group South Ukraine. The massed Soviet ground forces were supported by 1,700 aircraft. Against this the FARR could send just 161 sorties on 20 August, 304 on 21 August and 305 on 22 August. On 23 August Corpul 1 Aerien had to evacuate its advanced airfields. Within these few days, the Red Army had penetrated deep into the German–Romanian defences and a large-scale encirclement battle was in the making.

Now that Romania itself was threatened, King Mihai I was no

longer prepared to tie his country to Germany, which had now been forced onto the defensive. He ordered the arrest of Marshal Antonescu and proclaimed a 'change of fronts' for Romania. The German response was to make a few light air raids on Bucharest on 24 August, which only deepened the rift between the former allies. A day later Romania declared war on Germany.

The Royal Romanian Air Force and AA artillery, which had fought on the Axis side from 1941 to 1944, and claimed to have shot down 1,500 Soviet aircraft for their own personnel losses of 972 killed, 1,167 wounded and 838 missing,[59] accepted this sudden and dramatic change, if reluctantly and without any enthusiasm. Even after the official start of hostilities between the two former allies there were continuing friendly contacts between German and Romanian airmen, such as 'Edu' Neumann and the Romanian officers on his staff: 'We phoned each other for about three days afterwards, until our Stukas destroyed the telephone lines. Before that happened, we wished each other the best of luck for the future and au revoir!'[60]

The FARR pilots were distressed and depressed by the events that had delivered them to the Soviets. Vizanty could feel this mood among his comrades almost physically:[61]

A leaden mood, a fog of anxiety that one could almost feel, filled the officers' mess, as if we all had foreboding of the terrible times ahead. Nobody spoke. I looked at them with great sadness. The intuitive feeling that we would be facing dark years in the future tightened my throat, and had I been less strong, I would have broken down in tears, so great was my sorrow.

There were three reasons why the FARR joined this sudden volte-face: the false hope that the Western allies would protect Romania from the Soviets, their loyalty to the king, and the desire to snatch Transylvania back from the Hungarians. Only about 20 or 30 members of the FARR remained on the German side, where most were assigned to the Waffen-SS. One of these was Sgt Gheorghe Pana from the Romanian night fighter squadron. He left his homeland with IV./NJG 6, survived the war and later became a civilian pilot in South America.[62] Then there was Capt 'Buzu' Cantacuzino from Grupul 9, scion of an old Romanian lineage, and a highly decorated fighter pilot with 43 (or, according to other sources, 56) confirmed aerial victories: 'Rich, independent, a mixture of a man of the world and a playboy, but, as a fighter and aerobatics pilot – an eagle!'[63] He was selected by the Romanian government to take a memorandum to the Western allies. Cantacuzino took with him in his Bf 109G-3 Wk. Nr. 166133 the highest-ranking captured American officer, Lt Col James A. Gunn. On 28 August 1944 he took off for Foggia in southern Italy. But his mission was in vain: the memorandum was to have no effect on the occupation of Romania by the Red Army.

The Romanian aircraft not only changed their allegiance but also their national markings: instead of the yellow 'Mihael-Cross' they now received red/yellow/blue roundels. The 'new' FARR, with a personnel strength of 37,000 men and 1,131 aircraft[64] of which many were reserve and training types, was now subordinated to the 5th Soviet Air Army and participated in fighting against the Hungarians and Germans. Despite the new alliance, the Soviet AA guns and fighters often deliberately fired on Romanian aircraft, especially the Hs 129Bs from Grupul 8 Asalt. It seems they just could not forget the many causalities wreaked on the Red Army by these aircraft.[65] The Soviets also deliberately 'used up' some of the Romanian formations, because their loyalty to the throne did not fit in with the new, Communist Romania that came into being in 1947. Cantacuzino recognized the signs of the times and, in 1948, made his way to Spain where he was to die in 1958 at the age of 52 years. Dan Vizenty also managed to reach the West.

Much more unfortunate were members of higher Romanian military circles. The long-serving Undersecretary of State for Aviation, Gen Gheorghe Jienescu,[66] who had always energetically interceded on behalf of his air force in any dealings with the Germans, had to pay for his anti-Communist conviction with 17 years in prison. He was released in 1964 and died on 3 April 1971.

Hungary

Magyar Királyi Honvéd Légierö (MKHL)

The Treaty of Trianon of 4 June 1920 reduced the once mighty Hungarian kingdom to a small country. It lost 8.5 million of its 18 million inhabitants and had to surrender so many areas of its territory to its neighbours that only 93,030sq. km (35,919sq. miles) remained from the original 282,000sq. km (108,880sq. miles). The military conditions dictated by the victorious powers were no less severe: the Hungarian army was not permitted to have more than 35,000 men, military aviation was forbidden, and so was manufacture of military aircraft. Whatever was left in Hungary from the former Austro-Hungarian military aviation – 119 aircraft, 77 aero engines and more than 200 propellers[1] – had to be destroyed.

With this the victorious powers had prepared the ground for Hungarian revisionism. Hungarian politics, supported by public opinion, knew only one main goal: the revoking of the Treaty of Trianon. Despite the Allied military supervision committee that tried to oversee the observance of the treaty conditions until 1927, the Hungarians, unimpressed by these controls, began early on to take measures to create at least some foundations for an air force. The conclusion of the Hungarian–Italian friendship treaty on 5 April 1927, and an air convention with the victorious states signed in the same year ended Hungary's external political isolation. This brought some relief for the indigenous aircraft production.

Nevertheless, the creation of even the smallest air force still had to take place in secret. The post of an Inspector of the Air Force came into being in 1928, and infrastructures were created and pilots were trained under various guises, such as the 'Aero Club'. At that time the old British and Italian aircraft – later augmented by some German Udet U12 and U12As and Heinkel HD 22s – were completely unsuitable for military purposes. When Italy was asked, in 1928, to supply 400 aircraft, it offered to help out and exported Fiat CR.20 biplanes and Caproni Ca

101 parasol monoplanes. These were followed by further Hungarian orders. In 1935 and 1936 a total of 76 Fiat CR.32s reached Hungary. This biplane was the most significant fighter of the mid-1930s and helped the Nationalists to achieve aerial superiority in the Spanish Civil War. These deliveries were joined by a number of German aircraft. Altogether Hungary received 66 Ju 86K-2s, Heinkel He 46E-2s, five He 45s and 18 He 70s.[2] The size of the Royal Hungarian Air Force – Magyar Királyi Honvéd Légierö – (MKHL) expanded slowly from three fighter squadrons, three reconnaissance squadrons and eight bomber squadrons in 1935/36 to a total of 25 weak squadrons with 225 aircraft in July 1937. The intention was to form two air brigades with a total of 28 squadrons and 12,500 personnel, but this target was not to be achieved until 1942.

After the Treaty of Bled on 22 August 1938, under which the countries of the 'Little Entente' allowed Hungary the right to rearmament, the MKHL could finally leave its shadowy existence. On 1 September 1938 the Hungarian air force introduced the red/white/green chevron as the nationality symbol of military aircraft; this remained in use until March 1942 when it was replaced by a white cross on black background.

According to an order issued by the Hungarian Imperial Administrator and Vice-Admiral Horthy, from 1 January 1939 the MKHL would become an independent branch of the armed services. An Air Force Academy was established at Kassa, and Italy helped out in training Hungarian flying personnel; in 1939 and 1940, 200 Hungarian pilots at a time underwent flight training in southern Italy.

The Hungarian air force was to have its baptism of fire in March 1939, when it came to a short-lived conflict with the newly established state of Slovakia. The Fiat CR.32 fighters, with the red/white/green chevrons, kept the upper hand and the new Slovak air force lost a few Avia B.534 and Letov Š-328 planes.[3]

In 1939 the Hungarian air force comprised 6,075 men and 252 aircraft, representing a shortfall of 52 aircraft.[4] The promised deliveries from Germany faltered because Berlin feared that Hungary might use its aircraft against Romania. The situation was once again saved by Italy, who offered to supply more military aircraft. An existing 1938 contract for 42 Fiat Cr.42 fighters was augmented by an order or another 18 aircraft of the same type in 1939. Twenty-three Fiat CR.42s were delivered in 1939, and the remainder in 1940.[5] A further order was placed for 70 Reggiane Re 2000 Falco I (Falcon) fighters. The Hungarians also acquired the licence-production rights for this model and a total of 200 planes (known as Héja (Hawk) in Hungary) were built between 1940 and 1942. In summer 1940 the MKHL also received 35 Caproni Ca 135bis twin-engined bombers; and another 36 of these came later.[6]

The Hungarians did not always have happy experiences with the Italian aircraft. Of the 36 Ca 310s acquired between May and September 1939, they returned 33 to Italy in 1940,[7] but an Italian credit for 300 million lire and the impossibility of acquiring modern German aircraft led to the Honvéd air force flying mostly Italian aircraft until 1941. One of these was the Caproni Ca 135 bomber, which had been rejected by the Regia Aeronautica on account of its technical shortcomings and taken out of production.[8] In Hungarian service this bomber proved quite satisfactory – provided it could be made to fly! The bomber's frequent malfunctions and insufficient combat load-carrying capability set high demands on the mechanics maintaining it. A 50 per cent operational readiness of a Ca 135 unit on the Eastern Front was to be seen as a great achievement.

In August 1940 the Hungarian government put the MKHL and the army on standby. The growing crisis over Transylvania had reached a stage where a conflict with Romania seemed a real threat. The first Re 2000 fighters received from Italy were sent to Debrecen to strengthen the fighter defences. The Vienna Arbitration of 30 August prevented the war between the neighbours but did not resolve the territorial problem.

The Royal Hungarian Air Force had problems in retaining its independent status. The enforced inactivity in the aviation field, lasting almost 20 years, could not be made up in just two short years. The MKHL was also beset by organizational and procurement difficulties. All this led to the Hungarian air force losing its independence on 1 March 1941, when it was subordinated to the army command.

Four weeks later another crisis developed. After the anti-Axis *coup d'état* in Belgrade on 27 March 1941, Hitler ordered the destruction of the Yugoslav kingdom. Hungary became an assembly area for the German troops and Hitler asked the Hungarian Imperial Administrator, Horthy, to actively participate in the campaign against Yugoslavia. This created an awkward situation because the Hungarian Prime Minister, Count Pál Teleki, had signed a friendship treaty with Yugoslavia on 12 December 1940. As the majority of the Hungarian government pleaded for a march against Yugoslavia to recover the areas at Batschka and Banat lost after the First World War, Teleki could not see any other way out than to take his own life.[9]

Aircraft Park of the Hungarian Air Force on 6 May 1941

Fighters	174	incl. 69 Fiat CR.32, 68 Fiat CR.42, 3 He 112, numerous Re 2000 Héjas etc
Bombers	71	incl. 36 Caproni Ca 135 and numerous Ju 86
Short-range reconnaissance	123	incl. 38 He 46, 48 WM-21 Sólyom, 37 Romeo Ro 37
Long-range reconnaissance	13	He 111
Paratroop transports	4	Savoia-Marchetti SM.75
Target simulation	5	
Combat and practice aircraft	**390**	
Plus training aircraft	146	incl. Caproni Ca 101, Fw 56 Stösser, Fw 58 Weihe, Do 23, Fiat CR.30, Arado Ar 96, Bücker Bü 131 Jungmann etc
TOTAL	**536**	

Source: Gosztony, Peter, 'The military role of Hungary in World War II', Part II, in *Wehrwissenschaftliche Rundschau*, Issue 5/1981, p. 160

Even then, the Hungarian troops did not enter the conflict until 11 April, after an independent Croat state had been declared in Agram and the Yugoslav kingdom had ceased to exist. The Yugoslav air force on the other hand had begun to penetrate Hungarian air space already on 6 April, bombing railway stations and airfields.

The Hungarian command assembled the following air force units for their campaign against the disintegrating Yugoslavia: fighter squadrons 1/1, 1/2, 1/3, 1/4, 2/3, and 2/4; bomber squadrons 3/5, 4/3, and 4/4[10] as well as the independent reconnaissance group.[11] There were no major engagements or air combat because the Yugoslav air force had already suffered considerable losses and was in disarray. The heaviest MKHL loss occurred in the afternoon of 12 April, when four SM.75 transports loaded with paratroopers took off from Veszprém, and the leading aircraft (code E-101) crashed immediately afterwards. This disaster cost the lives of 23 Hungarians, including 19 paratroopers. Altogether, the Royal Hungarian Air Force lost three Fiat CR.32s, two Fiat CR.42s, one WM-21 and the above mentioned Savoia SM.75 in this brief campaign.

On the day of the German attack on the Soviet Union, 22 June 1941, the MKHL possessed 320 aircraft, although quite a few of these were outdated models. The planned build-up of the air force was not yet completed, but the degree of training and the morale of the aircrews gave no grounds for apprehension. The German plan for Operation *Barbarossa* did not envisage the participation of Hungary as an ally. Hitler feared the Hungarians would make further territorial demands regarding Romania if they took part, so there was no official German invitation for active Hungarian participation in this ostensibly 'anti-Bolshevik crusade'. However, there were powers within Hungary's leading circles who believed their country must take part in this altercation whatever happened. One of these advocates was the Chief of the General Staff, Col Gen Hendrik Werth. He summarized his thoughts as follows:[12]

We have to take part in this war because: 1) it would mean securing the territorial integrity of our land and the preservation of our social and economic order; 2) because the weakening of our Russian neighbour and removal of his presence some distance from our borders is of first-rate national interest for our future; 3) because our world outlook, based on Christian-nationalist foundations, and our position on Bolshevism in the past as well as the present obliges us to do so; 4) because we have finally put ourselves on the Axis side politically; and 5) because any further increase of our territory is also dependent on this.

When, on 26 June, a number of aircraft – whose identity has still not been established with certainty, but were most probably Soviet – bombed the north Hungarian towns of Kaschau (Kassa), Muncás and Raho, the ground forces prepared for Hungarian intervention.

On 27 June Prime Minister Bardossy announced that Hungary had declared war on the Soviet Union, and the Hungarian air force reacted with a reprisal raid. Early in the morning that day, 36 Ju 86K-2s from the 4th Bomber Wing and one squadron of Ca 311s escorted by nine Fiat CR.32s from the 2/3 Squadron bombed the town Stanislav. On 29 June 17 Ju 86K-2s and nine Ca 311s escorted by Fiat fighters from 2/3 Squadron attacked the town of Strij. On the same day Sen Lt Istvan Azakonyi, flying his Ca 135 from the 4/III Bomber group, managed to destroy an important bridge across the Pruth river with a 'trial drop' of just two bombs. This was followed by individual attacks on various targets east of the Carpathians. The first aerial combat over Hungary took place on 29 June, when seven Tupolev SB-2 bombers attacked the Csap railway station. Three of the raiders were shot down by Fiat CR.32s from 2/3 Fighter squadron.

The Hungarian Carpathian Group, which had been strengthened by a Rapid Corps with 160 dated tanks, began its advance eastwards on 28 June. The Rapid Corps, which was subordinated to the German 17th Army, was supported by a Hungarian air formation commanded by Lt Col Béla Orosz. This unit comprised the newly formed 4th Independent Bomber squadron, consisting of nine Ju 86K-2 bombers of 4/2 Squadron and six Ca 135s of 4/III Bomber group, as well as two short-range reconnaissance squadrons and 1/3 Fighter squadron with Fiat CR.42s.[13] On 7 August, the fighter strength was augmented by seven Re 2000s led by Capt László Gyenes. The bombers were based at Sutyska, near Vinnitsa in the

The fighting formations of the Hungarian Air Force, June 1941

Unit	Base	Aircraft
1st Fighter Wing		
1./I Group	Szolnok	Fiat CR. 32
1./II Group	Mátyásföld	Fiat CD. 42
2nd Fighter Wing		
2./I Group	Nyiregyháza	Fiat CR. 32
2./II Group	Kolozsvár	Fiat CR. 42
3rd Bomber Wing		
3./III Group	Debrecen	Ca 135
3./II Group	Kecskemét	Ju 86
(The unit was practically disbanded in June 1941)		
4th Bomber Wing		
4./II Group	Veszprém	Ju 86
4./I Group	Debrecen	Ju 86
1st Independent Long-range reconnaissance Group	Budaörs, Ungvár	He 70, He 111
11 squadrons of short-range reconnaissance aircraft	Ungvár and at the individual Army Corps	He 46, Wm 21 Sólyom

Ukraine; Sen Lt Szakonyi led the Caproni bomber detachment. On 10 August the six Ca 135s were ordered to attack the besieged town of Nikolayev on the Bug estuary at the Black Sea the following day.[14] The main target was a 2km (6,560ft) long bridge across the Bug river, the only withdrawal route for the defenders of the port. The Capronis took off at 0445hrs on 11 August. One machine had to turn back due to engine problems, but the other five, escorted by six Fiat CR.42s from 1/3 fighter squadron and five Re 2000s continued eastwards, reaching their target at 3,000m (9,840ft) altitude. On the approach, Szakonyi's Ca 135 (B-511) was hit by AA fire and lost its port engine, but the squadron commander remained in action. After one of his pilots, Capt Eszenyi, had succeeded in destroying the bridge, Szakonyi bombed the railway station of Nikolayev. On their way back the Capronis were intercepted by Soviet I-16 fighters. Their pilots were tenacious but inexperienced and Eszenyi's crew shot down an I-16, with five others falling victim to the escorting Fiat CR.42 fighters; only one Hungarian aircraft, an Re 2000, was lost. But the hero of the day was Sen Lt Istvan Szakonyi. With his crippled bomber struggling back on one engine his crew managed to shoot down another three Soviet I-16 fighters: quite an achievement! This Hungarian bombing success contributed considerably to the success of the German 11th Army in taking Nikolayev on 16 August and capturing 60,000 Red Army troops. The commander of Luftflotte 4, Col Gen Lohr, visited the Hungarians in person at Sutyska to decorate the aircrews.

The Hungarian flying formation was withdrawn from the Eastern Front in September 1941 for recuperation, re-equipment and rest in Hungary until December. After all, it had lost 56 aircraft, while the personnel losses amounted to 17 killed and six missing. That was the price the Hungarians had to pay for 1,454 operational sorties, dropping 217 tonnes of bombs and shooting down 30 Soviet aircraft.[15] Apart from a few units the entire Rapid Corps was also withdrawn back to Hungary at this time.

German pressure forced Horthy to increase the Hungarian contingent on the Eastern Front considerably. In addition to seven security divisions he sent the newly formed 2nd Army, comprising 200,000 men organized in three corps. The Hungarian troops were deployed on the Don front, between April and June 1942, and subordinated to the German Army Group South (Armeegruppe Süd). Initially it was not intended to furnish air support but finally it was decided to give the 2nd Hungarian Army a modest air umbrella. The 2nd Air Brigade was to provide the Hungarian army with tactical support and carry out reconnaissance sorties. This new brigade comprised 5,500 men and 90 aircraft, of which only 45 were combat types. According to reports, this formation was continuously receiving replacements throughout the summer and autumn of 1942.[16]

The fighter element of the 2nd Air Brigade consisted of 20 Re 2000s of 1/1 and 2/1 Fighter squadrons. Other aircraft were the 17 Ca 135s of 4/1 Bomber squadron, 12 He 45E-2s of 3/2 Short-range reconnaissance squadron, three He 111Ps, one Do 17K-2 (ex-Yugoslav) attached to 1/1 Long-range reconnaissance squadron and a few courier machines. Contact with the home-land was kept up by the Ju 52/3m trimotors from the Hungarian airline Malert, which had been allocated to the 2nd Transport squadron. In July 1942, aircraft of the 2nd Air Brigade were based at the Stary Oskol and Ilovskaya airfields, and were soon faced by a fierce Soviet resistance, suffering heavy losses in the process. Tragedy struck the unit on 20 August 1942, when the son of the Imperial Administrator, Sen Lt Stephan Horthy, lost his life in an accident. He was on his 25th operational sortie with his Re 2000 V-421 from 1/3 Fighter squadron when the pilot flying above him asked Horthy to increase height. He pulled up too hastily, and the Re 2000 stalled and crashed, killing the pilot.[17] The death of this young officer, which frustrated his father's plans to establish a new dynasty, aroused general sympathy among the Hungarian people.

The situation being what it was, the Germans now had to make good the Hungarian aircraft losses. The 1st long-range reconnaissance group was considered most important, and between July and September 1942 Luftflotte 4 supplied three He 111P-6s and four Do 215B-4s. On 1 September the Hungarian reconnaissance aircrews carried out their 100th operational sortie. Three weeks later the 2nd Air Brigade reported that it had shot down 25 enemy aircraft to date.

With the beginning of the rainy autumn weather some of the Hungarian flying formations were withdrawn from the front. Thus 3/2 Short-range reconnaissance squadron with its obsolete He 45E-2s was recalled to Hungary in late October. After 1,062 operational sorties and 265 bombing raids dropping 1,700 tonnes of high explosives on enemy targets 4/1 Bomber squadron also received orders to return home. It arrived at Debrecenon 15 November. Only one wing of 4/1 Bomber squadron remained at Poltava, where the pilots familiarized themselves with the He 111 before retraining on the Ju 88. This took place in January–February 1943 at Istres, in southern France. In spring 1943 this initial group was followed there by the remaining members of 4/1 Bomber squadron, as well as 3/1 Bomber squadron for retraining on the Ju 88A as part of IV./KG 3.[18]

This retraining also led to serious German–Hungarian discord. Although a state of war between Hungary and Great Britain had existed since 7 December 1941, and Budapest had declared war on the USA five days later, early in 1943 the Hungarian leadership began looking for contacts with the Western powers with a view to possible withdrawal from the conflict. For that reason, any actual hostile acts against the Western powers had to be avoided at all costs. On 2 April 1943 the German envoy in Budapest sent a report classified as 'state secret' (*Geheime Reichssache*) to the Foreign Ministry in Berlin: 'Hungarian General Staff has let it be known via the Chief of Operations Branch, Maj Gen Vörös, that the flying units at present retraining in France should on no account be used on operations. They are intended solely for operations against the Soviet Union.'[19] Hitler and Ribbentrop, who knew about the Hungarian peace feelers, expressed their annoyance about Vörös' instructions to Administrator Horthy during his visit to Klessheim Castle on 16 April 1943. His response was somewhat less than convincing: the Vichy-French Chargé d'Affaires had had an audience with Horthy and had pointed out that 'Hungary is not at war with France and therefore should not participate in the occupation.'[20]

In a personnel exchange in November 1942 the Hungarian air force command sent the staff of 5/I Fighter group and 5/2 Fighter squadron to the Don Front. In exchange, the staff of 1/I Fighter group and 2/1 Fighter squadron returned home to Hungary. Four of their pilots were retained for the time being on the Eastern Front to instruct the pilots of 5/2 Squadron on the Re 2000. A start was also made in retraining the Hungarian fighter pilots on the Bf 109. In October eight pilots from 1/1 Fighter squadron, led by Sen Lt György Bánlaky, were transferred to JG 52 at Stary Oskol. The retraining on the – for the Hungarians – unfamiliar German aircraft took place directly

Air Marshal Italo Balbo (second from right), here at the Castelbenito airfield, Tripoli, was instrumental in gaining an international reputation for the Regia Aeronautica in the 1930s. (Nino Arena)

Operations by the Corpo Aereo Italiano against Britain in the autumn of 1940 brought hardly any success. This Fiat CR.42 fighter of 83ª Squadriglia/18º Gruppo made a forced landing on the Belgian coast. (Author´s archives)

Macchi MC.200 fighters of 372ª Squadriglia in Albania. Note the open cockpits. (Author´s archives)

The three-engined SM.84, a progressive development of the proven SM.79, was disliked by its crews. (Author´s archives)

The Italian Expeditionary Corps in the Soviet Union had rather
weak air support. Macchi MC.200 fighters (above) and an SM.81
transport are shown here in the Russian snow. (Author's archives)

Max Peroli (left), pictured here after the successful bombing raid on Gura and Port Sudan in May 1943, flew the 6,000km (3,730-mile) trip between Italy and Ethiopia several times. (Nino Arena)

The SAS transport aircraft - here a Fiat G.12 in Sicily - suffered particularly heavy losses on their flights to North Africa. (Author's archives)

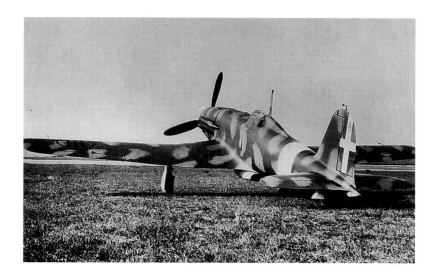

*Two aircraft of the famous 5ᵉʳ series that came too late for much
operational service and were only built in limited numbers: (above)
the Fiat G.55 `Centauro´ and (below) the Reggiane Re 2005
`Sagittario´ (Author´s archives)*

Funeral of Sen. Lt. Nicola Manzitti of the 2° Gruppo of the ANR, who was shot down and killed in an air combat on 30 April 1944. (Author´s archives)

An aged SM.81 (MM 20266) of the `Terraciano´ transport group of the ANR at Jelgava, Latvia, in August 1944. (Author´s archives)

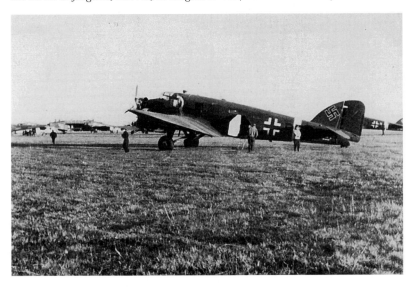

The Italian fighter pilot Luigi Gorrini was one of the many airmen who volunteered for the ANR. (Luigi Gorrini)

A Bf 109G-6 of the 1ª Squadriglia of the ANR warming up its engine at Ghedi, in November 1944. This particular aircraft displays both German and Italian national markings. (Author´s archives)

Pilots of the 1º Gruppo of the ANR, with Major Adriano Visconti on the right. (AuthorÕs archives)

An operational briefing demands the full concentration of these Romanian fighter pilots. (J.-L. Roba)

Last preparations before take-off by a Romanian Bf 109 pilot. (J.-L. Roba)

Two Romanian fighter pilots with their squadron mascot: Lt Ion Galea from 52nd Fighter squadron, operating from Mamaia on the Black Sea, leaning on his Bf 109E-4 `yellow 65´ in autumn 1943. Next to him is Lt Horia Pop. (J.-L. Roba)

More paintwork! Romanian Captain Constantin `Buzu´ Cantacuzino (front) has claimed another `kill´. (J.-L. Roba)

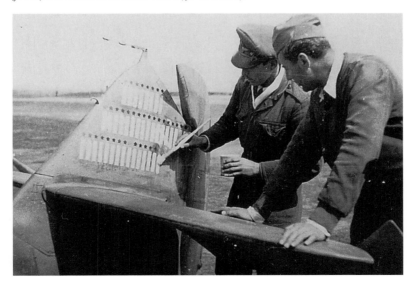

This IAR.81C was based at Popesti Leordani for the defence of the Romanian capital. (J.-L. Roba)

Kirovgrad, 5 June 1943. A visit by Marshal Antonescu to the front, with Romanian Ju 88A-4 bombers drawn up for inspection. (Dénes Bernád)

Pre-flight engine warming-up of a Romanian JRS.79B (J.-L. Roba)

30 November 1943: Constantin Boghean of 41st Squadron of the Romanian Grupul 8 Asalt has just returned in his Hs 129B from another operational sortie against Soviet armour. (J.-L. Roba)

Fiat CR.32 biplane of the Hungarian Air Force with the identity marking V.137. (Author´s archives)

Hungarian Bücker Bü 131B training aircraft. (Nino Arena)

Hungarian Reggiane Re 2000 fighters. (Author's archives)

This belly-landed Re 2000 of the Honvéd air force will have to spend some time in the workshops. (Nino Arena)

Brand-new Hungarian Messerschmitt Bf 109F, yet to receive individual markings. (Punka via Dénes Bernád)

After a successful operation the pilot of Bf 109G-6 `red 7´, deployed for Home Defence, is congratulated by his comrades. (J.-L. Roba)

A Bulgarian priest consecrating a DAR-3 biplane in 1937. (Todor Valkov)

Luftwaffe fighter pilot training school Werneuchen in 1938-39. The first Bulgarians are trained as fighter pilots and fighter-instructors. (Todor Valkov)

Avia B-534 biplane fighters, of which Bulgaria acquired seventy-eight examples in 1939. (Todor Valkov)

A Bulgarian Bf 109G-6 in 1944. (Todor Valkov)

at the front and was completed in just five days. Although the Hungarians had signed a licence production agreement for the Bf 109F and the Me 210 aircraft and the DB 605 aero engines on 6 June 1941,[21] for a while they had to make do with German Bf 109s because the first Bf 109 built at Gyor – a Bf 109Ga-4 with the markings V-7+51 – was not to leave the works until 21 December 1942, beginning its flight tests two days later. By that time Hungarian fighter pilots, led by Sen Lt Bánlaky, were already in action with their Bf 109F-4s from JG 52's inventory. Depending on data source, the number of aircraft available to the Hungarians varied between six and 12.[22] The Bánlaky group now acted as the 1.Ung.Jabostaffel (1st Hungarian fighter-bomber squadron) of JG 52. On 7 December the Hungarians were deployed to the Rossosh airfield. Nine days later Lt Imre Pánzél shot down four Ilyushin Il-2 armoured assault aircraft during two sorties. In their second operational phase, up to the end of 1942, the MKHL shot down 63 Soviet aircraft for the loss of 11 of their own. To this score one must also add the 260 Soviet aircraft shot down by the Hungarian AA guns and the Honvéd army.

The new year began depressingly bleakly for the Hungarians. Lt Pánzél, the first Hungarian ace with six confirmed victories, was lost on 11 January, when his aircraft (V0+04) was hit by Soviet small arms fire on a reconnaissance flight and crashed. The Hungarian fighter pilot was burned alive in the wreck of his machine. When the major Soviet offensive against the 2nd Hungarian Army began two days later the 2nd Air Brigade had only 15 operational aircraft – 5/2 Fighter squadron having seven Re 2000s, and the Bánlaky group eight Bf 109s. The thinly held front of the Hungarian 2nd Army was quickly penetrated and the MKHL units were also forced to retreat. On 14 January the 2nd Air Brigade at Ilovskoye received orders to prepare for an all-round defence. As the engines of their Re 2000 fighters refused to start in the extreme cold, the aircraft had to be blown up. Then came a Soviet ground attack, during which Lt Col Kálmán Csukás and at least another 50 members of the MKHL were killed while defending their airfield. After this Capt Aladár Heppes, known as the 'Old Puma',[23] took charge of the

surrounded Hungarian air force units. Despite his 39 years,
Heppes was still an active fighter pilot and a living example to
his comrades. In January 1943, when he was commanding the
5/I fighter group, all aircraft in his unit carried a red puma head
as their symbol. Later the same symbol decorated the Bf 109s of
101 Fighter group, his next command.

On 20 January 1943 Capt Heppes managed to evacuate
Ilovskoye, and together with the German 26th Infantry
Division, fight his way out westwards. The retreating allies took
with them 1,000 wounded and reached Novy Oskol on 23
January.[24] Two days later Heppes again took command of 5/I
Fighter group in Kiev. In the meantime the Bánlaky group had
been forced to give up Rossosh and provisionally assembled
at Kharkov on 18 January. Further stops were Kursk East,
Kharkov East and, early in February, Poltava. On 15 February
Bánlaky's group received eight brand-new Bf 109s and passed
their old machines to 5/2 Fighter squadron. The retraining of 5/I
Fighter group on the Bf 109 began.

The 2nd Air Brigade, which had lost about 50 per cent of its
aircraft and 75 per cent of its equipment, now had to be re-
equipped as a matter of urgency. On 25 March 1943 Lt Col
Sándor Illy took over command of this badly knocked-about
formation which, for the time being, remained as the only
Hungarian unit on the Eastern Front – if one ignores a few light
infantry divisions in the rear areas. The 2nd Hungarian Army
had lost 100,000 men killed in action and no longer existed.

The German Luftwaffe now had to re-equip its ally because
the Hungarian aviation industry did not reach its peak production until 1944. The Héja fighters – licence-built Reggiane Re
2000s, of which 98 had been completed in 1943 and another 72
were to follow in 1944 – were no longer suitable for combat
against modern Soviet fighters and should have served as fighter
trainers only. But the German Luftwaffe command were not
exactly generous when it came to supplying aircraft to the
Hungarians. For one thing, the deliveries went primarily to
the front-line formations, and, for another, the danger of a
Hungarian–Romanian conflict still existed and the German
government did not want to increase the tension over

Transylvania by making large-scale deliveries of combat aircraft to the opposing parties. Moreover, Hitler held an extremely bad opinion of the Honvéd airmen. In autumn 1942 he had reacted utterly churlishly to a Hungarian request for more fighters:[25]

> That would just suit the Hungarian gentlemen! They would not use the single-seaters against the enemy but just for pleasure flights! Aviation fuel is in short supply and I need pilots who attack and not ones who go on pleasure flights. What the Hungarians have achieved in the aviation field to date is more than paltry. If I am going to give some aircraft, then rather to the Croats, who have proved they have an offensive spirit. To date, we have experienced only fiascos with the Hungarians.

As a result of all this, only the following German aircraft were delivered to Hungary in more than 18 months, between summer 1942 and 1 March 1944:[26]

- 8 Do 215B-4 long-range reconnaissance aircraft
- 51 Ju 88A-4, Ju 88C-6 and Ju 88D bombers and reconnaissance aircraft
- 66 Bf 109F, Bf 109G-2 and Bf 109G-6 fighters
- 13 Ju 87D-3 and D-5 Stukas
- 16 Fw 189A tactical reconnaissance aircraft
- 10 He 111P long-range reconnaissance aircraft, of which five were returned to Germany

In addition there was an unknown number of courier, liaison and training aircraft (Fi 156, Bü 131) received directly from Luftflotte 4. This material was used by the Hungarians to modernize their air force formations as best as they could.

Early in January 1943 I./1 Long-range reconnaissance squadron received nine Ju 88s and a Bü 131. Another 12 Ju 88A-4s went to 102/1 Bomber squadron, reformed from 3/1 Bomber squadron.[27] From April 1943 until its retreat from the Eastern Front late in 1944, this formation carried out 1,000 operational sorties. The second squadron of this bomber group, 102/2, was a dive bomber unit equipped with 12 Ju 87Ds. Known as the

'Coconut squadron' and commanded by Capt János Kórosy, 102/2 excelled itself in the Kharkov area in summer 1943. It carried out 1,500 operational sorties for the loss of eight Ju 87s. Lacking modern aircraft material, 3/1 Short-range reconnaissance squadron, deployed to the Eastern Front in March 1943, had to make do with its WM-21 Sólyom biplanes, but only for a short while. At the front the unit was re-equipped with the Fw 189A.

At the end of June 1943, before the start of the Operation *Citadelle* (the German attempt to cut off the Soviet 'bulge' near Kursk), which began on 5 July, the VIII.Fliegerkorps had a strength of 1,100 combat aircraft,[28] which also included Hungarian aircraft. The Hungarian fighter pilots mainly flew as escorts for the German bombers, but they also carried out numerous fighter-bomber sorties. Sen Lt Bánlaky was no longer among his comrades; he had been recalled to Hungary in April 1943. On the opening day of the German offensive 5/2 Fighter squadron, which was temporarily based at Varvasovka together with 5/1 Fighter squadron (the former Bánlaky group), achieved five aerial victories. The total number of confirmed aerial victories achieved by 5/I Fighter group during the Battle of Kursk was 20. Some of the Hungarian pilots were flying up to five sorties a day, an operational rate that not only wore down the nerves but also reduced the operational readiness of the aircraft.

All this was noted, and in July the group received 16 new Bf 109Fs and Gs. This paid off immediately, as on 3 August 5/1 Fighter group gained seven aerial victories. All this had little effect on the overall situation of the Axis, however, which was steadily worsening. The Hungarians had to retreat, passing through the Poltava, Karlovka, Kiev and, late in September 1943, Ushin airfields. In November the Hungarian fighters were recalled home, except for 5/2 Fighter squadron. Up to December the pilots of both squadrons had shot down 132 enemy aircraft for just nine losses.[29]

From January 1944 onwards only a few Hungarian aircraft were on the Eastern Front. These were the 12 Fw 189As of 3/1 Short-range reconnaissance squadron, six Ju 83D long-range reconnaissance aircraft and 12 Bf 109G-6s of 5/2 Fighter squadron; the last-mentioned was redesignated 102/1 Independent Fighter squadron[30] and was commanded by Capt József Kóvacs.

In the meantime increasing efforts were being made in Hungary to strengthen the air defences of the country. Throughout 1943 there was practically only one unit available to protect the skies over Budapest and other large centres, this being 2/1 Fighter squadron, with 18 Héja II fighters and commanded by Capt Miklós Scholtz, which was transferred from Matyasföld to Ferihegy in October. The 5/1 Experimental night fighter squadron was also based there. In January 1944 the Héjas of 2/1 Fighter squadron took off twice to intercept Allied bombers that were flying over Hungary on their way to Germany. Fortunately for the Honvéd fighters it did not come into contact with any American four-engined bombers. Soon afterwards the fighting power of the Hungarian home defences was considerably strengthened with the arrival of licence-produced Messerschmitts built by the local manufacturers. According to the German–Hungarian agreement mentioned above, the Bf 109s were built by the Hungarian Railway Carriage and Engineering Works at Györ and the Me 210 by the Danube Aircraft Construction Joint Stock Co. in Budapest. The DB 605 aero engines for both aircraft were manufactured by the Weiss Manfred Works, also in Budapest. The licence-built aircraft and aero engines were split between the allies according to the following ratio:[31]

Model	RLM	Hungarian Ministry of Defence
Bf 109	1	1
Me 210	2	1
DB 605	2	1

At first sight it may seem surprising that the Hungarians had obtained the licence-production rights for the Me 210, as this aircraft had been one of the most dismal failures of the Luftwaffe. The aircraft behaved unpredictably in the air, this leading to many fatal accidents. In one March 1942 week alone,

17 Luftwaffe aircrew lost their lives, victims of the plane's flight characteristics. It has been estimated that the failure of the Me 210 had cost the Luftwaffe, in funds, raw materials and production capacity, the equivalent for at least 600 and possibly up to 1,000 aircraft.[32] Fortunately for the Hungarians their aviation industry was licence-producing a much-modified Me 210 version with two DB 605 engines and longer rear fuselage.

A total of 270 Me 210Ca-1 (a for *ausländisch*, foreign) were eventually to be built by the Danube Aircraft Construction Joint Stock Co, of which the MKHL received about 160, the remainder going to the Luftwaffe. In Hungarian service this extremely manoeuvrable machine, which could be used for reconnaissance tasks, as a fighter-bomber (the Me 210Ca-1 was capable of 618km/h/384mph at 6,800m/22,300ft), night fighter and destroyer (with 1 x 40mm Bofors cannon), was very well liked.[33] However, as it emerged later, this aircraft did not have such a convincing performance in action against the Allied bombers.

A somewhat similar case was the He 112, although it was never built under licence in Hungary.[34] A German–Hungarian agreement signed in May 1939 had envisaged permission for the Weiss Manfred Works to assemble a pre-series of 12 aircraft, but no parts were delivered to Hungary by Heinkel after the start of the war, so the planned licence agreement for series production had to be cancelled in December 1939. Hungary had ordered 36 He 112 fighters in 1938, but only four had reached the MKHL for evaluation, one being destroyed in an accident on 12 February 1939. The remaining three He 112B-1/U2s, with the identification numbers V.301 to V-303, were allocated to various fighter squadrons and, from 1941, had the task of protecting the Weiss Manfred works. All three fighters were probably destroyed during the American bombing raids in summer 1944.

The Bf 109Ga-4 and Ga-6, of which Hungary produced another 92 in 1943, were considerably better suited for the Home Defence than the Me 210Ca-1. Of course, for the Hungarian government it would have been better if none of their modern fighters had ever been used against the Western allies. Out of fear of the advancing Red Army and further loss of forces in the Eastern campaign, Budapest continued to try to establish contact with the Western allies. This effort culminated in a secret agreement between Hungary and the Western powers, signed on 9 September 1943, which envisaged an unconditional Hungarian capitulation if the Western allied troops reached Hungarian borders.[35] These Hungarian peace feelers did not remain hidden from Hitler, who consequently ordered the occupation of Hungary, which happened on 19 March 1944. It was to be the last of Hitler's 'flower wars' – the German forces generally received a friendly reception from the Hungarian population. Even after some members of the Hungarian government continued to look for some way out of the war most of the German-friendly Honvéd army rejected such an infamous change of alliance. However, the threads between Budapest and the Western allies continued to be spun, and the air force was also drawn into these secret dealings.

On 13 June 1944 Sen Lt Miklos Odescalchi and his rear gunner deserted with their Me 210Ca-1 (Z0+88) and tried to reach the Allies in southern Italy to deliver a secret message from the Hungarian government. Running short of fuel, Odescalchi was forced to land in German-occupied territory and was executed late in 1944.[36]

On the MKHL as a whole the German occupation had no noticeable effect. For a few days the Hungarian pilots were forbidden to fly until the Germans could assure themselves that the Honvéd pilots would not go over to the enemy.

The Hungarian pilots had had their first encounter with American bombers on 17 March. On that day two Bf 109Gs from 2/1 Fighter squadron were shot down and both pilots killed. The 'American season' – as the American overflights and raids were described by the Hungarian pilots – had begun. By early April 1944 the retraining of Hungarian fighter squadrons on the Bf 109 had yet to be completed. Units deployed for home defence had, at the most, 60 aircraft. Assuming an operational readiness of 70 per cent, this meant that only 42 fighters – many of which were outdated Héjas – could be put up against what were often more than ten times numerically superior American air fleets. The following formations were deployed for Home defence duties in April 1944:[37]

Unit	Base	Aircraft
2/1 Fighter squadron	Ferihegy	12 Bf 109G-4/G-6
1/1 Fighter squadron	Szolnok	4 Héja II
1/2 Fighter squadron	Szolnok	4 Héja II
5/1 Night Fighter squadron	Ferihegy	6-10 Me 210Ca-E
Destroyer squadron of the Experimental Air Force Institute (RKI)	Ferihegy	12 Me 210Ca-1
5/3 Fighter squadron	Tököl	2 Bf 109G-6
Fighter squadron of the Experimental Air Force Institute (RKI)	Ferihegy	4–6 Bf 109G-6
Acceptance and alarm unit	Tököl	2 Me 210Ca-1
Acceptance and alarm unit	Györ	2 Bf 109G-6

The first heavy blow was struck on 3 April 1944, when a formation of 180 bombers from the 15th USAAF, escorted by 170 fighters, bombed the Danube Aircraft Works in Budapest, among other targets. A total of 1,073 people were killed. After this, the leisurely life style of the Hungarian capital, which had hitherto been barely touched by the war, came to an end.

The fighter control centre situated in the Gellért hill near Budapest ordered up 2/1 Fighter squadron and one wing from 1/1 Fighter squadron. After the encounter the Honvéd pilots reported 11 aerial victories, of which six were confirmed. The Americans went one better and claimed no fewer than 27 enemy aircraft destroyed. In actual fact only two Hungarian airmen were killed.

On that day just two Me 210Ca-1s from the Experimental Air Force Institute (RKI) also took-off to protect Budapest. One machine developed a technical fault and had to turn back, and so the Me 210Ca-1 (Z0+60) crewed by Sen Lt Kornél Nagy and Sgt Istvan Kutay, was on its own. After a hard aerial combat with a dozen P-38 Lightnings from the 82nd Fighter Group, of which

Nagy managed to shoot down one, the Z0+60 was badly damaged and its Hungarian pilot had to make a forced landing. After his smoking Me 210Ca-1 came to a halt American P-38 Lightning pilots began to carry out a regular target practice on the wrecked aircraft, in which sat the badly wounded Hungarian pilot, who had lost an eye, and his dying gunner.[38]

This American raid of 3 April, when the Hungarians could put up only 25 machines, gave the Honvéd fighter pilots – who always had a high morale – food for thought.

Lt Tibor Tobak, born in 1923, who served with 101/3 Fighter squadron, observed the American bombing from the ground and was depressed and dejected watching the passing American bomber stream: 'That was the first time that I felt that our small country would be unable to stem the attackers. There were far too many of them, and they had such confidence in their power! They come from so far away and approached their targets with mathematical precision!'[39]

The next heavy bombing raid on the airfields at Ferihegy and Tököl, as well as the Györ aircraft works and Budapest, followed on 13 April. The Hungarians defended themselves with 33 machines: 12 Bf 109Gs from 2/1 Fighter squadron, six Bf 109Gs from 1/1 Fighter squadron, 12 Me 210Ca-1s from the Experimental Air Force Institute (RKI) and three Me 210Ca-1s from 5/1 Night Fighter squadron. The twin-engined destroyers carried the main burden of this battle against 535 American bombers and their escorts. They did manage to shoot down six enemies (four B-24 Liberators and two P-38 Lightnings) but suffered exceptionally high losses themselves: only four damaged Me 210Ca-1s regained their bases. According to Hungarian data, the Americans lost 20 aircraft that day, of which six fell victim to the AA guns. But the Hungarian losses, too, were very heavy, particularly because many MKHL machines were destroyed on the ground. The Hungarian air force drew the following conclusions from the events of 13 April 1944:[40]

• The effectiveness of a small number of fighters against hundreds of bombers is too slight.

- Co-ordination between the fighter guidance centre in the Gellért mountains and the fighters must be improved
- Daylight operations by the Me 210 destroyers against the US bombers are senseless and must be suspended.

This prohibition of daytime operations also related to 5/1 Night Fighter squadron. It had been equipped only with the Fiat CR.42 biplanes and Héja fighters until early 1944, but received some Me 210Ca-1s in April and also had three Bf 110G-2s. Its state of training in March and April still disallowed any nocturnal operations, but during that period this squadron was ordered to fly daytime sorties on several occasions. However, after two of the three Me 210Ca-1s had been shot down on 13 April, no night fighters were used on daytime operations.

After 13 April a deceptive calm ruled in Hungarian skies for six weeks. The USAAF was concentrating on the oil installations at Ploesti, and the Hungarians used this breathing space to build up a more effective home defence formation, the 101 fighter group. Undisturbed by Allied daytime raids, the Honvéd pilots could now train in formation flying and combat tactics. The former 2/1 Fighter Squadron had become 101/1, the 1/1 101/2, and the 5/3 101/3 Fighter squadron.[41] Each of these squadrons had 12 machines and 16 pilots, with Veszprém-Jutas as their base. The new formation was commanded by the 'Old Puma', Major Aladár Heppes, and some of the more successful Hungarian fighter pilots on the Eastern Front also joined the new group. Among these were Sen Lt László Molnár, who shot down two Soviet aircraft on 8 January 1944 and had achieved 18 confirmed victories by spring 1944, as well as Sen Lt Gyorgy Debrödy[42] who had 17 confirmed victories to his credit by this same time.

Debrödy had graduated from the Aviation Academy in 1942, and, together with his friend Miklos Kenyeres, was promoted to the rank of Lieutenant on 20 August 1942. Posted to 5/3 Fighter Group on the Eastern Front, Debrödy soon proved himself in combat. Then, in September 1943, he was shot down over enemy territory 20km (12.4 miles) east of the Dniepr river. After an agonizing and perilous march, and a swim across the river, he managed to regain his unit. In February 1944 he shot down another Soviet fighter but had to make another forced landing behind the Soviet lines. His No. 2, Kenyeres, vanquished the Yak-9 that had shot down Debrödy and afterwards landed close to his friend although Soviet troops were already in the vicinity. Debrödy squeezed himself into the narrow cockpit of the Bf 109, but both pilots had to throw away their winter flying jackets and the cockpit roof before they could take off again. In the icy wind both Hungarians were frozen in no time. In the draughty cockpit flying the plane was a shared task: Kenyeres was in charge of the control column while Debrödy looked after the rudder pedals. The ground crew of the Hungarian squadron at Uman could hardly believe their eyes when the overloaded Messerschmitt came in to land. Against all odds, Kenyeres had rescued his friend.[43] Two days later the rescuer was himself shot down by Soviet AA guns and had to bale out over enemy territory, where he was captured. Debrödy circled despondently over the area, but could not help his comrade.

The newly formed 101 Fighter Group first saw action on 20 May 1944. On this date 13 Bf 109Gs from 101/1 Squadron were involved in a hectic combat against American daylight raiders, but, for the loss of just two aircraft and one pilot, managed to shoot down one B-17 Fortress, three B-24 Liberators and one P-51 Mustang. On 14 June the entire Puma group was in the air, led by Capt Gyula Horváth, together with about 80 Bf 109s and Fw 190s from the German 8th Fighter Division (Jagddivision). Numerous dogfights took place over Veszprém and Perfürdö, during the course of which the Hungarians shot down eight American aircraft for the loss of two of their number. Only two days later there was another aerial combat over the Lake Balaton, in which the 'Red Pumas' encountered 658 American bombers with 290 escort fighters. The fighting was extremely harsh and bitter, with the American pilots deliberately firing on Hungarian airmen who had saved themselves by parachute, or strafing crash-landed aircraft. One of the victims was Sen Lt Jozef Bognár, who was killed by an American pilot while hanging helplessly beneath his parachute.[44]

These brutal measures did not help the Americans, and they

had to write off another 16–20 aircraft and the corresponding number of aircrew. But the Hungarian losses, too, were alarming: five pilots were killed and another two wounded. Six machines were lost and four others were 20–40 per cent damaged. But the morale of the Red Pumas remained unbroken, supported as it was by the pride of belonging to an élite unit whose task was the defence of the homeland against the terror bombing raids, and in so doing face an enemy that was often 20 times stronger. The most popular Hungarian hit song of summer 1944 was *Life does not last longer than a day* and the Hungarian fighter pilots, according to their temperament and talent, related this text to themselves with stoicism or assumed nonchalance. They did not allow themselves to show outward signs of fear, but it was there, especially before take-off. Once in the air it soon disappeared once combat began. Tibor Tobak from 101/3 Squadron put down his thoughts before his first operational take-off:[45]

> I did not sleep much that night. The morning comes, and with it a cloudless sky. In the car the tension seems to quiver in the air. They will definitely be coming today. The thoughts follow one another in quick succession: how is it going to happen? Are we really going to meet them? Will we succeed in reaching the bombers before interference from the escorts? Will luck be on our side? I admit without any shame: I am scared.

The summer months of 1944 were filled with major aerial battles over Hungary. The MKHL was supported by the Luftwaffe, but flew about 40 per cent of all defensive missions,[46] and more and more Hungarian pilots lost their lives:

Date	American Losses	Hungarian Losses
26 June	3 B-24, 1 P-38, 1 P-51	3 pilots killed
27 June	2 B-17, 1 B-24, 1 P-51	
30 June	3 B-24	1 pilot killed
2 July	5 B-24, 1 B-17, 4 P-51, 1 P-38	3 aircraft shot down, 1 pilot killed

On 7 July 1944 38 P-38 Lightnings from the 82nd Fighter Group had the task of escorting bombers from the 55th Bomber Wing and 304th Bomber Wing on their return from attacking targets in Germany. Altogether 560 American bombers and 250 escort fighters were in Hungarian airspace on that day. They were faced by just ten Bf 109s, led by Major Aladár Heppes. The Hungarians lost one machine, the Bf 109G of Lt Lajos Tóth, who had to take to his parachute for the fifth time just after achieving his 14th aerial victory. The 15th USAAF lost 25 aircraft that day, 8–10 of which went on the account of the Hungarian fighter defences.[47] By the end of July the Hungarian pilots had managed to shoot down another 15 enemy aircraft, losing only one of their own (Officer Cadet Leó Krizsevszky). But this phase of relatively light losses for the Pumas was not to last very long.

On 7 August 357 four-engined American bombers and 117 escort fighters flew over Hungary on their way to targets in Poland. The 101 Fighter Group was given the task of accompanying German Bf 109G-6 fighters. These 'Gustavs' carried additional cannon in underwing gondolas, which had a detrimental effect on their manoeuvrability. The 18 Hungarian fighters had to do their best under these circumstances to enable the 12 German machines to approach the bombers, but they did not succeed. The allies were intercepted by numerically far superior swarms of P-51 Mustangs and a massacre was in the making. Losing only two of their own, the Mustang pilots shot down eight Hungarian and at least nine German fighters. Among the dead Pumas was Lt László Molnár, whose score of 25 aerial victories (including seven American aircraft) had made him the most successful Hungarian fighter pilot to date.

On 21 August[48] the Americans carried out a series of heavy raids on Hungarian airfields. The heaviest blows fell on 102/1 Fast Bomber squadron, which had been active against the Red Army during the preceding weeks: all 12 Me 210Ca-1s were destroyed at Hajdub-Öszörmeny, the base of this unit. However, 102/1 Squadron soon received new aircraft and continued to operate against the Soviet forces.

Then came 23 August, when Romania changed sides and

Hungary, threatened by the Red Army on the Eastern Front and by the Western allies in the air, suddenly had another enemy.

The Pumas, 101 Fighter Group, who, until the end of August, had achieved 104 victories for the loss of 18 pilots, were temporally withdrawn from the very costly combat against the Americans. The Hungarian command now expanded the formation to full wing strength, comprising the following units: 101/II Fighter Group, with the 4th, 5th and 6th Squadrons at Kenyeri, and 101/I Fighter Group, which remained at Veszprém.

Despite the Soviet advance – by the end of 1944 they had occupied two-thirds of Hungary – the morale of the Hungarian airmen remained unbroken. Oberst Hajo Herrmann, the creator of the 'Wild Boar' night fighting method, who had visited the Red Pumas at Veszprém, described them as 'brave and frankly daring pilots.'[49]

On 15 October the Imperial Administrator, Admiral Horthy, attempted a defection from the alliance, which was nipped in the bud by the German troops and the local 'Arrow Cross' supporters. This underhand action by their leader had little support within the Hungarian army or air force. Lt Tobak described the mood of his comrades:[50]

We have vigorously condemned the Romanians for their desertion. To our minds they are traitors, because they have betrayed the Germans when their situation was hopeless. Are we to imitate them? What should we do? To be sure, we know that we are on the side of the losers today, but we cannot do anything about that. In a situation like ours only an irreproachable bearing and loyalty in further action seems honourable.

An upbringing oriented on the values of the k.u.k. (*kaiserlich und königlich*, royal and imperial) epoch, combined with a pronounced anti-Communist stance and an ardent patriotism prevented the disintegration of the MKHL in a situation that was politically and militarily desperate.[51]

To give up? Go over to the Russians or the British? The spirit, the tradition and the honour of my regiment does not allow me to do so. Each of us has the right to throw away the uniform and be free of further combat duties, but only one of us had made use of this choice, and that as a result of nervous depression.

In fact desertions to the Allies were few and far between. On 9 December 1944, on instructions from the Hungarian resistance movement, Maj Domokos Hadnagy, Chief of the Technical Department of the Hungarian General Staff, flew his He 111H-16 Wk. Nr. 8433, marked 2B+DC, to Italy and landed at San Severo near Foggia. On 26 February 1945 Maj Gen Ladislaus Havy took himself and his family to safety in Italy in a Fw 58 Weihe marked K3+58.[52] But these were exceptions.

In October 1944 the Red Pumas were operational only against the Red Army. On 12 October both 101 Fighter Wing and 5/1 Night Fighter squadron came under direct German command and were subordinated to the 8th Fliegerdivision. In the same month the two squadrons of 102 Fighter Group were also deployed from the Eastern Front back to Hungary.

Early in 1944 there had been only 30 Hungarian aircraft subordinated to Luftflotte 4 on the Eastern Front. These few machines were strengthened in the summer by the 12 Bf 109G-6s from the newly formed 102/2 Fighter squadron and 12 Ju 87D-5 Stukas, as well as some older models, which carried out 47 sorties from the end of June to August 1944, losing four aircraft.

Up to the end of 1944 the two squadrons of 102 Fighter Group flew 1,855 operational sorties, mainly on the Eastern Front, shooting down 85 enemy aircraft and losing 19 of their own. An additional 51 planes were written off in accidents, but only nine pilots lost their lives. For a short while some sorties were also flown by a night harassment squadron equipped with He 46 biplanes, which operated north-west of Lvov in June and July but was withdrawn to Hungary at the end of July. The planned used of this squadron against the Soviet troops in Romania could not be realized due to the poor technical condition of the aircraft. Even so, an entire night harassment group was formed in November. It consisted of three squadrons as follows: 102/1, also equipped with the He 46; 102/2, with a few He 111s; and

102/3 with the Bü 131B Jungmann, of which Hungary had received 100. However, this formation was never operational and ended the war in March 1945 at the Wiener-Neustadt airfield in Austria.[53]

The Red Pumas from 102 Wing, now supported by their comrades from 102 Fighter Group, went into action against the American bomber formations again up to 7 November. From that day onwards all combat activities against the Western allies were suspended because the MKHL concentrated all its efforts on stemming the Soviet offensive thrusts. At the end of the year the Hungarians were given a review by the German 8th Fliegerdivision, recording their successes from March to the end of November. This summary proves that the Hungarians were more effective in combating the enemy than their German allies.[54]

	101 Fighter Wing	Luftwaffe Day Fighters
Operational Sorties	649	932
Aerial victories, total	107	73
of which four-engined	61	53
twin-engined	32	
single-engined	14	20
Losses		
aircraft	78	88
pilots	30	43

These Hungarian successes must have had a decisive effect on plans prepared by the Luftwaffe command to retrain the Honvéd pilots on the Me 262 jet fighter. The initial group consisted of pilots from the short-range reconnaissance squadron that had been withdrawn from the Eastern Front in November 1944. The selected airmen were sent to Kölleda, near Gotha, but the conversion training did not progress beyond a technical introduction.[55]

On 24 December 1944 Budapest was surrounded by the Red Army. The MKHL, which had shot down 28 Soviet aircraft from 1 December to Christmas Eve, did all it could within its limited capabilities to break the encirclement. Among the participants in this action were the Me 210Ca-1s from 102 Fast Bomber Group, which was to celebrate its 2,000th operational sortie on 8 January 1945, as well as Hungarian Fw 190F-8s from 102 Close-support Group, which had begun to receive these machines at the end of 1944. To supply the surrounded capital, the Hungarian air force could provide only two Ju 52/3m transports[56] so that the Luftwaffe had to carry the main burden of this 'aerial bridge'. During the first 11 days of the Soviet investment of Budapest the Honvéd air force flew 291 sorties and shot down 16 Soviet aircraft. By comparison, the Soviet air force carried out no fewer than 8,490 sorties over the same period!

102 Fast Bomber Group[1]
Major Albert Martini

Unit	Established	Sqn Commander	Markings	Aircraft[2]
101/1 Fast Bomber sqn	Mar 1944	Capt Istvan Herszenyi[3]	Eagle with bomb in its claws	12 Me 210Ca-1
101/2 Fast Bomber sqn	Jun 1944	Capt Pal Bodo	Tiger	20 Me 210Ca-1 4 Bü131B 1 Fi 156
101/3 Fast Bomber sqn[4]	Oct 1944	Capt Adolf Péterdi[5]	Yellow lightning	15 Me 210Ca-1 1 Ju 88A 1 Fi 156 1 Fw 58

[1] The group was formally established on 1 November 1944
[2] The aircraft material relates to the original establishment
[3] Relieved by Capt Kalman Hary late in August 1944
[4] This unit was formed from the Me 210Ca-1 squadron of the Experimental Institute of the Hungarian Air Force (RKI)
[5] Captured on 23 December 1944 after a forced landing

Source: Mujzer, Péter, 'Les Messerschmitt Me 210Ca hongrois', Part 3, in *Avions* No.48, March 1997, pp. 22–30

On 6 January 1945 there was another change for the Hungarian fighter arm and a reassignment of the sole fighter wing: the headquarters of the German Jagdfliegerführer Ungarn

(Fighter Leader Hungary) was dissolved and the Hungarian as well as the Luftwaffe fighters operating in Hungary (I./JG 53, II./JG 52 and II./JG 51) were subordinated to Stab/JG 76, which had no other aircraft at its disposal.[57] With effect from 15 January, 101 Fighter Wing was expanded by adding a third group; 102 Fighter Group was incorporated into 101 Wing, 102/1 squadron becoming 101/7 and 102/2–108/8. The third group was also given an additional 9th squadron, comprised of members of the 'Reich' squadron that carried a green frog as its symbol. From May to August 1944 the pilots of this squadron had been in Hildesheim, Delitz and Neuruppin, where they had trained on the Bf 109 and Fw 190, and later flew as ferry pilots between the aircraft factories and the front. The plan to operate this Hungarian Fw 190 squadron during the German Ardennes offensive in mid-December 1944 was not realized.[58] At the end of December the pilots received new Bf 109s at Wiener-Neustadt and were subsequently transferred to the Kenyeri airfield.

German and Hungarian efforts to relieve Budapest failed, and the aerial victories achieved by the Red Pumas had no effect on the general situation. On 16 January 101/I Group sent six enemy aircraft to the ground, and on 20 January another four. But two days earlier the defenders had been forced to evacuate the eastern part of the metropolis, Pest. The Fw 190s of the Hungarian 102 Close-support Group circled in vain over the relinquished area of Budapest without releasing their bombs as the Red Army troops rarely provided a target. The aerial combat with the numerically far superior Soviet formations took on a fiercer character, but the Pumas nevertheless managed to shoot down another 69 Soviet aircraft during January. The lost Hungarian aircraft were quickly replaced, but the numbers remained modest. Early in February 101 Fighter Wing received a total of 26 brand-new Bf 109G-10/U4 fighters with the instruction that their engines had to be changed after just 30–40 operating hours. This did not disturb the Hungarian pilots in the least, as Tibor Tobak related: 'To remain for 30 hours in your aircraft without taking to the parachute or making a forced landing had in the meantime become almost a feat. As each operational flight lasted about 60–70 minutes, 30 hours was long enough to get killed, badly wounded or end up as a prisoner of war.'[59] Tobak was wounded and sent to a hospital in Osterode/Harz. On 14 February he 'deserted' with two other Hungarian pilots who also wanted to get back to their units. The three pilots made their way across the dying Reich without any personal documents, were temporarily 'collected' by the Hungarian SS-Division 'Kossuth' in Nuremberg, but finally managed to reach the Red Pumas at Veszprém on 25 February. 'Today three pitiful-looking air force lieutenants climbed down the slope to the airfield. We are thin, weak and dirty, but happy because we are finally back with our big family, the regiment'.[60] *Aeronautica patria nostra.*

On 11 February 1945 the last resistance of the defenders in Budapest was extinguished. The MKHL also supported the last Axis offensive at the Eastern front – Operation *Frühlingserwachen* (Spring Awakening) – which began in Transdanubia on 6 March, with, among others, the remainder of eleven German tank divisions, and was intended to recapture Budapest and secure the Romanian oil fields. In the air 850 German and Hungarian aircraft were met by 965 Soviet and Bulgarian machines. The German offensive began on schedule, but was soon choked in mud, and the Puma fighters were faced by a more dangerous and agile enemy, the Lavochkin La-7, which now appeared more and more frequently in the air.[61] But the Honvéd fighter pilots always attacked, even when they were numerically far inferior to the enemy. On 9 March eight Bf 109Gs from 101/3 fighter squadron dived onto a formation of 25 Soviet-crewed Douglas Boston bombers escorted by 16 Yak-9 fighters, and managed to shoot down three. This battle more or less repeated itself on 23 March, when eight Red Pumas attacked 26 Soviet aircraft south of Lake Balaton and shot down five without a single loss. A day later, the Hungarian fighter pilots were mentioned in the German High Command daily report. On the same day (24 March) 101 Wing began to transfer from Kenyeri to Szombathely. After landing on an airfield pockmarked with bomb craters, no fewer than 26 aircraft had to be written off.[62] But new fighters still arrived from the bomb-tormented Reich, and soon the Hungarians had more aircraft than pilots.

At the end of March the MKHL had to leave its homeland; the last part of Hungary was occupied by the Soviets on 4 April. The 102 Fast Bomber Group with its remaining Me 210Ca-1s withdrew to Parndorf, while the Red Pumas moved first to Petersdorf, then Wiener-Neustadt and Tulln, and then to Raffelding. The main body of the Honvéd air force assembled at Tulln. From there the Hungarian fighters still carried out numerous reconnaissance flights and attacks on ground targets, at times flying so low that their Bf 109s ripped off telephone wires. Their losses were dramatically high: in two days the Red Pumas lost ten aircraft and four pilots. The last Hungarian aerial victory of the war was achieved by Sen Lt Kiss, who shot down a Yak-9 on 17 April. The wing shrank to group size, but the fighting continued. When, late in April/early May, the Americans began to close in, the Hungarians set fire to their remaining aircraft at Tulln, Parndorf, Raffelding and Pöcking – where the survivors of their reconnaissance squadron had found their last base. The Magyar Királyi Honvéd Légierö had ceased to exist.

Bulgaria

Vozdushni Voiski

For the Western allies a Bulgarian air force in the Second World War does not seem to have existed at all – or only in insignificant size. In the 1946/47 edition of the respected encyclopaedia *Jane's Fighting Aircraft of World War II*[1] there is no mention of a Bulgarian air force – or a Romanian one, for that matter. And in the *Order of Battle* and *Handbooks of the Bulgarian, Hungarian and Romanian Armed Forces* published by the US War Department in 1944[2] the authors incorrectly disavow any indigenous Bulgarian aircraft production and describe the Bulgarian air force as 'numerically weak, inadequate in terms of maintenance, and of poor quality'.

The Americans estimated that only about 30 per cent of Bulgarian aircraft were serviceable. The pilots of this Balkan state were classed as 'good', yet the compilers of this handbook still displayed American arrogance towards this small country by adding that they were '... slow in learning and slow in reaction'.

When the balance sheets were drawn up in late summer 1944 the Western allies had no longer any grounds for presumptions: 329 of their airmen were in Bulgarian captivity, 187 had been killed over Bulgaria and another 69 had died in hospitals. The Bulgarians had shot down at least 53 British and American aircraft[3] and damaged another 71.[4] This was quite remarkable, considering that just 25 years before that it had not seemed likely that there would be a Bulgarian air force at all.

Bulgarian military aviation was, in fact, born on 19 August 1892. On that day Lt Vassil Slatarov carried out a balloon flight in the *La France*, owned by Frenchman Eugene Godard. It was only following an order from the War Ministry in Sofia on 24 April 1906, however, that an aviation detachment was founded and attached to the Army Engineers Railway Battalion. The first commanding officer of this detachment, which comprised 37 men and three spherical balloons by 1912, was Sen Lt Slatarov.

In the same year the Bulgarian government bought seven aircraft – three French, three German and one British – and established the 1st Aircraft Detachment under Sen Lt Khristo Topraktchiev. A total of 13 pilots, six mechanics and two balloon pilots then completed their training in the countries from which the machines were acquired. The Bulgarians established the fact that training a pilot in France took longer than three months, while in Germany pilot training was completed in a mere three days, with just three flying hours!

By the end of 1912 the number of Bulgarian aircraft had risen to 29, but there were only 12 qualified pilots, including eight foreigners. Bulgarian military aviation, now divided into three detachments, took an active part in the First Balkan War, involving Bulgaria, Greece, Serbia and Montenegro against the Ottoman Empire, which lasted from October 1912 to May 1913. The Bulgarian aircraft undertook reconnaissance and observation flights, and also carried out the first aerial bombing attack when, on 12 October 1912, the crew of an Albatros biplane dropped hand grenades over Adrianople (Edirne). One month after the First Balkan War Bulgaria attacked Serbia, starting the Second Balkan War, but Bulgarian planes hardly participated in this conflict. The Bulgarians could not hold out for long against the united front formed by Turkey and Romania, who had joined in to help the Serbs. Under the terms of the following peace treaty, signed in Bucharest, the Bulgarians had to give up Macedonia and Dobrudzha.

After this defeat, Bulgarian military aviation was reconstructed. The aircraft detachment and the balloon detachment now formed an Aviation Company, which, together with a searchlight detachment, was combined into a Technical Battalion, commanded by Major Zlatov and attached to the Army Engineering service. A base was established at Bojourishte, in the outer suburbs of Sofia, consisting of an airfield and a flying school, as well as the State Aircraft Factory, DAR (Darzhavna Aeroplanna Rabotilnitsa), which, however, did not start work until June 1917.

During the First World War Bulgaria joined the Central Powers on 1 October 1915, hoping to regain the territories lost in 1913. Although three years had elapsed since its foundation, Bulgarian air power remained weak. The aircraft park possessed only two Albatros C.Is, two Bleriot XI-2s and a Bleriot XI-1.[5] The German Kaiser had to support Germany's new ally, and the German deliveries totalled 66 aircraft by 1918: 12 LVG B IIs, six Roland D IIs, six Roland D IIIs, 13 Otto C Is, 18 Albatros C IIIs, three Fokker E IIIs and eight Fokker D VIIs.

Initially the Bulgarian air arm possessed just 124 men, mostly ground personnel. There were only seven pilots and eight observers, and, until the end of 1915, hardly any Bulgarian airmen were involved in combat. The training of Bulgarian fighter pilots began in spring 1916, after the arrival of three Fokker E III monoplanes intended for the defence of Sofia. Soon afterwards the Bulgarian air arm, now comprising two aircraft detachments, one flying school, one aircraft park, the DAR works and a balloon group, began taking an active part in operations, and recorded 497 combat sorties by the end of 1916. The air war intensified in 1917. By late April the French and British had about 60 aircraft on the Salonika front, opposed by just 35 German and Bulgarian aircraft, which nevertheless carried out 517 combat sorties that year. In 1918 the balance tilted even more in favour of the Entente: the Allies could field 200 aircraft arranged in 15 detachments while the Central Powers had only about 80 aircraft in nine detachments (seven German and two Bulgarian). To support the 1918 spring offensive on the Western Front the German command withdrew most of its troops from the Balkans. Bulgaria on its own was unable to hold out against the Allied offensive, starting on 14 September, and had to ask for an armistice. The demobilization of the Bulgarian forces began on 4 October. It was only then that the last Fokker D VII fighters arrived in Bulgaria, too late to be of any use for the Bulgarian air arm. During the war Bulgarian military aviation had lost nine aircraft, of which four had been shot down. In the same period the Entente had to write off 40 aircraft, of which five had been shot down in aerial combat.

The peace treaty of Neuilly, signed on 27 November 1919, was a hard blow for the small country: Bulgaria lost 8 percent of its pre-war territory. As regards its military aviation, the entire aircraft park had to be destroyed. Moreover, Bulgaria was not permitted to have or build any military aircraft for a period of 20 years. A total of 70 aircraft, 110 aero engines, three balloons and numerous accessories had to be destroyed in the Bojounishte hangars. The same fate befell the eight Friedrichshafen FF 33 reconnaissance seaplanes and two Rumpler 6B1 floatplane fighters that Bulgaria had bought from Germany as late as April 1918.

The Neuilly dictate meant the temporary end of Bulgarian military aviation – although Bulgarian personnel succeeded in clandestinely saving some aircraft from destruction.[6] The victorious powers had not forbidden every kind of air traffic, however, though restrictions were imposed on civil aviation – no aero engines of more than 180hp power were to be used in civil aviation and all civil aircraft had to be acquired from France, Britain or Italy. These injunctions were soon to be 'undermined'. An air gendarmery detachment was formed already in 1921. Two years later Sofia ratified the international civil aviation agreement, and, in 1924, an Aviation Directory was established as the first step towards an aviation ministry under the Minister for Railways, Post and Telegraph. In the same year Bulgaria bought 18 aircraft abroad – 16 French and two British.[7] In 1925 the Bulgarian government acquired another 17 aircraft, including two Italian floatplanes.

In Bojourishte, 12km (7.4 miles) outside Sofia, secret rearmament work was pursued on a modest scale. The first course of flying instruction had already begun in 1923. A few months later the DAR works resumed its activities and an indigenous Bulgarian aviation industry began to evolve. The groundwork for this industry was furnished by a German aircraft designer, Hermann Winter, who, with a small staff of technicians and experts, came to Bojourishte in 1925.[8] His first series-production aircraft was the DAR-U1, a copy of the proven DFW C VA general-purpose and reconnaissance aircraft, of which seven examples were built. The next small series of 12 aircraft comprised the DAR-2. This was a copy of the German Albatros C III reconnaissance aircraft. But Winter also designed several original aircraft, such as the DAR-1 (12 planes) and the

DAR-1a (eight), which, thanks to their robust construction, were to be seen in Bulgarian skies until the early 1940s. Other Winter designs were the DAR-3 reconnaissance aircraft, the DAR-5 fighter and the three-engined DAR-4 passenger aircraft (which were not built in series, however).

A second Bulgarian aircraft factory was established by the Czech firm Aero in Kasanlak in 1926. From 1928 onwards this factory produced only motor vehicles until it was sold to the Italian aircraft producer Gianni Caproni in 1930. Under the designation KB (Kaproni Bulgaria) the following different aircraft types were built at Kasanlak:

Model	Evolved from Italian Model	Function	Number Built
KB 1	Ca 100	Trainer	10, incl. two floatplanes
KB 2 UT	Ca 113	Trainer	8
KB 2 A	Ca 113	Trainer	6
KB 3	Ca 113	Trainer	20
KB 4	Ca 113	Trainer	28
KB 5	Ca 113	Trainer	45
KB 309	Ca 309	Transport	10
KB 11		Reconnaissance	42

On 15 September 1942 the Caproni-Kasanlak works were taken over by the Bulgarian state, which continued to employ the Italian chief designers Carlo Caligaris and Picini. From then on the works designation changed to DSF Kasanlak. Initially, only German and Italian technicians and engineers projected and built aircraft there. Bulgarian experts, such as Tsvetan, Lazarov and Boris Dinchev learned quickly from their foreign colleagues, however, and applied the knowledge acquired to their own original developments. Thus in 1931 Lazarov designed the DAR-6 two-seat trainer and, in 1936, the DAR-6a.

All these models were officially civilian ones, but they could just as well serve for military purposes, and became the foundation of the new Bulgarian air force, Vozdushni Voiski. In the mid-1930s Tsar Boris III started a rearmament policy, which more or less openly ignored the injunctions of the Neuilly treaty. The first Army Air Group, consisting of two

BULGARIA

reconnaissance, one fighter and one training squadron with their respective maintenance detachments, and the technical personnel, were established at Bojourishte in 1935.[9]

Despite all efforts by the indigenous aircraft industry Bulgaria lacked suitable aircraft models, so decided to purchase planes from Poland. A Polish delegation arrived in Bulgaria in 1937 to demonstrate various military models. The Balkan state subsequently ordered 14 PZL P.24B fighters, 12 PZL P.23 tactical bombers (redesignated P.43A after the fitting of Gnôme-Rhône radial engines) and five PWS-16bis trainers.[10]

Germany had resumed aircraft deliveries to Bulgaria in 1936, Sofia receiving 12 He 45s and 12 He 51s, as well as six He 72 Kadetts, six Fw 56 Stössers and six FW 44 Stieglitz trainers. The Bulgarians also acquired licence production rights for the Fw 44 and manufactured it in the new DSF Lovekh plant, which was opened in 1941, and was where the DAR with its entire personnel was transferred. In 1937 Göring presented Bulgaria with 12 Ar 65 fighters and 12 Do 11D bombers which had been discarded by the Luftwaffe as obsolescent. This gesture had of course ulterior political motives, the Third Reich wanting to extend its influence in the Balkans, which Italy considered to be strictly its own 'area of interest'.

In Salonika on 31 July 1938 the Sofia government reached an agreement with the Balkan League which envisaged a repeal of the armament restrictions. Almost simultaneously, Bulgaria obtained a French bank credit for 375 million francs for the purchase of armaments and railway and road construction materials. After the Agreement of Salonika, the Royal Bulgarian Air Force could at last be revealed to the public. Until October 1940, the aircraft of the Vozdushni Voiski displayed a very colourful emblem: a white circle containing a red, yellow-edged cross with swords with a yellow lion dominant in the centre. But the Bulgarian 'lion' was weak when one took into consideration the air force strengths of its potential enemies. To improve the balance, Sofia once again ordered a large number of fighters and bombers from Poland, including 42 PZL P.43B light bombers. But the Vozdushni Voiski received its largest boost in aircraft numbers after the German occupation of Czechoslovakia in

154

1939. The Third Reich sold most of the aircraft of the disbanded Czech air force to Bulgaria under extremely favourable conditions: the Germans guaranteed a discount of 60 per cent on the manufacturer's price and accepted payment in tobacco and other Bulgarian products. In this way the Bulgarian air force received 78 Avia B-534 fighters, 60 Letov Š-328 reconnaissance aircraft, 32 Avia B-71 (Czech licence-built Tupolev SB) bombers, 12 Aero M.B.200 (licence-built version of the French Bloch M.B.200) bombers, 28 Avia trainers and one Avia A-304 bomber.[11]

At the same time pilot training was intensified. Already in June 1938 seven Bulgarian air force lieutenants had been sent to Germany to be trained as fighter pilots and flying instructors:[12] Assen Kovatchev, Stojan Stojanov, Dimitar Lazarov, Alexander Guntchev, Dimitar Tamakhyarov, Vassil Zhishkov and Nikolai Jordanov. To begin with, the Bulgarian officers completed the aerobatic flying training course at Kaufbeuren. Then they underwent three courses at Werneuchen: as fighter pilots, leaders and flying instructors, and then as wing commanders of flying formations. The training sessions were completed successfully, and all Bulgarian officers were awarded diplomas as fighter pilot instructors. In March 1939 another batch of five Bulgarian airmen were sent to Werneuchen: Sen Lt Chudomir Toplodolski and Lts Dimitar Spissarevski, Bogdan Iliev, Georgi Genchev and Matei Todorov, of whom Genchev and Todorov were to lose their lives in a flying accident. The German assistance was not limited to fighter pilot training. During the second half of 1941 15 Bulgarians were trained as dive bomber pilots at the Stuka-Vorschule 3 (Stuka preliminary training school) at Bad Aibling and Stuka Schule 1 at Wertheim. On the conclusion of its training, the group was transferred to Italy, where it was supposed to gain practical experience under operational conditions. However, the Bulgarian High Command refused to allow its pilots to be used against Allied shipping in the Mediterranean, and the Bulgarian pilots returned home to be stationed at the Count Ignatievo airfield, where the 2nd Assault Regiment was formed.

Up to the summer of 1944 Bulgarian officers and other ranks

were continually passing through German training schools and other establishments to acquire further technical knowledge. In addition, there were the Bulgarian pilots who were instructed on French Dewoitine D.520 fighters at Nancy in France in 1943 (see Appendix 3). Italy, which had lost its position as the most important armament supplier to Bulgaria to Germany in 1939, also offered training facilities to the new generation of Bulgarian airmen. In summer 1940 20 Bulgarian pilots completed their training programme at the Accademia Aerionautica Militare in Caserta. Altogether, about 160 Bulgarian pilots were trained in Germany, Italy and Hungary.

At the end of 1939 the structure of the Royal Bulgarian Air Force was as follows:

Unit	Base	Commander	Squadrons	Aircraft
1st Army Air Group	Bojourishte	Maj V. Volkov	3 1 (training)	36 PZL P.43B 11, different models
2nd Fighter Group	Karlovo	Maj K. Georgiev	4 1 (training)	60 Avia B-534 12, different models
3rd Reconnaissance Group	Jambol	Maj E. Karadimtchev	4 1 (training)	48 Letov Š-328 12, different models
4th Army Air Group	Gorna Ornahovitsa	Maj I. Ivanov		
5th Bomber Group	Plovdiv	Maj C. Stoikov	3 1 (training)	36 Avia B-71 15 Do 11 + Aero M.B.200
Fighter training school	Karlovo			
Blind Flying Training School	Plovdiv			
Cadet Air Training School	Vrashdebna	Maj M. Dimitrov		62, mainly Fw 44 Stieglitz
Instruction school	Kasanlak	Maj G. Drenikov	3	52, different models

Source: Valkov, Todor, *The Story of the Bulgarian Air Forces up to 9 September 1944*, Part II, pp. 5–6

As can be seen from the above, the Bulgarian Vozdushni Voiski was equipped with a variety of German, Italian, Czech, Polish and other aircraft of indigenous manufacture, many of which fell short of modern requirements. Therefore the air force command in Sofia endeavoured to acquire high-quality fighters as a matter of priority, especially after the German occupation of Poland meant more spare parts could be obtained for the PZL P.24B fighters. France, for its part, could not fulfil a Bulgarian order for 20 Bloch 152 fighters, while a 1940 request to acquire 12 modern Avia 135 fighters, together with the licence to produce another 50, was torpedoed by the German Air Ministry in 1942. As a result the dozen available Avia 135 fighters had to be passed on to flying schools. Still, Germany had delivered ten Bf 109E-3s, 12 Do 17Ps, 14 Bü 131s, 24 Ar 96Bs and other aircraft models to Bulgaria[13] in 1940 so the Royal Bulgarian Air Force now possessed a total of 580 aircraft. On paper it was an impressive number, but qualitatively the Vozdushni Voiski remained second rate. The situation was hardly changed by a restructuring of the air force in summer 1940, when the Army Air Groups were reorganized into regiments (similar to Luftwaffe *Geschwader*, or wings).

The deficient equipment of the Bulgarian armed forces did not hinder achievement of some easy 'victories' on the diplomatic front. For example, in the Treaty of Craiova of 7 September 1940 Bulgaria acquired South Dobrudzha to the extent of its 1913 borders. Consideration of Bulgaria's safety and territorial promises induced Tsar Boris III to join the Tripartite Pact on 1 March 1941.

Although Bulgaria served as an assembly area for the German troops before the German attack on Yugoslavia on 7 April 1941, it did not participate in the conflict, despite the fact that Yugoslav and British aircraft carried out bombing raids on Bulgarian towns, causing panic among the local population. German Luftwaffe advisers had been in Bulgaria since the winter of 1940–1, had acquired a good general view of the installations used by the Vozdushni Voiski and had prepared airfields for the coming operations against Yugoslavia. The Bulgarians also laid out new airfields, which were eventually to total 50. The

BULGARIA

Bulgarians were to receive their reward for their passive participation in the Yugoslav campaign: Bulgarian troops were
allowed to occupy Greek Thracia and Serbian Macedonia. With
the territorial gains of September 1940 and April 1941 Bulgaria
expanded its area by 50 per cent and increased its population by
a third.[14] This was the birth of Greater Bulgaria.

Aircraft Inventory of the Bulgarian Air Force in 1941

Model	Translation of Bulgarian Name	Total Number
Fighters		
Bf 109E	'Arrow'	18
Avia B-534	'Hunting Eagle'	73
PZL P.24B	'Hawk'	11
Training Aircraft		
He 51	'Falcon'	1
Ar 65	'Eagle'	11
Fw 56 Stösser	'Gnat'	4
Avia 122	'Wasp'	29
Bombers		
Do 17	'Hurricane'	18
Avia B-71	'Crane'	32
Avia B-200	'Owl'	12
Close Support Aircraft		
PZL P.43B	'Gull'	33
DAR-10	'Snipe'	1
Training Aircraft		
Fw 44 Stieglitz	'Sparrow'	39
He 72 Kadett	'Canary'	5
Bü 131 Jungmann	'Swallow'	10
DAR-8	'Nightingale'	6
DAR-9	'Titmouse'	6
Communications and Transport Aircraft		
Me 108 Taifun	'Swan'	6
Fi 156 Storch	'Thrush'	3
Fw 58 Weihe	'Pigeon'	8
Ju 52/3m	–	2
KB 6	'Parrot'	9
Do 11	'Bat'	12

158

Reconnaissance Aircraft

He 45	'Stork'	10
Letov Š-328	'Crow'	60
DAR-3	'Raven'	22
KB 5 III	'Lark'	
42		

Training Aircraft

Ar 96	'Jay'	24
KB 3	'Lark I'	19
K 3	'Lark II'	25

TOTAL   **561**

Of these 561 machines 411 were operationally ready.

Source: Volkov, Todor: *Sofia*

With its strongly Russophile population, Bulgaria did not participate in the German attack on the Soviet Union. This was possibly partly why German aircraft deliveries were rather modest in 1941. The Vozdushni Voiski received 11 captured ex-Yugoslav air force Do 17Kb-1 bombers, among others. These had not been built in Germany, but manufactured under licence at Kraljevo in Yugoslavia.

Nevertheless, Bulgaria could not completely avoid taking an active part in the war in 1941. One day before the start of the Eastern Campaign, the German military attaché in Sofia asked the Headquarters of the Bulgarian Air Force to participate in the defence of German communications in the Aegean Sea, and the Bulgarian Chief of Staff immediately issued appropriate orders. The 5th Bomber Group organized a mixed formation, consisting of one squadron with nine Do 17s and one squadron with six Avia B-71s based at Kavalla, which was under Bulgarian civil administration and the base of the 443rd Bulgarian reconnaissance squadron since 5 May. Together with German reconnaissance seaplanes, the Bulgarians had the task of escorting German convoys north of Crete and keeping a lookout for British submarines. At that time Bulgaria was still not at war with the Western allies; the Bulgarian declaration of war against Great Britain and USA only followed on 13

December 1941. From 23 June 1941 to 3 January 1942 the Bulgarian bomber group carried out 304 sorties, but had only two visual contacts with enemy submarines.[15]

Another German request by the OKW (High Command of the Armed Forces) on 31 July 1941 concerned the protection of German convoys in the Black Sea. The Bulgarians assembled one squadron of Letov Š-328s (nine, later 12, reconnaissance aircraft). Its tasks embraced escort for convoys, search for mine-fields, protection of mine trawlers and the hunting of submarines insofar as these were operating in Bulgarian waters. As a matter of fact, Soviet submarines carried out about 60 operations in Bulgarian waters, mainly to set ashore groups of saboteurs of exiled Bulgarian Communists. By the end of 1941 the Bulgarian reconnaissance squadron had flown 68 sorties and attacked Soviet submarines five times with 20kg (44lb) bombs. Likewise the defence of the Bulgarian Black Sea coast by fighters was the result of German urging. On 10 October 1941, under the code name 'Galata', the formation of two fighter squadrons began. The 682nd Squadron of the 6th Fighter regiment, commanded by Sen Lt K. Atanassov, was based at Baltchik; the 692nd Squadron of the same regiment, commanded by Sen Lt D. Lazarov, at Sarafovo. Both squadrons were equipped with Bf 109E fighters. During the winter months of 1941/42, another nine Bf 109E-7s reached Sofia,[16] giving Bulgaria a total of 18 Bf 109E fighters.

The year 1942 passed peacefully for the Bulgarian air force even though Soviet aircraft had carried out bombing raids on Bulgarian towns as early as 1941, despite the fact that the two countries were not at war. Bulgarian lack of commitment led Germany to withhold deliveries of modern aircraft.[17]

On 11 June 1942 13 B-24 Liberator bombers took off from Fayid, in Egypt, to attack Ploesti, the centre of the Romanian oil industry. When, on their return flight, the American bombers over flew Bulgaria, there was no reaction nor any defence of Bulgarian airspace. This alarmed both the Bulgarian High Command and the Luftwaffe commission in Bulgaria. The Germans urged better co-ordination of defensive measures and promised deliveries of modern aircraft. To protect its capital the

Bulgarian High Command stationed the 612th Squadron/6th Fighter regiment at Vrashdena and the 622nd Squadron/6th Fighter regiment at Bojourishte. Both these squadrons were equipped with the obsolete Avia B-534 biplanes, however, and these could do little against the heavy four-engined bombers of the USAAF. It was not until December 1942 that the Air Ministry in Berlin finally agreed to supply 16 Bf 109G-2 fighters to Bulgaria, and even these were not delivered until the spring of 1943. It was Hitler himself who promised the Bulgarian War Minister, Nikola Mishoff, the delivery of modern weapons, during a meeting on 6 January 1943.[18] An OKW report drawn up five days after this visit to the Führer HQ stated:[19]

> Anti-aircraft defences and passive air defences in Bulgaria are still very weak. Very little is done for the civilians. Support and assistance is required especially by deliveries of AA equipment. (Ob.d.L./Lw.Fü.Stab, the C-in-C of the Luftwaffe, Luftwaffe Command Staff).
>
> For the time being the Bulgarian army and air force are only conditionally suitable for defence, but not for offensive tasks ...
>
> The requirements for the improvement of the Bulgarian air force will be presented separately to the Ob.d.L. by the air attaché. Far-reaching and quick realization of the requirements within the scope of what is possible for us considering the general situation has been promised to the Bulgarians.

Modern equipment was to take time in arriving, but earlier, in the winter of 1941–2, the Bulgarians had received 12 Ar 196A floatplanes, which equipped their 161th coastal squadron in the Black Sea.

Apart from 16 Bf 109G-2s delivered in March 1943 (followed by another 13 that reached Bulgaria that summer), when it came to modern fighters the Bulgarian command could at first only set its hopes on French aircraft. Although Berlin had prohibited delivery of Bloch 152 fighters by the Vichy government, a new situation arose after the Axis troops took over unoccupied France on 11 November 1942. A total of 1,876 aircraft of the Vichy-French air force fell into German hands, this number including 246 Dewoitine D.520 fighters and 37 Bloch 210 bombers.[20] These were to be passed on to the Balkan countries, but, in the event, only 96 D.520s found their way to Bulgaria. The majority of these excellent French fighters ended up in German fighter-training schools, while others were taken over by the Regia Aeronautica.[21] As it happened, not a single D.520 reached Bulgaria before August 1943; the Bulgarian fighter pilots were then still converting to the type with JG 107 at Nancy (see Appendix 3).

On 1 August 1943 the Americans made their second raid on Ploesti – Operation *Tidal Wave* – with five bomber groups taking off from Benghazi. Two Bulgarian squadrons, the 612th and the 622nd, based at Vrashdebna and Bojourishte, were supposed to intercept the American formations passing overhead, but did not succeed in doing so. For one thing, the old Avia B-534 biplanes could not climb rapidly enough, and, as the American bombers were flying at an altitude over 4,500m (15,000ft) and the Bulgarian fighter pilots had no oxygen masks, the whole undertaking was doomed from the outset. It was a different matter on the return flight, when the American bombers became separated from the main formations. Several lone B-24 Liberators gave the Bulgarian fighters a chance to intercept. The Liberator aircrews were struck by a sense of unreality rather than fear when individual Avia biplanes bravely dived on them: 'I could not believe my eyes,' a B-24 gunner from the 98th Bomb Group later reported, 'What kind of a war was this? The First World War? It was as if I was in a time warp. Suddenly there were these small biplanes, looking just like the old Curtiss Hawks. I was surprised to see they were firing at me – and then they were gone again.'[22] The low speed of the Avias precluded their making a second attack, but the Americans did not get away unscathed. A flight of Bulgarian Bf 109E fighters had taken-off from Karlovo. These 'Emils', displaying the new Bulgarian national markings – a diagonal black cross on white background that had replaced the colourful leonine coat of arms in October 1940 – succeeded in shooting down at least three and possibly five Liberators.[23]

In August 1943 a period of misfortune began for Bulgaria. Tsar Boris III, who had been a unifying figure for all Bulgarians, died suddenly on 28 August, His son, Simeon II, was under age and therefore could not govern the country, a task that was instead assigned to three regents. The strengthening of the air force had no effect on the beginnings of the political erosion in which this resulted. The Vozdushni Voiski finally received their urgently needed and much-requested modern fighters when Reichsmarschall Göring pledged to let the Axis partner have 48 Bf 109G fighters as a gift, and, furthermore, in September, the first 48 Dewoitine D.520 fighters were taken over in a ceremony held at the Karlovo airfield. In addition to these fighters, 12 Ju 87R-2/R4 dive bombers arrived in Bulgaria that autumn. The Allied bombing campaign became more intensive, the intention of the Allies being to bomb Bulgaria out of the Axis alliance. On 21 October 40 Allied aircraft appeared over Skopje, one P-38 Lightning being lost to Bulgarian fighters. The capital Sofia was the target again on 14 November, when a large-scale air raid was carried out by 91 B-25 Mitchell bombers of the 12th USAAF, escorted by 40 P-38 Lightnings. The Vrashdebna airfield was also attacked. As the air raid alarm had not been given in good time, the Bulgarian fighters from II and III Groups of the 6th Fighter regiment took off too late to mount an effective defence. In the developing air combat they lost one plane and one pilot, and two other aircraft were damaged in forced landings. The next raid on the Bulgarian capital followed on 24 November. Of the 60 B-24 Liberator bombers of the 15th USAAF detailed for this operation, only 17 reached their target, and this time the Bulgarian defences were ready. A total of 40 fighters took off, 24 D.520s from Vrashdebna and 16 Bf 109G-2s from Bojourishte, and effectively intercepted the bombers and the escorting 35 P-38 Lightnings. One Bulgarian fighter was lost and three had to make forced landings. The American losses were uncertain, but the Bulgarian pilots claimed four victories.[24]

The third raid on Sofia took place on 10 December, when 31 B-24 Liberators with an escort of P-38 Lightnings appeared over the capital.[25] The Bulgarian air defences sent up 39 fighters: six Dewoitine D.520s of II/6th Fighter regiment from Vrashdebna, 17 Bf 109G-2s of III/6th Fighter regiment from Bojourishte and 16 D.520s of I/6th Fighter regiment from Karlovo.

Subsequently, the Americans claimed to have shot down 11 D.520s for the loss of only one P-38 Lightning. In reality the Bulgarians lost just one Dewoitine!

The last air raid of 1943 on the Bulgarian capital took place on 20 December, when reportedly 110 Allied aircraft were involved. The Bulgarian pilots attacked the enemy force with great determination. Among the defensive fighters was that flown by Sen Lt Dimitar Spissarevski of III/6th Fighter regiment, who had completed his fighter training course at Werneuchen in 1939. Earlier in 1943 he had been temporarily attached to a German unit on the British Channel to study Luftwaffe defensive tactics. Now, over the capital of his country, he was determined to destroy an enemy bomber. After Spissarevski had used up all his ammunition, he rammed a four-engined bomber. Both aircraft exploded in a ball of fire and spun to the ground. The Americans claim to have shot down no fewer than 28 aircraft during this raid, but Bulgarian losses comprised only two fighters destroyed and two damaged in crash-landings. The Bulgarians claimed 12 aerial victories for themselves.

The morale of the Bulgarian civilian population began to waver under the impetus of the American bombing raids. The German envoy in Sofia, Adolf Heinz Beckerle, reported the following to the Foreign Ministry in Berlin one day before Christmas Eve:[26]

The Foreign Minister Shishmanoff asked me to see him today and expressed the apprehension felt by the Bulgarian government regarding the expected future enemy bombing raids. On the basis of the last bombing raid they are now really worried because the Bulgarian towns, and particularly Sofia, lack cellars and other potential shelters, and are thus particularly exposed to the effects of bombing raids. The Bulgarian people do not have the same powers of resistance as the Germans, and Bulgarian mentality might bring out some unpleasant consequences. For these reasons, the Bulgarian governments pleads with the German Reich government to consider the possibility of sending 100 German fighters with their appropriate ground crews to Sofia. Apart from this request, it also asks for the immediate delivery of 50 Messerschmitt fighters, which would be crewed by

Bulgarian pilots. The Bulgarian government believes it has the right to voice these requests because, on various occasions, it has been indicated that our military help would be at its disposal when necessary. The only defence against the enemy air raids are German fighters, which fly boldly against the attackers, but are diminishing numerically after each operation.

He also asked me to understand his country and pointed out how important it is psychologically that the Bulgarian people do not feel exposed and defenceless to the enemy air raids, but have the German air force coming to their aid.

The German Supreme Command also viewed the situation in Bulgaria as quite serious. In the OKW Diary there appears the following reference:[27]

The air raids on Sofia, of which the last one took place on 10 December, initially caused panic, but the shock effect has been overcome in the meantime. A point to be considered, however, is that these raids have so far been aimed at railway stations and installations, and many bombs have fallen on open fields, no serious damage thus has been caused.

The German Command promised the Bulgarians one Luftwaffe fighter Gruppe, the retraining of an initial batch of 50 Bulgarian pilots, and additional material help. More units of the Vozdushni Voiski were to be re-equipped with the Bf 109G-6, the remaining Bf 109E-3s and G-2s being used for training purposes. In January and February 1944, the following re-inforcements reached the Bulgarian allies: 32 Ju 87D-3s and D-5s (to combat partisans), ten Fw 58s, nine Bü 181s, five Ar 96Bs, 25 Bf 109G-2s and 40 Bf 109G-6s.[28] Unfortunately the fighters arrived too late to prevent the 'Black Monday' of the Bulgarian capital. On that day, Monday 10 January, at least 180 American bombers with a strong fighter escort arrived over Sofia. The defences put up 70 Bulgarian and 30 German fighters. In the evening, another 80 Allied bombers dropped their loads on Sofia. A total of 4,100 buildings were destroyed, 750 people were killed and another 710 were wounded. German and Bulgarian fighter pilots from the 6th Fighter regiment shot down eight bombers and five P-38 Lightnings. The Allies claimed to have brought down at least 31 fighters! In fact, the total fighter losses of the Bulgarian air force throughout the entire war amounted to only 42 planes, 24 of these being shot down and 18 destroyed in forced landings.[29]

The two raids of 10 January were to have grave consequences. A total of 300,000 inhabitants left the capital, schools were closed and public institutions suspended work.[30] Even two weeks after these raids, life in Sofia had still to return to normal. On 23 January the German Embassy apprehensively telegraphed the Foreign Ministry in Berlin to the effect that the Bulgarian government seemed to have lost its head and was reacting weakly, and that it did not have an administration at its disposal because the largest part of the civil service had left the city. 'Salvage work and clearing up is progressing only slowly; electric power and water function only partly, telephones not at all. Almost all shops are still closed.'[31]

During February the suffering population of Sofia had time to get life moving again in their capital, but the respite did not last long. New Allied bombing raids were launched on 16, 17, and 29 March, but they were only a prelude to the heavy attack of 30 March by (according to Bulgarian data) no fewer than 450 B-17, B-24 and Handley Page Halifax bombers, and 150 P-38 Lightnings. The Bulgarian defences brought everything that could fly against this armada. The 6th Fighter regiment, commanded by Col Valkov, could muster 73 aircraft: I./6th at Karlovo put up 28 Dewoitine D.520s, II/6th at Vrashdebna launched six D.520s and 19 Bf 109G-6s, and III./6th from Bojourishte joined in with 20 Bf 109G-6s. Even the Avia 135 fighter trainers were thrown against the enemy and managed to shoot down a B-24 Liberator. While more than 2,000 fires broke out in Sofia, bitter fighting was taking place in the sky above. The Allies lost at least ten aircraft – eight bombers and two fighters – and the Bulgarians five fighters and three pilots. Two planes had to make forced landings, and there was a nasty incident when Lt Kassianov was deliberately fired on and badly wounded while hanging helpless beneath his parachute.

On 5 April there were more aerial combats when 20

Bf 109G-6s from III/6th Fighter regiment intercepted Allied aircraft returning from Ploesti and shot down one enemy fighter without losses. The last raid on Sofia on 17 April caused the heaviest losses to the Bulgarian air force since the beginning of the war. The 350 attacking B-17s and B-24s were protected by 100 fighters. The defending II./6th Fighter regiment put up 16 Bf 109G-6s and seven Dewoitine D.520s. Up to that time the Bulgarians had only encountered P-38 Lightning fighters, but this time P-51 Mustangs provided the escort and, at first, the Bulgarians mistook them for their own Bf 109s. Before they realized their mistake the Americans had shot down seven Bulgarian Bf 109G-6 fighters. The Vozdushni Voiski pilots were now fighting for their lives. In desperation 1st Lt Bontchev rammed a four-engined American bomber from the rear and ripped off an elevator. Lt N. Stojanov shot down a P-51 Mustang, the first of this type to fall to the Bulgarians. The III./6th Fighter regiment also joined the battle, but to no avail. A total of 12 Bulgarian fighters failed to return to their bases: nine had been shot down and six pilots had lost their lives; three other fighters had had to make forced landings.

Despite these losses, on 1 May 1944, the Vozdushni Voiski still had 500 aircraft and about 13,500 men, of which 250 machines and 5,400 men were in direct front-line service.[32] The backbone of the Bulgarian air force was formed by the 145 Bf 109G fighters that had come from Germany. These carried the main burden of air combat in May and June. At that time the Bulgarian fighters were attacking enemy aircraft that crossed Bulgaria on their way back from bombing Romania or had bombed various targets in Bulgaria itself. From 18 May to 26 August, the aircraft displaying the diagonal black crosses shot down 15 Allied bombers and four P-38 Lightnings, losing eight of their own (four shot down and four forced landings). Once again, there was an unpleasant incident on 11 June, when a Bulgarian pilot was deliberately killed by American fighters while hanging helpless beneath his parachute. The last aerial combat over a Bulgaria that was allied to Germany took place on 26 August 1944.

From 6 April 1941 to the end of August 1944 the Allies had

bombed 187 inhabited places in Bulgaria, destroying 12,000
buildings; 1,828 people had been killed and 2,370 wounded. The
Anglo-American air raids were carried out almost exclusively
against civilian targets and were intended to wear down the
population. These terrorizing bombardments did not achieve
their goal, even if the Bulgarian population reacted with less
equanimity than German civilians to the air raids, and early in
1944 there were signs of a serious crisis. The Bulgarian air
defences consisted almost exclusively of the 6th Fighter regiment, which shot down at least 53 enemy aircraft and damaged
another 71. These successes were achieved by 66 Bulgarian pilots
under conditions of numerical inferiority, sometimes at a ratio
of 20:1.

Aircraft Equipment of the Combat Detachments of the Bulgarian Air Force on 28 September 1944

Units	Squadrons	Model	Total	In Repair	Operational
Air Regiment	Staff Sqn	Fi 156 Storch	2	1	1
2nd Assault regiment					
I Group	3	Ju 87D Stuka	29	8	21
II Group	1	Avia B-534	4	3	1
5th Bomber regiment					
I Group	2	Do 17	11	4	7
II Group	2	Avia B-71	20	9	11
6th Fighter regiment					
I Group	3	Dewoitine D.520	17	5	12
II Group	3	Bf 109G-6	13	7	6
III Group	3	Bf 109G-6	23	12	11
Reconnaissance Regiment					
III Group	3	Fw 189A	14	2	12
IV Group	3	Letov Š-328	9		9
		KB 11	9		9
		Do 17	5	4	1
Transport Squadron	1	Ju 52/3m	4		4

Structure of the Bulgarian Air Force

Bulgarian	Strength (aircraft)	English
Dvoika	2	Pair
Krilo	4	Flight
Jato	12	Squadron
Orlyak	40	Group
Polk	120	Wing (Regiment)

At the end of August 1944 the Vozdushni Voiski still had 186 operational front-line aircraft, including 70 fighters. The air force was badly hit, but not yet eliminated when the Bulgarian government initiated a change of side and a Communist uprising swept away the Tsarist system. Subsequently the Communists systematically destroyed the national intelligentsia. After 9 September, 18,000 so-called 'Fascist functionaries' were eliminated, and a further 3,000 were to be liquidated during the following years.[33] The number of victims of this 'blood purge' could be as high as 50,000. The brutality went to extreme lengths, even by Bolshevik standards: parts of bodies of people tortured to death were fed to the pigs. Naturally the Bulgarian air force did not escape the horror. Among others, the Communists ordered the execution of the following air force officers: Col T. Rogev, Maj Khr. Iliev (commander of 2nd Assault Rgt), Capt M. Petrov (commander of IV./6th Fighter Regiment), Capt N. Videnov, Sen Lt V. Shishkov and Lt Zhelev. The commander of the 6th Fighter Regiment, Col Vassil Valkov, was also liquidated. He had led the unit from 6 March 1942. This highly experienced officer had been in charge of the DAR works from 1934 to 1937, and a year later had taken over the command of the 1st Army Air Group. Col Valkov was arrested in October 1944, and, following five months of torture, was sentenced to death on 13 March 1945 and executed on the same day.[34] The fate of the Supreme Commander of the Bulgarian Air Force, Maj Gen Dimitar Airanov, remains uncertain to this day. A so-called 'People's Court' sentenced him to life imprisonment but this sentence was later reduced to five years in prison. But Airanov never regained his freedom and disappeared without a trace. There is

169

no mystery regarding the fate of the former War Minister Mishoff; he was executed on 8 February 1945.

The Bulgarian army and air force, robbed of their traditional leading élite, now had to fight on the Soviet side against their former allies. The Bulgarian armed forces obeyed these orders, hoping that by doing so they would ensure that Macedonia and Thracia would remain part of Bulgaria, but these hopes were dashed. In the event, about 30,000 Bulgarian soldiers lost their lives fighting against Germany and its remaining allies.

Croatia

Zrakoplovstvo NDH

An independent Croat state had already been proclaimed at Agram (Zagreb) on 10 April 1941, before the German troops – who had begun their attack against Yugoslavia on 6 April – reached the town. Carried by the extremely nationalistic Ustashi movement, the Independent State of Croatia (Nezavisna Drzava Hrvatska, NDH) never managed to achieve real consolidation, however; rather, the anti-Serb crusade propagated by the Ustashis resulted in immense growth of the Serb partisan movement, and the four years that the NDH was in existence were to be marked by an irreconcilable civil war fought with exceptional cruelty by all participants. It is obvious that with such a background there could be no continuous and uniform development of the Croat armed forces.

The Croat air force (Zrakoplovstvo NDH) came into being as early as 19 April 1941, just nine days after the proclamation of the independent Croat state. Its commander was Colonel Vladimir Kren, a former captain of the Royal Yugoslav Air Force who had deserted to Graz on 4 April and declared himself an Ustashi supporter. The first task of the new air force, which consisted largely of former members of the Royal Yugoslav Air Force, was the acquisition or salvage of aircraft, weapons and equipment that had survived the fighting and had not been confiscated by the German or Italian forces. Apart from that, the personnel of the new air force took over and reactivated the airfields at Zagreb, Sarajevo, Mostar, Banja Luka and Zemun – where there was a branch of the Wiener-Neustadt aircraft factory. Zagreb was selected as the 1. Zrakoplovna Luka (air force base), which at that time consisted of the newly formed 1. Skupina (group) with the 1. Jato (squadron). Sarajevo became the 2. Zrakoplovna Luka with the 7th and 8th Squadrons.[1] In July the Germans opened the FFS A/B 123 (initial flying training school) at Zagreb for the training of Croat airmen. The emblem of this pilot training school consisted of a red fez and a red-white chequerboard derived from the Croat coat of arms, dating back to the 11th century. The 4th Group, with the 10th and 11th Fighter squadrons, and the 5th Group, with the 12th and 13th Bomber squadrons, were formed in July 1941.

After the German attack on the Soviet Union, the Croat Chief of State, Ante Pavelič, wrote to the German dictator on 1 July, offering volunteers for the army, Luftwaffe and navy to fight on the Eastern Front. Apart from ideological motives, Pavelič's offer was also an attempt to avoid Italian predominance by participating in the war on the German side.

To began with the 10th and 11th Fighter squadrons and the 12th and 13th Bomber squadrons formed the Croat Luftwaffen-Legion, with 300 Croat airmen going to Germany for training. The fighter pilots of the 10th (Hptm Vladimir Ferenčina) and 11th Fighter squadrons (Hptm Zladko Stipčič) were trained at Fürth, near Nuremberg, while members of the 12th (Hptm Ivan Pelzej) and 13th Bomber squadrons (Hptm Vladimir Graovac) went to Greifswalde. All these Croat airmen were formerly active or reserve members of the Royal Yugoslav Air Force, some of whom had already gained experience on the Bf 109E or Hawker Hurricane. This accelerated their training, and the Croats were deployed to the Eastern Front as soon as October 1941. The bomber crews were assigned to the 'Blitz' Geschwader, KG 3,[2] and operated the Do 17Z from Vitebsk, Vyazma and Rzhev. The two squadrons had only 15 aircraft between them and formed respectively 10. and 15./KG 3.[3] On 6 January 1942 the Croat bomber crews were mentioned in the German High Command (OKW) report: 'With regard to air warfare a Croat formation has distinguished itself by daringly carrying out low-level attacks.'[4] But these attacks were also very costly. By January 1942 the Croats had lost six aircraft and four crews, including the squadron commander, Hptm Graovac. After 370 sorties and 13 Soviet aircraft destroyed, the Croat airmen attached to KG 3 were withdrawn from the Front and transferred back to Croatia, where, a short while later, they had to carry out operations against the partisans.

In June 1942 another batch of Croat airmen was sent to the Eastern Front, this time subordinated to KG 53 'Legion

Condor'. Equipped with 13 Do 17Z bombers – which remained the property of the Luftwaffe – these airmen formed the 15th squadron of the German wing – 15./KG 53.[5] Already in November 1942, on the express wishes of the Ante Pavelič government, this Croat bomber squadron was withdrawn from the Front, and this time permanently. From then on, this unit flew operations against the armed insurgents in Croatia and Bosnia and carried out reconnaissance flights over the Adriatic.

The Croat fighter pilots[6] of the 10th Jato were also deployed to the Eastern front in October 1941, and attached to JG 52. In November the Croat fighters went into action from Taganrog at the Sea of Azov. The unit was equipped with the Bf 109E and F. The 11th Jato did not join JG 52 until the end of 1941. Due to lack of aircraft the squadron was disbanded in January 1942, and its personnel were transferred to strengthen the 10th Jato (15./JG 52). After a phase of relative inactivity during the winter of 1941/42, the Croat airmen became active in the spring, and, by April 1942, had achieved 30 aerial victories. By that time the formation had become known as the 'Džal fighter group' after its commander, Maj Franjo Džal; it was also known as the 'Ustasha Legion'. The legionnaires wore the Luftwaffe uniform, which differed from the regular German issue solely by having the legion badge on the right-hand side of the uniform tunic or on the right sleeve. The Croat Bf 109 fighters carried the normal Luftwaffe markings with an additional Croat Legion badge – the red/white chequerboard – and a large letter 'U', the sign of the Ustasha, on the fuselage below the cockpit. Another coat of arms used by the Croat airmen showed 'a white posterior with a horsefly on it.'[7]

In May 1942 15. (kroat.)/JG 52 was temporarily redeployed from Mariupol to near Sevastopol and began operations against this Soviet fortress, which was not captured by the German 11th Army until 1 July. The Croats were rather dissatisfied with their old Bf 109E fighters and pleaded with the RLM in Berlin via their Air Attaché, Oberst Marian Dolanski, for the supply of more modern planes. Their plea was not in vain, and, early in July, they received seven brand-new Bf 109G-2 fighters. By 21 June the Croats had already recorded 1,000 operational sorties, and five days later a German High Command report mentioned the 50th aerial victory of the Džal fighter group.[8] By mid-September the Croat squadron was fully equipped with the Bf 109G-2. At that time relations between the Germans and Croats on the Eastern front were still good, comradely and co-operative. The Germans considered the Croats to be brave and always ready for action. A German eyewitness recalls that on one occasion 'despite enemy low-level attacks the Croat mechanics were standing on the wings of their aircraft and cranking the engines so that their pilots could take-off to intercept the attackers.'[9]

At that point there had been only one Croat defector fighter pilot, Oblt Nikola Vučina, who had deserted to the Soviet forces with his Bf 109E, Wk. Nr. 1506, 'green 9', on 4 May 1942. In October the Džal group received some newly trained fighter pilots, and in November they returned to Croatia for leave. By then the Croat fighter pilots had gained 164 aerial victories.

At home the Croat legionnaires had to face the fact that there was an ongoing and brutal civil war, and that the Croat government could only stay in power with German assistance. It is possible that some Croat fighter pilots established contacts with the partisans already during their leave, because it seems that on their return to action at Kertch on 30 March 1943 some of the pilots of 15. (kroat.)/JG 52 already planned to desert to the enemy when an opportunity presented itself.

In April and May the Croats were operational over the Kuban bridgehead[10] and gained 12 victories during 71 operational sorties, losing four of their own aircraft in the process. The first to go missing was Lt Andjelko Antič, who disappeared with his Bf 109G-2 Wk. Nr. 14824 after an aerial combat as early as 31 March. In April 15. (kroat.)/JG 52 flew 105 operational sorties and gained 18 victories. Their own losses were heavy too: nine aircraft, of which three had to be written off and six were over 30 per cent damaged. But heavier than the material losses was the fact that two pilots – Oblt Albin Starc with his Bf 109G-2 Wk. Nr. 14545 'green 11' and Hptm Bogdan Vujičič with Bf 109G-2 Wk. Nr. 13485 – had deserted to the Soviets on the same day, 14 May. On 15 June these two were followed by Hptm Nikola Cvikič with his Bf 109G-2 Wk. Nr. 14205 'green

2'. Five days later the Germans forbade the Croat legionnaires to fly any operational sorties, and in July this now unreliable unit was withdrawn from front-line operations.

The commander of the Zrakoplovstvo NDH, Gen Kren, announced punishment measures and relieved Franjo Džal as commander of the Croat fighter squadron. This was a mistake, as Džal was known to be trustworthy and friendly towards the Germans. As a result of this error Gen Kren was himself relieved of his duties and replaced by Oberst Adalbert Rogulja, who immediately reinstated and promoted Džal. As both the German and Croat aviation commands had lost trust in the old personnel cadre of 15. (kroat.)/JG 52 it was replaced by new pilots, who had either been trained at the FFS A/B 123 at Zagreb or the Italian pilot training school at Mostar. In spring 1943 they were posted to JG 104 for further training, which they completed on 10 September. A month later these newly trained fighter pilots were on the Eastern Front. The Croat pilots, equipped with the Bf 109G-4 and G-6, flew their first operational sorties from Beregovo, near Kertch. They were led by Hptm Mato Dukovač, the most successful Croat fighter pilot (see Appendix 1). The Croat fighters participated continuously in the defensive fighting against the increasingly stronger Soviet air force. In February 1944 they were based at Karankut on the Crimea. At that time the strength of 15. (kroat.)/JG 52 had shrunk to just four Bf 109G fighters.[11] On 15 March, after months of heavy fighting, the unit was withdrawn to Croatia for rest and re-equipment. Since October 1943 this squadron had achieved 51 confirmed and ten unconfirmed aerial victories at the cost of five of their own pilots killed in action. As the Croat squadron was no longer at the front, six young Croat pilots, who in the meantime had completed their training with JG 104 and II/Erg. JG.1, were allocated directly to the German III./JG 52.

In mid-June 1944 15. (kroat.)/JG 52 returned to the Eastern Front but ended up in Romania, waiting in vain for the promised Bf 109G-10 and G-14 fighters. Flying then over Slovakia and Poland this unit – now designated by the Luftwaffe as the 1. kroatische Jagdstaffel (1st Croat fighter squadron) – reached the Eichwalde airfield in East Prussia, together with the Croat assault/close support squadron. The Croat fighter squadron then received the anticipated Bf 109G-10 and G-14 fighters, and now became part of the 1. Fliegerdivision of Luftflotte 6. Already on 20 September, however, another two Croat fighter pilots had deserted to the Soviets, including Mato Dukovač, their foremost fighter ace! As a result the Germans forbade their Croat allies to fly anywhere in the eastern provinces of the Reich, and thus ended the operational service of the Croat fighter pilots on the Eastern Front. Less than three years before this inglorious turn of events it had been a different story: in 1941 alone, the Croat fighter pilots had achieved at least 259 aerial victories.[12] The Croat Luftwaffen-Legion was officially disbanded with the secret OKL (High Command of the Luftwaffe) Gen Staff Supply and Administration Branch order No 725/45 of 9 February 1945.

The airmen of the independent Croat state were fighting not only on the Eastern Front but also with almost 70 different aircraft types over their own country. In June 1941 the Germans had began to pass on to the Croats various captured Yugoslav aircraft[13], including five Bristol Blenheim I and five Potez 25 bombers. Most of the machines first had to be overhauled at the Wiener Neustadt aircraft works at Zemun, and it was not until 1943 that all these aircraft were delivered to the Croat forces.

In late 1941 the Zrakoplovstvo NDH had had 95 planes distributed in four groups and 12 squadrons, of which four were part of the Legion. About 50 per cent of the aircraft were serviceable. Fighting the partisans from the air had begun already in June 1941, when the Breguet 19 and Potez 25 light bombers[14] had proved to be most suitable. The first could carry a bomb load of up to 400kg (880lb), the second about half that amount. Altogether the Croat air force possessed 55 Breguet 19s and 45 Potez 25s.[15] These aircraft carried the red and white chequerboard insignia on the fin; in February 1945 this was replaced by the black and white trefoil cross of King Zvonomir.[16] The operational use of these light bombers was not limited to fighting the partisans; the aircraft were also used to supply strong points surrounded by the partisans.

In 1942 the Zrakoplovstvo NDH was able to increase its

fighting value by the addition two new aircraft models. The Italians delivered ten Caproni Ca 311M bombers, which had been ordered and paid for by the former Royal Yugoslav government, as well as ten F.L.3 trainers and ten Fiat G.50 fighters,[17] including one two-seat trainer variant. The fighters were allocated to the 16th Jato at Banja Luka. From Germany the Croats received six Do 17Es and 11 Do 17Ks. The latter were Dorniers built under licence in Yugoslavia and powered by Gnôme-Rhône radial engines. Armament comprised 1 x 20mm cannon and three machine guns.[18] Nine different Avia-Fokker types were acquired in addition from the German Protectorate of Bohemia and Moravia. Adding the aircraft delivered from the Zemun factory, the numerical increase of the Croat air force in 1943 amounted to 98 aircraft.

Thanks to this extended aircraft park the Croat air force could now form new units: in January the 1st and 2nd Squadrons were formed at Zagreb, and then the 2nd Group with the 4th, 5th and 6th Jato at Rajlovac.

At the end of 1942, the Zrakoplovstvo NDH had the following structure:

Unit	Station
1st Air Support Base	Zagreb
1st Group	
1st squadron	
2nd squadron	
3rd squadron	1 June–11 Nov 1942 in Banja Luka
19th squadron	from 1 June 1942
2nd Air Support Base	Rajlovac
2nd Group	
4th squadron	
5th squadron	
6th squadron	
3rd Group	
7th squadron	
8th squadron	
9th squadron	

Unit	Station
5th Air Support Base	Banja Luka
6th Group	
13th squadron	from 1 May 1942
16th squadron	from 1 June-31 Dec 1942 in Rajlovac
17th squadron	up to 1 Oct 1942 in Rajlovac
18th squadron	up to 1 June 1942 in Rajlovac

On 15 January 1943 the Axis troops began an offensive against the Tito brigades in south-eastern Bosnia. However, the bad weather of January and February hindered all aerial activities, and it was only in March that the Croat air force could record 250 anti-partisan sorties. A new 'cleansing action' against the 'proletarian brigades' in central Bosnia, Montenegro and the Herzegovina was started by the German, Italian and Croat formations as well as Serb Chetniks on 20 April 1943. This operation, too, was supported by the Croat air force, which flew 350 sorties. Another 325 sorties were flown in May, but only 130 of these had a direct combat purpose, the remainder serving reconnaissance and supply tasks, as well as leaflet dropping.

On 23 May the pilots of a Breguet 19 and a Potez 25 deserted to the partisans, and, in June and October, two crews with their Bristol Blenheim I bombers landed in neutral Turkey. The fighting morale of the Croat airmen was broken – many pilots did not want to participate in the murderous civil war and deliberately dropped their bombs away from the given targets. Something had to be done, and in June 1942 the Croat Ministry of Defence issued an order stipulating controls to verify that the crews had actually carried out their ordered operational tasks. On 2 July Croat aircraft for the first time dropped chemical warfare agents – bombs filled with teargas – over the village of Cuklici. In 1942 the Axis powers still had aerial supremacy over the territory of former Yugoslavia, but with all that the Zrakoplovstvo NDH lost 35 aircraft that year, 19 of which were destroyed by ground fire, four deserted and 12 were victims of accidents. From January to December 1942 Croat planes had carried out 4,800 flights, of which only about 30 per cent were actual combat sorties. By the end of the year the Croat aircraft park consisted of 160 aircraft, formed into 14 squadrons.

On 20 January 1943 the Axis troops tried once more to smash the Communist resistance movement. Known as *Unternehmen Weiss* (Operation *White*), this new attempt involved strong air support – three 'German' (including 15./KG 53, the Croat bomber squadron that had been withdrawn from the Eastern Front), seven Italian and four Croat squadrons with 150 aircraft altogether. Up to the end of the action, on 18 February, during which strong partisan forces once again managed to avoid being surrounded and escaped, the Croats (with the exception of 15./KG 53) flew only 97 sorties. The sequel to this operation, *Weiss II*, had begun already on 26 February, supported as before by German, Italian and Croat air formations. In this case, too, the Croat air force played a minor role, flying just over 100 sorties. In March 1943 the Zrakoplovstvo NDH received another batch of aircraft, consisting of 30 Do 17Es, which were allocated to 3rd Jato, 13th Jato and the newly formed 15th Jato at Banja Luka.[19]

The next major operation against some 20,000 Communist partisans, '*Unternehmen Schwarz*' (Operation *Black*) began at Sandschak on 15 May. As before, German, Italian and Croat squadrons, deployed to five airfields, were operational in support of the ground troops.[20] They bombed the positions occupied by Tito partisans and attacked them with machine gun fire. Despite this Tito managed to escape this 'cauldron' with some 3,000 men.

From mid-1943 onwards Allied aircraft began to appear over the Balkans in increasing frequency. The Croat air force command recognized the threatening danger and asked the Germans to let them have at least two squadrons equipped with the Bf 109. But the fighters that reached the Zrakoplovstvo NDH were of French origin and veterans of the Vichy-French air force: 36 Morane-Saulnier MS.406s in July, and another ten in December, which were allocated to the newly formed 11th Group, which comprised the 21st, 22nd and 23rd Jato. With the MS.406 the Croats could not effectively oppose either the threat from the air or the ground. On the night of 11 August Communist partisans made a surprise raid on the Rajlovak airfield and destroyed 17 Croat machines on the ground. Another 17 were damaged. After the Italian change of sides early in September 1943 and the disintegration of the Italian armed forces in the Balkans, the Croats succeeded in replacing some of their losses with captured Italian aircraft.

On 1 September 1943 the Croat air force had 228 machines at its disposal, of which 177 were operational. A month later the Zrakoplovstvo NDH was reorganized and four squadrons were disbanded. In the same month a secret agreement was reportedly reached between Croat and American diplomats according to which the Croats would forgo attacking Allied aircraft over their territory and the Allies, for their part, would not drop any bombs any Croatia.[21] However, it is more than doubtful that the Americans would have agreed to such a pact with the compromised Pavelič regime because they had no reason to fear the small Croat air force. In fact, they regularly fired on Croat aircraft, which makes the existence of any such pact even less plausible. In the whole of 1943 the Croats lost 61 aircraft, five of them through desertion.

By the end of 1943 parts of the Croat armed forces showed clear symptoms of disintegration. The German plenipotentiary general in Croatia made the following comments about the Croat armed forces at the time in his report of 31 December 1943:[22]

> On the other hand, the picture always painted by the German commanders during collaboration with the national Croat troops is anything but satisfactory. Lack of military discipline and fighting spirit, desertions, even by entire detachments led by officers who have broken their oath of allegiance, treason and collusion with the enemy are being reported time and time again, and overshadow the soldiery achievements that are still being accomplished ...
>
> The problem of the Croat air force is hardly less confused than that of the ground forces. In this case a legionary model, in which the Croat commanding officers could be given appropriate positions, is even more to be recommended than a purely

180

nationalistic organization. In their homeland this arm has had to overcome some personnel crisis, which have had not inconsiderable consequences for the officer class, which is largely of the Yugoslav school.

As the German command was of the opinion that mixed German-Croat formations under German command had a higher combat value, the Croat Luftwaffen-Legion was strengthened. Already in December 1943, the two Croat bomber squadrons of the Luftwaffe, 15. (kroat.)/KG 3 and 15. (kroat.)/KG 53, formed the 1st and 2nd Croat Bomber squadrons, which, in February 1944, were to provide the nucleus of the 1st Croat Bomber Group.[23] In January 1944 both squadrons received three Fiat BR.20 and three Cant Z.1007 bombers for training purposes, and, between March and April, additional Do 17s and three Ju 87B-2s, which were used to attack the partisans from the air.

By early summer the two squadrons had only five operational aircraft between them! In July the previously mentioned close support squadron equipped with Ju 87Ds was formed, within the framework of the Croat Luftwaffen-Legion. Together with the 1st Croat Fighter squadron, it operated for a short while from Eichwalde in East Prussia, but had to give up its aircraft on 1 November 1944.[24] On the other hand, a Croat short-range squadron that had been formed in 1943, equipped with the Hs 126, was to remain operational in the Balkans until the end of the war.[25]

By early 1944 the Allied Balkan Air Force was carrying out accurate strikes on railway and road traffic, bombing the ports and Axis airfields as well as supplying the partisans. An example of this took place on 12 April 1944, when American bombers raided the Zagreb airfields and destroyed 12 Croat aircraft on the ground. The Croat fighter arm was now in urgent need of reinforcements to defend Croat air space.

The Croat Luftwaffen-Legion then received a number of Italian fighters, Macchi MC.202s and 205s, which were allocated to the 2nd and 3rd Fighter squadrons of the Legion[26] but did not become operational until the summer of 1944. Modern

Bf 109G-10 and G-14 fighters reached Croatia only in January 1945, although even then five of the 15 planes supplied were lost during delivery.[27] In the meantime the general military situation had taken a dramatic turn for the worse, and a mere handful of Messerschmitt fighters no longer made much difference. Already in September the partisans had overrun the Croat strong point of Banja Luka with the Zaluzani airfield, capturing 11 aircraft, and, by the end of 1944 Tito controlled the largest part of Yugoslavia. Whatever led the Luftwaffe command, under these circumstances, to send completely unsuitable aircraft, namely eight Fieseler Fi 167 biplanes – once intended as shipboard torpedo-bombers for the aircraft carrier *Graf Zeppelin* (that was never completed) – to the Balkans, will probably remain undiscovered.

During the second half of 1944 those pilots of the Zrakoplovstvo NDH who knew that the best they could expect if they were captured by partisans would be a bullet in the back of the head, began to desert in increasing numbers. Either they went over to fight for the victorious side or tried to escape to the south or central Italy. From July 1944 to April 1945 the Allies recorded the arrivals of Croat aircraft as listed opposite.[28]

During the last month of the war, 30 Croat aircrews with their planes deserted from the airfields around Zagreb alone and surrendered to the partisans. If, by so doing, they managed to escape with their lives is uncertain. Certainly, the mass executions that followed Tito's victory surpassed all other revenge measures of the victors in Europe, not only quantitatively but also in brutality.[29] Even today there is no accurate general view of what really happened to the Croat airmen in the hands of Tito's 'People's Liberation Army', but judging by some of the individual fates known one has to assume the worst.

Among the executed fighter pilots were Oblt Ivan Jergovic, with 16 aerial victories to his credit; Lt Zivko Džal (12 victories) and Hptm Zlatko Stipčič, the former commander of the 11th Fighter squadron (also 12 victories), who were shot in the Zagreb prison camp. Oberst Franjo Džal (13 victories) was sentenced to death during a 'show trial' and executed immedi-

List of Croat aircraft that landed in Allied-occupied southern and central Italy between July 1944 and April 1945

Date	Place	Aircraft	Unit	Crew
13 July 1944	Alberobello	Do 17Z '0309'	1./kroat.KG1	Lt Dragou Ratkovicic and 5 men
30 July 1944	Southern Italy	Do 17Z-5 Z8 + AH Wk. Nr. 2899	1. kroat. Lw-Legion	Lt Albeiu Vonk and 4 men
10 Aug 1944	Nr Foggia	Do 17Z '0170'	3./kroat.KG1	Ofw Sulijman Kulenovic Ofw Zvonko Schweiger
3 Sep 1944	Amendola	Bü 181 '7415'	?	Off. candidates Ivan Mihalovic Nonrad Kovacevic
16 Apr 1945	Falconara	Bf 109G-10 ' black 4'	2nd Fighter Sqn	Fw Vladimir Sandtner
16 Apr 1945	Jesi	Bf 109G-14 'black 10'	2nd Fighter Sqn	Fw Josip Cekovic
21 Apr 1945	Falconara	Biplane ?		2 men

ately afterwards. Then there was Fw Kelez, who lost his life in Sarajevo, and Hptm Acinger (9 victories) who was shot while attempting to escape from the camp.[30] These executions, which were carried out without any regard for personal guilt or innocence, were intended not only to destroy the ideological enemies or opposition physically, they also served to extinguish any ideas of independence in Croatia. That this did not succeed has been proven by recent history.

SLOVAKIA

Slovenské Vzdušné Zbraně

On 14 March 1939 Slovakia proclaimed its independence. The Protection agreement signed five days later by the Slovak president Tiso with the German Reich made it quite clear that the fate of this young country of 2.7 million inhabitants was tied closely to Berlin. But this agreement did not prevent Hungarian troops pushing into Slovak territory on 23 March and carrying out 'border corrections' in their favour. The young Slovak air force (Slovenské Vzdušné Zbraně or SVZ), then just being formed under the command of Lt Col Ján Ambruš, was in no position to counter the Hungarian aggression. The SVZ had come into being from the 3rd Regiment of the Czechoslovak air force. Czechoslovakia no longer existed: Slovakia had separated itself and the Czech territory had been illegally taken over by the German government as the Reich Protectorate of Bohemia and Moravia.

The young Slovak air force mustered 300 aircraft, of which some were already hopelessly outdated. A bomber element, with only three modern aircraft, was still in the very early stages of formation. The bulk of the aircraft park was made up of 60 Avia B-534 and 11 Avia Bk-534 fighters, 73 Letov Š-328 and 14 Aero A-100 reconnaissance aircraft, and 41 Praga E-39 and 33 Praga E-241 trainers.[1] The Czech-built Avia B-534 fighter provided the backbone of the fledgling Slovak air force. This aircraft was also used in large numbers by the Luftwaffe as a fighter-trainer, and by Bulgaria.[2] First flown on 25 May 1933, the Avia B-534 was a robust biplane with a fixed armament of four 7.92mm machine guns, a range of 600km (373 miles) and a maximum speed of 380km/h (236mph) – good for its day, but distinctly inferior to most potential enemies in 1939.

Their unexpectedly early baptism of fire was scarcely auspicious for the SVZ.[3] Already, on 23 March 1939, Hungarian AA guns had shot down two B-534s and damaged another five, Oblt Ján Svetlik and Corp Stefan Devan becoming the first Slovak airmen to lose their lives in action. The following day was even worse. The 3rd Air Regiment had been weakened by the withdrawal of Czech pilots and had considerable personnel problems at the time of the clash with the Hungarians. There was bitter aerial combat, with the Hungarian Fiat CR.32 fighters and Ju 86K-2 bombers from Debrecen raiding the Slovak airfields at Spisska Nová Ves and damaging seven SVZ aircraft on the ground. But the losses in the air were more serious: Hungarian fighters and AA guns shot down two Slovak aircraft, six were so badly damaged that they had to make forced landings, and one B-534 fell into Hungarian hands.

That short Slovak–Hungarian conflict was over by 31 March, and the SVZ had a limited breathing space for reorganization. Already at that time it was clear that the Slovak armed forces did not unconditionally support the authoritarian Tiso regime. In June 1939 no fewer than five SVZ pilots deserted to Poland and Yugoslavia. Within the officer corps of the Slovak armed forces were numerous antifascists,[4] and moreover many Slovaks felt bound to the idea of a parliamentarian Czechoslovakian state. These were the factors that favoured the renunciation of the authoritarian Tiso government, and without which the Slovak national uprising in the summer of 1944 would have been unthinkable. On 5 August 1939 even the first commander of the SVZ left his homeland and joined the western powers. After arriving in Britain, Ján Ambrus was eventually to lead the 312 (Czech) Squadron of the RAF. In fact about 400 Slovaks served in the RAF during the war, of whom some 10 per cent lost their lives. Most of them belonged to Nos. 310, 312 and 313 (Czech) fighter squadrons, but there were also Slovaks with the Czech 311 Bomber squadron of the RAF.[5]

Slovakia was Hitler's only ally to join the attack on Poland in September 1939. Tiso sent 35,000 troops, although the Slovak contribution in the air was rather modest: 20 Avia B-534s from 39th and 48th (later 13th) Fighter squadrons and ten Letov Š-328s from 16th Observation squadron. The provision of these 30 aircraft had more of a symbolic character than anything else. Nevertheless, the Avias flew escort for the Luftwaffe Stukas and the Letovs carried out bombing raids and supported the Slovak infantry. Two Avia B-534s were lost, but on 26 September the SVZ could also celebrate its first aerial victory when Viliam Grúň shot down a Polish RWD-8 liaison aircraft.

After the end of the Polish campaign the Slovenské Vzdušné Zbraně began a phase of restructuring. This reorganization led to the formation of three fighter and three observation squadrons:[6]

Unit	Base	Aircraft
11th Fighter sqn	Piešťany	Avia B-534
12th Fighter sqn	Piešťany	Avia Bk-534
13th Fighter sqn	Spišská Nová Ves	
1st Observation sqn	Zilina	
2nd Observation sqn	Spišská Nová Ves	Letov Š-328
3rd Observation sqn	Nitra	

A flying training school was founded at Trencianské Biskupice, which at the outset had only Czech-built aircraft, such as the Praga E-39, Praga E-241, Avia B-534, Letov Š-328 and Ba/Bs-122. Later these were supplemented by German aircraft. In 1943 the flying training school was transferred to Tri Duby.

On 1 May 1944 the 11th, 12th and 13th Fighter squadrons were reorganized as the 2nd Fighter Group and the three observation squadrons as the 1st Observation Group. Seven weeks later Hitler launched his offensive against the Soviet Union. The Slovak state president Tiso let his troops march together with the Germans, although the German dictator had reservations regarding Slovak participation because he feared a 'Slav–Slovak fraternization' between his ally and the Russians.[7] Tiso's decision to join the German attack was based partly on his implacable anti-Communism and partly on his hopes that offering his armed forces would oblige the Germans to reject Hungarian demands for Slovak territory.

Slovakia sent a Fast Brigade and an Army Group consisting of two divisions to the southern flank of the Eastern Front, where the Slovak air force units also went into action. The 2nd Fighter Group, with the 12th and 13th Letky and 22 Avia

B-534s, was transferred to the western Ukraine, as was the 1st Observation Group with its three squadrons and 30 Letov Š-328s. Added to these was a Liaison squadron with nine aircraft. So that Slovakia was not left completely without protection, the 11th Fighter squadron, which was officially also intended for operations on the Eastern Front, was left at Piešťany.

At the front the Letovs carried out reconnaissance flights and also attacked the retreating Soviet troops, while the Avias often escorted the German Henschel Hs 126 short-range reconnaissance aircraft and attacked ground targets as well. On 29 June the 12th Fighter squadron shot down its first aircraft displaying a red star. During this early phase of the Eastern campaign the Slovak airmen fought with great commitment. On several occasions pilots forced to make emergency landings behind the Soviet lines were rescued by their comrades, who landed close to them with their Avia B-534s and lifted them out. As there was no room for them in the cockpit the rescued pilots had to hold on to the wing struts all the way back to their own airfield.

The susceptibility of the Slovak aircraft to ground fire, lack of spare parts and shortage of aviation fuel – the Avia B-534 used a special fuel mixture – all had an effect on the combat strength of the SVZ, which dropped quite quickly. For that reason the 2nd Observation squadron, after passing on the remainder of its aircraft to the 1st and 3rd squadrons, had to be withdrawn back to Spisška Nová Ves as early as 25 July. On 15 August, the 13th Fighter squadron was also recalled to Slovakia, followed two days later by the 3rd Observation squadron. This meant that only two Slovak squadrons were left to cover and support the Fast Brigade, made up to a weak division in the meantime, on its advance to Kiev. In September there was a marked increase in aerial activity and aerial encounters. Between 7 and 10 September, the 12th Letky shot down five Soviet aircraft without loss. These victories included three Polikarpov I-16 monoplanes, which, while of about the same vintage as the Avia B-534, were far more advanced, featuring a retractable undercarriage, and considerably faster.[8]

The first phase of the Slovak aerial operations on the Eastern front came to an end in October 1941. The 1st Observation squadron, which had only three Letov Š-328s remaining, and the 12th Fighter squadron, reduced to just four Avia B-534 biplanes, returned to Slovakia. Altogether, the Slovak airmen had flown 3,275 sorties, of which 1,119 were by fighters which had held their own in 58 aerial encounters.[9] As the obsolete Avia B-534s were no match for the more modern Soviet fighters, the German command decided to re-equip at least one Slovak squadron with more up-to-date aircraft. In February 1942 18 Slovak pilots and 98 mechanics were transferred to Karup-Grove airfield in Denmark for retraining on the Bf 109E. This Slovak group was led by Hptm Ondrej Ďumbala, one of the most successful fighter pilots of the young state, who was to shoot down 14 enemy aircraft by 1944. The Slovaks were assigned to 5./Jagdgruppe Drontheim (later 3./Jagdfliegerschule 3) and made familiar with the Ar 96 and Bf 109D and E. After successful conclusion of their training, the Slovaks returned home, where most of the pilots were assigned to the 13th Fighter squadron, which began to receive Bf 109E fighters from October onwards. However, the 27 aircraft delivered from Germany by the end of the year did not create much joy among the Slovak pilots: all were used machines, including some veterans of the Battle of Britain period and others that had been repaired after accidents. The Slovak government made some effort to modernize its air force, and, between 1942 and 1944 acquired a total of 185 foreign aircraft. These included 43 Bf 109s, two He 111H-10s, two Ju 52/3ms, six Savoia-Marchetti SM.84s and 84bis, as well as ten Caudron C.445 Goélands (Gu11), the last-mentioned being French twin-engined liaison and training aircraft captured by the Wehrmacht.[10]

Even before the Slovak fighter pilots had completed their conversion training in Denmark some SVZ units were once again deployed on the Eastern Front. On 13 June 1942 the 11th Fighter squadron, with 12 Avia B-534s, and the 1st Observation squadron, with just six Letov Š-328s, were sent to Zhitomir. This time, there were no front-line duties, both squadrons being intended as air support for a Slovak security division operating against Soviet partisans. (After a reorganization and the discharge of a large number of reservists, this security division and the Fast Brigade were to be the only Slovak units on the Eastern Front.) These operations wore down the morale of the Slovak airmen, 'particularly since the propagandistic influence of the "great Soviet brother nation" had an increasingly stronger effect'.[11] First the pilot of an Š-328 and then that of a B-534 deserted to the enemy, together with their aircraft. The Germans viewed their Slovak allies with strong suspicion and began calling them by the nickname 'Partisans No. 2'. Nevertheless, after transfer to the Obrukh and Minsk airfields the 11th Fighter squadron, with its obsolete aircraft, remained in Russia until August 1943. During the 14 months of the much disliked anti-partisan operations, the Slovaks lost two B-534s to groundfire.

The 1st Observation squadron had been withdrawn to Slovakia already in October 1942. In the same month, on the 27th, the 13th Fighter squadron, commanded by Maj Ondrej Ďumbala, was deployed to the southern sector of the Eastern Front. An initial seven Bf 109E fighters were augmented by another five in November. Back home in Slovakia, propaganda celebrated the fighter pilots as the 'Tatra eagles'. Their operational bases changed quite frequently. In January 1943 they flew from Maikop, then from Krasnodar and Kertch; in March it was Taman, and, from April onwards, Anapa, the Soviet Black Sea spa town. Afterwards, it was once again to be Taman and Kertch, and then finally Bagerovo. The first Slovak aerial victories with the Bf 109 were achieved on 28 November, when two pilots from 13th Fighter squadron defeated three Polikarpov I-153 biplanes. Beginning early in 1943 the 'Emil' version flown by the Slovaks was gradually replaced by more modern subtypes: the Bf 109F-2 and F-4 followed by the G-2 and G-4, and, from March onwards, the Bf 109G-6 as a 'loan gift' from Germany. At that time, the Slovak fighter unit functioned as the 13th Staffel of JG 52, commanded by Obstl Dieter Hrabak. The aircraft of the 13. (slow.)/JG 52 wore German national markings, although their propeller spinners had spirals painted in Slovak national colours of white/red/blue. Oddly enough, none of the Slovak fighters carried individual aerial victory markings.

Tiso's fighter pilots participated in the costly aerial combat over the Crimea, the Black Sea and the Kuban. They achieved relatively high aerial victory scores, which, however, they were to try to minimize after the war. In March 1943, for example, the Slovak fighters shot down 33 Soviet aircraft during 111 sorties. In April, in 84 sorties over and around Kuban, the Slovaks achieved 43 aerial victories, and, in May, during 90 sorties, they shot down 27 Soviet aircraft. It is also noteworthy that no Slovak aircraft were lost or damaged during the last-mentioned month, while JG 52 had to write off 61 Bf 109s, of which 27 were total losses.[12]

On the other hand, in the late summer of 1943, the 13. (slow.)/JG 52 lost several aircraft as a result of desertion by their pilots. These deserters came from the second group of pilots of the 13th Letky, whose training at Pieštany had progressed in somewhat desultory fashion. This second group of fighter pilots arrived at Anapa on 5 July, and it was soon evident that their morale was very low and that, whenever possible, they would try to avoid involvement in aerial combat! In September 1943, two months after the personnel of the squadron had been changed and the unit commander had become Hptm Jozef Páleniček, three pilots with their Bf 109G-4s defected to the Soviets simultaneously. One of the deserters, Alexander Gerič, was dropped by parachute over Slovakia to carry out a spying mission in 1944. He died on 26 August of that year while trying to escape with a Praga E-39 trainer from Pieštany. Another defector was Anton Matušek, who later joined the pro-Allied Czech fighter squadron that was formed on 3 May 1944 at Ivanovo, near Moscow.

What with the Stalingrad catastrophe, the defeat of the Axis forces in North Africa, the failure of the Operation *Citadelle* in the Kursk area and the defection of Italy to the Allied camp early in September 1943, Slovak fighting morale understandably declined. Accordingly, the commander of 13. (slow.)/JG 52 requested that his unit to be withdrawn from front-line duties. His request was granted, and, at the end of October 1943, the 'Tatra eagles' left Russia and settled in at their new airfield at Vajnory in Slovakia. They were allowed to take with them the old Bf 109E machines, of which five had survived, but the 'Gustavs' remained behind for use by the German parent unit.

Despite the dubious operational willingness of the second Slovak fighter group, the unit had not fought without success at the Eastern Front. In 2,000 operational sorties, 13. (slow.)/JG 52 had in fact shot down 215 enemy aircraft, of which 155 had been accounted for by the first Slovak contingent.[13] Even if these figures had been inflated for propaganda purposes, as the Slovak pilots were to insist post-war, they remain indicative of a high level of flying skill under harsh conditions of combat.

In the meantime, there had been more structural changes within the SVZ in Slovakia. The 41st Bomber and 51st Transport squadrons had been formed, the latter with five Cauldron C.445Ms, among other aircraft. There were also changes in the fighter component. On 1 June 1943 the SVZ command created the 3rd Fighter group, which was to consist of the 13th and 14th Fighter squadrons (that in the event were never formed). The pilots of the other two fighter squadrons, 11. and 12. Letky, now had to undergo conversion training to the Ju 87D-5, a decidedly questionable venture, as the future was to show that Slovakia needed modern fighters and not vulnerable dive bombers. There was an element of modernization, but this was confined to the reconnaissance component: the 1st squadron received some Fw 189A-2 machines.

The government in Bratislava was quite aware that the existing air force strength was insufficient to effectively protect the country. To improve the situation an expansion of the Slovenské Vzdušné Zbraně to three wings with 16 squadrons was planned for the summer of 1944. This ambitious project was to be thwarted by the political and military events of the summer months. But before the national uprising came the end of the 13th Fighter squadron, undoubtedly the best unit of the Slovak air force.

The 13th Fighter squadron, commanded by Oblt Vladimir Krisko, was transferred to Pieštany in February 1944. The Germans then provided the squadron with 14 Bf 109G-6 fighters and subordinated it tactically to the 8th Fliegerdivision in Vienna. The squadron was given the task of defending the capital, Bratislava, oil refineries and industrial plants against Allied bombing raids. However, the Slovaks were to avoid combat with enemy aircraft, an indication that the Slovak government, looking for a way out of the war, was anxious to preserve the unit. Naturally this directive did not escape the notice of the German Luftwaffe mission in Slovakia, which, understandably, criticized the lack of Slovak activity. Nonetheless, when, on 26 June 1944, strong American formations, coming from Italy on the way to Vienna, crossed Slovak airspace, they were intercepted and attacked by eight Slovak Bf 109G-6 fighters, led by the Eastern Front veteran Oblt Juray Puskar. These few fighters had no chance against the defensive fire from four-engined bombers of the 459th Bomb Group and its escorting P-51 Mustangs and P-38 Lightnings of the 52nd and 82nd Fighter Groups. To be sure, the Slovak pilots did shoot down a B-24 Liberator and damaged another three, but at a high price: five of the Bf 109G-6 fighters were lost, and two others were badly damaged. Three Slovak pilots lost their lives, one, Stefan Jambor, reportedly being shot while hanging from his parachute.[14] This engagement sounded the death knell of the 13th Letky.

The SVZ was to outlive the destruction of its best squadron by a mere two months. To support the East Slovak Army Corps in its defence of the Carpathian passes, the Slovak command managed to gather 40 aircraft. Commanded by Maj Julius Trnka, the 1st Reconnaissance squadron, 2nd Observation squadron and the 12th Fighter squadron – the last-mentioned possessing the last four Bf 109G-6 fighters – were supposed to hold up the Red Army. But the situation changed dramatically on 29 August. The army's national uprising – furthered by Czechoslovak orientated forces and supported by the Communists – spread to the air force. Almost the entire SVZ changed sides and joined the Red Army. On 31 August alone 28 Slovak pilots tried to reach Soviet-controlled territory. Only a tiny minority remained loyal to Tiso, for example the Slovak AA artillery at the Danube bridge in Bratislava. Initially disarmed by the Germans, the gunners were allowed to continue to serve their guns with the permission of the commander of the German troops in Slovakia, Waffen-SS Obergruppenführer (General) Berger.[15] In comparison, 60 former SVZ aircraft joined the fight against the German forces. After this Communist-supported uprising was overthrown, late in October 1944, both Berlin and Bratislava decided against the formation of another Slovak air force.

A notable non-participant in the Slovak uprising was the fighter pilot Ján Režnák. Born in 1919, this Slovak sergeant achieved 32 aerial victories between 17 January and 30 June 1943, including 15 LaGG-3, seven I-16 and three MiG-3 fighters. He was awarded many decorations, including the German Iron Cross 2nd and 1st Class, the German Cross in Gold and the Combat Aviation Clasp in Gold. In post-war Communist Czechoslovakia he must have presented something of a problem to the government. He was accepted as a flying instructor in the ČSSR air force, but dismissed in 1948. Three years later, the State Police confiscated his pilot's licence but Režnák managed to survive. This kind of repression was comparatively mild compared to the excesses that took place in Bulgaria and Croatia.

Losses of the 13. (slowak.)/JG 52

Date	Pilot	Aircraft	Wk. Nr.	Damage
14.3.1943	Uffz Kovarik	Bf 109G-2	10473	Enemy fighter, 70 per cent
21.3.1943	Uffz Stauder	Bf 109G-2	14814	Crash landing, 100 per cent
25.3.1943	Uffz Režnák	Bf 109G-2	13743	Landing after engine trouble, 75 per cent
29.3.1943	Uffz Jančovič (wounded)[1]	Bf 109G-2	14830	Enemy fighter, 70 per cent
16.4.1943		Bf 109F-4	13330	Collision while taxiing, 15 per cent
18.4.1943		Bf 109G-4	19492	Bomb damage, 40 per cent
21.4.1943		Bf 109G-2	14801	Bomb damage, 25 per cent
1.7.1943		Bf 109G-4	19506	Accident while landing, 40 per cent

193

Date	Pilot	Aircraft	Wk. Nr.	Damage
18.7.1943	Uffz Palaticki	Bf 109G-4	19292	Landing after engine trouble, 35 per cent
1.8.1943		Bf 109G-4	14968	Landing after engine trouble, 50 per cent
3.8.1943		Bf 109G-4	19763	Landing after engine trouble, 20 per cent
15.8.1943		Bf 109G-4	14967	Landing accident, 30 per cent
16.8.1943		Bf 109G-4	14979	Landing accident, 30 per cent
16.8.1943	Uffz Ocvirk (wounded)	Bf 109G-4	19756	Forced landing, 50 per cent
09.9.1943	Uffz Dobrovodsky	Bf 109G-4	19259	Missing, 100 per cent[2]
09.9.1943	Uffz Matušek	Bf 109G-4	19347	Missing, 100 per cent[2]
11.9.1943	Uffz Gerič	Bf 109G-4	14938	Missing, 100 per cent[2]
21.9.1943		Bf 109G-4	19330	Landing accident, 35 per cent
22.9.1943		Bf 109G-4	14895	Undercarriage damage, 35 per cent
26.09.1943	Uffz Božik (wounded)	Bf 109G-4	14761	Take-off accident, 90 per cent
26.09.1943		Bf 109G-4	19532	Engine failure, 40 per cent
29.09.1943	Uffz Geletko (wounded)	Bf 109G-4	14982	Crash landing, 75 per cent
06.10.1943		Bf 109G-4	19603	Undercarriage damage, 30 per cent
19.10.1943		Bf 109G-4	19248	Aerial combat, 100 per cent
22.10.1943		Bf 109G-4	14856	Landing accident, 35 per cent

[1] According to other information was KIA
[2] Actually deserted to the Red Army

Sources: Fast, Niko, *Das Jadgeschwader 52*, Vol. IV (Bergisch Gladbach, 1990)
Rajlich, Jiři/Sehnal, Jiři, *Slovak Airmen 1939–1945* (Kutna Hora, 1991),
p. 59

II
Special Cases

Finland

Suomen Ilmavoimat

When, on 30 November 1939, the Soviet Union, with its 180 million population, attacked Finland (4 million inhabitants), the air force of this small country was undergoing modernization. The Suomen Ilmavoimat consisted of three air regiments (Lentorykmentti 1, 2 and 3) and a few independent units. Most of the aircraft material was outdated and had originated in different countries: Dutch Fokker D.XXI, C.X and C.VEs were supplemented by British Blackburn Ripon IIFs, Bristol Bulldog IVAs, some Bristol Blenheim bombers, and obsolete German Junkers K.42 seaplanes. Altogether the Finns had only 145 machines to defend their land, of which 114 were ready for action.[1] The Finnish aviation industry consisted of the State Aircraft Factory Valtion Lentokonetehtas at Tampere, which had only a limited capacity and, in addition to the manufacture of indigenous aircraft types, also undertook licence production of some foreign models. In 1939 the Tampere works produced 35 Fokker D.XXI fighters, 22 VL Viima IIs and the first prototype of the VL Pyry I fighter-trainer.[2]

Against the weak Finnish forces the Soviets fielded 900 aircraft, and later even 1,400 planes. The very first days of hostilities made it clear that this was a new, total form of aerial war: Soviet low-level aircraft machine-gunned civilians on the streets of Helsinki.

Finland fought for its freedom and defended itself with the courage of desperation against an overwhelming enemy. The first Finnish aerial victory, over a Soviet Ilyushin DB-3 bomber, was achieved by Lt Eino Antero Luukanen with his Fokker D.XXI (FR-104) from 24th Squadron (Lento Laivue – LeLv).[3] The robust Fokker D.XXI fighters, with their 830hp Bristol Mercury VIII radial engines, were at that time the most modern Finnish fighters, but had outdated fixed undercarriages. The Finns fought with the utmost bravery against overwhelming Soviet numerical superiority. Eino Ilmari ('Illu') Juutilainen,

197

with 94 1/6 victories the most successful Finnish fighter pilot, has the following to say about the exhausting and hectic time of the 1939/40 winter:[4]

> It was a constant to and fro from morning till dusk, and our aircraft took off as soon as they were refuelled and rearmed. It was like that throughout the Winter War. We lived from day to day, and were relieved still to be in good health in the evenings. It became a habit to go to the sauna in the evenings and into the air in the mornings ... By day the operational sorties were continuous. While the aircraft were being refuelled we would eat something, but often we would have to run to our aircraft with a sandwich in one hand. It was normal to make six to eight flights a day. This hectic pace led to overstraining of both personnel and machines.

The mechanics, too, gave their best to keep up with the high standards of the Suomen Ilmavoimat. For example, the fitters of Luukkanen's unit, based on the snow-covered 'airfield' at Värtsilä, changed the engine of a Fokker D.XXI overnight – at night, under open skies, and at minus 14°C![5] This 'airfield' had neither permanent buildings nor electricity.

Alongside the fighter squadrons LeLv 24 and LeLv 26 – the latter equipped with the obsolete Bristol Bulldog biplanes – flew the two bomber squadrons LeLv 44 and LeLv 46 from the 4th Air Regiment, equipped with Bristol Blenheim bombers. They carried out reconnaissance flights and attacked enemy troop concentrations and airfields.[6] An additional bomber squadron, LeLv 42, was formed in January 1940, and received 12 Bristol Blenheim I bombers a month later.

Finland implored foreign countries despairingly for help in its war against Soviet aggression. What was needed most were volunteers – and additional aircraft. The first were easier to obtain than the second. Volunteers from at least 26 different nations supported Helsinki in its struggle against the Eastern aggressor. The strongest contingent was provided by Sweden, with 8,700 men, followed by about 730 Norwegians and some 700 Hungarians. Altogether, 200 foreign nationals tried to join the Finnish air force, but not all of them were suitable. Among the applicants were also mercenaries, adventurers, impostors and 'tourists'; individuals who were of little value to Finnish command. On the other hand, the Swedish volunteer airmen were most welcome. The Swedish volunteer unit, Flygflottilj 19 (F 19)[7] with 12 Gloster Gladiator IIs and two Hawker Harts, comprised 250 men and two medical nurses under the command of Maj H. Beckhammer. This squadron began operations on 12 January 1940, and carried out a total of 464 sorties, during which at least eight Soviet aircraft were shot down. Two Swedish pilots – Officer Candidate Gustav Mauritz Armfelt and Corp Sten Haraldsson – also served with the Finnish air force during the Continuation War 1941–4; Haraldsson was killed in action in summer 1942.

Denmark also sent some pilots.[8] Like the Swedish volunteers, they were all professionals. Two of them, Lt Christensen and Lt Kristensen, served with Fighter Group 'L', led by Luukanen, which received 12 Gloster Gladiator II fighters in February 1940. Luukanen valued his two volunteers as 'first-class pilots, extremely active and brave, even if they perhaps lacked in caution, which comes with experience.'[9] Lt Kristensen was killed in action on 29 February, in a dogfight with numerically superior Polikarpov I-153 and I-16 fighters. At least another three Danish pilots lost their lives in other aerial encounters with the Russians. Kristensen was not the only loss for the Finnish air force on 29 February. Fighter Group 'L', formed of aircraft from LeLv 24 and LeLv 26, lost five Gladiators and one Fokker D.XXI on that day, and managed to shoot down only one I-16. It was the worst defeat suffered by the Suomen Ilmavoimat until 1944.[10]

The line-up of foreign volunteers for the Finnish air force continued with a group of 16 British technicians, most of whom arrived at Turku in February 1940. Their task was to look after the aircraft of British manufacture on whatever airfields they were based. But there were also volunteer pilots from Poland, Britain, Canada and the USA, who served with LeLv 22, which was founded on 20 February 1940.[11] This unit was to receive American aircraft, but only a few Brewster B-239 fighters arrived in Finland before the Armistice. A few foreign pilots died in accidents: a Hungarian pilot, Lt Bekassy, crashed into the sea while ferrying a Fiat G.50 fighter (FA-7) to Finland, and an Italian volunteer, Diego Manzocchi, from LeLv 26, died on 11 March when his Fiat G.50 (FA-22) somersaulted during an emergency landing on a frozen lake.

Foreign Aircraft Deliveries to Finland 1939–40

Country	Number	Model	Delivery Date	Finnish Designation
Sweden	2	Bristol Bulldog IIA	11 Dec 1939	BU-214, BU-216
	3	Fokker C.VE	Dec 1939	FO-19, FO-23, FO-80
	3	J-6 Jaktfalk	Dec 1939	JF-219, JF-224, JF-228
	2	Koolhoven F.K.52	Jan 1940	KO-129, KO-130
	1	DC-2	Jan 1940	DC-1
Great Britain	30	Gloster Gladiator II	Jan–Feb 1940	GL-251 to GL-280
	12[1]	Hawker Hurricane I	Mar 1940	HC-451 to HC-460
	24[2]	Bristol Blenheim	Jan–Feb 1940	BL-122 to BL-145
	11	Westland Lysander	Mar–May 1940	LY-114 to LY-125
France	30	Morane M.S.406	Feb 1940	MS-301 to MS-330
	6	Caudron C.714	1940	CA-551 to CA-556
Italy	35[3]	Fiat G.50	Dec 1939–June 1940	FA-1 to FA-35
USA	44	Brewster B-239	May 1940	BW-351 to BW-394
South Africa	24	Gloster Gauntlet II	Mar–May 1940	GT-395 to GT-418

[1] Two aircraft lost in transit
[2] One lost in transit, one arrived in Finland on 5 June 1940
[3] Two aircraft lost in transit on 7 and 8 Feb 1940

The deliveries of more modern aircraft had a decisive effect on the further development of the Finnish air force. The American and Italian attitude in this respect was benevolent, that of Britain, France and Sweden dominated by their own interests, while that of the National Socialist Germany, tied by the Hitler–Stalin pact, was negative. To be sure, Finland had ordered 35 Fiat G.50 fighters from Italy before the outbreak of the war, but Germany hindered their transit. Due to this delay the first Fiat fighters did not reach LeLv 26 at Utti until February 1940. The Finns had also ordered 44 Brewster B-239 fighters from the USA, but strict export rules and overzealous customs officials delayed their delivery as well. France sent 30 Morane-Saulnier MS.406 fighters, which were allocated to LeLv 28, commanded by Major Jusu, between 4 and 29 February 1940. Before the Armistice these French fighters managed to carry out 259 operational sorties and shoot down 16 Soviet aircraft in 28 aerial encounters. The Finns lost one MS.406, and three others were damaged.

Sweden, which was urging Finland to make peace, let their threatened neighbour have a total of just ten aircraft, including one Douglas DC-2. Britain delivered the largest number of aircraft: in addition to 24 Bristol Blenheim bombers, the United Kingdom let the Finns have 30 Gloster Gladiators. The Finns were not exactly over-enthusiastic about these somewhat dated biplanes: they were not fast enough, too lightly armed, had insufficient armour protection, and tended to catch fire easily under enemy fire. In a few days the Suomen Ilmavoimat lost 13 of its Gladiators!

For 105 days the Finnish forces managed to defy the Red colossus, but the high losses and lack of support from the Western powers then forced Finland to sign a peace treaty in Moscow on 12 March 1940. The small country retained its independence, but had to give to the Russians the Karelian isthmus with the town of Viipuri (Viborg) and additional Karelian territory as well as part of the Fischer peninsula. The town of Hanko, not far from Helsinki, was to be 'leased' to the Soviet Union. When Finnish President Kallio signed the peace treaty, he commented: 'May the hand that was forced to sign such a paper wither away ...'[12] A few months later Kallio suffered a stroke, as a result of which his right arm remained paralysed.

The Finnish air force came out of the Winter War unbeaten. It had lost 42 aircraft to enemy action, and another 20 in crashes and accidents, but this was far outweighed by the 200 confirmed and 80 unconfirmed aerial victories over Soviet aircraft. Another 314 aircraft sporting the Red Star had been shot down by Finnish AA guns. When one adds the aircraft lost in accidents and on the ground, the Soviet air force had probably lost some 700–800 aircraft.[13] At the end of the Winter War the Suomen Ilmavoimat had 200 aircraft; more than at the beginning of the conflict. The most successful Finnish fighter pilot at this time was Lt Jorma Kalevi Sarvanto, who had achieved 13 confirmed aerial victories. On 6 January 1940 he shot down six Soviet DB-3 bombers in just four minutes, a truly remarkable achievement.

As for the Finnish bombers, the three squadrons (LeLv 42, 44 and 46) of the 4th Air Regiment flew a total of 423 sorties, lost 22 aircraft (including eight in accidents) and shot down ten Soviet aircraft.

The following months of peace were not free of tensions and Soviet provocations. On 14 June 1940 two Soviet SB bombers shot down the unarmed Ju 52/3m 'Kaleva' passenger aircraft of the Finnish airline Aero O/Y near the Estonian coast. The aircraft was flying over its regular route from Tallinn to Helsinki, and was clearly a civilian plane. The Finnish fighter pilot 'Illu' Juutilainen was ordered to search for the missing aircraft and found a surfaced Soviet submarine among the wreckage of the airliner. Beside himself with fury, he flew his Brewster B-239 in a low-level pass:[14]

> I made a few more passes over the submarine and was just waiting for the Russians to move their cannon a bit, then I would have shot the rats away from their guns, followed by the officers on the conning tower. And then I would have completed the job by shooting holes in the hull of that submarine.

But the Soviet submarine crew remained passive, and what could well have been the start of the Continuation War was put on hold!

The Finnish air force used the period of peace to modernize and build up its aircraft park. Up to May 1940 France delivered six Caudron C.714 fighters, and more Fiat G.50s arrived from Italy. Norwegian pilots, who wanted to escape the German occupation of their land, brought over seven aircraft (one He 115A-2 floatplane, three Høver HF.11s, two Fokker C.VDs and one Tiger Moth), all of which were absorbed into the Finnish air force. On the other hand, the capitulation of the Netherlands, on 15 May, meant that the fighters ordered from the Fokker works would not be delivered. Instead Germany suddenly stepped in as a supplier of military aircraft, although initially selling only its war booty. In this way a total of 57 Morane MS.406 and MS.410 fighters reached Finland between late 1940 and 1942, most of these being allocated to LeLv 28.[15] Further deliveries included 29 Curtiss Hawk 75A-3 and A-6 fighters captured in France and Norway, which, after the fitting of German instrumentation, provided welcome strengthening of the Suomen Ilmavoimat.

Shortly before the German attack on the Soviet Union the Finnish air force had five fighter squadrons organized into the 2nd and 3rd Air Regiments, three bomber squadrons and five independent squadrons. These formations totalled 550 machines, with an operational readiness of 50 per cent.[16] The aircraft park consisted of Russian, German, British, French, Italian, American and Dutch models, as well as some of indigenous construction. In fact the Suomen Ilmavoimat had the dubious status of the most 'cosmopolitan' air force in the world.

Finnish Air Forces on 2 July 1941

Unit	Commander	Aircraft	Base
LeR 2	Lt Col Lorentz		Pieksämäki
LeLv 24	Maj Magnusson	22 Brewster 239	Vesivehmaa
		8 Brewster 239	Selänpää
		4 Brewster 239	Mikkeli
LeLv 26	Maj Harju-Jeanty	28 Fiat G.50	Joroinen
		1 Fokker C.X	Joroinen

FINLAND

Unit	Commander	Aircraft	Base
LeLv 28	Capt Siren	21 MS.406	Naarajärvi
		1 Brewster 239	Naarajärvi
		9 MS.406	Joroinen
LeR 3	Lt Col Nuotio		Hämeenlinna
LeLv 30	Capt Bremer	22 Fokker D.XXI	Pori-Turku
		4 Hurricane I	Utti
LeLv 32	Capt Hanilä	7 Fokker D.XXI	Hyvinkää
		20 Fokker D.XXI	Hyvinkää
		8 Fokker D.XXI	Utti
LeR 4	Lt Col Somerto		Luonetjärvi
LeLv 42	Maj Eskola	10 Blenheim	Siikakangas
LeLv 44	Maj Stenbäck	8 Blenheim	Siikakangas
LeLv 46	Maj Jusu	1 Blenheim	Luonetjärvi
		1 DB-3m	Luonetjärvi
		1 DC-2	Luonetjärvi
LeLv 15	Capt Malinen	1 He 115	Vaasa
(seaplanes)		3 Ju W.34	Vaasa
		3 Blackburn Ripon	Vaasa

Independent Units

LeLv 6	Maj Ilanko	5 I-153	Nummela
		2 Koolhoven FK.52	Nummela
		3 SB	Nummela
LeLv 12	Maj Holm	2 Curtiss Hawk 75A	Mikkeli
		6 Fokker C.X	Mikkeli
		3 Gladiator	Joroinen
LeLv 14	Maj Larjo	2 Curtiss Hawk 75A	Utti, Padasjoki
		8 Fokker C.X	Utti, Padasjoki
		3 Gladiator	Selänpää
LeLv 16	Maj Pajari	8 Gladiator	Joensuu
		5 Fokker C.X	Joensuu
		4 Lysander	Rautavaara

The Finnish leadership in Helsinki was informed about the impending German attack on the Soviet Union, but for domestic and foreign policy reasons did not want to initiate anything, proposing to await Soviet actions and only then go over to the offensive. When, after 22 June 1941, Soviet artillery and aircraft actually attacked Finnish territory, Finland declared war on the Soviet Union on 26 June. The Continuation War, also known as the Second Defensive War, had begun.

In declaring war on the Soviet Union, Helsinki remained in a free position contractually in relation to Berlin. It was a brother-in-arms and a fellow warrior, but not an ally of the Axis. Apart from an anti-Bolshevik political stance there was hardly any ideological common ground between Germany and Finland. At first glance the blue swastika on white background carried on Finnish aircraft seemed to indicate a parallel and affinity to the National Socialist system and its symbols, but the Finnish swastika was much older and without any ideological significance. When the Finnish air force was founded on 6 March 1918 one of the first aircraft it acquired was a present from the Swedish Count Erik von Rosen, which was marked with his own good luck symbol, a blue swastika. The Suomen Ilmavoimat adopted and retained this symbol for the next 26 years.

In the Finnish officer corps, likewise that of the air force, there were hardly any pro-National Socialist sympathies, but a strong emotional bond to Germany. This had come about because many Finns had served in the famous 27th Royal Prussian Fusilier battalion (königlich preussischen Jägerbtl) during the First World War and now occupied high positions within the Finnish military hierarchy. The C-in-C of the Finnish air force, Lt Gen Carl Frithiof Lundquist, born on 15 August 1896 in Helsinki, had also served in that battalion, and latter attended the École Militaire de l'Artillerie and other military establishments in France. He was to lead his air force clear-sightedly and prudently from 8 September 1932 until 30 June 1945. Furthermore, the beginnings of the Finnish air force had strong associations with the air force of the Kaiser's Germany. In April 1918 two Finnish NCOs were ordered to Putzig to undergo naval aviation training. In August to September of the same year the Finns sent 18 pilots, 15 observers and 19 mechanics to Libau (Liepāja, in Latvia), Rügen and Kiel for training.[17]

The operations of the Finnish army in summer 1941 were very successful. The Finnish troops had reached the old

Soviet–Finnish border on the Karelian isthmus by early September, and captured East Karelia three months later. Marshal Mannerheim rejected more distant operational goals, and, in spring 1942, even demobilized 180,000 men from his army.

The Suomen Ilmavoimat played a decisive role in these offensive successes. The Finnish pilots were highly motivated and well trained, and went aggressively into aerial combat. It was to their benefit that the major part of the Soviet air force was fighting against the German armed forces, and that, until 1944, there were many novices among the Soviet airmen facing them.

The first demonstration of the Finnish air force's effectiveness came on 25 June, when Fiat G.50 fighters from LeLv 26 shot down 13 out of 15 Soviet SB bombers. Then there was the Brewster B-239, which had enjoyed so little success with Western Allied air forces: in Finnish hands, it contributed its share in securing Finnish aerial superiority. On 9 July 1941 LeLv 24 achieved nine aerial victories and on 12 August no fewer than 13 enemy aircraft were destroyed by the unit.[18] On the latter occasion, 'Illu' Juutilainen, who took part in 437 aerial combats without sustaining a single hit on his own aircraft, shot down two I-153s, and a day later, three I-153s. Because of its agility, the B-239 was very well liked by its pilots, and formed the back-bone of the Finnish fighter arm until 1943/44. 'Joppe' Karhunen, in 1941 Captain and commander of the 3rd flight of LeLv 24, recalls:[19]

> The Brewster Model 239 was good against the older Russian fighters, Polikarpov I-153 Chaika (Gull) and I-16. Hence the period 1941–2 was the best time for us. In 1943 it was already significantly more difficult when the Russians began to use their newer fighters against us… Later, with the Yaks, Hurricanes, Tomahawks, LaGG-3 and MiGs, it became a fight to the death.

'Joppe' Karhunen was an excellent pilot and tactician. By 4 May 1943 he had achieved 31½ aerial victories, including 25½ with the Brewster B-239.

The professionalism of the Finnish fighter pilots impressed the German general attached to the Finnish High Command, Waldemar Erfurth, who wrote:[20]

> The organizational capabilities of General Lundquist, commander of the Finnish air force, were remarkably successful and are now bearing fruit. The Finnish fighters can successfully hold their own against a very superior enemy. Numerous aerial combats, such as at Lahdenpohja on 9 July 1941, and over Rautjärvi on 1 August 1941, brought proof of the great flying skills and splendid fighting morale of the Finnish fighters.

Because of its hydraulic and pneumatic weaknesses, the French Morane-Saulnier MS.406 fighter, with its 'nose' cannon, did not prove as reliable as the Brewster B-239, but it was an excellent low-level attack aircraft. From then on, the MS.406 was to carry out most effective attacks on the supply and troop transport trains travelling along the Murmansk line.

On 28 March 1942 both LeLv 32 and LeLv 24 were assigned the task of covering the occupation of the Suursari island in the Gulf of Finland. A total of 12 Curtiss 75A-3s of LeLv 32 and five Brewster B-239s took off and were soon involved in a fierce aerial conflict, which the Finns decided unequivocally in their favour. Altogether they achieved 27 aerial victories that day. In August LeLv 24 was once again in the limelight. On 16 August 'Joppe' Karhunen led six B-239s on an interception mission towards Seiskari. The group found eight SB bombers protected by 15 Polikarpov I-16 and three LaGG-3 fighters. Karhunen gave the order to attack and the numerically much inferior Finns shot down 11 I-16s without suffering any losses. Two days later came the biggest aerial combat to date. Lt Hans Wind, with six Brewster B-239s, got involved in a running combat with some 60 Soviet aircraft near Kronstadt, and LeLv 24, with seven B-239s, took off to join in. Karhunen and Juutilainen hurried to help their comrades. 'When we got to the battle there were no grounds to complain of a lack of targets. Aircraft were coming in from all directions – I-16s, Hurricanes, and even a Pe-2 dived into the tumult.'[21] For many of the Russians this was to be their last flight. When the battle ended, 12 I-16s, one Hurricane and two Pe-2 bombers lay wrecked on the ground. The Finns lost just one Brewster B-239 (BW-378)!

On 5 September LeLv 32 remained victorious against 40 Soviet machines in the airspace over Lotinanpelto: 13 Red aircraft crashed to the ground but the Curtiss fighters returned home without a single loss. Despite these unquestionable successes, the Finnish air force faced the growing danger of being overwhelmed both quantitatively and qualitatively. In 1943 the training of Soviet pilots improved and, moreover, they now appeared at the Front with more modern aircraft. The Yakovlev Yak-9 and Lavochkin La-5 made their operational début in October 1942, and, in its developed 1943 version, the La-5FN, the Lavochkin was also a dangerous opponent for the German Bf 109G-2.

The Finnish air force command tried different measures to keep up with technological developments. The decision of 1941 to build 50 outdated Fokker D.XXI fighters with the Pratt & Whitney Twin Wasp Jr. radial engine of 825hp turned out to be a failure: the modified version proved less manoeuvrable and slower than the original model with the Mercury engine. On the other hand, the decision to replace the unsatisfactory Hispano-Suiza 12 Y-31 engine of the MS.406 with the Russian M-105P, which was a progressive Russian development of the HS12Y[22], was a complete success. The Russian M-105P engines, with a cannon fitted between the cylinder banks, had been captured in large quantities, and the engine switch created no difficulties for the state aircraft works. The modified fighter made its first flight on 25 January 1943, and the results were quite startling: the aircraft was 40km/h (25mph) faster than the original French version, and the service ceiling was increased from 10,000 to 12,000m (32,800 to 39,360ft). Work was immediately put in hand to re-engine all 41 remaining MS.406s and 410s with the Soviet aero engine of 1,100hp, and the Mörko-Moraani was born. But it took time, and the first front-line aircraft of this type did not reach LeLv 28 until July/August 1944; the entire re-engining programme could not be completed before March 1945.

The Finns had less success with their own indigenous

models.[23] The VL Pyry fighter-trainer, of which 41 had been built by June 1941, had revealed some teething troubles, such as stability problems when flown with a crew of two. More serious were the deficiencies inherent in the Myrsky (Storm) fighter, powered by a 1,115hp Pratt & Whitney radial engine. The prototype made its first flight on 23 December 1941, but fell far short of expectations. Although the technical problems could not be resolved satisfactorily, a pre-production series of three aircraft (MY-2 to MY-4) was built in 1943. All three aircraft were lost in accidents. Despite this poor showing, no fewer than 47 Myrsky II fighters had been built by the end of 1944. A few examples were allocated to TLeLv 12 and TLeLv 16 reconnaissance squadrons. The fighter squadrons, which in the meantime had received the Bf 109G, showed no interest in the Myrsky, which was disliked by the pilots. Another fighter project, the VM Pyörremyrsky with a DB 605A engine, did not advance beyond the construction of a single prototype (PM-1) in autumn 1945.

Under the circumstances, Germany had to help out in order to compensate for this lack of modern aircraft. During his visit to Germany on 17 January 1943, Göring promised Gen Lundquist Messerschmitt fighters and Ju 88 bombers. A mere five days later the Finns formed a new squadron, LeLv 34 within the Lentorykmentti 3, to take over the promised Messerschmitts. A German–Finnish agreement was then signed on 11 February 1943, according to which the Finnish air force was to receive 30 Bf 109G-2 fighters, of which 16 were to be brand new, and the remainder completely overhauled ex-Luftwaffe machines. Any losses suffered by these aircraft were always to be made good by Germany. This resulted in the Suomen Ilmavoimat receiving 48 Bf 109G-2 fighters altogether (MT-201 to MT-248) by 1 June 1944.[24]

The newly formed LeLv 34, the command of which was taken over by Maj Eino Luukanen on 27 March, took on élite pilots from all Finnish fighter squadrons. On 10 February 1943 17 of these leading Finnish fighter pilots flew to Germany to familiarize themselves with their new planes. The Finns certainly did not suffer from any lack of self-assurance. A few of them visited the German capital, where they were surprised by a heavy bombing raid. Oiva Tuominen, who was to increase his score to 44 victories by the end of the war, had a personal explanation for this raid: 'I wonder how the British knew we were here in Berlin!'[25]

On 10 March the Finnish pilots brought their first Bf 109G-2s to the Helsinki-Malmi airport. For the time being 1./LeLv 34 remained there to protect the capital, while the rest of the squadron was based at Utti. The pilots were most enthusiastic about their new machines. Luukanen explains: 'It was love at first sight. The smooth powerful lines of the Messerschmitt were in such great contrast to the portly contours of the Brewster that I could hardly hide my excitement when I first swung myself into the cockpit.'[26] The aircraft was ideal for the courageous Finnish fighting style. By 4 October 1943 LeLv 34 had achieved 100 aerial victories for only five losses. Luukanen proudly said of his pilots: 'As individuals they were remarkable, as a team they were magnificent, and I could not think of a greater honour than to be a commander of these men.'[27] But the Bf 109G-2 also had its tricky side: two aircraft caught fire in the air for in-explicable reasons. Apart from this the poor supply of spare parts from Germany resulted in several machines staying on the ground at times.

Germany delivered not only fighters but also bombers. Early in 1942 Göring presented the Finns with 15 Do 17Z-2 bombers from Luftwaffe stocks. These aircraft were allocated to LeLv 44, which handed over its Bristol Blenheims to LeLv 48. But the most welcome boost for the Finnish bomber fleet did not come until 1943. On 19 April the Finnish plenipotentiary signed a contract with the Junkers Flugzeug- und Motorenwerke AG for the delivery of 24 Ju 88A-4 bombers.[28] A group of 41 pilots, observers, gunners and mechanics from LeLv 44 had arrived in Germany in February to familiarize themselves with and train on the new model at Tutow. The first 12 Ju 88A-4 bombers were in Finnish hands on 10 April, before the contract deadline, and were ferried via Helsinki-Malmi to Pori. The remaining machines left Germany on 20 April, one Ju 88A being lost during the ferry flight.

Each of the four flights of LeLv 44 at Onttola received four Ju 88s, the other machines remained in reserve at the LeR 4 (4th Air Regiment). The Finnish Ju 88A-4s flew their first operational sorties on 30 May 1943, their target being the Leningrad–Murmansk railway line. In August followed diving attacks on partisan camps and railway bridges.

An attack by 35 bombers from LeR 4 and LeR 5, including 14 Ju 88s, against Soviet airfields on the Lavansaari island took an unfortunate turn on the return flight. In thick fog seven aircraft lost their way and had to make emergency landings on different airfields. Some were damaged and out of service for several months. An accident such as this pointed to insufficient training of the aircrews in blind flying and navigation, and for that reason training in these areas was intensified during the following weeks.

On 15 November the 3rd Flight of LeLv 44 had to be disbanded due to a shortage of aircraft; the entire squadron had only 13 Ju 88A-4 bombers. Apart from one sortie on 29 December, the following weeks passed quietly. On 14 February 1944 LeLv 44 as well as LeLv 42 and 48 were redesignated Pommituslento Laivue (PLeLv, bomber squadrons); a short while later Maj T. Meller replaced Lt Col T. Gabrielsson as squadron commander.

In the same month the Soviet air force carried out three heavy bombing raids on Helsinki with the intention of forcing the Finnish government into suing for peace.[29] The first attack took place on 6 February. Even as the Finnish government were discussing the Soviet demands on 26 February, another Soviet bombing raid meant the session had to be suspended. After this, LeR 4 was ordered to raid Soviet airfields in the Karelian Isthmus. During the period from March to May the regiment carried out six successful bombing attacks against Soviet targets; the participating units, apart from PLeLv 44, included PLeLv 42 (squadron commander Maj K. Kepsu) and PLeLv 48 (squadron commander Maj E. Ahtiainen). The two additional squadrons comprised three flights each and were equipped with Bristol Blenheim bombers.

PLeLv 48, founded on 23 November 1941, had had to make

do with captured Soviet bombers for two years before it could re-equip with the Blenheim. This unit was not the only one to fly captured Soviet bombers. During the Winter War of 1939–40 Finnish fighters and AA guns had shot down 200 Tupolev SB bombers, of which more than 50 were salvaged by Finnish teams and taken to depots. Four repaired and refurbished SBs were allocated to LeLv 6,[30] based at Turku in June 1941. This first batch was augmented by more Tupolevs after Finland acquired 16 captured, lightly damaged SB bombers from Germany. These reconditioned aircraft carried out reconnaissance and surveillance flights over the Gulf of Finland, and made a mark for themselves by attacking several Soviet submarines. It is questionable, however, if LeLv 6 actually sank four Soviet submarines as the Finnish crews believed. Nevertheless, on 21 October 1943, the squadron recorded its 100th operational sortie with the ex-Soviet bombers. The unit lost a total of seven aircraft, none of them due to enemy action.

The LeR 4 began its bombing raids on 9 March 1944, when 21 bombers attacked three Soviet airfields north of Leningrad.[31] Under the protection of darkness the Finnish bombers mingled with Soviet bombers returning from a raid on Tallinn, in Estonia, and enjoyed an element of surprise in their attack as they dropped their bombs over the Soviet airfield. Ten Soviet bombers and the fuel reserves of Gorskaya were destroyed. Other Finnish actions followed on 22 and 30 March, as well as 3 April and 19 and 20 May. On 3 April alone 34 Ju 88A-4 and Blenheim bombers attacked Lähy and managed to destroy 17 Soviet aircraft on the ground. These attacks had a notable effect on the Russians, who now suspended their bombing of Helsinki.[32]

The Suomen Ilmavoimat did not have a single night fighter unit of their own to counter nocturnal Soviet bombing raids effectively. Only a handful of Finnish airmen were trained as night fighter pilots in Germany. It is known that two of them, Corp Bengt Ringbom and Lt Matti Tervo, lost their lives in August 1944.

In spring 1944 the relations between Berlin and Helsinki became strained and a diplomatic crisis was in the making. This was caused by Finnish contacts with Moscow and consultations regarding a separate peace, which caused quite a stir in Berlin. The National Socialist government immediately imposed sanctions. The Foreign Minister, von Ribbentrop, decided early in April 1944 to suspend armament deliveries to Finland, but not to inform the Finnish government of this action. Instead a strategy of quiet postponements and delays was to be initiated.[33] Hitler confirmed this secret delivery blockage on 18 April. However, the export of armaments was to continue, insofar as the weapons were essential and indispensable to the Finnish forces.[34] This crisis was settled for the time being when the Finnish President Risto Ryti gave the German dictator his personal assurance, on 25 June 1944, that Finland would continue fighting alongside Germany until the Soviet threat to the small countries was eliminated. In addition he also pledged that any armistice discussions would only take place in agreement with the Reich government.

The deliveries of the Messerschmitt planes were completely unaffected by this German–Finnish quarrel. On 15 March the unequal brothers-in-arms had signed another contract, according to which the Reich would deliver 30 Bf 109G-6 fighters. Half of these machines were on the way to Finland in the next three days; the remainder arrived there by 1 May. The new G-6s were allocated to HLeLv 34, which had passed its G-2 fighters to HLeLv 24. These squadrons had been redesignated Hävittäjälentolaivue (HLeLv, fighter squadron) in February.

The expected major Soviet offensive in the Karelian Isthmus began on 9 June. The Russians attacked with two armies, totalling 260,000 men, four mechanized brigades, eight tank regiments, eight assault artillery regiments and a strong air force commitment. They could deploy more than 1,500 aircraft, which flew 1,150 operational sorties on the first day and 800 on the second. The goal of this powerful thrust was the capital, Helsinki, which should have been taken within 31 days. Although the Finns had only 75,000 men available at the front, and during the early phase of this major offensive could put up only 48 fighters (14 Bf 109G-2s from HLeLv 24 at Suulajärvi, 16 Bf 109G-6s from HLeLv 34 at Kymi and 18 Brewster B-239s from HLeLv 26 at Heinjoki),[35] the Soviets failed to achieve their target, although they took Viipuri, something they had not managed to do during the Winter War. In ten days the Finns lost more territory then during the 105 days of the Winter War of 1939–40. Marshal Mannerheim pleaded with the Swedish government for urgent deliveries of weapons and ammunition, but Stockholm turned him down.

However, help came from Germany when it was most needed, in the form of aircraft and a special Luftwaffe formation. Up to the end of June the Germans delivered 41 Bf 109Gs, followed by 18 more in July. Finnish pilots were flying into the Reich almost daily to collect the Messerschmitt fighters – not always to the pleasure of the pilots, who would have rather stayed at the front defending their homeland. As 'Illu' Juutilainen put it, 'I would have preferred to fight in the skies over Kannas rather than play an unwilling tourist for an undefinable time.'[36] Altogether the Finnish air force received 162 Bf 109G fighters[37] by September 1944, which enabled the Suomen Ilmavoimat to cope during the heavy fighting of summer 1944.

The aerial fighting at that time was characterized by great bitterness because the Finns always suffered numerical inferiority. Eino Luukanen, who achieved 11 aerial victories in June, described the situation during the Soviet offensive as follows: 'The sky was full of La-5s, Yak-9s, Airacobras, Pe-2s, Yak-4s and Il-2s every day. Sometimes the enemy aircraft appeared in great waves of several hundred, sometimes they came in smaller groups, but no matter when we took off we knew that we would not have much ammunition left when we landed again.'[38]

Symptomatic of the combat at that time were the events of 30 June 1944. On that day seven Bf 109Gs from HLeLv 34, led by Maj Luukanen, and seven Bf 109Gs from HLeLv 24, led by Lt K. K. E. Karhila, attacked a formation of over 100 Soviet aircraft and, without suffering a single loss, shot down 17 planes. During the period from 9 to 22 June 1944, the total Soviet losses at the Finnish Front amounted to 423 machines.

The Finnish bomber aircrews for their part tried to help their comrades on the ground to stem the dangerous Soviet offensive from the air. From 12 June to 9 August the three squadrons of HeR 4 were in the air almost every day, bombing the Soviet troop and tank concentrations and artillery positions. But it became a war of attrition of a kind, because the continuous operations not only wore out the material but also the nerves of the Finnish pilots, who would climb out of their aircraft after each operation bathed in perspiration and with trembling lips due to the exhaustion and nervous strain. 'Illu' Juutilainen observed:[39]

Our pilots began to show signs of over-exertion because the stand-by now lasted 24 hours a day. We slept in tents next to our fighters. Whenever we landed after our operations we immediately took in a hatful of sleep. Usually we were so tired that even the roar of aircraft engines could not wake us. However, when the relatively quiet alarm telephone happened to ring we were on our legs at once and running like lightning to our machines.

The German command was worried about the northern flank of the Eastern Front and dispatched not only fighters to help the Finns but also organized and sent out a special formation, the 'Gefechtsverband Kuhlmey' (combat task force), to Finland.[40] This *ad hoc* task force, commanded by Obstl Kurt Kuhlmey, was withdrawn from Estonia and composed of units from different squadrons:

4. and 5./JG 54 with Fw 190s (fighters)
1./NAGr 5 with five Bf 109G-8s (tactical reconnaissance)
I./SG 3 with 23 Ju 87D-5 Stukas
1./SG 5 with Fw 190Fs (close-support aircraft)

A total of 46 planes from this task force landed at Immola, Finland, on 16 June. The technical personnel were brought in by 19 SM.81s of Transportgruppe 10 (ital.), also known under its Italian designation as Gruppo Aerotransporti 'F. Terraciano'. The German formation immediately joined the fighting and, on 20 June, shot down seven Soviet aircraft in 16 sorties. At the same time the Finnish air force achieved 49 victories in 126 sorties. On 2 July a heavy Soviet air raid on Immola accounted for four Ju 87Ds, two Fw 190Fs and three Fw 190As from the German formation; another 21 aircraft were damaged.

However, these material losses were relatively quickly made good again by replacements. On 8 July the fighter-bombers of Kuhlmey's task force, covered by Finnish Bf 109Gs from HLeLv 24, destroyed a Soviet landing attempt at Uuras. But this period of direct German assistance was soon over: on 21 July the Kuhlmey task force was withdrawn from Finland, although the Fw 190F fighter-bombers of 1./SG 5 remained there for the time being and continued to support the Finnish defenders. The local population, who had witnessed the withdrawal of the German airmen, were in tears; they knew that their small country could not hold out alone against Soviet superiority.

Even today some of the Finnish people have not forgotten the actions of the Kuhlmey task force, which helped to stop the Soviet offensive and thus secured the independence of Finland. In 1994, 50 years after the events, a memorial to the German airmen was unveiled at the Immola airfield. Among the guests at the ceremony was the President of the Finnish Parliament.[41]

In the end the Finns and their German allies had achieved a decisive defensive victory. During the 38-day battle, which was discontinued by the Soviets on 16 July, no fewer than 1,000 Soviet aircraft had been destroyed, including 126 by the pilots from JG 54 'Grünherz'.[42]

This was only a temporary respite. The Finnish government, which had ordered the evacuation of Eastern Karelia by 19 July, knew that another Soviet offensive would mean the end of the freedom and independence of their republic. On 1 August Marshal Mannerheim took over the post of State President from Ryti. On 19 September 1944 a Finnish delegation signed an armistice agreement in Moscow with both the Soviet Union and Great Britain. That the country retained its independence was in no small part due to its brave Ilmavoimat, which had suffered the following losses during the Continuation War:[43]

A total of 215 aircraft were lost in combat. Of these, 85 were shot down by Soviet aircraft, 67 became victims of Soviet AA fire and 23 were destroyed on the ground; 22 remained missing, and 18 machines were lost due to other causes. Another 208 aircraft were lost in crashes and accidents. Set against these Finnish losses were 1,567 confirmed aerial victories, not counting the Soviet aircraft shot down by AA guns. Looked at from another viewpoint, 663 of these aerial victories were achieved by the Finnish-flown Bf 109G fighters, of which only 27 were lost in action, giving a ratio of 25:1 in favour of the Finns.[44] An even more favourable ratio was achieved by the Brewster B-239 fighter during the first phase of the Continuation War: no less than 32:1.[45] From this point of view and taking into consideration all the circumstances, the Suomen Ilmavoimat was – and is – probably the most successful fighter arm in the history of aerial warfare.

After the brief Lapland war against the German forces to clear Finland, which was dictated by the armistice requirements, the Finnish air force was materially and personnel-wise drastically reduced. However, German aircraft models remained in Finnish service for many years. The Ju 88As were withdrawn in September 1948, but the Bf 109Gs were still flying over Helsinki, Turku and Tampere in 1954.

Balance Sheet of the Finnish fighter squadrons 30 November 1939–4 September 1944

Squadron	Aircraft	Aerial Victories	Aircraft Losses	Personnel Losses (KIA)
HLeLv 24	Fokker D.XXI	96		
	Brewster B-239	477		
	Bf 109G	304		
		877	55	27
HLeLv 26	Bulldog IIA	4		
	Fokker D.XXI	25		
	Gladiator	30		
	Fiat G.50	99		
	Brewster B-239	19		
		177	41	16
HLeLv 28	Morane MS.406	118		
	Bf 109G	15		
		133	39	18

FINLAND

Squadron	Aircraft	Aerial Victories	Aircraft Losses	Personnel Losses (KIA)
HLeLv 30[1]	Fokker D.XXI	36		
	Bf 109G	3		
		39	24	11
HLeLv 32[2]	Fokker D.XXI	5		
	Hurricane	6		
	Curtiss 75 A-3	190		
	LaGG-3	1		
		202	29	16
HLeLv 34[3]	Bf 109G	345	30	12

[1] HLeLv 30 was formed in March 1940
[2] HLeLv 32 was formed from LeLv 22 in March 1940
[3] HLeLv 34 was only formed in 1943

Vichy-France

L'Armée de l'Air de l'Armistice

The German–French armistice negotiations in June 1940 also decided the future fate of French military aircraft. At the conclusion of hostilities the French air force still had an imposing strength at its disposal. An Italian inventory of July 1940 mentioned a total of 3,685 aircraft in unoccupied France and the French colonies.[1] Even if this figure was not exactly accurate – in all probability far too high[2] – the remaining strength of the Armée de l'Air was still impressive.

Article 4 of the armistice agreement between Berlin and Paris covered the demobilization and disarmament of the French armed forces on land, at sea and in the air. Article 5, which gave the victors the right, if they so desired, to demand the handover of all military aircraft, led to long-lasting discussions between the French and German delegations. In the end, the French managed to ameliorate this clause, it being agreed to include in the article a stipulation stating that the surrender of military aircraft could be waived if they were all disarmed and put under German control.[3] This seemed to seal the fate of the French air force, for although France was permitted 100,000 men under arms, no air component was included in this force.

Table of Armée de l'Air de l'Armistice formations

G.C.	=	Groupe de chasse	Fighter group
G.R.	=	Groupe de reconnaissance	Reconnaissance group
G.B.	=	Groupe de bombardement	Bomber group
G.T.	=	Groupe de transport	Transport group
E.C.	=	Escadrille de chasse	Fighter squadron
E.B.	=	Escadrille de bombardement	Bomber squadron
E.R.	=	Escadrille de reconnaissance	Reconnaissance squadron
E.O.	=	Escadrille d'observation	Observation squadron

It was the British, who, albeit unintentionally, made it possible for the French to retain their own air force. On 3 July a British naval force made a surprise attack on French warships anchored at Mers-el-Kebir, near Oran, with the intention of sinking them and thus preventing them from falling into Axis hands (Operation *Catapult*). The French naval units and the yet-to-be-demobilized air force defended themselves staunchly during this attack by their former allies. French Curtiss H-75A fighters of G.C. I/5 and II/5, as well as Dewoitine D.520s of G.C. II/3 and III/3, took off and attempted to intercept the attacking British torpedo-bombers, while French bombers turned on the British warships. A day later the Vichy French government, led by Marshal Petain, broke off diplomatic relations with Great Britain and the Vichy Admiralty ordered reprisal attacks on Gibraltar. These were carried out the same night by three Leo H-257 bombers of Escadrille B1 and three Glenn Martin 167Fs of Escadrille B13, but with little noticeable effect.

The British attack had cost the French navy dear: the battle-ship *Bretagne* had been sunk, many other naval units had been damaged, and nearly 1,300 French sailors had been killed. Impressed by the energetic defence against this British attack, however, the Axis powers decided against disbanding the French air force, only limiting it numerically and operationally. Thus the Armée de l'Air de l'Armistice was born.

The French air force also participated in the defence of other French warships attacked by the British at Dakar in Senegal. In this action the new French battleship *Richelieu* was badly damaged. However, the Armée de l'Air de l'Armistice was unable to prevent French Equatorial Africa from renouncing the Petain regime in August and going over to the Free French under de Gaulle. The same happened with Tahiti, the New Hebrides and New Caledonia, where Vichy could not give any effective material support. But not so with Senegal. Under the pretext of preventing the surrender of Dakar to the Germans, the British launched their Operation *Menace*. On 23 September 1940 a force of Royal Navy vessels, including two battleships and an aircraft carrier as well as some Free French warships, attempted to take Dakar by surprise attack. The French Governor-General Boisson rejected the British ultimatum, stating: 'The French government has entrusted Dakar to me. I shall defend Dakar to the end.'[4]

He had the necessary air power at his disposal, as Vichy had in the meantime considerably strengthened the local garrison: 19 Curtiss H-75A fighters of G.C. I/1 and 43 Glenn Martin 167 bombers of G.B. I/62, II/62 and I/63 were available for the defence. The Vichy pilots reacted aggressively to the attempted seizure of Dakar, and, together with the naval artillery of the French warships at anchor, repelled the Allied attack. The British lost 11 aircraft: eight Swordfish, two Skuas and one Walrus amphibian. The Vichy-French lost just two aircraft (one Curtiss H-75A and one Liore 130).[5] An air raid on Gibraltar was then ordered in reprisal for this attack on Dakar.[6] On 24 September 64 Vichy-French bombers took off from Meknès, Mediouana, Oran, Port Lyautey and Tafaraoui, and dropped 41 tonnes of bombs on the British port. One day later no fewer than 83 bombers of the Armée de l'Air de l'Armistice raided 'The Rock', one LeO 451 from G.B. II/23 being shot down. The damage caused was allegedly light, but Vichy had demonstrated that France was prepared to repay provocation with the same coin.

Despite this success Vichy had to suffer another humiliation only a few weeks later. On 10 November 1940 Gabon was captured by the Gaullist forces, and Free French troops moved into Libreville. Earlier the only aerial encounters between the Armée de l'Air and the Gaullist pilots of the FFAF (Free French air force) had taken place: on three occasions shots were exchanged in air combat between the two French air arms. The situation being what it was, Marshal Petain could not always rely on his pilots. Some were inclined to join de Gaulle, others were 'war-weary' or deserted for other reasons. From the armistice until the end of October 1940 no fewer than 23 Vichy pilots went over to the Allies, and another six 'dissidents' were recorded during the next three months.[7]

These desertions caused irritation among the Germans and Italians and led to sanctions, but did not hinder the further build-up of the Armée de l'Air de l'Armistice. On 1 December 1940 the occupying powers had granted the Vichy government

– 'temporarily, for defence against British aggression' – an air force strength of 1,040 planes, stationed in the motherland, its colonies and the mandate regions. This total included 435 fighters, 292 bombers, 275 reconnaissance aircraft and 38 torpedo-bombers.[8]

Vichy-French Air Force (Armée de l'Air de l'Armistice) as permitted 'for the time being' by the occupying powers, as on 1 December 1940

Area	Units	Number of Aircraft
France	*Armée de l'Air*	
	6 fighter groups	156
	6 bomber groups	78
	3 reconnaissance groups	39
	2 fighter squadrons	16
		289
	Aéronavale	
	1 reconnaissance squadron	6
	2 torpedo-bomber squadrons	20
		26
	Total in France (including 52 reserve aircraft	**367**
Tunisia	*Armée de l'Air*	
	1 fighter group	26
	2 bomber groups	26
	1 reconnaissance group	13
		65
	Aéronavale	
	2 reconnaissance squadrons	12
	2 bomber squadrons	12
	2 torpedo bomber squadrons	12
		36
	Total in Tunisia	**101**

Algeria	*Armée de l'Air*	
	3 fighter groups	78
	3 bomber groups	39
	3 reconnaissance groups	39
		156
	Aéronavale	
	2 fighter squadrons	24
	2 bomber squadrons	12
	2 reconnaissance squadrons	12
		48
	Total in Algeria	**204**
Morocco	*Armée de l'Air*	
	2 fighter groups	52
	4 bomber groups	52
	2 reconnaissance groups	26
	Total in Morocco	**130**
French West Africa	*Armée de l'Air*	
	1 fighter group	26
	4 bomber groups	52
	1 fighter squadron	12
		90
	Aéronavale	
	1 reconnaissance squadron	6
	Total in French West Africa	**96**
Syria	*Armée de l'Air*	
	1 fighter group	19
	1 bomber group	11
	1 reconnaissance group	13
	6 reconnaissance squadrons	36
	1 bomber squadron	6
		85
	Aéronavale	
	1 surveillance squadron	6
	Total in Syria	**91**

Area	Units	Number of Aircraft
Indochina	4 reconnaissance groups	59
Madagascar	1 bomber squadron	10
	1 fighter squadron	13
		23
New Caledonia	1 reconnaissance squadron	7
Oceania (South Sea Islands)	1 reconnaissance squadron	7
French Antilles	1 reconnaissance squadron	7
Total		1,040

Source: Garello, Giancarlo: *Regia Aeronautica e Armée de l'Air 1940–1943,* Part 2 (Rome, 1975), p. 84

This was a considerable force, particularly as regards the fighter arm, which totalled 14 groups (of two squadrons each) and five independent squadrons. At first the French could equip only four groups – G.C. I/3, II/3, III/6 and II/7, and two squadrons of the Aéronavale (naval air arm) with the best fighter, the Dewoitine D.520.[9] Its prototype, the D-520-01, had first flown on 2 October 1938 at Toulouse-Francazals. On 8 February 1939 the second prototype, D-520-02, allegedly achieved no less than 825km/h (512mph) during a diving test. In April 1939 the French air ministry ordered 200 D.520 fighters, followed by another 400 in June 1939. Later additional orders raised the number to a total of 2,200 aircraft. The D.520 was powered by a Hispano-Suiza 12Y Y-45 engine, developing a take-off power of 910hp, had an armament of one 20mm HS-404 cannon firing through the propeller hub and two 7.5mm machine guns in the wings, and had a maximum speed of 535km/h (332mph). The first unit to receive the D.520 was G.C. I/3, and the pilots were enthusiastic about their new mount. During the Western campaign the D.520 proved to be about 30km/h (18.6mph) slower than the Bf 109E, but it was

224

considerably more manoeuvrable than the German Messerschmitt. Of the 350 confirmed aerial victories by the Armée de l'Air in May/June 1940, no fewer than 114 were reportedly achieved by the D.520. By 25 June 1940 a total of 437 D.520s had left the final assembly halls at Toulouse. Of these, 328 were still in service after the armistice – 153 in the unoccupied zone of France and 175 in north Africa. A German–French agreement signed in 1941 envisaged the production of another 550 D.520 fighters and as many as 349 were in fact completed until the German occupation of the remaining free French zone in November 1942. According to the plans of the French air force command, the D.520 was intended in time to replace the other fighters in service, the Curtiss H-75A, Bloch 152 and Morane MS.406. The programme envisaged the re-equipment of 17 fighter groups of the Armée de l'Air de l'Armistice with the D.520 by 1 June 1944, with another 37 going to the Aéronavale. With that, the French air force in 1944 would have had a fighter strength of 475 D.520s. This optimistic plan could not have foreseen that a Vichy air force would no longer exist by that time.

Even though the Axis powers allowed the French to retain an air force of 1,040 aircraft – all planes surplus to this number being dismantled and stored in depots – they also tried, by means of far-reaching injunctions and restrictions, to reduce the effectiveness of the Armée de l'Air, which, for its part, endeavoured to evade the controls. No formations larger than a group (two squadrons) were allowed, and the number of airfields was limited to 41 (five in France, 17 in North Africa, four in West Africa, eight in the Levant and five in Indochina). The pilots were not allowed to fly more than two training/instructional hours a week, and had to remain within 15km (9.3 miles) of their airfield. All lengthier flights required special permission from the occupying powers. Initially no flying schools were permitted to function at all, but this restriction was only temporary.

The French were never satisfied with what they had achieved and continually put in additional requests to increase the fighting power of their air force. Their efforts were not entirely in vain, and on 29 March 1941 the occupying powers granted more concessions: the total number of aircraft was increased to 1,071, and air force personnel strength was established at 38,354 men. From 1 July 1941 Vichy was also permitted to operate flying training schools. As far as civil aviation was concerned, the French had received permission already in August 1940 to operate 67 machines on airline services, with another 50 aircraft for airmail services with the colonies and 75 for communications with North Africa.[10]

The Armée de l'Air had increasingly to avail itself of the aircraft of Air France to supply the threatened distant territories. The British had imposed a complete naval blockade of French Somalia (Coté Française des Somalis), which had led to a famine in the country, and a shortage of medicines, so Vichy established an air bridge to the Red Sea. The Italians agreed to this, but insisted that the French would allow them to use Djibouti airfield in return. But there was no guarantee that their aircraft would be safe there: on 5 October 1941 the SM.75 I-LUNO fell victim to an attack on Djibouti by aircraft of No. 3 SAAF squadron.

From November 1940 to October 1942 the French carried out 17 supply flights to Somalia, 5,500km (3,415 miles) away.[11] For these they used a variety of aircraft types, such as the Amiot 356, Amiot 37, Laté 522 and Glenn Martin 167F. The Amiot 356 F-BAGP needed 17 hours for the trip. This air bridge enabled the Vichy-French to hold Djibouti for quite some time, the Somali coast not falling into Gaullist hands until 1 January 1943.

In the meantime other events had taken place that had considerably weakened the French Empire, and therefore also Vichy. In May 1941 the Germans had decided to help Iraq – which was striving for full independence and wanted to shake off British protection – and perform a 'heroic gesture' to that effect. Due to the distances involved, a prerequisite for this action was a measure of support from France, Syria being the only suitable intermediate landing place on the way from Greece to Iraq. In return for some more concessions, the French government agreed to supply arms to Iraq and allow German aircraft to land on some Syrian airfields. But the specially appointed 'Fliegerführer Irak' (Sonderkommando Junck/Special detachment Junck) had far too few aircraft at its disposal (some Bf 110s and He 111Hs from 2./ZG 26, 4./ZG 76 and 4./KG 4) to bring this operation to a successful conclusion.[12]

On 6 May 1941 the Armée de l'Air in the Near East received orders to allow flights over Lebanon and Syria by Axis aircraft, as well as transit landings in the French mandate region.[13] The British reaction was swift. A number of British aircraft attacked Palmyra on 14 May and destroyed two German aircraft parked on the airfield; other attacks on airfields in Damascus and Aleppo followed. The Vichy fighter strength in that area was very weak, comprising just 20 MS.406s of G.C. I/7, based at Rayak, and they hardly interfered in the action. Therefore the German Armistice commission granted permission to the French High Command to deploy G.C. II/6 from Algiers Maison-Blanche to the Levant. The French had to make all the arrangements, no logistical help being offered by the Luftwaffe.

Comparison of Forces in the Levant on 8 June 1941

Armée de l'Air de l'Armistice

Area	Units	Aircraft Strength
Rayak	G.C. III/6	25 D.520
	G.B. I/39	3 Martin 167F
	E.O. 592	6 Potez 25 TOE
Estabel	G.C. I/7	12 MS.406
Aleppo-Nerab	G.C. I/7	6 MS.406
	G.A.O. 583	5 Potez 63.11
	E.O. 593	6 Potez 25 TOE
Madjaloun	G.B. I/39	10 Martin 167F
	E.B. 3/39	6 Bloch MB.200
Damascus-	G.R. II/39	12 Potez 63.11
Mezzé	E.O. 594	6 Potez 25 TOE
Palmyra	E.O. 595	6 Potez 25 TOE
Deir Ez Zor	E.O. 596	6 Potez 25 TOE
Tripoli	Esc. 19 S	5 Loire 130

227

Royal Air Force

Area	Units	Aircraft Strength
Habbaniya	203 Sqn	4 Blenheim IV
Mossul	84 Sqn	3 Blenheim IV
Aqir	11 Sqn	12 Blenheim IV
	80 Sqn	2 Hurricane II
	208 Sqn	7 Hurricane II
Haifa	80 Sqn	6 Hurricane II
Jenin	3 RAAF Sqn	12 Tomahawk IIB
Lydda	252–272 Sqn	3 Beaufighter
	803 Sqn	6 Fulmar
Amman	X Flight	8 Gladiator
H-4	203 Sqn	2 Blenheim IV
	208 Sqn	2 Lysander
Cyprus	80 Sqn	4 Hurricane II
	815 Sqn, FAA	6 Swordfish
Gaza	208 Sqn	3 Hurricane I
		1 Lysander
Abukir	806 Sqn, FAA	6 Hurricane I

The British strength include aircraft based in Iraq, Palestine, Transjordania, on Cyprus and in Egypt intended for Operation Exporter.
Sources: Ehrengardt, Christian J./Shores, Christopher F., *L'Aviation de Vichy au combat, Vol. II: Le campagne de Syrie, 8 juin–14 juillet 1941* (Paris, 1987), p. 43. Also Shores, Christopher F., *Dust Clouds in the Middle East* (London, 1996), pp. 202, 206

That the Free French, who were prepared to side with the British to conquer Syria, still had their doubts, uncertainties and orientation difficulties is indicated by the fact that on 19 May a Gaullist pilot, Lt Labat, changed sides to join the Armée de l'Air de l'Armistice. On the same day the conflict escalated, when, for the first time, British Hurricane fighters attacked French aircraft at Damascus-Mezzé – the Potez 63.11s of a reconnaissance group based there, and some Potez 25 TOEs of E.O. 594.

On 28 May the expected French reinforcements arrived: 25 D.520s from G.C. III/6. The group had left Algeria on 24 May and transferred, via Tunisia–Catania–Brindisi–Athens–Rhodes, to Rayak.[14] Among the French fighter pilots was Lt Pierre Le Gloan, who had achieved 11 confirmed aerial victories during the fighting in France. He was to achieve another seven victories in Syria, but was killed in an accident while flying an Airacobra fighter on 11 September 1943.

On 28 May 1941 the Vichy-French reported their first aerial victory of the Syrian campaign: Lt Vuillemin of G.C. I/7 destroyed a British Bristol Blenheim IV from No. 211 Squadron at Nerab. Two days later the national uprising in Iraq had collapsed and Prime Minister Rashid Ali left the country. From then on the British were able to concentrate all their forces in the Levant.

At that time there were some voices in Vichy that supported a military alliance with the Reich, provided Berlin recognized France as a full partner. This political idea failed to advance much further, not only because of the deviousness of Hitler, but also because the majority in the Vichy cabinet wanted to avoid total confrontation with Britain.[15] When it came to the confrontation in the Levant, France had to face the British on its own.

When, on 8 June, the British and Free French troops of de Gaulle invaded Syria, the Allies had no numerical superiority either in the air or on the ground. The Syrian campaign was not going to be a walkover, that was clear from the outset. The Vichy-French fought back. On that day Lt Le Gloan of G.C. III/6 achieved his first aerial victory (his 12th altogether) when he shot down a Hurricane from No. 208 Squadron.

During the afternoon his fighter group managed to shoot down another three aircraft, Fairey Fulmars from No. 803 Fleet Air Arm Squadron, but by the evening G.C. III/6 itself had lost four D.520 fighters. The next day Le Gloan was once again successful, intercepting and shooting down two Hurricanes. On that day the French also tried to attack the British fleet and lost two obsolete Bloch 200 bombers from Escadrille 3/39 in the attempt. Altogether the French bombers flew 12 operational sorties that day, the fighters 23. On the ground, too, the French troops loyal to Marshal Petain put up a staunch resistance to the attackers. On 10 June the Armée de l'Air de l'Armistice received a welcome reinforcement in the form of nine LeO 451 bombers from G.B. I/31, which landed at Aleppo. Reinforcements also arrived on the British side, in the shape of No. 829 Fleet Air Arm squadron with six Fairey Albacores. The following day, 11 June, turned out to be a black day for the newly arrived G.B. I/31, which lost three LeO 451 bombers during a disastrous night landing at Damascus-Mezzé. A day later G.C. III/6 flew a total of 34 operational sorties, but for the time being had only 12 serviceable D.520 fighters. General Dentz, the French High Commissioner in the Levant, asked Vichy to request the use of German Stukas against the British fleet, but that was turned down on political grounds by the French government.

Additional reinforcements for the Vichy air force arrived on 13 June: nine LeO 451 bombers from G.B. I/12 from Istres, in southern France. An attack on the British fleet by G.B. I/31 on the following day did not result in any success. But the Vichy government were determined and the French received more reinforcements: G.B. I/25, with initially seven LeO 451 bombers, was transferred from Tunisia to Aleppo-Nerab.

After one week of extensive fighting, the French aerial superiority remained unchallenged. But the Air Levante made the mistake of not using it to the best advantage. Moreover, the French fighter pilots acted too individualistically and did not maintain formation in the air (as was also to happen in north Africa in November 1942). The net result of this was that the British lost only two aircraft during the second week of fighting as compared with nine French losses. These could be made good, however, by additional reinforcements: a total of 17 Dewoitine D.520s from G.C. II/3 and Flotille 4F of the Aéronavale.

On the other hand, the visit on 17 June by General Bergeret, the French secretary of State for Air, brought hardly anything positive. Quite the contrary, in fact, because his instructions to avoid losses at all costs could only have a negative effect on the morale of the Armée de l'Air de l'Armistice. Bergeret had sown doubts in the minds of his officers that their actions were really necessary, even if they fulfilled the wishes of their government.[16] It is of interest to add that, late in 1942, this defeatism-spreading General was to go over to the Allied side and, under their protection, become the Police Prefect of Algiers.

Bergeret's defensive instructions did not fail of their effect, because, on 19 and 20 June, when Damascus was seriously threatened by Allied troops, the Vichy air force noticeably held back. This lack of action had catastrophic results, for Damascus was captured on 21 June. The main ground fighting now moved in the direction of Palmyra, the ancient trading town in the Syrian desert.

The day that marked the beginning of the end of the Vichy position as a political power in the Near East was 23 June. The numerically inferior RAF now changed its tactics, and, instead of direct confrontation with the Armée de l'Air, began to attack the poorly defended French airfields. French reaction was slow, and they were unable to find any effective countermeasures against these attacks. They also made the mistake of attacking Allied troops near Palmyra with small, isolated groups of aircraft. Thus, on 25 June six LeO 451s (three from G.B. I/12 and three from G.B. I/31) were sent to attack targets in the Palmyra area without any fighter escort. All three planes from G.B. I/12 were intercepted by P-40 Tomahawks of No. 3 RAAF squadron and shot down. The Tomahawk IIB was not an exceptional aircraft, but the Australians of 3 RAAF squadron used it in masterly fashion. On 26 June their Tomahawks attacked and blew up an ammunition train in the Homs railway station. The explosion was so powerful that it destroyed three of G.C. II/3's D.520 fighters parked on the nearby airfield.

On that day nearly all French aircraft were concentrated on the Aleppo-Nerab airfield, an unfortunate circumstance because this airfield was situated too far away from the focal points of the fighting. This third week of fighting had cost the French dear: by 27 June they had lost 24 aircraft (not counting accidents), against only five British aircraft lost in combat. The greatest single tragedy for the Armée de l'Air occurred on 28 June when six Glenn Martin 167F bombers of Flotille 4F were ordered to attack targets in the Palmyra area, once again without any fighter escort. All six were shot out of the sky by Australian Tomahawk pilots within three minutes, and 20 French airmen died. It was a painful lesson, and from then on the French bombers flew only with a fighter escort. But by then the Vichy air force was already dwindling. By the evening of 30 June the

Armée de l'Air and Aéronavale together could only muster 53 operational aircraft, including 11 D.520 fighters. An air bridge to the motherland, for which the Vichy government also took 18 Dewoitine 538s of Air France, could not prevent the wasting away of French fighting power. On 2 July the hard-fighting defenders of the Palmyra oasis had to surrender owing to the shortages of ammunition and water.

The situation of the Vichy forces was now desperate. In another week of fighting to 3 July they had again lost 21 aircraft, the British only four. More reinforcements arrived on 4 July, three Morane MS.406 and five D.520s from the Armée de l'Air and 12 D.520s from Escadrille 1AC, as well as six Laté 298s from Escadrille 1T of the Aéronavale. They came too late. On 7 July the Australians were just 7km (4 miles) from Beirut, and Vichy authorized General Dentz to arrange an armistice with the Allies. Before that the French air force gathered up its remaining strength and a total of 14 LeO 451 bombers, covered by 12 D.520s, took off to attack the British ships and Allied troop concentrations at Damour. On 8 July all formations of the Armée de l'Air de l'Armistice received an order to transfer to Athens in Greece. The official reason – that the squadrons would be re-equipped there with new material for fighting in the Lebanon – was rightly regarded by the aircrews as a mere pretext. As if to give the lie to this order, three completely obsolete LeO H.257 biplanes from Escadrille 1E arrived in the Syrian combat zone the same day. All three veterans were finished off by Australians from Nos. 250/450 Squadrons within one hour of their arrival at Aleppo.

The exodus of Vichy-French aircraft from Syria began on the morning of 9 July. The first to leave were the 14 remaining D.520 fighters of G.C. III/6. On 10 July another large aerial combat took place when D.520s from Escadrille AC intercepted 12 Bristol Blenheim bombers from No. 14 RAF Squadron, escorted by seven Tomahawks from 3 RAAF Squadron between Beirut and Zahle. The Allies lost three bombers and the French two D.520s in this final aerial clash. The armistice between Vichy and the Allies came into force at 00.01 hours on 12 July 1941. Nonetheless, on the morning of the armistice day,

MS.406s from G.C. I/7 made an attack on Allied motor vehicles north of Raqqa! That evening most of the serviceable Vichy aircraft were in the Axis-occupied Greece, later to continue their way to North Africa and France.

The losses of the Vichy-French air force in the Levant amounted to 77 dead, 24 POWs and 11 wounded flying personnel. Of the total of 273 aircraft operating there, which had flown 3,090 operational sorties, 169 had been lost.[17] These losses were painful enough, and still more machines were written off on the flight to the Lebanon or on the way out from Syria. The British losses totalled just 41 aircraft.

As the captured Vichy troops were officially members of a 'neutral' country they had the alternative of either repatriation or joining the Gaullist forces. Only 5,331 soldiers decided to fight for de Gaulle; 33,000 men returned home to France. In 1945 General Dentz, who had so faithfully carried out all orders of the Vichy government, was sentenced to death by a Parisian court, degraded, and his financial means and property confiscated. De Gaulle reduced this sentence to life imprisonment, and General Dentz died in Fresnes prison hospital.[18]

Allied attacks on the French Empire continued after the Syrian campaign. Before that, the Armée de l'Air could claim for itself another success – this time at the conference table. In September 1941 the occupying powers had made some more concessions, among them being the agreement to form a new transport squadron at Oujja, in Morocco, equipped with 20 Amiot 143 aircraft. At the end of September 1941 the total of all military and civil aircraft controlled by Vichy France reached the quite considerable figure of 1,611 machines.[19]

There was a shortage of aircraft in the French colonies, however. In Madagascar[20] a Groupe Aérien Mixte (GAM) was organized in February 1942. It was made up of two squadrons: Escadrille 565, with 18 Morane MS.406 fighters, and Escadrille 555, with obsolete Potez 25TOEs and six of the more modern Potez 63.11s. The French garrison on the island consisted of 9,500 men. Against this small force the Allies prepared a major concentration of forces for Operation *Ironclad*. The British invasion fleet that assembled in the Indian ocean consisted of 34 vessels: one cruiser, four destroyers, six corvettes, six mine sweepers, seven landing ships, four transports and one tanker, protected by an escorting group made up of one battleship, two aircraft carriers, one cruiser and seven destroyers. Aboard the aircraft carrier *Illustrious* were four squadrons with 41 aircraft, and on the *Indomitable* another five squadrons with 45 aircraft. This effort was reinforced by SAAF formations operating from the mainland.

The landing operation began on the night of 5 May 1942. The French GAM suffered heavy losses right at the beginning: five MS.406 fighters were destroyed and two others damaged during an air strike on the Arrachart airfield. Within the next three days a total of 12 Moranes and four or five Potez 63.11s were lost, and the capital, Diego Suarez, capitulated on 7 May. But the French had no intention of surrendering the whole island, and withdrew inland. It was only in September that the Allies renewed their efforts to capture the island. What was left of the GAM could hardly join the action now, having no spares or other supplies. After an air raid on the Ihosy airfield, where the remainder of the GAM had withdrawn, virtually the entire Vichy air force on the island consisted of one MS.406 fighter, No.815. On 6 November 1942 the French had to surrender and Vichy had again lost a part of its colonial empire.

The État Français under Marshal Petain also had to swallow defeats and humiliations in the Far East. French Indochina, with an area of 740,400sq. km (285,868sq. miles) and a population of 25.3 million, was now under Japanese control. The Armée de l'Air had 100 aircraft in Indochina, although most of them were quite obsolete. In detail, the Vichy air force there consisted of the following formations:[21]

Unit	Aircraft Type	Base
E.R. 1/41	Potez 25TOE	Pursat/Cambodia
E.B. 2/41	Farman 221	Ton/Tonkin
E.R. 1/42	Potez 25TOE	Pursat
E.B. 2/42	Potez 542	Tan Son Nuut/Cochinchina
E.O. 1/595	Potez 25TOE	Dong Hoi/Annam
E.C. 2/595	MS.406	Bach Mai/Tonkin
E.O. 1/596	Potez 25TOE	Tourane/Annam

In addition there were 20 seaplanes. After the French defeat in Europe the colony came under the sphere of influence of the expanding Japanese Empire. At the end of September 1940 the French Governor-General, Admiral Decoux, had to sign an agreement that allowed the Japanese to use the port of Tonkin and the territory of Indochina as an assembly area for their troops. In return the Japanese Empire 'guaranteed' the sovereignty of Indochina. But the substance of this sovereignty came into question before this agreement was even signed, when, on 22 September, the Japanese invaded the French colony to emphasize their demands. During the four-day battle the French lost two Potez 25TOE aircraft. On 26 September Sgt Labussière managed to shoot down a Japanese Ki.48 bomber, but this aerial victory was not recognized by his superiors 'for political reasons'.

In October 1940 the French fighter force in the Far East received welcome reinforcement. Seven MS.406s, which had really been intended for China, were discovered in crates in the port of Haiphong and assembled, forming a new unit, 2/596. In the same month the French High Command transferred 33 aircraft to Laos and Cambodia because the Siamese Kingdom (modern Thailand) wanted to exploit the French weakness and demanded territorial concessions. The Vichy-French air force had two units in Laos, E.O. 1/596 and E.C. 2/596. Beginning on 23 November 1940, aerial encounters took place between the French and the Siamese, who were equipped with Japanese and American aircraft, and both sides suffered losses during the following weeks.

On 8 December a French MS.406 shot down a Siamese Corsair, and on 10 January 1941 Sgt Tivollier achieved two aerial victories over Siamese-flown Japanese Ki.30s. On 15 January Siamese aircraft managed to carry out an attack on the French airfield at Dong Hene and destroy two Moranes and two Potez 25TOE on the ground. If the aircraft losses were more or less equal, the strength of the French air force was continually weakening while the Siamese were regularly supplied by their new Japanese allies. Some relief to the French was brought by the clear victory of their Indochina naval command formation over the Siamese fleet on 17 January 1941, when three Siamese ships were sunk. Despite this the French had to sign a peace treaty in Tokyo on 11 March 1941, which brought the Siamese some territorial gains. The air force of the French colonial empire had now shrunk to 63 operational machines, including 14 MS.406 fighters and 34 Potez 25TOEs. The decline of the Armée de l'Air in south-east Asia was accelerated by shortages of materials and spare parts, and the desertion of various pilots to the Allies. One visible result of this had been the disbandment of 2/596 fighter squadron in mid-1941.

Responding to force of circumstances the Vichy authorities now moved closer to Japan. This collaboration by Admiral Decoux protected some 40,000 French colonial civilians from Japanese camps. But the French did not give in to all Japanese demands, such as the request that the pilots of the Armée de l'Air should support the Japanese air force in the defence against Allied air attacks. The operational strength of the Vichy air force in that area sank at an alarming rate. Another blow came on 27 January 1942, when the Japanese shot down two MS.406 fighters from E.C. 2/595 in error, mistaking them for American aircraft. This led to the disbandment, in summer 1942, of the last remaining French fighter squadron, 2/595. When the Japanese finally stepped in to disarm the French colonial forces, on 9 March 1945, they found only a handful of French aircraft.

The curtain for the final act of the tragedy of the Vichy air force was already raised in autumn of 1942, in North Africa.

The Allied attack on the French North Africa in November 1942 was backed by enormous material superiority. For this invasion the Anglo-Americans had concentrated 300 warships and 370 other vessels, carrying the 63,000-man landing force. Nevertheless, the Vichy armed forces, particularly the navy, tried at least to hinder this landing operation. The French naval forces were supported by many – but not all – Armée de l'Air squadrons, which attacked the invaders.[22] In highly disciplined fashion they followed the orders of their government. Moreover, there was no doubt that many of them were anti-British in the aftermath of the British attacks on the French fleet at Mers-el-Kebir and Dakar, and the invasion of Syria and Madagascar. The Allies were very much aware of this Vichy-French anglophobia and tried to counter it; for example, the British 'camouflaged' their aircraft as American machines. But these measures proved to be of little help.

On 8 November, as part of Operation *Torch*, the Americans attacked French North Africa in three places[23] – Casablanca, Oran and Algiers. At this time 47 D.520 fighters from G.C. II/3 and G.C. III/6 as well as six Potez 63.11s were parked on the Maison Blanche airfield at Algiers. Thick fog prevented their take-off, and American troops managed to capture Maison Blanche at 10.00hrs that morning. There were just 13 Potez 63.11s on the other airfield in the Algiers region, Sétif, which for the time being was to remain untouched by Allied attack.

Fighting in the Oran region took quite a different turn. Although the Americans managed to overrun the seaplane base at Arzew, where the French kept 13 Latécoère 298 torpedo-bombers belonging to Flotille 5F, the pilots of G.C. III/3 based at Oran and commanded by Commandant (Major) Engler were far from ready to surrender. They had 26 D.520 fighters and the will to use them. Seven D.520s took-off from Oran at 07.20hrs, and within a short period of time had shot down three Fairey Albacore biplanes from No. 822 FAA squadron; another three Albacores had to make forced landings and their crews were captured. In a counter-action, Sea Hurricanes from No. 800 FAA squadron, based on the British aircraft carrier *Biter*, intercepted and shot down three D.520s. The fighting swayed back and forth the whole day, though the LeO 451 bombers of G.B. I/11 were held back and did not attack the invasion fleet.

The D.520s from G.C. III/3 were more aggressive than ever. Commandant Engler, who had described the operations of his unit as *le dernier baroud d'honneur* (the last offering of honour) of the French fighter arm, was killed during an attack on the Tafaraoui airfield, which was already occupied by British Spitfires. His fighters got their own back among the Dakotas of the 60th Troop Carrier formation, carrying American paratroopers. On the evening of 8 November only 20 of the 39 C-47s of that unit were still serviceable. At this stage G.C. III/3 had just nine operational D.520s left and had to record the loss of three dead and two wounded pilots. On the credit side the French unit could claim 17 confirmed and seven unconfirmed aerial victories. The most successful French pilots that day were 1st Lt Blanck with five, and Corporal Poupart with four victories. On 9 November the French resistance in the air collapsed. Admiral Darlan issued an order to cease fire, which was promptly countermanded by the Vichy government, but the French troops in North Africa obeyed their Admiral.

There were seven French airfields in the Casablanca landing zone, with 200 Armée de l'Air and Aéronavale aircraft, including 40 D.520 fighters. The fighting there began with a great victory for the Allies. During an air attack on the Rabat-Salé airfield they destroyed 32 French aircraft on the ground, among them nine LeO 451 bombers from G.R. I/22 and 16 Potez 29s from G.T. I/15. It was a real massacre. A group of 20 aged Curtiss H-75 fighters from G.C. II/5 took off from Casablanca and attacked the American F4F Wildcats from the carrier *Ranger*. The French had to pay a high price for their seven confirmed and three unconfirmed victories: 13 Curtiss H-75s were lost, including two destroyed on the ground. Five G.C. II/5 pilots were killed and four wounded.

In the Port-Lyautey sector the D.520s from Flotille 1F and Glenn Martin 167F bombers from Flotille 3F joined the battle. However, American F4F Wildcats from VGF-26 squadron, based on the carrier *Sangamon*, surprised the French as they were taking off and wreaked havoc. Within two hours Flotille 1F of the Aéronavale had lost 11 D.520 fighters. But the French did not give up. At midday on 8 November ten LeO 451 bombers from G.B. II/23, based at Meknès, and two Douglas DB-7s from G.B. I/32, escorted by nine Curtiss H-75s from G.C. I/5 and II/5, attacked the invading Allied troops along the beach of Fédala.

All these operations reduced the aircraft inventory of the Armée de l'Air and Aéronavale in Morocco. On the morning of 9 November Flotille 1F at Port-Lyautey had only nine of its original 26 D.520 fighters left, while the strength of G.C. I/5 at Rabat had shrunk from 26 to 16 Curtiss H-75As. Nevertheless, at 07.30hrs a force of 30 French aircraft again attacked the Allied landing zones.

In the ensuing aerial combat G.C. I/5 lost four Curtiss H-75A fighters. Numerous other French aircraft were destroyed on the ground. At dawn the following morning, 10 November, only 90 of the original 200 French aircraft in the Casablanca region were still operational. The Allies now had an unlimited aerial superiority.

The fighting ceased on 11 November 1942. In three days the Vichy-French had lost 44 pilots killed and ten wounded, a high score by any reckoning. The French airmen had repeatedly displayed bitter resistance, but 30 months of inactivity, together with stagnation in the development of air combat tactics had placed them at a distinct disadvantage, particularly so since much of their aircraft material had become dated. The end for the Armée de l'Air de l'Armistice came on 11 November 1942, when the German Wehrmacht occupied the previously free zone of France. Only three days before that it had seemed that the pressure of circumstances might lead to a German–Italian–French alliance, but events had overtaken all such considerations. The air forces of the État Français were officially disbanded on 27 November 1942. The Germans and the Italians now began taking possession of the French air arm's equipment, the actual quantity of which went unrecorded. Be that as it may, by the end of 1942 the Germans had already listed 1,876 French aircraft by model.[24] In addition at least 500 French aircraft had fallen into Italian hands. Much of the Vichy-French aircraft park was no longer suitable for modern aerial warfare, but there were some exceptions. One of these was the LeO 451, which, no longer considered adequate as a bomber, was suitable for conversion to a high-speed transport. Another was the Dewoitine D.520 fighter. The German forces confiscated 246 D.520s, while another 169 were still under construction at the Toulouse works.[25] The D.520 was later used operationally as a fighter against the Americans both by the Italians and the Bulgarians. In the German Luftwaffe the D.520 found use as a fighter trainer, mainly with JG 101, 103 and 105.

Unfortunately this elegant fighter also cost the lives of quite a few German trainee pilots because, like all French and Italian aircraft, it differed from the German models in one decisive point: the way the throttle lever worked.

Independently of the aircraft thus captured the German Luftwaffe had in fact been a purchaser of French planes in preceding years. On 28 July 1941 the German and French authorities had signed an agreement concerning the production of aircraft by the French aviation industry ('Programme áero-nautique commun franco-allemand'), which had a timespan of 24 months and a value of 15 milliard francs. According to this, 30 per cent of the produced aircraft would go to the French, the remainder to the German Luftwaffe.[26] Under this agreement the French achieved some modernization of their air force, a reduction of the enormous unemployment problem – the number of people employed in the French aviation industry rose from 34,000 workers in mid-1941 to 95,000 in March 1944 – and prevented the dismantling of the factories and their transfer to the Reich. After the total occupation of France the French aviation industry worked exclusively for the occupying powers. When it came to transport aircraft, French aircraft production was a decisive factor for the Luftwaffe as shown by the following statistics:

The French Industry Share in the Production of Transport Aircraft for Germany[27]

1st half 1942	5.2 per cent
2nd half 1942	27.0 per cent
1943	47.0 per cent
1st half 1944	49.0 per cent

Altogether, from 1941 to 1944, the French aviation industry delivered a total of 11,219 aero engines and 3,606 aircraft to the Reich (see Appendix 2). For their own use, the French aviation industry produced 1,237 aero engines and 536 aircraft up to the end of 1942.

III
Foreign Flying Personnel
in the German Luftwaffe

Introduction

During the early stages of the war the German National Socialist leadership had a most negative attitude towards the use of foreigners in the German armed forces.[1] Initially an exception was made for the 'Germanic' volunteers, who were assigned to the national legions of the Waffen-SS. These foreigners of good racial background, from the Netherlands, Flanders and Scandinavia, were supposed to be the pioneers for the planned Greater German Reich. As far as the other foreign nationals were concerned, Berlin was torn; on the one hand it believed it could do without them, and on the other it did not want to take the risk that the subjugated countries might later make demands on the Reich on the grounds that many of their nationals had fought in German formations, or rejected the use of foreigners because from the racial point of view they did not fit in with the National Socialist concept.

With the expansion of the war and resultant increased personnel requirements, the National Socialist dogma of the Germans as the only people fit to bear arms was undermined from without by events. By 1941 there were Croats, Spaniards, French and Belgian Walloons serving in the German armed forces.

However, the basic ideological reservations and prejudices of Hitler and other leading personalities of the Third Reich did not change in the least. In a speech made on 7 November 1943 the Chief of the Operations Staff of the German armed forces (Wehrmachts Führungsstab), Generaloberst Jodl, expressed an even more emphatic warning: 'But the drawing upon foreign nationals as fighting soldiers must be viewed with great caution and scepticism.'[2] By then the recruitment of foreigners for the German armed forces had already long since developed its own momentum.

Ultimately Russians, Ukrainians, Indians, Tunisians, Vietnamese, Serbs, Icelanders and many other foreign nationals were fighting for a cause that had mostly nothing to do with them and was already lost in any case. Most of these foreigners served in the Waffen-SS or the Wehrmacht, but the Kriegsmarine (navy), too, had non-Germanic personnel. The Luftwaffe, however, held back from recruiting foreigners, at least insofar as flying personnel were concerned, but the AA units and the various ground elements made widespread use of them. The reason for this was quite simple: the foreigners were mistrusted, and the Luftwaffe command did not want to entrust them with aircraft with which they could, without great difficulty, abscond to the enemy or to neutral countries.

Other countries did not make it so difficult for foreign nationals to join their air forces. During the Spanish Civil War of 1936–9 foreign airmen served both on the Republican and Nationalist sides. The Frenchman André Malroux organized the international Escuadrilla España for the Madrid government, the pilots of which were either idealists or mercenaries. Foreign pilots are also known to have served on the Nationalist side, mainly Portuguese. At least 20 Portuguese airmen fought as members of the Franco air force;[3] five of them were officers from the Portuguese military mission, Missão Militar de Observação, and flew as air gunners on the Ju 52/3m and the Italian SM.79 bombers. In the Finnish–Russian Winter War of 1939–40 about 200 foreigners volunteered for the Finnish Suomen Ilmavoimat, and the Swedish-crewed F19 volunteer squadron gave valuable service in that conflict. During the Second World War the RAF readily accepted the services of foreign personnel and eventually had Czech, Polish, Norwegian, Belgian, Dutch, French, Yugoslav and Greek squadrons. Even Stalin allowed the formation of the French fighter regiment 'Normandie-Niemen', a Czech fighter regiment and a Latvian night bomber regiment within the Soviet air force.

In the event, the German Luftwaffe, too, gave up its categorical refusal to accept foreign airmen, but never carried out an active recruitment campaign to win over non-German pilots. But they came forward just the same, and by 1943–4 several hundred foreign flying personnel were in Luftwaffe service. These airmen came from right across Europe – there were flying personnel from Alsace-Lorraine, Spaniards, Italians, Russians, Croats, Danes, Norwegians, Czechs, Estonians, Latvians,

Dutch and Belgians. There was even a South American among them. A Brazilian of German origin, Egon Albrecht was born on 19 May 1918 at Curitiba, Parana, emigrated to Germany and later began his Luftwaffe career with ZG 1, taking over command of III./ZG 1 in October 1943. Decorated with the Knight's Cross of the Iron Cross, Albrecht was killed in action over France on 25 August 1944 as commander of III./ZG 76.[4]

There were also cases where the pragmatism of front-line units simply swept aside the racial policies of National Socialist dogma. For example, there was the Dutch Feldwebel Wilhelm Eduard de Graaf of I./KG 200, who before the war had served with the KLM airline.[5] His mother was Indonesian and he was scarcely an example of the ideal of the 'Germanic warrior'. Or there was the German JG 77 that operated in North Africa from October 1942 to May 1943. This well-known fighter formation had few scruples about distancing itself from the National Socialist racial delusions: a number of former South African POWs, whose skin colour was far from white, served as members of its ground personnel. And there were others.

The reasons the Luftwaffe command started admitting foreigners to the flying personnel were various. Some were classed as Germans (such as volunteers from Alsace and Lorraine); others were allies or ideologically trustworthy, such as Croats and Spaniards. Then there were isolated cases where a fundamental exception was made, as in the case of Danes, whose country was not at war with Germany. Others, such as the Estonians, had formed their flying units practically on their own initiative, were flying for the Kriegsmarine, and proved indispensable for naval reconnaissance. Entirely national units, such as were organized by the Wehrmacht and the Waffen-SS, were formed only to a limited extent in the Luftwaffe. Two examples were the Estonian and Latvian formations, which were disbanded in October 1944, although their fighter pilots remained operational with different German Luftwaffe units. Then there were the Spaniards and the Croats who served with their squadrons in German Luftwaffe formations, and, following the episode with the Russian 'Ostfliegerstaffel' (Eastern Squadron), the national Russian airmen of General

Vlassov. There was also a proposal for a Danish fighter squadron, the formation of which was quite within the realms of possibility, but it came to nothing.

Otherwise the foreigners were distributed to various Geschwader, Gruppen and Staffeln, and individual aircrews of the Luftwaffe. Assigning individual foreigners to a German bomber crew – as often happened with Belgian volunteers from Eupen-Malmedy – also guaranteed the best possible control in service. But the reluctance to form additional nationally homogenous foreign units also had its negative side because it meant forgoing the chance to use these units for propaganda purposes to win over new volunteers.

Nevertheless, due to the large number of foreign personnel in its ranks, the Luftwaffe High Command found it necessary to establish a special department, and the post of General for Foreign Personnel was established in May 1944.[6] He was responsible for the treatment and control of all foreigners within the Luftwaffe without differentiating between volunteers, deserters, auxiliaries, soldiers of allied countries or POWs who were serving in the Luftwaffe. Further, it was the responsibility of the General for Foreign Personnel to intercede on their behalf with other command headquarters and duty stations as necessary. This post was initially held by Generalleutnant Grosch, and then General der Flieger Julius Schulz. The interests of the 'Eastern personnel' of the Luftwaffe (Russians, Ukrainians, Caucasians and so on) were looked after by a specially created post of Inspector for Foreign Personnel (Inspizient für ausländisches Personal), held by Generalleutnant Heinrich Aschenbrenner. From December 1944 onwards this post was directly subordinated to the Chief of the General Staff of the Luftwaffe and renamed Inspekteur für ostvölkisches Personal der Luftwaffe (Inspector for Eastern Personnel of the Luftwaffe). General Aschenbrenner was especially concerned with building up the air forces of the National Russian armed forces led by General Vlassov.

The reasons why foreigners joined the Luftwaffe of Hermann Göring were equally varied. The aggressive anti-Bolshevik stance virulent among the Estonians, Latvians and Spaniards would not have been the governing factor for, say, a professional Danish officer, who, with the permission of his government, chose to serve under a foreign flag. It is likely that he saw this as an opportunity to gain additional qualifications with modern aircraft; perhaps a chance to serve his country in the future under the National Socialist 'New Order' that would follow the German victory. The treatment and status of the occupied countries under such a 'New Order' would have to take into account the participation of citizens from the individual countries in active fighting on the National Socialist side.

Others, again, answered emotive calls of German propaganda that, with the gradually worsening military situation, constantly called for European solidarity against Soviet savagery, presenting the battle for the German Reich as a struggle for Europe.

Finally there were the young men from Alsace, Lorraine, Estonia and Latvia who were under threat of forced mobilization – at least into the Waffen-SS – and for whom volunteering to join the Luftwaffe offered a possibility of avoiding the trenches of the Eastern Front and better chance to survive the conflict. True enough, the longer the war, the higher the losses of the Luftwaffe. By mid-1944, 50 per cent of fighter pilots were shot down before their tenth operational sortie.[7] Training times, too, were continually shortened, being reduced for pilots from 210 flying hours in 1942 to just 160 in 1944. Nonetheless, the Luftwaffe still needed many months to train its aircrews to fully operational standard, and, furthermore, was known to be less 'Prussian' than other branches of the German armed forces. Another favourable point was that the Luftwaffe looked after its personnel better from the point of view of provisions and supplies. For a young man from the Baltic states or from areas annexed to the German Reich – who was under obligation to serve in the German armed forces in any case – these were grounds that would give him a marked preference for the Luftwaffe.

The totalitarian system that had gathered them in gave them no way of avoiding military service – save that of desertion – but individuals did have a chance to choose the 'lesser evil' of the

Luftwaffe. There were also some foreign members of the Waffen-SS who, by 1944, had come to realise that the war was lost and that they were hopelessly compromised, but as there was no chance to quit the military service they could at least try to get a transfer to the Luftwaffe.

So, as far as the motivation of the foreign members of he Luftwaffe flying personnel was concerned, there was no uniform scheme or pattern. Idealism, patriotism, political conviction, love of adventure and the wish to improve professionally or advance a personal flying career, could have led to the Luftwaffe, just as much as an attempt to evade enforced active military service or the horrors of the Eastern Front as long as possible.

Norwegians

The headstrong Norwegian Vidkun Quisling, who functioned as a powerless Prime Minister under German control from 1 February 1942, held a political creed from which he did not deviate throughout the war years. He demanded untiringly that Hitler create a 'Germanic Commonwealth', an alliance of countries in which a separate and autonomous Norway would play a privileged role. According to Quisling's conception, this independent Norway would also have its own armed forces. These ideas were detailed already in his memorandum of 25 October 1940, in which Quisling proposed a national Norwegian army, as well as a joint 'Greater Nordic' navy and an air force.[1] The draft of a preliminary peace treaty that Quisling submitted to Hitler during a visit on 13 February 1942 also envisaged 'a joint Germanic navy and air force, but an independent Norwegian army'.[2] However, all these proposals and visions by Quisling fell on deaf ears in Berlin.[3] Quisling's youth organization, Hirdens Flykorpset, was allowed to train with gliders, but never evolved even to the preliminary stage of a 'Nordic' air force.

While the Waffen-SS, the NSKK (National Socialist Motor Corps) and the German navy all smothered the country with large recruiting posters to attract volunteers,[4] the Luftwaffe held itself aloof from such activities in Norway. For all that, some Norwegians succeeded in joining the Luftwaffe on their own initiative. Their number was likely to have been small, probably no more than 75 men,[5] of which only a few got so far as to become aircrew. It is doubtful if the few Norwegian members of the Luftwaffe were even noted separately by the Third Reich bureaucracy. A working report by the Higher SS and Police Commander 'Nord', dated 30 September 1944,[6] lists the numbers of Norwegians in the Waffen-SS, the Germanic SS, the Navy and with the German Red Cross, but does not mention anything about the Luftwaffe.

The reverse was true on the Allied side, where the Norwegians had the opportunity to form their own units. In May 1945 the Norwegians manned Nos 331 and 332 Fighter

Squadrons of the RAF with a total of 2,582 personnel (although this included some Danes). Another 1,600 Norwegians served in other RAF units.[7]

Among the few Norwegians who found their way to the German Luftwaffe was Harald Hougen. Born on 3 May 1922, he passed his school leaving examination in 1941 and wanted to qualify as a mechanical engineer. He did the practical work necessary for this degree at the Weserhütte works in Bad Oeynhausen and matriculated at Munich University, where almost 100 other Norwegians were studying at that time. In late autumn 1942 Hougen began to worry about the military situation. He feared the Soviet Union and hoped the Western powers would limit their armament and supply deliveries to Russia to give Europe a chance to build a dam against Communism. This distinct anti-Bolshevism was a sign of the times and was by no means limited only to the middle class and the Norwegians. The Belgian André Leysen, who wanted to volunteer for fighting on the Eastern Front in 1944, has this to say: 'To us Communism was the arch-enemy. In our youthful idealism, Germany represented a bastion against such a movement ... I recall that the victory of the 'Godless Bolshevism' seemed to me so dreadful my powers of imagination refused even to consider such a possibility.'[8]

Late in 1942, while considering his choice between continuing his studies or enlisting on behalf of the occupying power, Hougen made up his mind to join the German armed forces. Decisive factors in this move were both his political conviction and his wish to make an active contribution to the defence of Europe, which he regarded as being in danger.[9] At this time the German 6th Army was fighting for its survival in the 'cauldron' at Stalingrad. Still, it must be added that Hougen's idealism was paired with a love of adventure. On 1 January 1943 he reported as a volunteer at the German District Command in the Akershus Fortess in Oslo. When the 20-year-old told the duty officer he was induced to join up because of the worsening prospects of the Reich in the war the reception there was quite cool. After a thorough medical examination Hougen elected to join the Luftwaffe.

He received his basic training in a former French barracks near the Maginot Line. The training company consisted of about 120 volunteers from a wide selection of countries, including representatives from South America, Russia, Scandinavia – among them four or five Norwegians – France and the Netherlands. On reflection, Hougen describes the training as a 'hard time with arduous duties, little to eat and much swearing'.[10] But there were no physical assaults by the German cadre personnel, just shouting. The extremely hard drill and frequent punishment exercises to the state of complete exhaustion led some recruits to break down in tears.

After the completion of this basic training the young Norwegian received orders to report to an air gunnery and aircraft mechanics training school 30km (19 miles) west of Danzig. He was to be trained as an air gunner, and underwent an intensive six-week course of theoretical and practical instruction. As the participants of this training course who did not manage to pass the final tests were transferred to the Luftwaffe ground personnel, some fellow trainees saw this as a good way of avoiding the dangers of aerial warfare. Hougen did not take this route and successfully completed the training course. He was then posted to Aalborg in Denmark, where there was a transport detachment of the Luftwaffe; it was also the base of VI./KG 30, the 'Adler-Geschwader'. Hougen recalls: The unit, KG 30, was a dive bomber formation and known for its operations particularly against shipping targets. To be posted there was looked upon as a death sentence. And that is where I was sent.'[11] The Geschwader had made a name for itself by its attacks against the Allied Russian convoys PQ 16, 17 and 18. If an aircraft happened to crash in the icy sea the crew had hardly any chance of surviving.

However, Hougen saw being a member of this formation as a mark of distinction, because 'foreigners were seldom allowed to join the flying crews, but an exception was made in my case because I was a Norwegian and an academic.'[12] After another medical examination Hougen underwent 'private training' as an observer with the aircrew of a training course instructor. The normal training period of three to five months was considerably condensed. The period of the practical navigation training flights by day and by night, radio navigation and handling of the Ju 88 during bombing in horizontal and diving attacks remain as 'thrilling and exciting weeks' in Hougen's memory. Only the first dive was a fiasco: 'On that first dive, I completely lost my self-control. The unusual position – I was hanging on my harness straps – the engine noise and the howling airflow, the wild dive at about 200m/sec (650ft/sec), and the fear that everything might break up, really scared me.'[13] But after a few more training flights it all became a matter of routine. During these tests the Ju 88 always carried two 250kg (550lb) concrete bombs under each wing. The diving attacks would start from about 3,500m (11,480ft) altitude and the crew had about 15 seconds to drop the bombs before pulling out of the dive. 'The centrifugal force was so strong that we could not move our heads, and the lower jaw dropped so much and became so feeble that it looked like the lower lip of a boxer dog.'[14] Hougen made his first operational flight from Oldenburg in late autumn 1943. It was a raid on London docks. This nocturnal attack went according to plan, but the massing of bombers in the air brought greater problems with it than the British AA fire or night fighters. The formation was flying so close together that the young Norwegian observer dreaded a collision. 'The only thing that one could see was a faint glow from the exhaust pipes of the aircraft in front and the luminous instruments of aircraft flying close to our flanks. Occasionally there was also a slight vibration when one got too close to another aircraft, only there was nothing one could do about it, just take note of it.'[15]

After some more operations over England and an operational sortie over Italy between, when Hougen's Ju 88 was hit and the crew had to take to their parachutes, his formation was transferred to Munich at short notice in March 1944. On 19 March the Germans began their Operation *Margarethe* – the occupation of Hungary. In a period of frenetic activity Hougen's Ju 88 was loaded with bombs. These were then unloaded and replaced by leaflet containers, which, in turn, were removed and replaced by bombs once more. This performance was repeated several times, but the tension eased when it became clear that Hungary would not offer any resistance to the German forces.

A few weeks before the Allied invasion of France Hougen took off with his pilot Hans Hutz from an airfield near Orleans for a night bombing raid on Bristol. The aircraft carried a load of incendiaries and was difficult to fly. Near Cherbourg the overloaded Ju 88 was attacked by a night fighter and went into a spin. The crew jettisoned the cockpit roof for an emergency exit and fought for survival; despite the strong slipstream Hougen managed to guide the aircraft to a safe landing at an airfield near Paris. At the end of May Hougen took off from Orleans with 12 other crews, and his Ju 88 carried out two diving attacks with armour-piercing bombs on shipping targets at Portsmouth. Such pin-pricks did not hold up the invasion fleet, and, on 6 June, the Allies landed in northern France.

In fighting against the invasion forces, the strength of the 'Adler-Geschwader' soon melted away, and Hougen's group (III./KG 30) had to be withdrawn from the front. 'After the heavy losses in northern France, our group was almost dissolved. Only a few crews had survived and the aircraft park was almost completely destroyed.'[16] In July III./KG 30 had to be disbanded, and Hougen's crew was posted to Nordhausen in Oldenburg, where they were supposed to make operational aircrews out of recruits in record time.

In autumn came another transfer, this time to a base near Prague 'for special operations'. Harald Hougen was given the exacting task of being an instructor for the 'Beethoven-airmen'. That was the cover name for the pilots who would fly the upper component of the 'Mistel' (Mistletoe) combination, a Bf 109 or a Fw 190 perched atop a structure attached to an unmanned Ju 88 carrying a large explosive charge. The pilot controlling this contraption would approach the target in 'pick-a-back' fashion, detach himself by explosive charges from the unmanned explosive carrier before reaching the target and fly home after setting the autopilot in the unmanned bomber that would guide it towards its target in the final dive. For these 'Mistel' sorties, I and II./KG 30 were operationally subordinated to KG 200, the secretive 'special task' formation of the Luftwaffe. These flights 'in a yoke' were quite risky: 'Controlling this contraption in flight was extremely difficult and at times barely possible, and for that reason only very experienced pilots were selected for this task.'[17] Accidents with loss of aircrew and machines were the order of the day. Despite this, the instructors managed to train a large number of pilots to fly the 'pick-a-back' planes, although the planned attack on Soviet power stations in the Moscow area and beyond the Ural mountains could no longer be realized.[18]

In spring 1945 Hougen was posted to an airfield north of Berlin. There he had an understanding commanding officer who issued him with marching orders to join the Norwegian SS-Ski Fusilier battalion in Norway just before the major Soviet offensive that broke through the Oder front. In this way Hougen arrived in Oslo on 6 May 1945. But after the German capitulation the attitude of Hougen's own people towards him and his family became understandably hostile. Harald Hougen tried to avoid being arrested at home as a 'dangerous traitor' in a pragmatic way. 'I packed a few books and the most essential clothing in a rucksack and took my weapons – an army rifle, my service pistol, a couple of hand grenades and some ammunition – and then got onto a tram to the town and reported to the police at Möllergatte 19. I told them who I was and where I had served, surrendered my weapons and was then asked to wait in the entrance hall.'[19] A short while later, Uffz Hougen, who had survived 25 operational flights, was taken to the Ilebu camp and sentenced to three years imprisonment. He had destroyed his documents, especially his Luftwaffe logbook, beforehand – 'Otherwise I would have been given at least ten years on account of my operational flights against England.'[20]

Another Norwegian who got caught in the wheels of the post-war and 'cleansing' justice was Alf Lie.[21] At the time of the German occupation of Norway, in April 1940, he was 19 years old. His mother came from Germany and his family had close contacts with the Reich. Between August 1937 and summer 1938 Lie had attended a commercial high school in Göppingen and thought of Germany as his second fatherland. In pre-war Norway large sections of the population were German-friendly.

The German language was compulsory in further education, the cultural exchange between the two countries was extensive and German influence was dominant in the intellectual and natural science fields, as well as in technological development. Furthermore, numerous Norwegian artists and literati had been educated in Germany or owed their recognition to their successes in the German society. (However, for most Norwegians, their view of Germany as the leading cultural nation was completely reversed when Reichskommissar Terboven forced the country under the yoke of National Socialist occupation.)

At the time of the German invasion, Lie was actively serving as a medic. He had managed to gain his school-leaving certificate in the same year and had begun to study social economy at Oslo University. When Norwegians were asked to volunteer for the SS-Regiment 'Nordland' in January 1941, Lie did not find the idea appealing. When he eventually joined the voluntary Norwegian Legion after the German attack on the Soviet Union it was more by chance than intent. Lie knew the first commander of the Legion, Jørgen Bakke, who applied pressure on him on 19 July 1941, pointing out how important a Norwegian contribution on the Finnish front would be. The young student was caught off guard, and before long found himself on a German troop training ground at Fallingbostel.

In January 1942 the Norwegian unit was sent by train to Stettin, and from there by air transport to the Leningrad Front. Nobody said anything more about fighting in Finland. When the Norwegian Legion was disbanded in May 1943, Lie – who, in the meantime, had attained the rank of Oberscharführer (Colour Sergeant) – was posted to the SS-Panzergrenadier Regiment 'Norge'. Early in 1944 he was seriously wounded three times, and, after convalescing in several hospitals, was transferred to another hospital at Regensburg. During his convalescence leave in August he submitted a formal request for discharge from the German military service, but it was rejected. By this point Lie had come to realize that the war was lost and wanted to get away from the Eastern Front. A way out was to attempt to join the Luftwaffe. His request was granted, and, on

3 November 1944, Lie was posted to the Flieger-Ersatz (replacement) battalion at Nagold.

However, he did not get to do any flying. In December he saw action as a member of the 4th Company/II. Luftwaffe Brigade Oberrhein: four weeks infantry fighting near Müllheim in Baden. Then came strict and hard air force training at the Flugzeugführer-Doppelschule (Pilot Double School) A 43/I at Crailsheim. Lie could only look longingly at the aircraft based there. By then he had developed a real interest in flying, but the chronic fuel shortage allowed only theoretical flying instruction. In March 1945 Lie was transferred to the airborne training school, also at Crailsheim. It was clear to him what was in the wind, but he managed to evade a further bout of front-line duty by requesting a transfer to Oslo-Fornebu. Luck was with him, and he spent the final days of the war with the Flieger-horstkompanie (Airbase Protection Company) Fornebu. His paybook carried the statement: 'Belongs to the flying personnel and must be made available on request from the OKL (Luftwaffe High Command'. But it never came to that. Instead Lie faced a Norwegian post-war justice process, accused of 'supporting the enemy'.

After the war the Norwegian front-line volunteers were treated severely during the ongoing 'cleansing' campaign. The authorities handed out a total of 14,729 prison sentences, in addition to 25 death sentences, and another 2,489 cases where the accused agreed to a prison sentence without actually going through the trial process.[22] Lie was sentenced to a prison term of three years and one month, and was released after serving two-thirds of his sentence.

The first Dewoitine D.520s of the disbanded Vichy-French air force arrive at Karlovo in September 1943. (Todor Valkov)

The commander of the 6th Bulgarian Fighter Regiment, Colonel Vassil Valkov, was executed by the Communists on 13 May 1945. (Todor Valkov)

A Bulgarian squadron commander issues his orders. In the background are Bulgarian Do 17Ka-2 bombers. (CEGES, Brussels)

A Croat Fiat G.50 fighter with the symbol of Sisak town on its engine cowling. (Dénes Bernád)

A Croat pilot proudly presents himself in front of his Rogožarski R.100. The Croat air force used these parasol monoplanes as light bombers. (Mitja Maruško)

Worried looks all round at the 15.(kroat.)/JG 52 on the Eastern Front! Left, Major Franjo Džal, next to him Major von Bonin, Major Hrabak and General der Flieger Unger. (Niko East)

Taganrog, the operational base of the 15.(kroat.)/JG 52. In the Bf 109 cockpit is Franjo Džal and next to him is Lt Ivanič. (Eric Mombeek)

An Avia B-534 of the 12th Fighter squadron of the Slovak Air Force on the Eastern Front in autumn 1941. (Dénes Bernád)

13 (slowak.)/JG 52 at Anapa, Black Sea coast, in 1943. The Slovak machines could only be distinguished by the white-red-blue rings on their propeller spinners. (CEGES, Brussels)

A Hawker Hart of the Swedish volunteer formation F 19 in flight over Finland in 1940. (Krigsarkivet Stockholm)

This Koolhoven F.K.52 with the individual marking KO-130 was a present of the Swedish Count von Rosen, and reached Finland in January 1940. (Tapio Huttunen)

With ninety-four confirmed aerial victories achieved between 19 December 1939 and 3 September 1944, Eino Ilmari Juutilainen was the most successful Finnish fighter pilot. (Keski Suomen Ilmailumuseo)

1942: Lt Lauri Vilhelm Nissinen leaves his Brewster 239 (BW-384) after a successful operational sortie. (Keski Suomen Ilmailumuseo)

Morane-Saulnier 406 MS-624 was flown by 2./LeLv 26 from Hirvas in 1942. (Keski Suomen Ilmailumuseo)

Curtiss Hawk 75A CU-568 of LeLv 32 taking off on 28 March 1942 to join the aerial battle over Gogland, where the Finns shot down seventeen Soviet aircraft without loss. (Keski Suomen Ilmailumuseo)

Suulajärvi, 7 May 1943. Staff Sgt Y.O. Turkka and Captain Karhunen, with the squadron mascot Peggy Brown, resting on Karhunen´s personal Brewster 239, BW-366, displaying twenty-nine victory markings. (`Joppe´ Karhunen)

BL-129, pictured here at Onttola in 1943, was the most famous Blenheim bomber of the Finnish Air Force. This aircraft carried out more than eighty reconnaissance sorties during 1942-43. (Keski Suomen Ilmailumuseo)

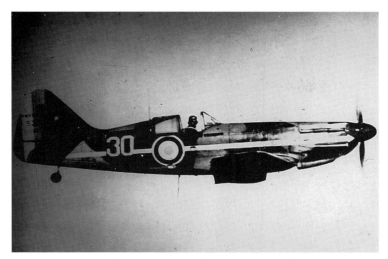

A Dewoitine D.520 from G.C.III/6 of the Vichy French Air Force in North African skies in 1941. (Gaston Botquin)

This three-seat Latécoère 298 torpedo bomber of the Vichy-French Air Force made a refuelling stop at Rhodos on its way to Syria. (Nino Arena)

Four Danish volunteers in their pre-war national uniforms: Poul Sommer (top left) flew with JG 27 and JG 54 and then transferred to the Waffen-SS; Wolfgang Fabian (top right) was killed in action as a member of 9./JG 51 near Rzhev in the Soviet Union on 21 August 1942; Peter Horn (below left) served with I/JG 54 and survived the war; and Ejnar Thorup (below right) participated as a volunteer in the Finnish Winter War of 1939-40, and died in a crash landing on 5 June 1942 while flying with 3./JG 54.

René Darbois of Lorraine deserted to the Allies in Italy on 25 July 1944 while a pilot of 3./JG 54. (J.-L. Roba)

Darbois´ Bf 109G-6, `yellow 4´, Wk.Nr.160756, at Santa Maria in southern Italy after his desertion to the Allies. (J.-L. Roba)

Alsatian volunteer Charles F. Kern from Strasbourg, who flew with 2./NJG 4. (Charles F. Kern)

Guido Rombout (right) of 6./JG 1 was probably the only Belgian pilot in the Luftwaffe. (J.-L. Roba)

Charles F. Kern´s Ju 88G night fighter with FuG 220 Lichtenstein AI radar at Mainz-Finthen early in 1945. (Charles F. Kern)

Spanish Major Muñoz Jimenez from the 1st Escuadrilla Azul, killed in action on the Eastern Front on 27 November 1941, with the German fighter ace Werner Mölders. (Author's archives)

Toulouse Coulomiers 1943. The German fighter ace Major Hermann Graf meets the Spanish volunteers. (Eric Mombeek)

Orel airfield, 20 February 1943. Sen Lt Gavilán of the 3rd Spanish Escuadrilla with his Bf 109. (Author's archives)

Commander of the 5th Spanish Escuadrilla, Major Murcia Rubio, at EJG Süd (Ergänzungs-Jagdgeschwader, *Replacement Fighter Wing South*) in Bergerac, southern France, early in 1944. (Heinrich Heuser)

Members of the 2nd Spanish Escuadrilla on a visit to the Werneuchen fighter training centre in Germany. (Author´s archives)

Heinkel He 50s of Nachtschlachtgruppe 11 (estnisch) on the Eastern Front in winter 1943-44. (Gebhard Aders)

1./SAGr.127 (See) naval reconnaissance squadron at Ülemiste near Tallinn in July 1944. In the Ar 95 cockpit is Lt Remi Milk, with his observer, Lt Korneli Kallas, behind him. (Remi Milk)

*Flying activity at FFS A/B Libau-Grobin (Liepäja-Grobiņa) in
Courland, Latvia, in spring 1944. Swinging the propeller on a
Bü 131B Jungmann trainer (via Alex Vanags-Baginskis)*

*Fw Harijs Klints (killed in action on 1 January 1945), Lt Mencis and
Lt Abrams from the Latvian NSGr.12 on the Eastern Front in early
1944. Behind them are aged Ar 66C trainers adapted as night
harassment bombers. (Gebhard Aders)*

Danes

After the peaceful occupation of Denmark by German troops on 9 April 1940 the country's parliamentary system remained untouched for the time being. The personnel strength of the Danish armed forces was reduced by two-thirds, although this restriction did not apply to the Danish officer corps.

After the German attack on the Soviet Union a Danish Free Corps was created, which was intended to accept Danish volunteers prepared to fight on the Eastern Front. The Danish government did not object to this plan – quite the opposite, in fact. A circular was issued by the Danish Defence Ministry on 8 July 1941, stating explicitly that active and demobilized officers of service age, NCOs and other ranks of the Danish army were permitted to join the Free Corps. As a parallel measure Danes were also permitted, for the time being, to join the Finnish army.

Eight Danish officers, including seven military pilots, volunteered for the Finnish air force.[1] Among them were Capt of Naval Aviation Poul Sommer, born on 13 October 1910, and Lt of Army Aviation Alf Aggerbøl, born on 24 September 1917. Peter Horn, born on 15 October 1915, was of the same rank. Other volunteers who wanted to take part in the Finnish 'Continuation War' were Capt of Army Aviation Knud Erik Ravnskov (born on 29 October 1911), Lt of Naval Aviation Wolfgang Rudolf Fabian (born on 10 June 1914), Lt of Army Aviation Ove Terp (born on 10 November 1914) and Capt of Army Aviation Ejnar Thorup (born on 7 January 1912). Thorup was a veteran of the Finnish Winter War; he was one of the 24 Danish pilots who had hastened to help the Finns in 1939–40, and had served with Finnish LeLv 32.[2] That war had cost the lives of five Danish volunteer pilots. In spring 1940 Thorup, who held the Danish pilot's licence No 187 of 1937, flew operationally in the Viipuri area. After the end of the Winter War he completed an advanced instructional course in Finland, lasting from 4 August to 24 October 1940. Anker Tage Harild (born on 21 October 1905) did not quite fit into this category: he was an infantry captain, but held a private pilot's licence.

In summer 1941 the Finnish air force no longer needed foreign volunteers, and the eight Danish officers reported to the German Luftwaffe. They were posted to the Flug-zeugführerschule (Pilot Training School) A/B 120 at Prenzlau in Uckermark, where they were told they should really join the Danish Free Corps. This was not what the eight Danish pilots had in mind, but on their way back to Denmark they made a stop-over in Berlin and called at the German Air Ministry. This personal approach proved successful and at the end of August the eight tenacious Danes were flown from Copenhagen-Kastrup back to Prenzlau. After an examination the eight were sent to different fighter-training schools except for A. T. Harild, who joined a bomber training course. This RLM (German Air Ministry) decision to accept Danish airmen remained an exception, however. Other Danish airmen who tried to join the Luftwaffe were, as a rule, assigned to the Waffen-SS.

Three of the Danish pilots were killed in action during the following years. Oblt Wolfgang Fabian, who was trained at the Jagdfliegerschule (Fighter Training School) 4 at Fürth and the Blindflugschule (Blind Flying School) 4 at Copenhagen, died in his Bf 109F-2 'yellow 6' Wk. Nr. 12601, as a member of 9./JG 51, when it was hit by Soviet AA fire near Rzhev on 21 August 1942.[3] Lt Peter Horn, who achieved a total of 11 aerial victories and was decorated with 2nd and 1st class Iron Crosses, served in the same Gruppe but with 1./JG 51, and survived the war. So did his compatriot A. T. Harild, who flew a Ju 88 over Orel in summer 1943. He served with 9./KG 1 'Hindenburg' and was promoted to the rank of major. Ove Terp came to JG 54 'Grünherz' and was badly wounded in action. After the war he worked as a technical adviser in the USA. In the 1950s he took on German citizenship and served with the German Bundesluftwaffe, retiring with the rank of Lt Col on 26 March 1979.

The Luftwaffe career of Knud Erik Ravnskov was very short in comparison. He had served in the Danish air force from 1 January 1930, and, after volunteering for the Luftwaffe, was posted to Jagdfliegerschule 5 on 16 October 1941, subsequently transferring to Jagdfliegerschule 1. On 1 March 1942 Ravnskov was posted to Blindflugschule 4 at Copenhagen-Kastrup, later serving with 1./Erg. Gruppe Ost (reserve and replacement group East). He lost his life on 7 September 1942, when his Bf 109F-1 'white 18' (Wk. Nr. 6609) turned over while making an emergency landing at Krakow, in Poland. Hptm Ejnar Thorup received his transfer orders from FFS A/B 120 (pilot training school) to Jagdfliegerschule 5 at Villacoublay, in France, on 11 September 1941. Afterwards he flew with JG 54, as did Terp. Thorup died on 5 June 1942 near Bol. Obshivalovo, 12km (7 miles) south of Chudovo, in Russia, as a member of 3./JG 54. His Bf 109F-2 'yellow 5' (Wk. Nr. 9663) was totally destroyed. In the loss report preserved at the Wehrmachtauskunftstelle (German armed forces information centre, a post-war establishment), this incident is described concisely as follows:[4]

> During an operational flight, Hptm Thorup was fired on from the ground. His engine began to smoke, and Hptm Thorup attempted to make an emergency landing behind his own lines. While doing so the aircraft broke up, Hptm Thorup was thrown from the aircraft together with his seat, and was recovered dead.

Poul Sommer, decorated with the Iron Cross 2nd and 1st Class and promoted to Hauptmann on 1 January 1943, left the Luftwaffe late in autumn 1943. After graduating from the Jagdfliegerschule 1 in autumn 1942 he had served with JG 27, and later JG 54. While with IV./JG 27 he had served for a while as captain of 10./JG 27. Flying operationally over the southern theatre of war he shot down three enemy aircraft[5] in the period October 1942 to March 1943. He is believed to have achieved another three victories while flying with JG 54. After his return to Denmark Sommer organized the Guard Corps of the German Luftwaffe (Vagtkorpset de Tyske Luftvaaben in Denmark), which eventually comprised five companies with a total of 1,200 men.[6] This unit did not only have the task of guarding German airfields in Denmark, but also took an active part in fighting against the Danish resistance movement. By order from Heinrich Himmler, dated 11 January 1945, Poul Sommer was seconded with the rank of reserve SS-Hauptsturmführer (equivalent to Captain) to the SS-Hauptamt (main office), Amtsgruppe D (Office Group D) and subsequently transferred to the SS-Ersatzkommando Dänemark (SS Replacement Department Denmark), Germanic control branch. After the war he managed to hide on a farm until autumn 1946. He subsequently served several years in prison, and died in 1991.

At least one other Danish pilot is known to have served in the Luftwaffe – Uffz Börge Darr, born at Silkeborg on 11 September 1919. His family had moved from Germany to Denmark around 1910, and, after his marriage to a Danish woman, the German citizen Darr was also given Danish citizenship. Against strong opposition from his father, young Darr volunteered for the Luftwaffe in 1940. He passed through the Flugzeugführerschule (Pilot Training School) A/B 11 and, from 4 December 1941, FFS (C) 16, which trained bomber and transport pilots. After becoming an instructor he submitted several applications for transfer to the fighter arm, but his wish was not granted until 1943. From 11 November 1943 Darr finally flew operationally with 4./JG 11, but was killed in action over Dollendorf in the Eifel just three weeks later, on 1 December 1943, flying his Bf 109G-6 'white 3', Wk. Nr. 20467. His grave is in the Catholic cemetery of Schleiden.

French

The French voluntary legion (Légion des Volontaires Français contre le Bolshevisme), formed after the German attack on the Soviet Union, was a product of collaborationist parties who temporarily buried their differences to form the LVF in occupied Paris. A member of the Central Committee of the LVF was the collaborator Pierre Costantini,[1] the leader and founder of the small Ligue Française. Costantini was a First World War fighter ace, who, despite his disability, had served as commandant of the Coulommiers airfield in 1940. A cavalier of the Légion d' Honneur, an ardent admirer of Napoleon and an anglophobe, he had personally declared war on Britain, and, in addition to the LVF, planned to organize an independent Aviation Legion, the Légion des Aviateurs Français.[2] In fact he seemed to have found a sufficient number of demobilized airmen, active members of the Armée de l'Air de l'Armistice or aviation enthusiasts who had expressed their interest in this project, because the German Ambassador in Paris, Otto Abetz, reported the following to the Foreign Ministry in Berlin on 7 July 1941: 'The number of trained airmen who have put down their names for the LVF has increased to 50, including 30 well-known bomber pilots.'[3] Costantini's phantom legion moved into its first residence in Paris in Rue de la Chaussée d'Antin 5; from there it moved to the former British Railways building in Rue Godot de Mauroy 1 on 1 November 1941. Costantini hoped that the German Embassy would support his ambitious project but he was to be disappointed, as the National Socialists wanted to limit the French contribution in their 'crusade against Bolshevism' to a symbolic force of no more than 15,000 men so that the importance of a defeated France would not be raised. French military aviation was undesirable.

That being the official German policy, the efforts of Costantini and the French aviation Captain Caël, who had already started training courses in preparation for flying training, did not lead to anything. Perhaps the fact that he did not succeed in forming a French Aviation Legion saved

Costantini's life after the war: Gaullist justice, not known for its forgivingness, declared the accused collaborator as 'mentally not accountable for his actions' and spared him from the death sentence.

Instead of enlisting airmen, in 1942 the establishment at Rue Godot de Mauroy 1 housed the NSKK (National-Socialist Motor Corps) Luftwaffe group and served to recruit young Frenchmen for this organization. The French motor vehicle drivers of the Luftwaffe were formed into seven companies and, among other tasks, were used as infantry in ground fighting against the partisans in northern Italy.

After the Vichy armed forces were disbanded the German occupation authorities tried to transfer French servicemen into non-flying formations of the Luftwaffe. The following note appeared in the German High Command War Diary, dated 27 November 1942:[4]

> On request from the Luftwaffe, the Führer has declared that personnel from the disbanded formations of the French armed forces can at once be taken over for service in the German armed forces, preferably for air defence reporting tasks, in AA artillery and coastal artillery; the men are to be put up and looked after according to the pre-war French conditions and put under the German military law.

Transfer to flying personnel was (still) not possible, but even the intended recruitment for other tasks within the German armed forces proved unsuccessful. Already on 29 November 1942 Luftflotte 3 had to report to the Luftwaffe Operations Staff that 'the demobilization of the French air force had taken place so quickly that the servicemen could not be taken over for the German service use.'

Despite all resistance and obstacles a few aviation enthusiasts and Frenchmen willing to collaborate managed to serve as pilots in the Luftwaffe. One more or less homogenous French squadron came into being in 1943. The transport squadron 'Hansa' was established in that year[5] – possibly already at that time with French personnel – and began operations with

LeO 451 aircraft. These planes, produced by the Lioré et Olivier concern, were really four-seat bombers, but of such good quality that the Vichy government, with German agreement, had ordered another 225 examples in August 1941.[6] A transport version, the LeO 451T, was produced after the total German occupation of France in November 1942, with at least 30 aircraft of this type completed. A large number of LeO 451 transports served with the Luftwaffe IV./TG 4,[7] and there were 110 LeO 451s in the Luftwaffe inventory on 31 March 1944, including 73 in operational service.[8] All ferry flights for the Luftwaffe within France were carried out by French pilots from Air France, a fact that was to cause them some trouble after the war.

In summer 1944 LeO 451s from the disbanded IV./TG 4 were used to reinforce the 'Hansa' transport squadron. An OKL (Luftwaffe High Command) order of 8 August 1944 regarding the disbandment and redesignation of TG 3, TG 4, and TG 5[9] also allocated the following planned posts for French personnel within this squadron: nine crews with nine pilots, nine radio operators, nine flight mechanics and 28 maintenance men, mechanics and other ground personnel. In fact, two months after the successful Allied invasion, French airmen were still reporting for duty with this squadron. These were probably former members of the Vichy-French air force, ex-Air France airmen or Frenchmen trained in Germany. By then the Allied air superiority had already considerably diminished the operational scope of Luftwaffe transport aircraft, and the Luftwaffe High Command reached the inevitable conclusion: an order of 18 September 1944 requested 'immediate disbandment'[10] of the 'Hansa' transport squadron by the Luftflottenkommando 3 (air fleet headquarters).

But the products of the French aviation industry remained in German service. Another aircraft model that found use was the Bloch M.B.220, a cantilever monoplane designed to carry 16 passengers and used before the war by Air France to serve its European routes. In 1944 the German Lufthansa adopted this model from Air France stocks as it did not have enough planes left to serve its remaining routes. From the beginning of the war the Lufthansa aircraft park had shrunk dramatically. On 1 January 1939 Lufthansa had 151 aircraft, including 73 Ju 52/3m trimotors; by 31 December 1943 there were only 47 aircraft left in service.[11] A total of 11 Bloch M.B.220s had fallen into German hands in November 1942, but as these were commercial aircraft they were not at first considered as booty,[12] and Lufthansa came to an agreement with Air France to lease them. In June 1944 Lufthansa still had ten M.B.220s in service and Air France flight mechanics supposedly flew aboard these aircraft.[13] They preferred this occupation to unemployment, the alternative – as, at that time, the French were forbidden to have either military or civilian air services. It seems that the reliability of the M.B.220 was not particularly good, for by the end of June only one of the ten examples remained in service, the others being either under maintenance or kept in reserve.[14]

Rather doubtful – from the National Socialist point of view – was the motivation and operational willingness of many young men from Alsace and Lorraine, who, from 1942 onwards, came under the German obligation to serve in the armed forces and had been mobilized. Thousands of these 'recruits' attempted to evade German military service, and fled to unoccupied France or neutral Switzerland. One young man from Lorraine chose another way: he deserted to the Western Allies with his aircraft.

René Darbois,[15] born in Metz on 23 October 1924, was one of the few Frenchmen known to have served as a pilot in the Luftwaffe.[16] After basic training at Oschatz he had attended the Luftkriegsschule (Officer Candidate School) 7 at Tulln near Vienna. Fighter pilot training with JG 103 at Chatereau and Orleans followed until May 1944. Additional training took place with Erg.JG 1, Erg.Gr.West (Replacement Fighter Wing, Replacement Group West) at Stargard, in Pomerania, which was completed on 26 June 1944. To his comrades, Darbois gave the impression that he wanted to be an engineer officer of the Luftwaffe. This leaves open the question of whether Darbois would have reached the flying personnel of the Luftwaffe if he had been one of those compulsorily mobilized. The Luftwaffe command had little faith in 'recruits' from Alsace and Lorraine. It would seem possible that he volunteered for the Luftwaffe to forestall threatened mobilization into the Wehrmacht or the Waffen-SS and the inevitable transfer to the Eastern Front. It is also quite possible that this young man from Lorraine had already planned to defect to the Allies at the time he enlisted.

After completing his training Darbois was posted, via brief intervals with JG 54 and JG 77, to 3./JG 4 in Italy. On 25 June 1944 eight Bf 109Gs from 1./JG 4 and eight Bf 109Gs from 3./JG 4 were on a ferry flight from Maniago to Ghedi, where they were to be transferred to JG 77. None of the pilots, who included Darbois, had any operational experience. They were ordered to keep strict radio silence. Darbois, from his 'yellow 4', used sign language to indicate to his wingman that he was not well and then sheared away from the formation. Once out of sight he climbed to 7,000–8,000m (23,000–26,000ft) and turned southwards, landing behind the Allied lines at Santa Maria. During his interrogation he stated that he considered himself French and had for some time intended to change sides at the first opportunity.[17] His aircraft, a Bf 109G-6 Wk. Nr. 160756, was shipped to the USA and restored during the 1970s; today it is on display in the National Air and Space Museum in Washington.

Darbois's military career did not end with his desertion. A short time later he was flying again, this time under the name of Guyot, for the de Gaulle Groupe de Chasse 'Corse'. The false name was necessary, because, if he had been captured by the Germans, Darbois would have faced certain execution had his identity been known. After 1945 he became a member of the well-known French aerobatics squadron 'Patrouille d'Etampes'. Darbois alias Guyot also participated in the war in Indochina, and distinguished himself by flying 122 helicopter sorties. After returning from South-East Asia he committed suicide on 14 February 1955. So ended an unusual airman's life, the study of which leaves quite a few questions unanswered.

There was no doubt whatsoever about the loyalties of another Luftwaffe pilot from Alsace-Lorraine, Robert Ernst[18], who was born on 4 February 1897 in Hürtingheim, Alsace. After obtaining an emergency school leaving certificate he joined the Lower Saxony Infantry Artillery Regiment No. 10. He transferred to aviation in 1917 and flew operationally over northern France as an observer with the Fliegerabteilungen (aviation detachments) A 256 and A 284. After the war he settled in Baden and completed his studies in national economy with a graduation certificate. Politically he was one of the leading Alsatian autonomists who were drawn into the National Socialist orbit. Ernst joined the NSDAP (National Socialist Workers Party) in 1933, and completed his pilot training four years later. After the defeat of France in 1940 he became the Lord Mayor of Strasbourg and general arbiter to Gauleiter (NSDAP regional chief) Robert Wagner, who was pushing ahead the 'Germanization' of Alsace. In 1943 Maj Dr Ernst submitted a request to the C-in-C of the Luftwaffe to serve with the flying personnel on the Eastern Front. This application had a political purpose as it was connected with the introduction in Alsace of the obligation to serve in the German armed forces[19], and Ernst intended to set an example.

In April 1944 he joined KG 55 'Greif' at Stalino, and, as a fifth man aboard an He 111, without any specific functions, he took part in 84 operational sorties in four months. These included night bombing raids on Astrakhan, Saratov and Gorki, and daytime attacks on Kursk as part of Operation Citadelle. Members of KG 55 paid high tribute to this NS party member: they believed Ernst had joined them 'to help out',[20] while in reality his action had been politically motivated. This same political activity led the French to sentence him to ten years imprisonment after the war.

Not political grounds but pragmatic considerations dictated the decision of Charles F. Kern to join the Luftwaffe. Born on 3 January 1924, this Alsace citizen was in 1941 living with his family in Strasbourg. His father, who was employed by the chief of the German Civil Administration, knew that the veiled German annexation would sooner or later be followed by a compulsory mobilization of some age groups of the male population of Alsace-Lorraine, and that a voluntary enlistment in the Wehrmacht had the advantage that it allowed the volunteer to choose his branch of service. And so Charles F. Kern, who had discovered his love for flying through being a member of the

Flieger-HJ (Aviation Hitler Youth), volunteered for the Luftwaffe late in 1941 as an engineer-officer aspirant.

'My father's belief proved correct. While, after two years, I was still in training, thousands of my Alsatian comrades had already fallen on the Eastern Front.'[21] From 1 December 1941 to 24 February 1942 Kern served in the 2.Fliegerausbildungs-regiment (Luftwaffe Pre-Flight Training Regiment) at Eger, then, until 31 January 1943, at the Luftkriegsschule (Officer Candidate School) 3 at Werder an der Havel. He spent the next three months at the Flugzeugführerschule (pilot training school for blind/all-weather flying) (C) 10 at Fürstenwalde/Spree, and then, until August 1943, at the Blindflugschule (blind flying school) at Belgrade-Zemlin. After an interval at 1./NJG 101 at Schleissheim, Kern by now promoted to Lt, was posted to 2./NJG 4 on 15 September 1943. He flew his first operational sortie from Laon-Athies on 3 January 1944. On 30 May 1944, after taking off from Florennes in Belgium, he succeeded in shooting down a B-24 Liberator from the 801st Bomb Group.[22] A short while later, the Alsace-born pilot himself became the victim in an aerial combat. Following an operational sortie over the English Channel on 17 June the starboard engine of his Ju 88 (3C + KK) failed and Kern was forced to attempt an emergency landing at Laon-Athies. But an RAF Mosquito night fighter was waiting and shot him down. Kern's crew was killed, but he survived with second-degree burns on his face.

Kern witnessed the end of the war at the Eggebeck airfield in Schleswig-Holstein, and was released from the POW camp on 19 January 1946. He was lucky that he had not fallen into French hands: 'Had I gone back home right after the capitulation, the French would have certainly arrested me and put me in front of a court martial, as happened to a comrade of mine. He was sentenced to five years of forced labour as well as ten years loss of civil rights and ten years prohibition from residence in Alsace.'[23]

Belgians

During the war some 9,000 Flemings and about 6,000 Walloons served as volunteers in the Waffen-SS.[1] Others enlisted in the Wehrmacht, the Kriesgmarine or the auxiliary formations of the collaborationist parties. In addition 2,000 Belgians formed the Flämische Flakbrigade (Flemish AA brigade) in 1944. However, hardly any Flemings or Walloons can be traced to the flying personnel of the Luftwaffe.

It was another story on the Allied side. The RAF formed two Belgian squadrons, Nos 349 and 350, whose pilots later flew Spitfires over northern Europe.[2]

As a rule, former members of the Belgian air force and Sabena airline who had decided to join the Axis found their way barred when it came to operational flying, as shown by some known examples. Léon Closset,[3] born at Liège on 29 May 1911, served in the Belgian air force until 1934 and then moved into civil aviation. From February 1938 to May 1940 he was captain of a Sabena airliner. The Belgian armistice took him by surprise in Algiers. While some of the Sabena crews escaped to Britain, where their two DC-3s and seven SM.73s were allocated to Nos 24 and 271 Squadrons of the RAF, Closset managed to get back to Belgium.

In 1941 Closset joined the newly founded Legion Wallonie (Infantry Btl 373 of the German Wehrmacht), which left Brussels for the Eastern Front on 8 August. He distinguished himself in fighting at Gromovabayalka in February 1942, and, at the end of the year, commanded the rearguard of the Legion in the Caucasus. Closset returned to Belgium in February 1943, but not to continue his flying career. Instead he took over the leadership of the Walloon Labour Service (Service des Volontaires du Tavail pour la Wallonie). At the end of the war he held the rank of Oberfeldmeister (equivalent to Lt Col) of this service.

His colleague Albert Lassois[4] also had to give up his flying career. Born in Liège on 15 February 1905, Lassois was also engaged as pilot for Sabena before the war. Like Closset, he belonged to the first contingent of volunteers for the Legion Wallonie, where he served as an adjutant. He left front-line service in 1943 and began working for the welfare of the Walloon front-line volunteers, later to join the Garde Wallonie, an armed local security force of 6,000 men.

Another Belgian officer of the Legion, which was incorporated into the Waffen-SS in June 1943 as the 5.SS-Frewilligen-Sturmbrigade Wallonie (5th SS-Volunteer Assault brigade), had better luck. Adolphe Rénier,[5] born on 18 July 1915, had served as a lieutenant in the pre-war Belgian air force and afterwards volunteered for the Legion Wallonie. There he was appointed a special duties officer, serving in the headquarters company of the Sturmbrigade. After the brigade broke out from the Cherkassy cauldron, achieved at terrible cost, Rénier managed to transfer to the Luftwaffe. Once in Luftwaffe uniform he found that the increasing shortage of aviation fuel and inadequate training facilities dragged out his flying training, and it was only on 6 May 1945, two days before the unconditional surrender, that Hptm Rénier reached an operational unit with his Fw 190.

Similarly slow flying training was also experienced by Alfons Labeau,[6] a former pilot of the Belgian air force who succeeded in transferring to the Luftwaffe as an Oberscharführer (colour sergeant) of the Waffen-SS in June 1944. The stations in his training odyssey were Straubing, Crailsheim, Platting, Weiden/Oberpfalz, Germersheim and Mannheim. As a Luftwaffe Feldwebel, Labeau hardly got to do any flying – there was either no aircraft or no aviation fuel.

One of the very few Belgian airmen who evidently flew operationally for the Luftwaffe was the Fleming Guido Rombaut.[7] Born the son of a Belgian officer at Vlaarschot, near Ghent, on 27 April 1923, Rombaut spent part of his youth in the Belgian Congo. However, at the time of the German attack on 10 May 1940 he was in Belgium. His parents were Fleming nationalists who had wanted to free themselves from the decades of oppression by the French-speaking upper levels of the local society. The weakness of the Brussels parliamentary system and Rombaut's anti-Communism did the rest, and he fell for the propaganda of the German occupiers. It has to be pointed out, however, that the decision of this young Fleming to join the German side was based purely on idealistic motives, and that was also the attitude of most Belgians who joined German military formations.[8] Rombaut enlisted in the Allgemeine SS Flandern (General Fleming SS), but, already in 1941, he submitted a request for transfer to the Luftwaffe, something that initially seemed completely out of reach. But Rombaut was determined and sent in request after request to get a transfer to his desired arm of the services. His persistence finally paid off: he was taken on and began his Luftwaffe career. Rombaut underwent his pilot training at Nenndorf and Gumpersdorf and, on 5 April 1943, was posted to JG 102 (fighter training unit). Just over three months later, on 20 July 1943, he was with Jagdgruppe West.[9] On 7 September 1943 he received his posting orders to JG 1 'Oesau', where he was detailed to 6.Staffel. By that time Rombaut was no longer convinced of a German victory and felt depressed and disillusioned, but there was no legal way for him to quit military service.

On 27 September JG 1 received orders to intercept an American formation, consisting of 308 heavy bombers escorted by 262 P-47 Thunderbolt fighters, which was attacking Emden. The two Gruppen took off at a 30-minute interval – I./JG 1 at 10.30hrs, II./JG 1, including Guido Rombaut with this Fw 190A 'yellow 12' (Wk. Nr. 550523), at about 11.00hrs. From that moment all trace of him is lost.[10] On that day the P-47s of the USAAF 63rd Fighter Squadron claimed three Fw 190s and two Bf 110s near the island of Borkum. Initially reported as missing, Rombaut was officially declared dead by a court in Münster on 26 January 1961.

Another Belgian who wore the Luftwaffe uniform was Joseph Christian. Born at Faymonville on 20 March 1921, he served as a radio operator in I./KG 54. Early in 1944 I. and II./KG 54 were part of IX.Fliegerkorps on the Western Front and had the task of intensifying the air offensive against the British Isles (Operation Steinbock). Christian was killed in action on 18 April 1944 during a raid on Britain.

Many Belgians had no choice about taking the risk of joining the German armed forces. These were the young men eligible for military service living in the former German areas of Eupen and Malmedy and the former condominium (jointly ruled region) of Moresnet. These had been allocated to Belgium after the First World War, but were once again annexed to the German Reich by an edict by Hitler's of 18 May 1940. From June 1940 onwards some 700 men from Eupen and Malmedy volunteered for service in the Wehrmacht. But once their citizenship had been established, the other Eupen-Malmedians who were liable for military service were simply called up, even those possessing dual citizenship.

One of those mobilized at that time was the mechanic Henri Dannemark, who was born on 26 November 1921. He received his call-up papers late in March 1942. As he was already interested in flying, having joined the NSFK (National Socialist Flying Corps) in 1941, he naturally choose to join the Luftwaffe. Dannemark received his training in the Netherlands and France, as well as in various training schools in Germany, such as the Fliegerwaffenschule (See) (Aircraft Armament School – Naval Aviation) at Parow. On completion, he was posted as a flight mechanic to 2.Seenotstaffel (ASR squadron). The crew of his Do 24T turned out to be quite multinational: Dannemark himself was of Belgian origin, the pilot was German, the navigator came from Poland, and the radio operator from Alsace.

Dannemark's Do 24T (Wk. Nr. 1075) was based at Kunda Bay in Estonia. On 5 June 1944 his aircraft was shot down by Soviet fighters in the map grid square 7041 (Gulf of Finland), north-east of Narva. Of the six-man crew only the badly wounded Dannemark survived. Dannemark heard of the failed attempt on Hitler's life on 20 July 1944 in a hospital at Plauen. There he witnessed a heated argument between fanatical National Socialists and wounded soldiers who had had enough of the war. The tensions exposed during these arguments were so extreme that, for the first time, the Eupen-Malmedian experienced real fear for the regime he was serving.[11] At the end of August, at his own request, Dannemark was discharged and returned to his own unit at Grossenbrode. There he met an understanding commander and a doctor who was willing to help, both of them making sure that the still only partly recovered airman would be sent home. Dannemark received his leave papers and a special safe conduct permit, because his home village was very close to the combat zone. When he arrived there, on 9 September 1944, the last German soldiers were just leaving, and an American reconnaissance troop arrived the next day. Luftwaffe Gefreiter Henri Dannemark had survived the war, and was once again a Belgian.

The involuntary military career of a laboratory assistant, Joseph Justin, also ended quite undramatically.[12] Born in Malmedy on 16 February 1924, he was ordered to attend the registration for the draft in autumn 1941, and chose to join the Luftwaffe. After several examinations and tests in Cologne and Münster he was accepted for flying personnel. Justin received his orders to report for active duty in July 1942, and was detailed to Flieger-Regiment 42. In winter 1942–3 he was in Russia to prove himself in the compulsory 'combat competence' in action against partisans. In March 1943 Justin finally began his training in the air gunner's school at Stolp, in Pomerania, and was afterwards sent to the Blindflugschule (blind flying school) 2. After completing his training he was posted to 12./KG 6, later 9./KG 6, the newest bomber formation of the Luftwaffe, which had been formed in the late summer of 1942. He did fly as a crew member of a Ju 88, but not in action. In December 1944 Justin was transferred to Flak-Regiment 159. After the capitulation in May 1945 he became a POW of the Americans at Aschaffenburg but, as he was a compulsorily mobilized Belgian he was released a month later.

Dutch

After the end of the war the Dutch psychologist Dr A. F. G. van Hoesel examined the motives of 450 young Dutchmen who had volunteered to serve in the German armed forces and who were then interned for 'military collaboration', a punishment that affected some 50,000 Dutchmen. In his research Dr van Hoesel found adventurers and idealists, politically convinced and previously convicted criminals, and youngsters who had joined the Waffen-SS during the 'hunger winter' of 1944–5. Only 2 per cent of those imprisoned – that is just nine young men, who had described themselves as mechanics and pilots – claimed to have joined up because they wanted to receive professional training in the German armed forces.

It seems doubtful, however, if these findings could be generalized and applied to all Dutch pilots serving in the German Luftwaffe, and the information on individual cases available to the author is insufficient to allow an accurate analysis. In any case, it has been established that only a few Dutchmen served as flying personnel in the German Luftwaffe. Wilhelm Eduard de Graaf, born at Sukabumi, in Java, on 11 January 1908, and who joined the Luftwaffe at an indeterminable point in time, has already been mentioned. He first served with the Versuchsverband Ob.d.L. (Experimental formation of the C-in-C of the Luftwaffe) and then with I./KG 200. He was known to be an excellent pilot and carried out numerous dangerous missions. In 1944, as part of the secret Operation *Maria*, he flew agents into the Soviet Union and set them down behind the Soviet lines.

Another volunteer was Dr Jan (Johannes) de Vliegher, born at Roosendaal on 30 July 1918. According to the meagre details found in the Bundesarchiv/Zentralnachweisstelle (Federal Archives, Central Information Office), he underwent training at Flugzeugführerschule (Pilot Training School) A/B 4, and after completing that he went Jagdfliegerschule (Fighter Training School) 2 on 18 March 1943; then, with effect from 11 July 1943, Dr de Vliegher was a member of JG 50, a short-lived fighter formation that only existed between August and December 1943. His next unit was JG 11, in which he was allocated to the staff on 7 December 1943. This fighter formation was based in northern Germany and had the task of combating the heavy four-engined American bombers approaching from the British Isles. Uffz Dr de Vliegher was killed in action at the start of the 'Big Week', the concentrated American bomber offensive against German industry. On 20 February 1944 he intercepted and attacked a B-17 from above, but the defensive fire from the bomber ripped off the tail plane of his Bf 109G-6 Wk. Nr. 29091 'blue 6'. The Dutch pilot managed to bale out of his stricken fighter, but did not survive the parachute descent. He died near Eggstedt in Schleswig-Holstein.

Another Dutch pilot, who was killed in action on 12 December 1944, was Klaas Visser of 9./NJG 1. More fortunate was Johannes Kuhn, born in Amsterdam on 15 November 1908. He served in the Militaire Luchtvaart (Dutch air force) from 1932, and in 1937 volunteered for a six-year term with the Dutch Indies air force, which he joined on 14 August 1937. However, due to an illness, doctors pronounced him unfit for service in the tropics in 1938, and Kuhn had to return to the Netherlands. From April 1939 onwards he flew with I-2 LvR (1st Reconnaissance Group of the 2nd Air Regiment/Army Aviation). At the end of that year Kuhn was transferred to V-2 LvR(Army Aviation Fighter Group) and retrained as a fighter pilot. He was shot down over the Pijnacker area on the first day of the German western campaign, on 10 May 1940. Kuhn saved himself by parachute, but owing to a bad knee injury had to spend several months in hospital afterwards. His wound did not heal until 1942, and on 15 October of that year he was officially discharged from the Dutch military service. On the same day he volunteered for the German Luftwaffe. To his British interrogation officers, Kuhn was to declare in the summer of 1944 that his German wife had talked him into joining the Luftwaffe, probably a 'protective' statement given to veil his real motives. In any case, until April 1943, he underwent the hardest training stage with the Flieger-Ausbildungsregiment 63 (Pre-Flight Training Regiment) at Toul, and passed the Flugzeugführerüberprüfungsschule (Pilot Re-Examination School) at Prenzlau, graduating in early July.

From 2 July 1943 Kuhn was with Schlachtgeschwader 101, a close-support training formation, flying the Hs 129 armoured assault aircraft from Paris-Orly. In February 1944 he was assigned to the Flugzeugführerüberprüfungsschule at Quedlinburg, and in May was posted to his last unit, 3./Über-führungsgruppe West (3rd Squadron of Ferry Group West). The pilots of this unit, consisting of four squadrons and a staff squadron, were engaged in ferrying aircraft from industrial establishments and assembly plants to the various front-line units. After the Allied invasion of France the losses of Ferry Group West rose dramatically, the pilots having to fly in all weather conditions and their aircraft often being damaged while touching down on improvised airstrips.

By then Kuhn had realized that the war was lost for the Reich and decided to defect. A favourable opportunity came on 30 August, when 14 Fw 190s had to be ferried to JG 26 at Brussels-Melsbroek. Kuhn took off from Wiesbaden, and, as the weather was poor, managed to disengage from the others without being noticed. His course now led over Ostend and the English Channel in low-level flight straight to southern England. Kuhn avoided landing on an RAF airfield, where he would have risked being shot down by AA guns. Instead he made a perfect belly landing in a field near Monkton, in Kent. His Fw 190A-8, Wk. Nr. 171747 was only slightly damaged.

Spaniards

Spain was probably the only European country in which large sections of the population saw the German attack on the Soviet Union on 22 June 1941 with satisfaction, even delight and spontaneous enthusiasm. The Nationalists in the country, still marked by the scars of the Civil War from 1936 to 1939, remembered only too well that Soviet weapons and instructors had supported the People's Front government. Already in the evening of 22 June the Spanish Foreign Minister, Ramón Serrano Suñer, offered the German ambassador in Madrid volunteers for the 'Crusade against Bolshevism'. Hitler agreed, hoping that this would tie Spain closer to the Axis powers. On 24 June a massed demonstration against the Soviet Union took place in the Spanish capital. Serrano Suñer made a brief speech culminating in the sentence 'Russia is guilty!' The enthusiastic crowd, including many students and supporters of the anti-Communist Falange Party, replied with 'Arriba España!' and 'Viva Franco!'[1]

For the cunning Spanish chief of state the dispatch of volunteers was not only an expression of his pronounced anti-Communism. He could pay off the debt to the German and Italian nationalists who had participated in the Civil War without being directly involved in a war against the Allies, the outcome of which was uncertain. He wanted to keep his options open, so that in the event of an Axis victory he could put forward some territorial claims in North Africa. Furthermore, the daring fighting of his soldiers in Russia would scare off any potential invaders by clearly demonstrating what sacrifices an attacker would have to make when trying to march into the Iberian peninsula. Finally, the Caudillo had another aim of a domestic nature: many Falangists were not satisfied with the reactionary nature of the Franco regime, but their energies could now be diverted to the Soviet battlefields and thus neutralized.

All this led to the formation, preparation and operational service on the Eastern Front of an infantry formation – the 250.ID (infantry division) of the Wehrmacht, also known as the 'Blue Division'. A total of 47,000 Spaniards served in this unit on the Eastern Front[2]. Like the members of the Spanish aviation formations, they were relieved in turn.

Strange to relate, these Wehrmacht formations never fought together, the 'Blue Division' always serving in the northern sector of the Eastern Front while the Spanish airmen were in the central sector.

The 1. Escuadrilla de Cazo (fighter squadron) left the Spanish capital with 130 men, including 17 pilots, on 25 June 1941. The Spanish had sent the cream of their fighter pilots with this unit: during the Civil War these 17 pilots had shot down a total of 79 Republican aircraft between them. The squadron was led by Comandante Angel Salas Larrazábal, whose personal score stood at 17 aerial victories. A rapidly advancing career awaited him in Franco's Spain after his return from Russia. After some time as an air attaché in Berlin and Paris, Larrazábal was to be appointed Chief of the Spanish Air Defence Forces in 1956. Later he was to become the Director of the Supreme Research Centre for Defence Studies. He died in Madrid at the age of 88 on 19 July 1994.

Although most of the Spanish pilots knew German air combat tactics and were familiar with German aircraft types, having fought with the German Condor Legion during the Civil War days, they still had to undergo additional, more comprehensive fighter training in Germany. When Larrazábal and his men arrived at Berlin-Tempelhof there was an embarrassing gaffe: the National Spanish airmen were not greeted by the Luftwaffe band with their own anthem but that of their former enemies, the 'Red' Republic!

There followed training and retraining at the Luftwaffe fighter establishment at Werneuchen. To the veterans of the Civil War all this dragged on too long, and they protested: they wanted to be at the Front. On 5 September 1941 the Spanish pilots finally received their new aircraft – Bf 109E-7s. Their swearing-in had already taken place in August. The Spanish swore the usual Wehrmacht oath, but with an adjunct – 'in fighting against the Communists' – which made it clear that they would not be drawn into combat against the Western Allies. In the meantime they had also exchanged their elegant Spanish uniforms for the German Luftwaffe outfits, which, however, displayed certain differences:[3] on the right upper sleeve of the uniform tunics and greatcoats was a shield-like national emblem in red/yellow/red with a black outline and the inscription ESPAÑA on top. Their steel helmets bore a smaller replica of this emblem.

In addition, many airmen, like the infantry soldiers, wore the blue Falange shirt under their uniforms, which was often turned up over the collar and eventually gave the unit its nickname of 'Escuadrilla Azul', the 'Blue Squadron'. On their uniforms, in addition to the awards earned during the Civil War, the Spanish soldiers often carried the Falange emblem or that of the student association SEU. The squadron had also brought along its own flag: next to the symbol of the San Fernando Order it displayed a circle with three birds in the centre – a falcon, a bustard and a blackbird. A similar illustration with the inscription 'Vista Suerte y al Toro' decorated many planes of the five Spanish formations. This was the emblem of the well-known Morato squadron of the Civil War years. With 40 aerial victories, Joaquin García Morato was the most successful Spanish fighter pilot.

On 26 September 1941 the 1st Spanish fighter squadron, with its 12 Bf 109E-7s, was sent to Minsk, and from there on to their operational airfield at Mozhna. The Spanish squadron was now listed as 15.(span.)/JG 27 of VIII. Fliegerkorps. Their operational début was not very encouraging: Sen Lt Luis Alcocer was killed on 2 October, when his Bf 109 turned over during an emergency landing. Three days later the Commanding General of VIII. Fliegerkorps, Wolfram Freiherr von Richthofen (1895–1945), who knew and valued 'his' Spaniards as a former commander of the Condor Legion, paid a visit to their airfield and awarded the Iron Cross, 2nd class, to the squadron commander Larrazábal, who had in the meantime shot down one I-16 Rata and a Pe-2 reconnaissance-bomber. But the highly qualified and motivated southerners were not satisfied: instead of 'free chase' they were repeatedly ordered to fly low-level attack sorties.

The German offensive against Moscow (Operation *Taifun*) forced the Spaniards to change their bases time and again. Places like Bieloy, Konnaya, Kalinin South and Russa were their stations in this hectic war of movement, and the ground services could hardly keep pace. A severe blow was suffered by the squadron on 27 November, when the deputy squadron commander, Comandante José Muñoz Jiménez, and another pilot failed to return from an operational sortie. Both remained missing.[4] A day later the squadron was transferred again, this time to Klin. This airfield was the deepest into Soviet territory, and the fall of Moscow then seemed only to be a matter of time. But the Russian cold paralysed the strength of the attackers and affected their equipment. At minus 35°C the aircraft engines would not start and the Soviet counter-attacks with fresh Siberian troops stopped the German formations. On 5 December 1941 Army Group Centre was forced to go on to the defensive.

The Spanish airmen, too, had to retreat, first to Duguino, where they celebrated Christmas in the biting cold and invited their German colleagues to join them. Uffz Walter Tödt from I./JG 52 still recalls the time: 'Yes, we had little to celebrate then. But our Spanish comrades in arms had received their Christmas presents from Generalissimo Franco, flown in by a Ju (Ju 52/3m transport), and they shared them with us. That was real comradeship!'[5]

The retreat of 15. (span.)/JG 27 ended at Vitebsk, where, on 6 January 1942, they received an order recalling them to Spain. After 460 operation sorties, ten confirmed aerial victories, the destruction of four Soviet aircraft on the ground and the loss of five of their own pilots, the first Spanish volunteer squadron returned home again.

Its replacement took some time to organize. The 2a Escuadrilla Azul came into being at Morón de la Frontera on 6 February 1942. It was formed by Comandante Julio Salvador Diaz-Benjumea, who had achieved 24 confirmed aerial victories in the Civil War, and who was destined to be appointed Minister of Aviation by Franco in 1969. Salvador functioned as chief inspector, while the squadron was led by Capt Noriega. With a personnel strength of 150 men, the second Spanish squadron, too, was first sent to the Jagdfliegerschule (Fighter Pilot Training School) Werneuchen, where they were trained between March and June. On 8 June 1942 the Spanish squadron was deployed to Orel. From then on the unit was listed as 15. (span.)/JG 51 and received new aircraft, the Bf 109F-4, with improved armour protection, and the faster-firing MG 151/20 cannon, while the German pilots of JG 51 still had to make do with the Bf 109F-2.[6]

When, on 28 June, the Wehrmacht started its summer offensive, with which Hitler hoped to force a decision at the southern wing of the Eastern Front (Operation *Blau*), the Army Group Centre, which also included the Spanish squadron, was not immediately involved. As Orel was at the boundary of the Army Group Weichs, however, the Spanish pilots were frequently in action. By November they had flown 403 operational sorties and shot down 13 Soviet aircraft for only two losses. In the meantime 3a Escuadrilla was being formed at Morón. Its captain was Comandante Carlos Ferrandiz Arjonilla and its training took place at S. Jean d'Angeli in France. The official relief of the 2nd Spanish squadron by the 3rd took place at Orel on 30 November 1942 but, as the new unit was still short of pilots, six from the 2nd Squadron temporarily remained with the replacement unit.

The 3a Escuadrilla, whose pilots and ground crews were still suffering from acclimatization difficulties, had to record its first loss on 1 December, when Capt Andrés Asensi Alvarez-Arenas was shot down and captured by the Soviets. He was not to return home until 1953. While in the Soviet camp, Asensi led a group of Spanish POWs who refused to bend to Soviet pressure and that of the NKVD (Soviet Internal Security) commissars. The National Spanish soldiers refused to be converted to 'anti-Fascists' for an extra portion of soup. The ethnic German POW Johan Urwich, who witnessed this, describes the group as 'very hard, very proud; they were impenetrable and reserved, true examples of the Spanish magnanimity. A perfect Hidalgo who looked like Don Quixote, was the pilot Captain Arensio [sic].'[7] After release from the Soviet camp Asensio (born in Murcia on

21 May 1912) had an exemplary career in post-war Spain. He became the Chief of the General Staff of he Spanish air force and commander of the Canary Islands Air Zone. He died as a Lt General on 20 December 1987.

After just two aerial victories the hard Russian winter, with its penetrating cold, prevented further action by the Spanish fighters for some weeks. But on 27 January 1943, six days before the capitulation of the remains of the German 6th Army in Stalingrad, they were once again successful with seven victories. Between 22 and 24 February the Spanish pilots sent 11 Soviet aircraft to the ground, followed by another seven between 7 and 10 March. The remaining pilots of the squadron also arrived from Spain that month, so that the veterans of the 2nd squadron could at last be relieved.

March was also the month when an important decision was made regarding the aircraft used by the Spanish fighters. The German Luftwaffe command had decided to let their Spanish allies have the Fw 190.[8] This piece of news was received with great joy by the Spaniards because their Bf 109Fs were 'flown out' and prone to all kinds of mishaps. On 21 April 1943 the new Fw 190A-3 fighters landed at Sestchinskaya. Powered by a BMW 801D double-row radial engine of 1,730hp, a total of 509 of this version were built between 1941 and 1943. The Spanish pilots of 15. (span.)/JG 51 'Mölders' first spent four days getting acquainted with their new planes before they were ready for action again.

A painful loss was the death of Sen Lt Juan Roselló Simonet, whose parachute failed to open after an accident on 5 May. But the Spanish pilots soon mastered the Fw 190A-3 and shot down a total of 29 Soviet aircraft with this fighter.

Beginning on 16 May, new Spanish pilots, intended as relief for the 3rd squadron, had begun arriving at the French airport of Toulouse-Blagnac.[9] They were then trained, if not particularly thoroughly, on the Fw 190, the conversion being completed after 15 hours. On 16 June the first of the newcomers touched down at Sestchinskaya and the exchange of personnel began. The command of Luftflotte 4 was very satisfied with the performance of the 3rd Spanish squadron: after all, they had achieved 62 aerial victories and the Ju 87 Stukas they had escorted had not lost a single aircraft. The Kommodore of JG 51 'Mölders', Karl-Gottfried Nordmann, discharged the 3rd Spanish squadron on 8 July 1943 with the following martially cordial speech:[10]

> Apart from the harshness of the war itself, with your iron will you have overcome the unaccustomed cold of the winter, the dirt and mud of the spring, as well as the dust and heat of the summer. You have done your duty as only soldiers know how to do it, and the proof and reward for it are the magnificent successes of the squadron.

It has to be said that the Spaniards and Germans respected and appreciated each other at the front and relations between them were generally cordial. The charm and cheerfulness of the individual Spaniards, who always had their beloved *vino tinto* brought up by the Ju 52/3m transports, conjured up some bright spots on the otherwise stern grey of the Wehrmacht. To be sure, the *señores* from Madrid, Valencia, Barcelona or Alicante did not think much of the rigid Prussian discipline, but their temperament, enthusiasm and audacity made them feared opponents.

One of the Spanish Junkers supply aircraft was flown by Indalecio Rego, who was never molested by Soviet fighters, but often got into the range of rifle fire from the partisans during low level flights that punched holes in the aircraft. After the war Rego continued flying for the Iberia airline, piloting such planes such as the DC-3 and DC-4, as well as the DC-8 and Boeing jets. In later years his considered opinion, based on very considerable flying experience, was that the best planes he had flown were the Boeing 747 – and the indestructible Ju 52/3m![11]

A few of the 'old hands' of the 3a Escuadrilla remained with the 4th replacement squadron, led by Comandante Mariano Cuadra Medina, because the pilot cadre was not yet quite complete. The new arrivals from Spain – apart from the squadron commander there were three captains, eleven senior lieutenants and five officer candidates among the flying personnel – came just at the right time to participate in the last major German offensive on the Eastern Front, Operation *Citadelle*, an attack from the Orel and Belgorod areas against the protruding Soviet frontal bulge at Kursk. At that time, there could no longer be any talk about German aerial superiority – after all, the Luftwaffe had lost 488 aircraft, equivalent to a complete air corps, at Stalingrad alone. The Spanish squadron of JG 51, like JG 54, had the task of providing fighter cover for the German 9th Army of Generaloberst Walter Model (1891–1945). In the event the Kursk offensive, for which the Germans had concentrated 3,000 tanks and assault guns and 1,800 aircraft, had to be broken off already on 13 July, not only because of the Soviet resistance but also because of the Allied landings in Sicily (Operation *Husky*), which forced the transfer of German reinforcements to Italy.

The morale of the Spanish airmen nonetheless remained intact. The 4a Escuadrilla became the most successful of all the Blue Squadrons. In 391 operational sorties in July, they shot down 12 Soviet aircraft; in August 21, and in September 15.[12] And this time it was mostly the latest Soviet models that were shot to the ground in flames, such as the Lavochkin La-5 and La-7, Petlyakov Pe-2 and Ilyushin Il-2m3 armoured assault aircraft. Two engagements were mini replays of the Spanish Civil War, when National Spanish pilots flying German aircraft were suddenly involved in aerial combat with 'red' Spaniards flying Soviet aircraft, and the hostile brothers swore at each other over the radio.

October 1943 became the 'black month' in Spanish–German military collaboration on the Eastern Front. As the Axis armies were now fighting defensively on all fronts Generalissimo Franco changed his stance from 'non-conduct of war' to 'neutrality' status. One of the first things he did was to order the withdrawal of the Blue Division, which was replaced by a much smaller (1,500 men) 'Blue Legion', led by Col Navarro.

The Spanish airmen, as they were not numerically so significant, were allowed to remain on the Eastern Front for the time being. On 19 November 1943 they lost an ace with eight victories – Sen Lt Sánchez-Arjona, who died in a crash. Six days later the 15. (span.)/JG 51 'Mölders' was transferred to Bobruisk.

The following two months were relatively peaceful and saw Spanish pilots victorious in another two aerial encounters. They achieved their last aerial victory of the war on 12 January 1944, when Sen Lt Valiente shot down a Soviet-flown Douglas Boston bomber. Altogether the 4a Escuadrilla had achieved 52 aerial victories and destroyed another 22 Soviet aircraft on the ground, but its own loss rate was also high: almost 50 per cent. Of the 20 pilots seven had been killed in action and three badly wounded.

Their replacement – 5a Escuadrilla – had in the meantime completed its training at Bergerac, in France. The flying instructor responsible for the training was Heinrich Heuser from the Ergänzungsjagdgruppe Süd (Replacement Fighter Group South), who was to recall: 'The training lasted until early February 1944. The pilots brought along with them good flying ability, a high morale and a great operational willingness. During their stay with the Erg. Jagdgruppe Süd we also developed a good personal relationship between us.'[13] The Spanish airmen, led by Comandante Javier Murcia Rubio, reached the Eastern Front, via Berlin, late in February. To their great surprise they now received Bf 109G-6s although their training had been mainly on the Fw 190A. With their 'Gustavs' the southerners carried out 86 more operational sorties, contested six more aerial encounters and lost one pilot. Then Caudillo Franco finally gave in to Allied pressure and recalled all Spanish volunteers from fighting on the Eastern Front.

After the Legion Azul received its repatriation orders on 6 March 1944 a similar order went out to 5a Escuadrilla in April. The last of the 89 Spanish pilots of the Blue squadrons – who had flown more than 3,000 operational sorties, achieved 159 aerial victories[14] and had suffered a loss rate of 30 per cent (including wounded) – were now back home. This recall back to Spain did not give the highly motivated Spanish fighter pilots any joy; instead, their feelings were dominated by bewilderment, fury, disappointment and bitterness. When Comandante Murcia Rubio read out the disbandment order to his officers, their response was a resounding 'NO!'[15] For propaganda reasons the German leadership in Berlin kept quiet about this withdrawal of Spanish troops. Spain itself, which had so enthusiastically and exuberantly celebrated and taken leave of the first volunteers in 1941, remained silent when the last legionnaires and airmen arrived back home. Franco, who had now prepared himself for an Allied victory, thus let it be known that he no longer backed the Axis card.

Successes of the Spanish Fighter Pilots by Squadron

Squadron	Operational Period	Victories
1a Escuadrilla	October–December 1941	10
2a Escuadrilla	June–November 1942	13
3a Escuadrilla	December 1942–July 1943	62
4a Escuadrilla	July 1943–January 1944	74
5a Escuadrilla	February–May 1944	–
TOTAL		159

Losses of the Five Spanish Fighter Squadrons 1941–4

Squadron	Killed in Action	Missing	POW
1a Escuadrilla	3	2	
2a Escuadrilla	2		
3a Escuadrilla	5		1
4a Escuadrilla	7		
5a Escuadrilla	1		
TOTAL	18	2	1

Estonians

After the Soviet occupation of Estonia in June 1940, and enforced annexation by the Soviet Union, the Estonian armed forces were first purged of 'untrustworthy' officers and then integrated into the Red Army. The Estonian army was formed into 22nd Territorial Rifle Corps and the air force, the size of a group, was reduced to a squadron. The Soviets concentrated all Estonian civil and military aircraft at Jägala, and in September 1940 transferred part of this booty, including the Ju 52/3m aircraft of the Estonian airline AGO, to the Soviet Union.

With the strengthening of the Soviet occupation forces to some 650,000 men in all three Baltic republics, June 1941 saw the beginning of the subduing and purging of 'class enemies' and 'bourgeois elements'. Thousands of Estonians were arrested, deported and murdered, increasing the hatred of the population of the Soviet occupiers. Against this background it is not difficult to imagine the frame of mind prevalent in the Soviet-dominated Estonian flying unit: 'The mood in the squadron was, like everywhere else, hopeless. Arrests were the order of the day, and a feeling of insecurity prevailed.'[1]

After the German attack on the Soviet Union on 22 June 1941 the Wehrmacht quickly advanced into the Baltic region. Vilnius, the capital of Lithuania, was captured on 24 June, and the German spearheads pushed deeper and further north-eastwards. The Estonian airmen were ordered by their Soviet superiors to transfer to Russia 'for retraining', as it was officially designated, but most of the flying personnel ignored this. Officer candidate Remi Milk, born on 18 July 1921, who had joined the Estonian air force in November 1938, was one of those who declined to obey this order and made an open stand against Soviet despotism instead. 'On 27 June 1941 we received orders to go to Russia by train, but we, 85 per cent of the flying personnel (about 45 men), escaped into the forests instead and fought as 'forest brothers' against the Soviet occupiers.'[2] These 'forest brothers', nationalist partisans, harried the Soviet troops to the extent that parts of Estonia were already liberated from the Red Army before the arrival of the German Wehrmacht.

Contrary to the expectations and wishes of the Estonians, the German National Socialists had no intention of restoring the independence of the Baltic States, and Estonia, Latvia and Lithuania became part of the Reichskommissariat Ostland. Nevertheless, many Estonians fought in various German formations as they believed Communism to be the main evil, and never gave up the hope that they would somehow still succeed in achieving the freedom and independence of their country in some shape or form. This desire was also expressed in numerous petitions submitted to the German National Socialist occupation authorities by the Estonian self-administration: 'Unfortunately the Estonians, who would want to protect their land from Communist Russia, have to do this in German uniform, but with the blue/black/white escutcheon on the sleeve and free Estonia in their hearts.'[3]

The Estonian Luftwaffe units were founded by an ethnic German, Gerhard Buschmann. Born in Tallinn, he had been a sports pilot in Estonia before the war, and also an officer of the German Abwehr (counter-intelligence service)[4] who, within the scope afforded by his responsibilities, always supported Estonian interests. He had already tried to form an Estonian detachment to be attached to the Suomen Ilmavoimat, but the Finns feared complications with the Germans so the plan could not be realized. The fact that the Estonian Aero Club had managed successfully to hide five aircraft (four unarmed PTO-4s and one Polish RWD-8 trainer) from the Soviets gave rise to the idea of forming an Estonian aviation unit equipped with this material. Of course that could only be done with official approval of the German occupying powers. However, Buschmann had good contacts and was able to gain the support for his project from both Luftflotte 1 and the Admiral of the Eastern Baltic Sea. This 'private squadron' was conceived as a coastal and naval reconnaissance unit. However, as neither the navy nor the Luftwaffe could at that point simply take on Baltic personnel and put them on the official payroll, they had to find another ally. Finally, the SS and Police Commander in Estonia declared himself prepared to recognize this unusual formation officially as a 'police unit'. In this roundabout way Buschmann had brought into being one quite unique squadron, which was listed as 'Sonderstaffel Buschmann' (Buschmann Special Squadron), usually abbreviated to SB, which received its equipment from the Luftwaffe, its operational tasks from the German navy and its provisions and pay from the SS.[5] Its aircraft carried German national markings, but had their propeller hubs painted in the Estonian colours, blue, black and white. Buschmann received definite permission to form the unit on 12 February 1942, and the four Estonian PTO-4s were at last able to fly their first operational sorties over the Gulf of Finland. The aircraft were of course unarmed and carried no radio equipment, and the outfits worn by the pilots were anything but conventional: they were German uniforms without any rank insignia, pre-war Estonian uniforms or a mix of civilian clothing.

By early summer 1942 the Germans had to supplement the four PTO-4s (identification letters SB+AA, SB+AB, SB+AC and SB+AD) with a Miles Magister (SB+AF), a de Havilland D.H.89 Dragon Rapide (SB+AH), another RWD-8 (SB+AJ) and five Stampe SV-5s. The last-mentioned was a Belgian training biplane of which six examples had been built under licence in Latvia. This plane would have graced any sports aviation association, but was only of limited use for operations over the sea. It soon became obvious that these light trainers were not up to the task assigned to Sonderstaffel Buschmann, so were replaced by He 60 floatplanes during the summer of 1942.

In the meantime Buschmann did all he could to acquire more aircraft for the squadron carrying his name. In Germany he unearthed some 'mothballed' Arado Ar 95 multi-purpose reconnaissance floatplanes that had originally been intended for Chile, but that could not be delivered to Latin America because of the outbreak of hostilities.[6] After some negotiating he succeeded in having these aircraft passed on to his Estonian airmen. He was less successful in his attempt to transfer to Estonia the Bf 109T fighters originally intended for the aircraft carrier *Graf Zeppelin*: the Luftwaffe refused to release these aircraft.

In autumn 1942 it seemed that the Estonian flying unit had reached the end of its existence when Hitler ordered its disbandment.[7] Sonderstaffel Buschmann was more like a national partisan unit than a regular flying formation, and its close ties with the navy must have irked Göring, while having Baltic airmen as equal comrades in arms with their own aircraft must have aroused Hitler's mistrust. However, the Estonian flying formation, which had by early 1943 grown to 50 aircraft and about 200 personnel, was never completely dissolved. Various German military command headquarters, not least the navy in the Baltic, had an interest in keeping the unit going – now known formally as the Nachrichten- und Verbindungsfliegergruppe z.b.V. (Communications and Liaison Aviation Group for Special Purposes) – while Buschmann negotiated for its incorporation into the Luftwaffe.

His persistence paid off in spring 1943. Sonderstaffel Buschmann was officially taken over by the Luftwaffe as 16./Aufkl.Gr.127 (See), backdated to July 1942, although the actual and complete acceptance of the Estonians in the Luftwaffe did not take place until April 1943.

The unit was now reorganized into three squadrons, of which only one was to continue carrying out naval reconnaissance tasks, while the other two were to be equipped with He 50 land planes newly supplied from Germany. Originally designed as dive bombers, these sturdy biplanes were now classed as multipurpose trainers and were suitable for conversion into night harassment aircraft.

There was no lack of volunteers for the new unit. One of these was Valdo Raag, born in 1925:

I volunteered for the Luftwaffe in June 1943. Why? That is not easy to explain. Perhaps because I received a patriotic upbringing in the Estonian democratic republic and could not get over the Soviet occupation of Estonia in 1940–1. When, after the start of the war [22 June 1941], a number of people were arrested and executed, the youth of Estonia was ready to fight the Bolsheviks at the first opportunity. And this opportunity came in 1943. At that time, several Estonian units were formed within the

Wehrmacht[8] and, quite by chance, I saw an article about Estonian airmen in a newspaper. That immediately aroused my interest and I decided to join the Luftwaffe.[9]

But it was not only volunteers who joined the Estonian flying formation. In 1943 young Estonians were mobilized for German military service under the pretext of labour service duty, beginning with those born between 1919 and 1924. Among those mobilized was Benno Abram, born in 1923, who followed the call of the Luftwaffe without much enthusiasm. 'I was not exactly enthused about my call-up in 1943, but I accepted it because I felt a duty to my country.'[10] Many of his countrymen felt the same because the German defeats on the Eastern Front made them fear a renewed Soviet occupation of their land. Whatever else, Estonia had to be defended.

Both land-based squadrons of Aufkl.Gr.127 (See) were transferred to the northern sector of the front where the Estonian airmen began operations as night harassment bombers south of the Ilmen Lake, at the Lovat river and near Leningrad. They were also deployed to attack Soviet partisan bases. In the meantime 1./Aufkl.Gr.127 continued its naval reconnaissance flights over the Gulf of Finland, patrolled the mine barrages and tried to prevent Soviet submarines from breaking out of Kronstadt into the Baltic Sea.

The single-engined Ar 95 could carry bombs and thus attack the submarines on its own, or inform the German and Finnish naval forces about their presumed diving positions. But it was not an easy task. Combating submarines was made very difficult by the murky water of the Gulf and the numerous oil spills leaking from sunken Soviet vessels. Nevertheless, the Commander of the German Mine Sweeping Formations East reported to Aufkl.Gr.127 on 4 June 1943, that, thanks to its successful reconnaissance flights and timely reporting to submarine chaser forces, it had contributed to the destruction of five enemy submarines during the period 21 May to 1 June. One Soviet submarine was reportedly sunk on 21 May in map square 6015, another a day later in map square 5018, the third on 26 May in map square 4016, the fourth on 28/29 May in map square 5019 and the last on 1 June in map square 4019.[11] However, the unfavourable conditions in the Gulf of Finland made it difficult to confirm the success or otherwise of anti-submarine attacks and led to exaggerated sinking claims. Post-war research reveals that only two Soviet submarines – *Shch-408* on 26 May and *Shch-406* on 1 June – were in fact destroyed during the above period.[12] Thus reports claiming that no fewer than 18 Soviet submarines were destroyed thanks to the assistance of 1./Aufkl.Gr.127[13] do not stand up to closer analysis.

By that time Hptm Buschmann had been relieved of his duties as commander of the Estonian flying formation because he was far too 'Estonian-friendly' for the liking of the National Socialists. His successor, Hptm Paul Lehmann, also proved to be a competent officer and friendly towards the Estonians. Nevertheless, it is surprising that the seven former Estonian members of the Luftwaffe interviewed by the author could recall no negative experiences during their collaboration with their German aviation comrades. Their descriptions of relations with the Germans range from 'normal' and 'comradely' to 'very good' and 'of solemn mutual respect'. Unfortunately, the German command headquarters and other administrative centres all too frequently treated foreign fellow soldiers in an overbearing racial manner as 'second-class people' and 'inferior mercenaries'.

The Aufkl.Gr.127 was redesignated Seeaufklärungsgruppe (Naval Reconnaissance Group) 127 in June 1943. An important restructuring followed in October: the 1. and 2. Staffeln of SAGr.127 now formed the 1. and 2. Staffeln of the newly established Nachtschlachtgruppe 11 (estnisch), the Estonian Night Harassment Group, abbreviated to NSGr 11 (est.). A 3rd squadron was formed in December 1943, and was equipped with Ar 66C trainers adapted for night bombing. The first squadron, 1./SAGr 127 commanded by the Estonian Oblt (later Hptm) William Laanekörb, remained in action for naval reconnaissance purposes. In September 1943 the Luftwaffe established a training centre for Estonian and Latvian pilots at Liepāja-Grobiņa in Courland, Latvia, which also functioned as a Flugzeugführerschule (pilot training school)

A/B and was renamed Ergänzungsnachtschlachtgruppe Ostland (Night Harassment Replacement Group Baltic) in January 1944. This establishment was commanded by a German major, Walter Endres, an experienced bomber pilot and leader. Liepāja-Grobiņa was not only a training centre for pilots but also Estonian air gunners and Estonian and Latvian aircraft mechanics and other specialists. The first group of airmen who passed through were Estonian reserve pilots, who, after this refresher and orientation course, were posted to NSGr. 11. The training of new pilots began in November 1943, and 26 beginners left the school as fully trained pilots in June 1944. In the same month the Estonian personnel of Erg.NSGr. Ostland were transferred to Tartu, in Estonia, where the training was continued. By that time most of the instructors were Estonians themselves. In Tartu another six former Estonian pilots completed their refresher and orientation course, but the training of 26 beginners had to be suspended in September due to the shortage of aviation fuel.[14] Some Estonian members of the Luftwaffe were then attached for a while to German formations to complete their training and gain some experience. Arvo Putmaker, born in Tallinn on 8 September 1921, who had enrolled in the technical high school there, volunteered for the Luftwaffe in March 1943, underwent an air gunner's training for three months and then flew a few naval reconnaissance sorties in an Ar 95 before being transferred. He recalls:[15]

> My friend and I (we had completed the air gunner's course as the best of 13 trainees) and another three of our group were then sent to Pskov to gain more experience while serving with the German unit. From there my friend and I were sent further on, to Dno (about 100km/61 miles from Pskov), to join 3.(F)/22 (long-range reconnaissance squadron) equipped with Ju 88s. Another two comrades were also posted to Ju 88 long-range reconnaissance aircraft, while the fifth of our group remained in Pskov where there was a night long-range reconnaissance squadron equipped with Do 217s.

In August came another reorganization of the Baltic airmen serving in the Luftwaffe. A secret order from the Quartermaster General of the OKL (Az.: 8 Nr. 12042/44 g. Kdos 2, Abt. IIB), dated 11 August 1944, divided the Erg.NSGr. Ostland into Erg.NSGr. Estland and Erg.NSGr.Lettland.[16] The aircraft park for both units was listed as 16 Bü 131s, 16 Ar 66/Go 145s and three additional Ar 66s for instrument flying training each. Provision was also made for three additional Ar 66s with rotating gun rings in the rear cockpit for Estonian air gunner training.

The reliability and operational willingness of the Estonian airmen was high, factors that were recognized by both the German naval and Luftwaffe commands. For instance, on 6 January 1944 the Chief of Luftflotte 1 sent a message to 1.(S)/Aufkl.Gr.127: 'By the exemplary completion of the given tasks in 1,000 operational sorties against the common enemy, the squadron has demonstrated great flying skills and outstanding operational willingness. I would like to express my thanks and special appreciation both to the flying and to the ground personnel for their brave and untiring efforts.'[17]

The reputation enjoyed by the Baltic airmen must have been a contributing factor to the secret order from the Quartermaster General at the OKL (Az.: 11b 16.10 Nr. 10570/44 g. Kdos 2, Abt. IIB), dated 31 May 1944,[18] requesting the formation of one Estonian and one Latvian fighter squadron. The execution of this order was assigned to Luftflotte 1. On the strength of this order ten Estonian pilots were selected from NSGr.11 and posted to Germany to begin their fighter raining in May–June 1944. These potential fighter pilots were sent in two groups of five men each:[19]

1st Group	2nd Group
Lt Juri Kukk	Lt Voldemar Eller
Oblt Karl Lumi	Lt Harri Kollo
Oblt Lembit Raidal	Oblt Edgar Martensen
Oblt John Sepa	Oblt Anatol Rebane
Obfrh Aksel M. Kessler	Oblt Albert Vaart

(Obfrh = Oberfähnrich, Senior Officer Candidate)

293

At least three of these Estonian pilots lost their lives while training: Voldemar Eller, Juri Kukk (on 12 August 1944 at Jagdgruppe Ost) and Lembit Raidal.

In February 1944, as the Red Army had reached Narva and therefore Estonian territory, NSGr.11 was moved back into Estonia itself. It was concentrated on the Jöhvi and Rahkla airfields, and continued to fly operational sorties to relieve the Narva front until the end of August. In February the unit received 'new' aircraft in the form of about 20 Fokker C.VEs. These aged biplanes had originally belonged to the Danish air force and had been confiscated by the Germans. 'It was said in a joking way that these were Dutch aircraft that the Germans had taken them off the Danes and given them to the Estonians to fight the Russians.'[20]

Translation of German Naval Order
Dated 11.2.1944

Commanding Admiral   11 February 1944
Baltic

1./Aukl.Gr.127
Personally to Sqn Commander Oblt Laanekörb

With the help of the Naval Commander Baltic the squadron was built up from the smallest beginnings in 1942. Since that time, it has been in spirited action that has extended over the Gulf of Finland to the Bay of Kronstadt. Later on the squadron obtained valuable reconnaissance data for the navy before the capture of the Tüttere Island.

As a naval reconnaissance squadron the unit has continued its operations over the Gulf of Finland in 1943, and has to date completed over 1,000 operational sorties, often faced by enemy countermeasures. It is thanks to the untiring reconnaissance activities of this squadron that successful attacks could be carried out against enemy submarines by our naval forces, reported by the reconnaissance airmen.

The number of decorations awarded to the members of this

squadron are proof of their constant readiness for action.

I would like to express my fullest appreciation to all members of the squadron for the services provided to the Navy since the establishment of this unit.

Signed
Viceadmiral

In summer 1944 the NSGr.11 shifted the concentration of their efforts from around Narva to the Tartu area, and the unit moved to a new airfield at Adavere and Kärevere in central Estonia. By then the shortage of aviation fuel was becoming serious and the pilots were unable to carry out many sorties even under the most favourable conditions. Understandably, the Estonian airmen who wanted to defend their country reacted with incomprehension and fury to these circumscribed conditions.

But Estonia could not be held. On 29 July the German Army Group North in Estonia and Latvia was cut off from its land connections with Germany by a Soviet breakthrough and advance to the Gulf of Riga. Although the Soviet spearhead was checked and beaten back by a German counter-attack, the pressure continued and the gradual evacuation of German forces from Estonia to defensive positions around the Riga area began in mid-September. The Estonian flying formations, which by then had flown 7,000 operational sorties on the Eastern Front, received orders to retreat further inland. On 18 September NSGr.11 (est.), which still had 17 He 50s, 13 Ar 66Cs and seven Fokker C.Vs, was assigned to the Blome airfield in northern Latvia; from there its way led over Liepāja-Grobiņa to Tirksliai, in Lithuania, and finally to Heiligenbeil, in East Prussia.[21] On 22 September 1./SAGr.127 flew from Tallinn to Pillau, near Königsberg.

At this point many Estonians could see no sense in further fighting. Their homeland, for the freedom of which they had fought and sacrificed so much, was now lost once more, and the end of the war was drawing closer. For these reasons some aircrews decided to flee to neutral Sweden. On 22 September three Ar 95s (6R+LL, Wk. Nr. 2346, 6R+BL, Wk. Nr. 2350 and 6R+UL, Wk. Nr. 2351) from 1./SAGr.127 alighted on Swedish territorial waters. The 6R+LL was piloted by Lt Remi Milk, who set down not far from Stockholm. The Swedish authorities took over all three Ar 95s and brought them into their own service. Milk's aircraft was given a new identity as SE-ANT and remained in Swedish service for six years, until it was destroyed during an unsuccessful take-off on 30 July 1951. It is interesting to note that Milk also had a strange meeting with the German Luftwaffe attaché in the Swedish capital in November 1944. Milk was told that he had been awarded the Iron Cross, 1st Class, and the Combat Flight Clasp in gold, as well as being promoted to Oberleutnant. Furthermore, the Estonian flying formation was expecting him to return. In fact by that time there were no independent Estonian flying units any more.

Secret Command Matter – Teleprinter Message from Uebe Nr. 026

Teleprinter message   Secret Command Matter
L UEBE Nr. 026
4.10.(1200) = to OKL FUEST – (Robinson 7)*

Re: Estonian (flying) units

The flights to Sweden undertaken by aircraft of Estonian flying units during the last few days indicate, after hitherto proven behaviour, serious symptoms of morale decline since the loss of Estonia. As a first countermeasure the Estonian flying units have been grounded by an order from Luftflotte 1. They have also been deprived of aviation fuel. Beyond that, instructions have been issued to disband all Estonian flying units, insofar as this does not go against political considerations (continuation of fighting against Bolshevism by Estonian formations). The following would be affected by this disbandment order:

Commander of Luftwaffen-Legion Estland (Estonia) at HQ of Luftflotte 1. In his place will be appointed an Estonian liaison officer. Naval Reconnaissance Squadron 1./127; NSGr.11; Erg.NSGr.Estland (for the time being subordinated operationally to G.D.S., in official matters to Luftflotte 10). Apart from some technical personnel there are no other possibilities for the employment of Estonian personnel within the Luftflotte 1 area. The intended formation of Estonian AA units is only in its early stages. It is proposed to leave suitable, proven and operationally willing AA personnel as well as Estonian volunteers serving in German signals troops where they are. All other Estonian personnel, however, will be offered to the Waffen-SS or conveyed to the State Labour Service.

The remaining personnel within German units can stay where they are in smaller groups and be employed as voluntary auxiliary personnel.

The above conditions do not apply to the Latvian units as yet.

Luftflotte Command 1 Chief of General Staff
Signed Uebe – Roem One – Secret Command Matter No.4383/44

* Code designation of Göring's command train

On 1 October 1944 the three Arado Ar 95 floatplanes from 1./SAGr.127 were followed to Sweden by another two aircraft from NSGr.11 with Estonian pilots, a Fokker C.VE (3W+OL) and an He 50 (3W+NO, Wk. Nr. 1260). The Luftflotte 1 staff were dismayed by this desertion of five aircraft within a week. Until then the Estonian squadrons, with a personnel strength of 1,000 men including about 200 flying crews, had not shown any signs of dissolution, quite the opposite. The Estonian airmen had been known for their high operational morale. Luftflotte 1 now had to issue an order grounding the Estonian airmen, and, with a teleprinter message to the OKL of 4 October 1944 requested the disbandment of all Estonian flying units. This request was granted with a teleprinter message from the Quartermaster General at the OKL (Az.: 11b16 No. 13215/44 Secret Command Matter IIB of 7 October 1944), which ordered the disbandment of all Estonian and Latvian flying units 'with immediate effect'.[22] This order did not specify the planned Estonian and intended Latvian fighter squadrons, which were not mentioned. However, their pilots never saw action as an independent formation, but were allocated to various German fighter formations. The disbandment order was announced to the personnel of NSGr.11 at Heiligenbeil on 12 October. One day later a Fokker C.VE (3W+OD) managed to cross the Baltic Sea to Sweden, and on 31 October an Estonian mechanic stole a Do 24 flying boat, which was also to alight on the waters of the neutral kingdom.

All members of NSGr.11 and 1./SAGr.127 and the Estonian fighter pilots were initially gathered together at the Kunersdorf airfield. There followed a further dispersion of the Estonian airmen and ground personnel. Only the Estonian fighter pilots, of whom at least Lumi and Sepa had already flown operationally with JG 54 in September, were permitted to continue flying, and, at the end of 1944, arrived at different German units. Some Estonian officers were assigned to the 20th Waffen-SS Grenadier Division (estn.Nr.1), but most of the Estonian airmen and ground personnel were ordered to join the Baltischen Legion der Fallschirmarmee (Baltic Legion of the Parachute Army) forming near Esbjerg, in Denmark. It was supposedly intended to form a parachute regiment with one Estonian, one Latvian and one Baltic ethnic German battalion, but this never came to fruition. Instead the Estonians were ordered to Dortmund in December, where they were trained on the 88mm flak guns and underwent further dispersal among German AA detachments in Germany or were assigned to the Estonian units of the Waffen-SS.

The Estonian fighter pilots were operational on the Eastern Front (and also on the Western Front) until the last days of the war. It is known that Oblt Karl Lumi of 7./JG 4 was killed in action. To avoid capture another two Estonian fighter pilots later escaped to neutral Sweden. On 19 April 1945 Officer Candidate Aksel Kessler of II./JG 4 flew his Fw 190A-8 'black 10' Wk. Nr. 961076 there, and was followed eleven days later by Oblt Anatol Rebane of 6./JG 4 with his Fw 190A-8 'white 15', Wk. Nr. 739136, who landed at Malmö.[23]

Those Estonian airmen who fell into Soviet hands could expect a standard penalty: 25 years hard labour, confiscation of property, loss of rights and banishment for five years. The living and working conditions in Soviet prison camps were terrible, and most Estonian soldiers had to suffer this harsh existence until 1955 or even 1956. Kaljo Alaküla, born on 20 April 1923, had served as a volunteer with the Estonian self-defence from October 1941 to May 1943, afterwards with the Aufkl.Gr.127, NSGr.11, an AA unit and finally with the Waffen-SS. He reports:[24]

> Life in the Soviet prison camp was very rough. Every day we had to work hard for 12 hours. When one considers the march there and back, our forced labour amounted to 16 or 17 hours a day. Food was extremely sparse and poor. Men who weighed some 80kg (176lb) were soon down to just 40 or 50kg (88–110lb), and the mortality rate among us was very high. We were permitted to write two letters a year, which almost never reached our homeland.

The 'people's enemy' Alaküla also had to divorce his wife to prevent her deportation to Siberia. Other Luftwaffe comrades of his had better luck. Benno Abram, Lt of the Luftwaffe (Rtd), was released from an American POW camp quite early and returned illegally to Estonia in 1946. The Soviet authorities had no evidence against him because all his personal documents had been destroyed. After a while Abram joined Tartu University to study medicine. In the lecture hall he spotted some fellow students who, like himself, had been in the Luftwaffe but did not venture to talk to them for fear of informers. The former airmen could only talk openly about their past experiences after Estonia regained its independence in 1991.

Latvians

After the forced occupation of Latvia in June 1940 the Soviets behaved in the same way as they had in Estonia. The Latvian army, after a brief period as 'People's Army' and a purge of 'unreliable' officers, became the 24th Territorial Rifle Corps of the Red Army. The Latvian Army Air Force, founded on 7 June 1919 during the War of Liberation and numbering some 90 aircraft (including 26 Gloster Gladiator II fighters) and more than 500 personnel at the time of the Soviet occupation, was reduced to just one squadron equipped with Belgian Stampe et Vertongen SV-5 trainers and a personnel strength of just 175 men. There was also a Home Guard (Aizsargi) aviation element, consisting of 30 aircraft and 300 personnel, which was completely disbanded. Following the German attack on the Soviet Union on 22 June 1941, the small Latvian unit, known as 24th Squadron, was deployed near Gulbene and ordered to carry out local reconnaissance flights. One SV-5 was lost at night.[1] A few days later the Soviets ordered this Latvian unit to transfer to Rzhev on the Upper Volga, where it arrived on 2 July. The Latvian airmen were then supposed to travel by train to Moscow, but the train was attacked by German aircraft on the way and several of the Latvians were killed. The remaining members of 24th Squadron were then assigned to various aviation units, aircraft repair trains and bases; some pilots were also engaged as flying instructors.[2] It was not until spring 1943 that the Soviet authorities resurrected the Latvian flying unit. Starting as a single squadron equipped with old Po-2 biplane trainers adapted for night harassment bombing, this unit eventually expanded to regimental size, although only about 70 per cent of its personnel were of Latvian origin.[3] Official Soviet data stated that this Latvian formation carried out a total of 6,450 operational sorties up to the end of hostilities in May 1945. It was one of only three 'national' units of the wartime Soviet air force, and was disbanded in June 1946.

After two years the German occupying powers in the Baltic States had lost most of the goodwill and sympathy of the inhabitants, but they could still count on local support when it came to active opposition to the Bolsheviks. This was clearly shown by the fighting record of the many thousands of Latvian volunteers and, later, mobilized soldiers of the Latvian Legion, particularly during the bitter defensive battles in Courland in 1944–5.

Preparations for the formation of a Latvian aviation unit in the Luftwaffe had begun in September 1943. The establishment of the FFS (Flying Training School) A/B Libau-Grobin (Liepāja-Grobiņa) in Courland opened the way for former pilots of the Latvian Army Air Force and Home Guard, as well as interested sports and glider pilots and younger aviation enthusiasts. It gave them an opportunity to be trained as pilots of German aircraft or as technical personnel. There was no open recruiting by posters or public announcements; most of the younger age group learnt of this new training school by chance.[4] As with the Estonians, anti-Communist conviction also played an important role. 'One year of Soviet occupation was a traumatic shock for the Latvian people.'[5]

For nine months the training facility at Leipāja-Grobiņa was shared by Estonian and Latvian Luftwaffe volunteers under the overall command of a German major, Walter Endres. The first graduates were exclusively former Latvian Army Air Force and Home Guard pilots, who completed the refresher and familiarization course in February 1944.[6] Of the 25 Latvian pilots eight remained behind at Leipāja-Grobiņa as instructors.

Some experienced airmen of the former Latvian Army Air Force or Home Guard, who were already serving in the Latvian Legion, police battalions or other German units, found it very difficult to transfer to the Luftwaffe; others were luckier. Indulis Ozols, born at Valmiera on 16 October 1923, who had volunteered for the RAD (State Labour Service) in summer 1943, received his call-up papers for the Waffen-SS after his RAD service, but volunteered for the Luftwaffe instead and was accepted without any problems.

Altogether five Latvian pilot refresher and training courses took place at Liepāja-Grobiņa until September 1944; the sixth course was planned but not implemented. A total of 140 airmen completed these courses, including 50 former pilots of the Latvian Army Air Force, 50 Home Guard pilots and 40 members of the Latvian Aero Club and glider pilots. There were three fatalities: one pilot on the first course, Lt Jānis Stukáns, was killed in a crash after becoming disorientated during a searchlight affiliation exercise, and two young trainee pilots, Flg Degimuss and Martini, died after a mid-air collision on 22 August 1944.[7]

In February 1944 the first 17 Latvian pilots were formed into 1./NSGr.12 (lett.), of which only the headquarters and this squadron existed at that time. It was planned to establish three squadrons, but this target proved too ambitious and the group was never to exceed two squadrons.

Squadron 1./NSGr.12 (lett.), commanded by the Latvian Hptm Alfreds Salmiņš, had a strength of 19 pilots and 105 ground personnel, among whom there were only five Germans. The unit was equipped with 18 Ar 66c training biplanes adapted for night harassment bombing, and began operations from the Vecumi airfield in Latgale (eastern Latvia) on 23 March. For their night sorties the aircraft were flown individually, in single-seat configuration, and could penetrate up to 50km (31 miles) behind the enemy lines. Their usual operational altitude was about 1,000m (3,280ft), and the average sortie would last about two hours. The aircraft carried an offensive load of two to three 50–70kg (110–154lb) bombs, the aiming of which was assisted by diagonal 'inclination' lines painted on some aircraft on the starboard fuselage next to the pilot's seat. The squadron was especially active during the period 12–22 May, when it dropped 1,000 bombs on enemy targets in eight nights. On 28 May the squadron was moved to the Salas airfield.

On 22 June 1944 2./NSGr.12 (lett.) was formed at Leipāja-Grobiņa, and left the base to join the first squadron at Salas airfield four days later. The second squadron comprised 17 pilots and 70 ground personnel, and was commanded by the Latvian Hptm Augusts Graudiņš. It began operations within a day of its arrival on the airfield. While both squadrons were led by Latvian officers, the overall command of NSGr.12 (lett.) was temporarily in the hands of a German officer, Hptm

Rademacher, who held that post until mid-September. He was succeeded by a Latvian officer, Obstl Nikolajs Bulmanis, while another Latvian officer, Major Aleksandrs Tomass, took charge of the Leipāja-Grobiņa training base.[8]

In July 1944 both Latvian squadrons were based at the Gulbene airfield. The massive Soviet offensive involving the 1st Baltic as well as the 1st, 2nd and 3rd Byelo-Russian Fronts, with their main drive towards Vilnius, had begun on 4 July, and that meant intensified operations for both Latvian night harassment squadrons. Their 1,000th night sortie was recorded on 25 July. Two days prior to that 2./NSGr.12 (lett.) had experienced its 'black day': of the 16 Ar 66s that had taken off on operations only nine had returned to base! Bad weather had surprised the largely inexperienced pilots, of whom two managed to make emergency landings elsewhere behind their own lines. One young pilot returned the following afternoon lightly wounded; he had made a forced landing in a rough field. Another, older pilot also managed to make a forced landing, but was captured wounded by Red partisans. Somehow he succeeded in gaining their trust; so much so that he managed to escape and return to his unit in mid-August, with his wounds still not healed.[9] Three Latvian pilots remained missing, however, and one of them, Flg Juris Kiršteins, was 'turned' as a Soviet POW. Under the massive pressure by interrogation experts, he agreed to work for the Soviet intelligence service. In March 1945 he was dropped by parachute in the Pāvilosta/Courland area, landing in German hands, and was executed shortly afterwards.[10]

Attempts to form a third Latvian squadron in July 1944[11] failed for lack of aircraft. The same applied to the planned re-equipment with Ju 87D-5/D-7 special night bombers.

In June 1944 Erg.NSGr.Ostland was renamed Erg.NGSr. Lettland and received more volunteers, who kept arriving until early August. The last batches were flown in direct from Riga-Spilve by Ju 52/3m transports, making a detour some distance from the coast of Courland to avoid Soviet-occupied areas.[12] Whereas many of the earlier volunteers were really interested in aviation, this time there were only a few such enthusiasts. Apart from some mobilized older aviation mechanics, most were young Latvians who wanted to avoid being called up for the Latvian Legion and hoped to find an easier life in the Luftwaffe.

Uffz Indulis Ozols, who was one of the instructors at that time, described his new charges as 'escapees from the trenches'.[13] However, training at the base was demanding, and the activities of the Latvian night harassment squadrons by no means offered a guarantee of an easy life. On the night of 1 August alone, 35 aircraft from NSGr.12 (lett.) flew nearly 300 operational sorties and dropped 50 tonnes of bombs in the Jelgava area.[14] Early in August both Latvian squadrons moved to the Salaspils airfield near Riga. Within a week bad weather struck once more and, on the night of 12/13 August, NSGr.12 lost two aircraft in a storm south of the Peipus lake.

Under an OKL order of 11 August 1944 the Latvian flying units were combined into the Luftwaffen-Legion Lettland, and the training centre at Liepāja-Grobiņa became Erg.Flg.Gr.Lettland (Latvian Replacement Training Group). The Latvian Obstl Janis Rucels was appointed commander of the Luftwaffen-Legion Lettland, but this organization, like the Luftwaffen-Legion Estland, remained a paper formation.

The Latvian night harassment bombers effectively supported the hard-pressed Army Group North from the air until October. Records show that by 7 October 1944 1./NSGr.12 had flown 3,000 operational sorties, and by 8 October 2./NSGr.12 was close behind, with 2,658 sorties; but then the units were grounded. The flight to Sweden by several Estonian airmen with their aircraft also meant the effective end of the Latvian night harassment group. True enough, NSGr.12 (lett.) had official support from the Chief of Staff of Luftflotte 1, Generalmajor Uebe, who sent a teleprinter message to the OKL on 4 October, pointing out that there had been no attempts to abscond to Sweden by any Latvian airmen, but the mistrust of the OKL had been aroused. An order disbanding the Latvian flying units followed shortly afterwards.

The nominal commander of the LLL (Luftwaffen-Legion Lettland), Obstl Janis Rucels, tried to prevent this from happening by sending a detailed letter to the Luftflottenkommando 1, in which he stated (among other things) that 'the Latvian people and its military are proud to have their own Luftwaffe formations. It has to be feared that the disbandment of the Latvian Luftwaffe formations, especially those already in operational service, which have been praised for their actions, will be misunderstood and taken as an affront to the honour of the Latvian people.'[15] This appeal proved in vain, however. Berlin had lost its trust in the Baltic night harassment airmen, despite the fact that 80 per cent of the Latvian flying personnel had been decorated with the Iron Cross and other awards for meritorious service. Lt Teodors Abrams, who had served with a Luftwaffe reconnaissance unit before the formation of NSGr.12, was the most combat-experienced Latvian airman. In October 1944 he was recommended for the German Cross in Gold (DKG), but he never received it due to the disbanding of the Latvian flying formations. In the event only one Latvian pilot flew to neutral Sweden, and that was after the grounding order. On 8 October 1944 Fw Žanis Tamsons of 1./NSGr.12 (lett.), the most decorated Latvian night harassment airman, made his way to Gotland with an Hs 126 (6A+NL), taking his mechanic with him.

However, Latvian fighter pilots were not affected by this disbandment order. Following an OKL order of 31 May 1944 regarding the formation of one Estonian and one Latvian fighter squadron, two groups of five Latvian pilots each were selected from 1./NSGr.12 (lett.) and sent to Germany for training:[16]

June 1944	July 1944
Oblt Eduards Millers	Uffz Vitolds Berkis
Lt Arnolds Mencis	Uffz Valdemars Lívmanis
Lt Jánis Lècis	Uffz Júlijs Stars
Uffz Haralds Makars	Flg Roberts Dumpis
Uffz Harijs Klints	Flg Edgars Lazdins

The first group travelled via Berlin, where they were met by Oblt Lützow, the Inspector of Fighters, before being sent to the Jagdfliegervorschule (Preliminary Fighter Training School) at Parow, near Stralsund, where they were trained on four different types of aircraft in succession. Afterwards the five were posted to Plathe, Lignitz and Sagan for training on the Fw 190A. On completion the five newly qualified Latvian fighter pilots were sent to Bromberg to collect brand-new Fw 190As, and flew them to the Riga-Spilve airfield. All five were now members of I./JG 54 'Grünherz', and managed to fly about ten operational sorties each from Ventspils, in Courland, by early October. Artur Gärtner of 3./JG 54 carried out several 'free chase' and air surveillance sorties with the Latvian pilots, and remembers his foreign wingmen as 'splendid comrades who participated in operations with much zeal and eagerness.'[17]

By this time, autumn 1944, most of the Latvian airmen no longer believed they would return home again. The parents of one Latvian pilot owned a well-established farmhouse near Cësis, in northern Latvia, and when the Red Army closed in the pilot attacked his parents' premises and sent them up in flames rather than allow them to fall into Soviet hands.

At the end of October these first five Latvian fighter pilots were ordered to Stettin-Altdamm to join the Luftwaffen-Legion Lettland, evacuated from Courland and awaiting disbandment. However, Maj Endres, commander of Erg.Flg.Gr.Lettland, managed to get the grounding order for these fighter pilots revoked, who consequently were allowed to continue flying operationally – in the West.

This group of five Latvian fighter pilots was posted to JG 1 'Oesau' at Greifswalde, where the pilots were allocated to different squadrons. On 5 December Lt Janis Lecis of 3./JG 1, flying the Fw 190A-8 'yellow 3' Wk. Nr. 738248, was shot down over Neuruppin, but managed to bale out. On that day JG 1 suffered a terrible bloodletting: in a wild aerial combat against 700 American P-51 Mustang escort fighters it lost 26 pilots, while another 14 were wounded.[18]

Oblt Millers of 1./JG 1, flying the Fw 190A-8 'white 22', Wk. Nr. 739385, was shot down over the Eifel mountains on 27 December. The aerial combat ended when, just 200m (330ft) above the ground, his engine was hit. Millers baled out but collided with the tail plane of his aircraft and badly injured his shoulder; his parachute only just had time to open before he alighted near Kelberg. Fw Harijs Klints of 2./JG 1 and Lt Arnolds Mencis took part in Operation *Bodenplatte*, the tactically poorly planned low-level strike by 1,000 German fighters against Allied airfields in the West early on New Year's Day 1945. Klints was shot down and killed in his Fw 190A-8 'black 5', Wk. Nr. 739235, over the St Denis-Westrem airfield by a Polish Spitfire pilot from RAF 308 Sqn.[19] He appears to have attempted a forced landing, but was thrown out of his machine on impact near a Polish AA unit on the airfield. Indulis Ozols, who researched this event locally in the 1970s, is convinced that Klints survived the crash, albeit badly injured, but was killed afterwards, possibly by hostile civilians.[20] After a provisional burial as 'an unknown German airman', the mortal remains of Harijs Klints were reinterred in the German military cemetery at Lommel in Belgium.

The other Latvian participant in Operation *Bodenplatte*, Arnolds Mencis, was born in Riga on 25 April 1915. Although he had joined the Latvian Army Air Force in 1936, Mencis did not qualify as a pilot-mechanic until April 1939. Between 1941 and 1943 he served in a guard battalion in Riga before joining the Luftwaffe, and was promoted to the rank of lieutenant. After some operational service with 1./NSGr.12 Mencis was selected for fighter training, beginning this new stage in his career on 21 June 1944. Following a brief sojourn with JG 54 he was posted to JG 1 'Oesau' late in October 1944. On 20 November he was badly injured (brain trauma) in a forced landing but remained in operational service. 'Because of the situation at the Front it was a matter of honour for me not to take notice on my own injuries and make an effort to continue flying on operations.'[21] During Operation *Bodenplatte* Mencis claimed to have shot down two Spitfires, although these aerial victories cannot be confirmed either by eye witnesses or documentary evidence. Mencis then had to make a forced landing about 10km (6 miles) from the Hengelo airfield when his fuel tank was damaged, and was taken wounded to the Quedlinburg hospital.

The second group of five prospective Latvian fighter pilots was destined to have a much shorter operational career. After a quick visit to the Luftwaffe fighter allocation centre at Berlin-Kladow they had begun their training at Plathe, north of Stettin, on 21 July 1944. Unlike the first five, all were young airmen with only limited flying and hardly any operational experience. Although the need was urgent, training was prolonged and frequently inter- rupted owing to roving American long-range fighters and fuel shortages. On 10 October Uffz Júlijs Stars lost his life in an acci- dent. On his second solo flight with a Fw 190A the engine failed, and Stars, wanting to save the aircraft, attempted a wheels-down landing in a field. Contrary to instructions, he had left his cockpit closed, and when the aircraft turned over the pilot was suffocated by petrol fumes in his cabin.

A short while later the four remaining Latvian fighter trainees were ordered to Stettin-Altdamm, where Major Endres success- fully pleaded for his charges. Initially the Sichtungsstelle (Sorting Centre) for the Luftwaffe fighter pilots sent the four Latvians to Ergänzungs-Jagdgeschwader (Replacement Wing) 1, but then three of them – Livmanis, Dumpis and Lazdiņš – were posted to JG 4 at Jüterbog, near Berlin, and assigned to 5.Staffel after completing their abbreviated fighter training course in March 1945. Uffz Berķis, who could not come to terms with the enforced idling during training, had in the meantime volunteered for the Latvian Legion, and his request was granted. After the war he was recruited by the British Secret Service and covertly sent back to Latvia.[22]

The remaining three newly trained Latvian fighter pilots posted to JG 4 suffered various fates. The unit was mostly engaged on low-level ground support tasks, and in April 1945 the still operational elements of JG 4 were transferred to Schleswig-Holstein. On 16 April Uffz Lívmanis was sent to Dresden to collect a new Fw 190 fighter and was never heard of again. Lazdins, who was to carry out a similar task, was captured by Soviet troops but was then liberated by a local German coun- terattack. Uffz Dumpis continued flying operationally until the end of April and claimed a 'probable', a Yak-9 fighter, on the Oder Front.[23] JG 4 was disbanded on 1 May, but one day later Uffz Dumpis, Lazdins and Oblt Millers from the first group of Latvian fighter pilots, who had recovered from his injuries, received orders to report at Erlangen for conversion training on the Me 262, probably with Erg.Jagdgeschwader 2, but the end of the war made this order superfluous.

The other Latvian Luftwaffe personnel who had been assembled at the Stettin-Altdamm airfield in October 1944 had to submit to the disbandment of the Luftwaffen-Legion Lettland. 'This did not take place smoothly and created much resentment, bitterness and disappointment among the airmen who had fought with such great fervour.'[24] Some officers were transferred to the Latvian Legion, including Hptm Salmiņš, former commander of 1./NSGr.12, who volunteered to rejoin the Latvian 19th Grenadier division in Courland where he became a Soviet PoW after the capitulation in May 1945. Ten groups of eight experienced mechanics were each posted to various German aircraft factories and airfields to dismantle unwanted bombers, some older officers transferred to Latvian construction regiments, and, late in November, six officers and 100 NCOs and airmen were posted to the Schw.Flak Ers.Abt.11 (Heavy AA Artillery Replacement Detachment) at Königsberg. But the largest group of the disbanded Luftwaffen-Legion Lettland – 25 officers and about 600 NCOs and airmen – was selected as paratroops, and late in October transferred to Nymindegab (west of Esbjerg) in Denmark, where their training was to take place. According to an entry in their pay books they were now part of the 'Baltic Legion of the Parachute Army, Einheit Fix'. However, they were more impressed by all the things they could buy or trade in peaceful Denmark – smoked fish, white bread, whipped cream and chocolate. All Latvian troops were paid in Danish currency and their relations with the local Danish people were good. But their enjoyment of these Lucullan delights did not last long. The already experienced Latvian soldiers found the new, very harsh drill humiliating; even officers were treated like raw recruits. The commanding German officer, Obstl Fix, rumoured to have fought against the Latvians after the First World War, treated the Latvian Luftwaffe soldiers very dismissively. The situation was also strained by the unanimous refusal by the Latvian officers to fight against the Western allies,[25] and German–Latvian relations grew worse from day to day. Some of the training was deliberately repetitive or senseless, and there were even several searches for 'hidden weapons'. Finally a compromise was reached at a higher level and all Latvian members of the Luftwaffe in Denmark were transferred to the Schw.Flak Ers.Abt.11 (18.Flak Division) in Königsberg, where they arrived early in December. Combined with the previously posted airmen from Stettin-Altdamm, they now numbered 29 officers and about 970 NCOs and airmen. Soon 60 NCOs and men were posted for flak calibration training to Schöngau and another 330 for training on 88mm flak outside Königsberg – 90 to Marienburg, 90 to Graudenz and 150 to Elbing. Of the first detachment, one group went to Schw.H.Flak Batt. I/222 at Marienburg-Tessensdorf. After the start of the Soviet offensive in January 1945 the personnel of this battery were hurriedly sent to Marienwerder, the rest remaining in Marienburg, where they were later involved in the prolonged defensive fighting. The Marienwerder detachment took over the guns of the Schw. H. Flak Abt. I/316 (o). They were overrun by a Soviet tank attack on the night of 19/20 February. The Graudenz group was divided between Schw.H.Flak Batt.215/1 and 220/1, and was soon in action against the Soviet ground forces attacking the local airfield and the town. Some of the wounded from this battery were fortunate in being sent to Denmark, where they later became British POWs. Those Latvian flak gunners who managed to escape from these two batteries were assembled at Stolpmünde and hurriedly retrained on 37mm flak before being dispersed by another Soviet tank advance. A number of experienced Latvian pilots went missing at that time, while the rest retreated to Danzig and ended up as infantry defending Oliva, a northern suburb of the town.

After some hard defensive action the Elbing group, too, was dispersed by the Soviet advance. Some survivors retreated to Danzig and others to Krampnitz near Berlin, where they were captured by the Soviets on 24 April 1945.

In the meantime the 29 Latvian Luftwaffe officers and some 600 NCOs and airmen remaining in Königsberg were also split up and, except for the Latvian officers, shared the fate of the other defenders of the town. The original proposal to post some of the officers to separate Latvian flak units was rejected by 18.Flak Division. Instead they were first to be trained as flak officers. On 25 January 1945, following an intercession by Obstl Rucels, commander of the already disbanded Luftwaffen-Legion Lettland, the Latvian officers were given permission to leave Königsberg for Danzig, and eventually Neubrandenburg, the appointed assembly centre for the Latvian Legion.

Most Latvian airmen, who had to remain in the 'Fortress Königsberg' to the end, understandably resented this and felt abandoned.[26] Only one Latvian Luftwaffe liaison officer volunteered to remain behind, Oblt Ludvigs Gráve. Of Belgian-Walloon origin, he had settled in Latvia before the war and was known for his linguistic skills. He was also an exemplary officer to his men. Gráve was captured by the Soviets during the final stages of fighting in Königsberg in April 1945.[27]

By the end of January the East Prussian metropolis had been cut off from all land connections, although a German counter-attack temporarily restored contact with Pillau on 19 February. The Latvian airmen had been distributed among various flak batteries covering the approaches to the town, such as those at Grossfriedrichsberg, Jummerau and Neuendorf, and, after the destruction of their guns, continued fighting as infantry until the end.

The captured or surrendered Latvian airmen received different treatment in Soviet hands. Initially most had to endure physical violence and even extreme brutality, followed by special camps for 'traitors'. As a rule, the former Latvian Luftwaffe soldiers were released after a few years, but there were exceptions. No fewer than 11 Latvian airmen were sentenced to 25 years forced labour and five years loss of civil rights; another three to 15 years, and 41 to 10 years hard labour. Most of the Latvian ex-Luftwaffe men were released from Soviet labour camps in 1955, two years after Stalin's death, but after eight to ten years in Kolyma or other notorious Soviet Gulag camps they were never to regain their full health. A still unknown number of former Latvian airmen died in Soviet camps.[28]

Lt Mencis was captured by the Americans on 23 April 1945, taken to Paris and handed over to the Soviets. During the deportation to the East he managed to escape and hide in Brest-Litovsk until late autumn 1945, afterwards returning to his parents' home in Riga. He was arrested on 14 July 1952, and six days later sentenced by a tribunal to 25 years forced labour and five years loss of civil rights for his voluntary service in a police POW guard battalion between 1941 and 1943 and subsequent service in the German Luftwaffe. Like many other prisoners Mencis was released during the Khrushchev regime, being set free on 5 November 1955, but that did not mean an end to his sufferings. 'As politically unreliable I was spied upon and tormented for many years, and had to live under difficult conditions, doing casual jobs.'[29] The renewed independence of his homeland was to signify an end to such discrimination against this former Lieutenant of the Luftwaffe.

In June 1993 many surviving Latvian airmen met in Riga to celebrate the 50th anniversary of the founding of the flying training school at Leipāja-Grobiņa. It was to be the first time that many former Latvian members of the Luftwaffe still living in Latvia could meet their comrades from abroad and reminisce freely about their experiences, while celebrating the regained independence and freedom of their homeland.

Russians

During the period 22 June to 20 December 1941 a total of 980 aircraft of the Soviet air force (VVS) fell into German hands.[1] When one adds the Soviet aircraft captured afterwards as well as those flown voluntarily by Soviet pilots to the German side – 66 in 1943, 20 during the first three months of 1944 alone – it would have been possible to form several wings with these aircraft and the Russian volunteers. That it never came to this was due to the National Socialist concept of a 'master race', which attributed the status of an inferior class of people to even the most co-operative Russians – never that of allies. Moreover, because the captured material was classed as 'second-grade', most of the available Soviet aircraft were simply scrapped. A small number were sold to the Finns, others served briefly in various German flying training schools; for instance, the FFS (C) 2 used the Tupolev SB bombers and the Jagdfliegervorschule (Preliminary Fighter Pilot Training School) at Vienna-Schwechat had some Polikarpov I-153 fighters,[2] but that was all.

Given the political-ideological framework established by the National Socialist regime, the beginnings of a Russian anti-Communist flying formation within the German Luftwaffe could only be modest in scale. Thus a flying unit composed of former Soviet pilots, observers, air gunners and radio operators came into being under Major Filatov as part of the Russian National People's Army (RNNA), set up in late summer 1942 in the German Army Group Centre Area.[3] However, as there was no special permission from the highest command headquarters for this unit, which only existed until February 1943, it had to limit its activities to theoretical training. A more serious attempt was the formation of the 1.Ostfliegerstaffel (russisch), the 1st Eastern Squadron, Russian, by Luftflotte 1 in December 1943.[4] It was recruited from Russian volunteers and was equipped with German Ar 66s and Go 145s, as well as captured Soviet Po-2 biplanes. Early in 1944 this squadron was within the command region of 3.Fliegerdivision in Daugavpils/Latvia; in March 1944 it was transferred to Lida, where it was subordinated to Fliegerführer 1. After the German retreat from the Eastern Front the Luftwaffe command seems to have become apprehensive that this squadron might become unreliable, so it was disbanded in July 1944. Up to that point it had carried out 500 operational sorties. The Russian flying personnel serving with various German fighter, bomber and reconnaissance formations, who, without being formed into a national unit, were fighting against the Soviet Union were not affected by this disbandment order. Their exact number is unknown.

The role of the initiator of an independent national Russian air force was played by Obstl (General Staff) Holters, Chief of the Auswertestelle Ost (Evaluation Centre East) at the Luftwaffe Operations Staff.[5] Holters was in charge of the interrogation of captured Soviet air force officers and, as he could not fail to pick up the frequently expressed anti-Stalinist sentiments of the Soviet POWs, he evolved the idea of forming a flying unit staffed by such POWs and deserters. His Russian counterpart for this project was Col Viktor Ivanovich Maltsev. This former commander of the Red air forces in the Siberian district and later Chief of the Civil Air Fleet was caught in the Stalinist purges in 1937, and the tortures he had to suffer in the NKVD cellars had made Maltsev into an ardent anti-Communist. He came over to the German side in 1941 and in October 1943 was assigned to the Auswertestelle Ost. Holters took him into his confidence and authorized him to recruit volunteers for a future national Russian air force in Soviet POW camps.

The recruited personnel were collected in a camp at Suwalki, in German-occupied Poland, and underwent a two months' long examination and checks. Following the attestation and classification according to ranks they were sent to the Gruppe Holters at Moritzfelde, near Insterburg in East Prussia. There the Russian volunteers were allocated to a variety of tasks: pilots and technical ground personnel began their retraining on German aircraft models, others were put to work on repairing captured aircraft, while the approved Russian pilots began their new service duties by ferrying German aircraft from workshops to the front.

These members of the Holters-Maltsev group were not mercenaries. They were men fighting for a free, non-Communist Russia that would be allied to the German Reich but would not be its vassal. Early in 1944 Maltsev had an opportunity to voice his views about these matters over the radio to the Eastern workers in Germany:[6]

> Millions of honest Russian people have been tortured to death. The peasant class is ruined and has been transformed into a herd of desperately poor and hungry slaves reduced to silence. The life and the working conditions of the Soviet workers is now worse than it was before the October revolution ... I have broken consciously with the Soviet power. I am taking up arms again and, together with hundreds of thousands of other Russian volunteers, am going into mortal combat against the Soviets.

Recruiting for the future national Russian air force was helped by the fact that Soviet POWs of the Luftwaffe were better off in terms of treatment and food than those in army hands. Soviet propaganda had hammered into Russian airmen that they would be mistreated and killed once they had fallen into German hands. Many of those who actually became POWs consequently felt they had been deceived by the system that had kept them walled off from the Western world. Senior Lt Bronislav Romanovich Antilevsky and Capt Semyon Trofimovich Bytchkov, both highly decorated Heroes of the Soviet Union (Gold Star), reported their first impressions after capture:[7]

> Not only did nobody torment or torture us, as had been predicted, but quite the opposite – we encountered warm-hearted and comradely behaviour from German officers and soldiers, respect for our shoulder tabs (rank insignia Tr) and war decorations, and our military merits. Nobody tried to persuade us in any way, but we were given the opportunity of learning about the life of the German people.

Both officers of course overlooked the fact that they were privileged and thus enjoyed certain favours not granted to the ill-treated Eastern workers and the majority of the Soviet POWs.

In February 1944 General Vlassov, the Russian de Gaulle, visited the camp of the Evaluation Centre East, situated among the Masurian lakes in East Prussia. The discipline, honesty and political morale of the prospective air force soldiers convinced him personally as well as his German escorts that Holters and Maltsev were on the right track. The Baltic German Sergei Fröhlich, who served as a liaison officer to Gen Vlassov, participated in this inspection:

> The former Soviet airmen were young men in brand-new, well-fitting German Luftwaffe uniforms with the appropriate rank insignia. Gen Vlassov was impressed by the good morale that prevailed. We left Moritzfelde, the first preliminary stage of the ROA[8] air force, with the best impressions and the hope that this small group of airmen would soon develop into the air force formations planned by Col Maltsev.[9]

But it was to be months before anything would happen.

Even though Vlassov's airmen still did not fly at the Front, some of them nevertheless already fulfilled tasks of military importance. In summer 1944 about 25–30 Russian pilots served with 3./Gruppe Süd Flugzeugüberführungsgeschwader 1 (3rd Squadron of Group South, Aircraft Ferrying Wing 1), which ferried planes from the Messerschmitt industrial establishments to various Luftwaffe airfields. These Russian pilots made an excellent impression on their German superiors, although technical problems and lack of knowledge of the Bf 109 led to the fatal crashes of at least six ROA pilots *(see* table opposite).

As it happened, it was Himmler's recognition of the ROA on 16 September 1944 – on the grounds of usefulness – that helped the Russian liberation movement and with it their air force to achieve a breakthrough. From that moment planning of an independent Russian air force could take on more concrete forms. Col Maltsev's proposal for this branch of the national Russian armed forces envisaged an initial strength of 2,594 officers,

Russian Losses on Transport Duties

Name	Aircraft	Wk. Nr.	Date	Place
Lt I. Sevkin	Bf 109G-14	760698	18 August 1944	Darmstadt
Lt A. Yakovlev	Bf 109G-14	780807	18 August 1944	Darmstadt
Lt Aleksei Chassovnik	Bf 109G-14	782159	3 September 1944	Bavarian Forest
Lt C. Karelin	Bf 109G-14	782211	11 September 1944	Panyöfö, Hungary
Capt Peter Vorontsov	Bf 109G-14	785730	20 November 1944	North of Olmütz
Oleg Gorbatchov	Bf 109G-14	332519	6 January 1945	

NCOs and other ranks, 1,800 training personnel and 25 front-line and 21 training and liaison aircraft, in addition to 96 AA guns.[10] Generalleutnant Heinrich Aschenbrenner, who had in peacetime been the Luftwaffe attaché at the German Embassy in Moscow and now served as an Inspector for Foreign Personnel of the Luftwaffe East, and the Chief of the 8th (War History) Department of the Luftwaffe General Staff, Generalmajor Hermut von Rohden, fully supported Maltsev's proposal. It was also thanks to their support that the Luftwaffe command released Russian personnel as well as motor vehicles, weapons and aircraft in Luftwaffe service for the ROA. However, there were difficulties when it came to the allocation of aviation fuel, already in short supply. The airfields at Eger and Karlsbad, in Bohemia, were put at the disposal of the Russian flying personnel, while the AA units were concentrated at Brüx, in the same region.

The Russian Liberation Army received a further lift from the state ceremony in Prague on 14 November 1944, when Gen Vlassov – despite considerable difficulties and reservations – was able to announce his political creed and the founding of the Committee for the Liberation of Russian Peoples. On 19 December 1944 Reichsmarschall Göring signed the order authorizing the formation of the air force of the Russian Liberation Army. It was to consist of the following units:[11]

317

One fighter squadron with 15 Bf 109G-10s
One close support squadron with 12 Ju 88s
One bomber squadron with five He 111s
One courier squadron with two Fi 156s and two captured
    Po-2 biplanes
One replacement squadron with two each of He 111s, Ju 87s,
    Bf 109s, Bf 108s and three Po-2s
One AA regiment
One paratroop battalion
One signals company

The war strength of the ROA air force was set at 4,500 men
for the time being, and the initial organization and formation, as
well as the command of the air force of the Russian Peoples, was
left in the hands of the ROA. On 28 January 1945 Gen Vlassov
became the Commander in Chief of the ROA, and, during a
discussion with Maltsev and Vlassov at Karinhall on 2 February
1945, Göring also agreed that this Russian air force would be
subordinated to Gen Vlassov. Whether the C-in-C of the
German Luftwaffe actually understood anything about the
Russian Liberation movement and its ideals is doubtful. During
a discussion about the military situation with Hitler on 27
January, less than a week before meeting the Russian commanders, Göring had expressed the following opinion about
members of the Russian Liberation Army: 'They cannot do
more than desert to the other side. Then we don't have to feed
them any more.'[12]

An order dated 4 March 1945 separated the National Russian
Air Force from the German Luftwaffe. By that time the Vlassov
movement had attained the status of an ally of the Reich.
Maltsev, promoted to Maj Gen, became the Chief of the Air
Force of the Russian Peoples, and its flying formations,
composed of foreign Russians, old émigrés and former Soviet
officers, also underwent an external change. All members of this
new air force now exchanged their German cap badges for
Russian ones and attached the ROA insignia to their uniform
sleeves; their aircraft were decorated with the blue Andreas
Cross on a white background. The structure of the air force was

also reorganized. The 1st Air Regiment of the ROA, commanded by Col Baydak, was formed at Eger, while the bomber squadron was abandoned; instead, work was put in hand to form a transport squadron and a reconnaissance squadron. By an order of 28 March 1945 the close support squadron was transformed into a night harassment squadron. The formation of an air force signals-telegraph and construction regiment had started in Dresden already in February.

The Air Force of the Armed Forces of the Russian Peoples Situation at the End of March 1945[13]

Field Post Number	Designation of Unit	Aircraft
60 962	ROA Close Support Squadron[1]	12 Ju 88
60 975	ROA AA Regiment 9	
61 853	High Command of the Luftwaffe – Inspectorate of the Eastern Personnel	
61 904	ROA Liaison Squadron 14	?
62 899	ROA Fighter Squadron 5	16 Bf 109G-10
62 956	ROA Training (Replacement) Squadron	2 Bf 109, 2 Ju 88 2 Fi 156, 2 Po-2 1 Do 17, 1 He 111
62 978	ROA Signals Company 6	
63 892	ROA Bomber Squadron 11[2]	
63 914	ROA Parachute-Infantry Battalion 3	
63 966	ROA Aviation Signals-Telegraph-Construction Regiment 12	
?	ROA Transport Squadron 4	2 Ju 52/3m
?	ROA Reconnaissance Squadron 3	2 Fi 156, 1 Me 262

[1] Transformed into a night harassment squadron by an order of 28 March 1945
[2] The formation of this squadron was broken off

In mid-April the combat units of the ROA air force – Night Harassment Squadron 8 and Fighter Squadron 5 'Kazakov' – were ready for action. On 13 April aircraft from Night Harassment Squadron 8 supported an attack by the 1st ROA Division against a Soviet bridgehead at Erlenhof at the Oder. This action remained the one and only operation to be carried out by the ROA Air force.

With the end of the war imminent, Gen Vlassov tried to save

the substance of his troops, and, with the XV.Cossack Cavalry Corps, the Russian Rifle Corps and other anti-Communist formations of various peoples and nationalities, form a 'third power'. He anticipated altercation between Stalin and the Western Powers, giving his 'third power' the chance to play a key role. This hope very soon proved illusory. When Vlassov realized this he tried to save as many Russian airmen and ROA soldiers as possible from falling into the hands of the Red Army and certain death. On 24 April the following ROA flying formations were in the Reichsprotectorat Bohemia and Moravia: Fighter Squadron 5 'Kazakov' at Deutsch Brod, Night Harassment Squadron 8 with detachments at Eger and Deutsch Brod and the Replacement Squadron, also at Deutsch Brod.

Gen Aschenbrenner, in his function as the adviser to the ROA air force, and the Russian expert Hptm Professor Dr Dr Oberländer established contact with the Americans, and smoothed the way to enable most members of the Air Force of the Russian Peoples to become American POWs. These ROA men put down their arms at 10.00hrs between Zwiesel and Regen on 27 April 1945. The overwhelming majority of the 4,800 men managed to avoid repatriation to the Soviet Union. However, in September 1945 the Western allies delivered 200 National Russian air force officers from Cherbourg to their sworn enemy, Stalin; and Maj Gen Maltsev was flown to Moscow in 1946. He was hanged in the Soviet capital, together with Gen Vlassov and other anti-Communist officers, on 2 August 1946.

Appendices

1. The Most Successful Fighter Pilots

It is not possible to compare the number of aerial victories achieved by pilots of different nations. The criteria for the recognition of aerial victories were different, as were the aircraft material, the enemy situation and the length of operational service. For example the Spanish pilots were only operational for six months at a time at the Eastern Front, and the Bulgarians were only involved with the Western Allies in 1943–4. However, the record of the Finnish airmen call for special remark. Despite quantitative inferiority and having to cope with partly obsolete aircraft material (such as the Fiat G.50 and Brewster B-239) their fighter pilots nevertheless achieved an exceptionally high number of aerial victories.

Where the lists show fractions (Hungary, Finland) these indicate participation in collective aerial victories.

Italy

Name, Rank	Aerial Victories	Of which were with the ANR	Killed
Corporal T. Martinoli	22		25.8.1944[1]
Lieutenant L. Ferrulli	21		5.7.1943
Captain F. Lucchini	21		5.7.1943
Sen Lt F. Bordoni-Bisleri	19		
Sergeant Luigi Gorrini	19	(4)	
Captain M. Visintini	16		11.2.1941[2]
Captain Ugo Drago	15	(11)	
Major M. Bellagambi	14	(11)	
Corporal Luigi Baron	12		
Captain Luigi Gianella	12		
Sergeant Carlo Magnaghi	11	(2)	12.5.1944
Major C. M. Ruspoli di Poggio Suasa	11		
Sen Lt G. Solaroli di Briona	11		
Corporal Mario Veronesi	11	(2)	
Sergeant Amedeo Benati	10	(2)	
Captain Fernando Malvezzi	10		
Captain Giulio Reiner	10		
Captain Giuseppe Roberto	10	(3)	

Name, Rank	Aerial Victories	Of which were with the ANR	Killed
Captain Claudio Solaro	10		
Sergeant Ennio Tarantola	10		
Captain Giulio Torresi	10	(2)	1.7.1944
Major Adriano Visconti	10	(4)	29.4.1945[3]

[1] Martinoli was killed on a practice flight
[2] Visintini's aircraft crashed into the Mt Nefasit in Eritrea.
[3] Visconti was murdered by Red partisans after the capitulation

Another 54 pilots achieved more than five aerial victories.
Not included in this list are the collective aerial victories. For example, Sen Lt Duilio Fanali, commander of 155° Gruppo C.T., participated in at least 32 aerial victories.

Romania
(up to 23 March 1944)

Name, Rank	Aerial Victories	Killed
Captain Alexandru Serbanescu	45 (52)[1]	18.8.1944
Captain Constantin Cantacuzino	43 (56)[1]	
Lieutenant Ioan Milu	32 (40)[1]	
Captain Dan Vizanty	32 (39)[1]	
Staff Sergeant Ion Mucenia	24	
Sen Lt Tudor Greceanu	20	
Lieutenant Tiberiu Vinca	16	September 1943
Lieutenant Hristea Chirvasuta	14	
Captain Cheorge Popescu-Ciocanel	12	August 1944

[1] A new assessment system was introduced in 1944, which allocated higher value to downed multi-engined aircraft. According to this new system the Romanian fighter pilots would have achieved the number of victories shown in brackets.

Hungary

Name, Rank	Aerial Victories	Killed
Officer Candidate Deszö Szentgyörgyi	32 (2)[1]	
Sent Lt György Debrödy	26 (2)[1]	
Lieutenant László Molnár	25	7.8.1944
Lieutenant Lajos Tóth	24 (1)[1]	11.6.1951[2]
Lieutenant Miklós Kenyeres	18 (1)[1]	

Name, Rank	Aerial Victories	Killed
Sergeant István Fábián	15.5 (1)[1]	
Sen Lt Ferenc Málnássy	13 (2)[1]	13.3.1945
Captain László Pottyondy	13 (1)[1]	
Lieutenant Kálmán Nánási	12	
Officer Candidate István Kálmán	12	
Lieutenant Joszef Málik	11 (1)[1]	16.4.1945
Sen Lt László Dániel	11.75	
Lt Col Aladár Heppes	8 (4)[1]	

[1] Figures in brackets show aerial victories for which there is no official confirmation.
[2] Tóth was executed by the Communists.

Bulgaria
(up to 6 September 1944)

Name, Rank	Aerial Victories	Type of shot-down aircraft
Sen Lt Stojan Stojanov	5[1]	3 B-24 Liberator 2 P-38 Lightning
Lieutenant Petar Botchev	4	4-engined bombers
Captain Chudomir Toplodolski	3	1 B-24 Liberator 2 P-38 Lightning
Lieutenant Ivan Bonev	3	2 B-24 Liberator 1 P-38 Lightning
Lieutenant Gentcho Dimitrov	3	1 B-24 Liberator 2 P-38 Lightning
Sen Lt Nedeltcho Bontchev	2	2 B-17 Fortress II
Lieutenant Petar Kirov	2	2 B-24 Liberator
Lieutenant Khristo Kostakev	2	2 B-17 Fortress II
Sergeant Khristo Zankov	2	1 B-24 Liberator 1 P-38 Lightning

[1] According to other information Stojanov achieved six aerial victories.

Croatia

Name, Rank	Aerial Victories	Killed
Major Mato Dukovač	40 (5)[1]	
Hptm Cvitan Galič	38 (8)[1]	6.4.1944[2]
Lt Dragutin Ivanič	18	
Oblt Ivan Jergovic	16	1945[3]
Stabsfw Josip Jelačič	16	
Oblt Ljudevit Bencetič	15	
Lt Stepan Boškič	13 (3)[1]	
Oberst Franjo Džal	13 (5)[1]	1945[3]
Hptm Zlatko Stipčič	12	1945[4]
Lt Zivko Džal	12	1945[4]
Stabsfw Stjepan Martinasevič	11	
Major Mato Culinovič	10 (8)[1]	1944 (?)[5]
Hptm Vladimir Ferenčina	10 (6)[1]	
Stabsfw Tomislav Kauzlarič	10 (2)[1]	
Fw Eduard Martinko	10 (2)[1]	
Obfw Veco Micovič	10 (1)[1]	20.7.1942[6]
Obgfr Zdenko Avdič	10	
Hptm Josip Hellebrandt	10	

[1] Figures in brackets show aerial victories for which there is no official confirmation.
[2] Killed by an attack of US P-51 Mustangs on the Sarajevo airfield while sitting ready in his aircraft.
[3] Executed by Communists.
[4] Shot by Communists in the Zagreb prison camp.
[5] Shot down by Communist partisans during a low-level strike sortie and killed afterwards.
[6] Killed in action at Rostov as member of 15./JG 52 in Bf 109G-2 Wk. Nr. 13411 'black 13'.

Slovakia

Name, Rank	Aerial Victories	Killed
Hptfw Jan Režnák	32	
Stabtw Izidor Kovarik	29	11.7.1944[1]
Sen Lt Ján Gerthofer	27	
Stabfw Stefan Martiš	19	
Stabfw Stefan Ocvirk	10 plus ?	
Stabfw Anton Matušek	10 plus ?	
Maj Ondrej Ďumbala	14	

[1] Kovarik was killed during a practice flight.

Spain

Name, Rank	Aerial Victories	Killed
Capt Gonzalo Hevia	11	
Capt J. Ramon Gavilán	9	
Sen Lt Fernando Sanchez-Arjona	8	19.11.1943
Officer Cadet Vicente Aldecoa	7	
Maj A. Salas Larrazábal	6	[1]
Sen Lt Bernardo Meneses	6	
Sen Lt Luis Azqueta	6	
Sen Lt Francisco Valiente	6	
Maj Mariano Cuadra Medina	5	
Capt M. Sanchez-Tabernero	5	
Capt Antonio Alós	5	

[1] Larrazábal died on 19 July 1994

Finland

(Winter War 1939–40 and the Continuation War 1941–4)

Name, Rank	Aerial Victories	Killed
Staff Sgt Eino Ilmari Juutilainen	94 1/6	
Captain Hans Henrik Wind	75	
Major Eino Antero Luukanen	56	
Staff Sgt Urho Sakari Lehtovaara	44 1/2	
Staff Sgt Oiva Emil K. Touminen	44	
Captain Risto Olli P. Puhakka	42	
Lieutenant Olvai Kauko Puro	36	
Corporal Nils Edvard Katajainen	35 1/2	
Lieutenant Lauri Vilhelm Nissinen	32 1/2	17.6.1944
Lieutenant Kyöstil K. E. Karhila	32 1/4	
Major Jorma Karhunen	31 1/2	
Corporal Emil O. Vesa	29 1/2	
Corporal Turo Taipo Järvi	28 1/2	
Corporal Klaus J. Alakoski	26	
Lieutenant Altto K. Tervo	23 1/4	20.8.1943[1]
Lieutenant Jorma K. Saarinen	23	18.7.1944[2]
Staff Sgt Eero A. Kinnunen	22 1/2	21.4.1943[3]
Corporal Antti J. Tani	21 1/2	
Lieutenant Urho P. J. Myllylä	21	

[1] Missing since that date.   [2] Killed during an emergency landing.
[3] Killed by AA gunfire hit.

In addition, another 32 Finnish fighters had 10 or more aerial victories.

Vichy-France

(26 June 1940–10 November 1942)

Name, Rank	Aerial Victories	Of which individually achieved
Lieutenant Pierre Le Gloan	7	5
Captain Léon Richard	7	4
Sen Lt Georges Blanck	5	2
Corporal Poupart	4	4
Captain Roger Duval	4	1
Sen Lt Michel Madon	4	1
Sen Lt Georges Pissotte	4	1

2. Aircraft Production of Germany's Allies, including Finland and Vichy-France

Italy

Year	Number	Number of Exported Aircraft
1939	1,750	138
1940	2,723	204
1941	3,487	112
1942	2,818	138
1943	2,741	54
1944	1,043	268
Sub-total	14,562	914
Total	15,476	

The above-listed 14,562 aircraft were of the following classes:

Fighters	6,101
Bombers/torpedo bombers	3,773
Reconnaissance	2,344
Transports	480
Training aircraft	1,864

Not included in this list are aircraft that Italy had to deliver on request by the German RüK-Stab (Armaments and War Production Staff) from 1943 onwards.

Romania

Model	1939	1940	1941	1942	1943	1944	Total
IAR 37/38/39	125	70	25	50	50	60	380
Fi 156					3	7	10
PZL 24	35						25
IAR 80			119	151	130	50	450
Bf 109G		13		23	24	7	67
Fleet	50			40	39		210
IAR 27	9	21		50			80
FM 305		40	30		4		74
Totals	209	176	223	314	250	130	1302

Hungary

Period	Delivered Aircraft	Of which were Me 210c	Of which were Bf 109G
1939	21		
1940	26		
1941	65		
1942	91	1	1
1943	371	104	92
1944	872	167	378
Totals	1,446	272	471

Bulgaria

Period	Model	Number
1939	DAR-3a	12
from 1940	DAR-9	42
1941	DAR-10a	1
1945	DAR-10F	1
1939–42	KB-5	45
1940–2	KB-11	44
1940–1	KB-309	9
1944 (?)	Bf 109G (rebuild)	2
Total		156

Slovakia

Model	Number
Skoda-Kauba SK 257	5
Ju 87D-5	12
Total	17

Finland

Year	Licence Production	Number Production	Own	Number	Totals
1939	Fokker D.XXI	35	VL Viima II	22	
			VL Pyry I	1	58
1940			VL Pyry II	3	3
1941	Fokker D.XXI	50	VL Pyry	37	
	Blenheim Mk I	15	VL Myrsky	1	103
1942	Fokker C.X	5			5
1943	Blenheim Mk I	30	VL Myrsky	3	33
1944	Blenheim Mk IV	10	VL Myrsky	47	
	Fokker D.XXI	5	VL Humu	1	63
1945			VL Pyörremyrsky	1	1
Total					266

Vichy-France

(summer 1940–summer 1944)

Year	Number of French models	Number of German models	For Germany	For France
1940–1	1,001		925	76
1942	791	330	661	460
1943	272	1,172	1,444	
1944		576	576	
1940–4	2,064	2,078	3,606	536

Total number of aircraft produced: 4,142

3. Training of Foreign Personnel

Training of foreign airmen within the area controlled by the General der Fliegerausbildung (airmen training) as on 1 September 1943

In training	147	
Training completed during the period 1.8.–31.8.1943	–	
Training prepared for or intended	5	
Relieved from training	10	(incl. 2 killed in crashes)

In Detail

A. In training

1. Croatia

FFS A/B 123, Graz (pilot training school)	8	flying instructors
	29	trainee pilots
JG 104, Fürth	39	fighter trainees
Ln-Schule 2, Königgrätz (signals school)	19	aircrew radio operator candidates
Blindflugschule 6, Wesendorf (blind flying school)	6	trainees
FFS C 6, Kolberg (advanced instrument flying)	12	trainees

2. Bulgaria

Fl.Bildschule Hildesheim (aerial photography school)	2	aerial photography officers
	30	candidates

3. Hungary

II./ZG 102, Bad Aibling (destroyer training unit)	3	trainees

B. Training completed during the period 1.8.-31.8.1943

–

C. Training prepared for or intended

1. Hungary
Fl.Bildschule Hildesheim   2   officers
(aerial photography)

Training to officer grade   3   candidates

D. Released from training

1. Croatia
FFS A/B 123, Graz   2   trainee pilots

JG 104, Fürth   8   trainee pilots (incl. 2 killed in crashes)

Training of foreign technical personnel within the area controlled by the General der Fliegerausbildung

In training   160
training completed during the period
1.8.–31.8.1943   16

Training prepared for or intended   1,973

In Detail

A. In training

1. Bulgaria
Fl. Techn. Schule 5,Wischau   40   techn. officer candidates
     8   techn. officers
     15   NCOs

JG 107, Nancy (instruction on
Dewoitine D.520)   40   men

2. Spain
Fl. Techn. Schule 1, Giessen   36   men

Fl. Techn. Schule 3, Munich   10   men

Fl. Waffentchn.Schule 1, Halle   11   men
(aircraft armament school)

B. Training completed during the period 1.8.–31.8.1943

1. Bulgaria
    Höh. Fl. Techn. Schule Jüterbog
    (higher aviation-techn.school)   16 men

C. Training prepared for or intended

1. Romania

Höh. Fl. Techn.Schule Jüterbog	125 men
Fl. Techn. Schule 3, Munich	382 men
Fl. Techn. Schule 4, Krosno	362 men
Ln. Schule 1, Nordhausen	700 men
Fl. Waffentechn. Schule	
Halle-Merseburg	404 men

Source: BA/MA RL2 III/699 (microfiche), Strength, Increase and Losses of the Luftwaffe (Personnel, Aircraft) from Summer 1943 to November 1944. Copy in author's possession.

4. British Interrogation Report
of Major Neumann

RESTRICTED

C.S.D.I.C. (Air) C.M.F.
Report No. A.599.
File No. 967

24th October 1945
Jafü Oberitalien

Preamble

The following brief notes have resulted from the interrogation of Oberst Neumann, Jagdfliegerführer (Chief Controller of Fighters) in central Italy from September 1944 to the capitulation, and go to show the perilous state in which this arm of the Luftwaffe found itself during the final eight months of the war.

The Situation as Encountered

On my appointment as Jafü Oberitalien in September 1944 I found the situation as follows:

• All German fighter units had been removed from Italy for the defence of the Reich.
• The Italian fighter units had been disbanded as they did not wish to join the proposed Italian Air Force Legion under German commanding officers.
• In the event of emergency developments (code name 'Drohende Gefahr Süd', Threatening Danger South), approximately four fighter Gruppen were to be despatched to Italy.
• Night fighters were not available.
• Operational headquarters were on Castle Hill, near Verona, with sub-HQs at Udine and Milan.

• The radar system was still usable.

• A draft agreement relating to the re-formation of Italian units was submitted to me for consideration. It provided for a fighter Gruppa, a torpedo Staffel and a signals company with German COs. I arranged that Italians should take command of their own units, to which German liaison officers with small liaison units would be attached.

Formation and Conversion of Italian Units

To begin with II. (ital.) JG, with Lt. Col. Alessandrini as CO, was equipped with Me 109 G-6s. The Gruppe had already flown sorties with this type of aircraft. In addition an Italian torpedo Staffel of the Faggioni Gruppe, with Major Marini as CO, was formed to fly SM.79s.

In November 1944 I. (ital.) JG, whose CO was Major Visconti and which had previously flown Italian aircraft, was sent to Holzkirchen (Oberbayern) to train on to the Mo 109 G-10. The Gruppe made its first training flights in the Milan area in February 1945.

At the same time a Staffel of selected Italian pilots was sent to Germany for training on the Me 163 rocket fighter. Training had to be broken off as the fuel was required for other purposes (V-2). German fighters were similarly handicapped. In January 1945 III. (ital.) JG, under command of Captain Malvezzi, proceeded to Holzkirchen. They never advanced beyond the preliminary stages of conversion.

Political Alignment of the ANR

In contrast to the Air Ministry, the purpose of which was not immediately apparent, the General Staff of the ANR with its economical establishment, its sense of duty and its spartan outlook made an excellent impression.

The CGS, Lt. Col. Baylon, an exceptionally capable man, was the moving spirit behind the operational sections of the air force. He and his QMG, Lt. Col. Bonzano, were known to me from Africa days, when they were both Gruppenkommandeure, and

I well remembered their keenness on operations. Our former good relations now stood us in good stead. Whereas there was no pronounced political trend among the officials at the Air Ministry, the General Staff and the flying personnel cannot be regarded as Fascists. Baylon was in fact suspected of being an 'A-Fascist', a euphemism applied to anti-Fascists when reports had to be submitted to Mussolini.

The thinking members of the air force wanted an organized state control, and frequently criticized the corrupt Fascist functionaries.

Factors that determined their continued adherence to the German cause were a desire to avoid going down in history for a second time as a people who could not keep faith, and the fear that an Italy without firm leadership would be driven to anarchy. The bulk of the rank and file, who had formed no political opinions of their own, clung to leaders who were familiar to them.

The Pilots

• Remarkably gifted in the art of flying, able and high-spirited.
• The Italian's inclination to do what promises the most fun led the pilots to attach far greater importance to aerobatics than to combat flying and gunnery.
• The Italian, fundamentally a 'lone wolf' flyer, thinks too little of the tactical aspects of formation flying.
• Technically he is exceedingly able and resourceful.
• As he has a strong tendency to dissipate his energies in a non-productive manner, the organization required tactful German guidance.
• Their performance and bearing won for the Italian fighter pilots the genuine respect of their German colleagues. It must be said that their morale was appreciably higher than that of most of the Italian fighter units I encountered in Africa.
• There was much potentially valuable material among them.

Operations

• II. (ital.)/JG first began operating from Villafranca; later they took off from Aviano-Osoppo and Lonste-Gallarate.
• Flying control was centralized at Verona, with branches at the sub-HQs. Both the Y and the Egon procedures – principally the latter – were employed.
• The intercept service furnished useful material from the enemy bomber formations, but none from recce (205 Group's good W/T discipline was still in evidence).
• The Italian fighters were for the most part sent out to attack the formations bound for targets in the Etschtal, as at the outset the latter flew without fighter protection. These missions also required a minimum expenditure of petrol.
• On these operations the Italians proved their mettle, but their attacks were not sufficiently co-ordinated.
• Allied fighter-bomber formations were seldom challenged as there was no certainty of visual contact owing to poor radar coverage. It was impossible to fly free-chase patrols continuously due to the petrol shortage.
• Take-off became increasingly difficult as a result of the ever-increasing enemy air activity in the Verona district, and in November 1944 the fighters transferred to Aviano and Osoppo.
• Operations from these airfields were chiefly directed against Allied t/e formations from Corsica, but four-engined stragglers were occasionally challenged on their return flights.
• After the Allies had overrun Hungary the American heavy bomber activity became still more intensified in the eastern zone, grounding the fighters at their peak operational period. This, together with bombing attacks, necessitated a constant change of airfields.
• Our own tactics had to be varied continually with a view to achieving optimum results with a minimum of loss. Any attempt to ward off attacks on vital targets was out of the question.
• From September 1944 until the Italian capitulation, the Italians, as far as I can remember, shot down 30 Allied aircraft, mostly t/e, for the loss of approximately 15 of their own. Write-offs due to accidents were remarkably few.

Plans

• Me 163 Rocket Fighters were to have operated from various airfields in the Verona and Brescia areas. These were to be very heavily defended by flak to safeguard landing as far as possible.
• Preliminary preparations to operate Me 262 jet fighters in the projected JG 44[1] (see CSDIC Report No. A.582), under the command of Generalmajor Galland, from Gallaste airfield were also in train. The runway, camouflage and dispersal facilities at this airfield rendered it ideal for this purpose.
• All these schemes had to be abandoned due to the shortage of petrol, supply difficulties and the deteriorating war situation in general.

(illegible signature)

For J. B. Newton W/Cdr.,
Commanding,
C.S.D.I.C(Air) C.M.F.

Distribution:

C.I.O., R.A.F., MED/ME, Cairo. (3)
S.I.O., A.H.Q., R.A.F., Italy

O.R.S.
A-2, A.H.Q., R.A.F., Italy
C.I.O., A.H.Q., Gibraltar.
  "   "D.A.F.
USAF D. of Int. Ser.
Washington, D.C. (2)
2677th Regiment OSS (Prov.) (3)

A.D.I.(K). (17).

G-2, A.F.H.Q.
Arty Section, A.F.H.Q. (Att'n Major Darlow)
S.O.(I), Med.
Cmdr. U.S. 8th Fleet. (NIU).
J.I.C.A. (4)
A.F.S.C., ACC (W/Cdr. W. L. Minter).
H.Q. Occupational Air Force

Capt. T. M. Webster, A-2 Combat, AAF/MTO (4)
C.I.O. 205 Group.

[1] Galland's unit was not intended to be a fighter squadron (JG) but a smaller fighter unit (JV).

Source: Eduard Neumann, Munich. Copy held by author.

5. Air Force Ranks in the Second World War

Luftwaffe	Abbreviation	RAF	USAAF
Reichsmarschall	RM	–	
Generalfeldmarschall	GFM	Marshal of the RAF	
Generaloberst	Gen	Air Chief Marshal	General (4-star)
General der Flieger	GdFlg	Air Marshal	Lt Gen (3-star)
Generalleutnant	Genlt	Air Vice Marshal	Maj Gen (2-star)
Generalmajor	Genmajor	Air Commodore	Brig Gen (1-star)
Oberst	Obst	Group Captain	Colonel
Oberstleutnant	Obstl	Wing Commander	Lt Col
Major	Maj	Squadron Leader	Major
Hauptmann	Hptm	Flight Lieutenant	Captain
Oberleutnant	Oblt	Flying Officer	First Lt
Leutnant	Lt	Pilot Officer	Second Lt
Stabsfeldwebel	StFw	Warrant Officer	–
Hauptfeldwebel	HptFw	–	–
Oberfeldwebel	Ofw	Flight Sergeant	Master Sgt (1st grade)
Feldwebel	Fw	–	Techn.Sgt (2nd grade)
Unterfeldwebel	Ufw	–	Staff Sgt (3rd grade)
Unteroffizier	Uffz	Sergeant	Sergeant (4th grade)
Stabsgefreiter	Stgefr	–	–
Hauptgefreiter	Hptgfr	–	–
Obergefreiter	Obgefr	Corporal	Corporal (5th grade)
Gefreiter	Gefr	Leading Aircraftman	Private 1st Class
Flieger	Flg	Aircraftman	Private

In addition, there were the Luftwaffe ranks of Fähnrich and Oberfähnrich (Officer Candidate and Senior Officer Candidate), which had no equivalent in the RAF or USAAF.

Notes

INTRODUCTION

1   The only exception is the book *Horrido*, by the Hungarian authors Dénes Bernád, Péter Mujzer and János Hangya (Budapest, 1992), and the two-volume work *Sojusznicy Luftwaffe*, by Polish authors R. Rajlich, Z. Stojczew and Z. Lalak (Warsaw, 1997/8), of which only Vol. 1 (Bulgaria, Slovakia and Romania) is available.

2   Cooper, M., *Die Luftwaffe 1933–1945* (Stuttgart, 1988), p. 249.

3   Cp 'Bell P-39 Airacobra' in *Aircraft*, Issue 200 (1996), pp. 5,590–5,597.

4   16,000 victories are mentioned by Musciano, W. A., *Die berühmten Me 109 und ihre Piloten 1939–1945* (Augsburg, 1994), p. 214.

5   The exceptions so far are the aviation formations of Slovakia and Croatia. These states had hardly been founded when they were drawn into the war, and a part of their population and their elite held distinct sympathies for the Allied cause.

6   Roba, J-L./Craciunoiu, C., *La chasse de nuit germano-roumaine 1943–1944* (Bucharest, 1997), p. 82.

7   Gaiser, G., *Die sterbende Jagd* (Frankfurt/Hamburg, 1957), p. 190.

8   One example should suffice here: from the Hungarian 101st Fighter regiment alone three pilots were killed in the air between June 1944 and March 1945 after they had baled out of their stricken aircraft.

I THE ALLIES

ITALY: REGIA AERONAUTICA

1   Rochat, G., *Italo Balbo, aviatore e ministro dell'aeronautica 1936–1933* (Ferrara, 1979), pp. 38–40; Pelliccia, A., *La Regia Aeronautica. Dalle origini alla Seconda Guerra Mondiale (1926–1943)* (Rome, 1992), pp. 18–19.

2   Re personality of Balbo cp Rochat, loc. cit.; Segrè, C. G., *Italo Balbo* (Bologna, 1988); Taylor, B. *Fascist Eagle. Italy's Air Marshal Italo Balbo* (Missoula/Montana 1996), pictorial book with text largely from Segrè's book; Gatta, B, *Gli uomini del Duce* (Milan, 1986), pp. 44–57; Cannistraro, P. V., *Historical Dictionary of Fascist Italy* (Westport/London 1982), pp. 57–9.

3   Segrè, loc. cit., pp. 204–5.

4   Rochat, loc. cit., pp. 118–9; Pelliccia, loc. cit., p. 23 ff; Segrè, loc. cit., p. 189 ff

5   Cp Beith, R., *The Italian South Atlantic Air Mail Service 1939–1941* (Chester, 1993)

6   A tabulation of some of the records established between 1930 and 1940 is in Emiliani, A./Ghergo, G. F./Vigna, A., *Regia Aeronautica: periodo prebellico e fronti occidentali* (Milan, 1975), pp. 52–3.

7   The record-breaking aircraft MC.72 (construction number MM.181) is at present in the Aviation Museum at Vigna di Valle, near Rome.

8   Cp Segrè, loc. cit., pp. 237–319; Rochat, loc. cit., pp. 62–9; Rocca, G., *I Disperati* (Milan, 1991), pp. 50–4; L. R., '1 Luglio 1933–1 Luglio 1993' in *Storia Verità*, No. 12 (August–December 1993), pp. 16–21.

9   Segrè, loc. cit., p. 302.

10   Rocca, loc. cit., p. 59.

11   Rochat, loc. cit., pp. 140, 191.

[12] Segrè, loc. cit., pp. 338–340.

[13] Rochat, loc. cit., p. 151; cp also Rocca, loc. cit., pp. 61–7.

[14] Pelliccia, loc. cit., p. 66.

[15] Pedriali, F., 'L'Aviazione del Negus' in *Rivista Storica*, No. 9/1995, p. 29.

[16] An accurate account regarding the use of gas is in Gentilli, R., *Guerra aerea sull'Etiopia 1935–1939* (Florence, 1992), pp. 95–6, 100.

[17] Pelliccia, loc. cit., p. 79; although Pelliccia has different personnel losses on p. 167; cp also Gentilli, loc. cit., p. 118 ff.

[18] Pelliccia, loc. cit., p. 81 ff, 170 ff; D'Avanzo, G., *Ali e poltrone* (Rome, 1976), pp. 209 ff, 877 ff.

[19] Minniti, F., 'Aspetti della politica fascista degli armamenti dal 1935 al 1943', in De Felice, R. (publisher), *L'Italia fra tedeschi e alleati* (Bologna, 1973), p. 128.

[20] Re the odyssey of the 12 SM.81s see also Pedriali, F., 'Disastro aereo nel Mediterraneo', in *Rivista Storica*, No. 3/1995, pp. 35–40; Malizia, N., *Ali nella tragedia di Spagna* (Modena, 1986), pp. 20–2; Alfocar Nassaes, J. L., *La aviación legionaria en la guerra española* (Barcelona, 1975), p. 18 ff; Pelliccia, loc. cit., p. 99 ff.

[21] Various figures are given in the literature, cp Alfocar Nassaes, op. cit., p. 342; Coverdale, J. F., *La intervención fascista en la Guerra Civil española* (Madrid, 1979), p. 347; Pelliccia, loc. cit., p. 140; Rocca, loc. cit., p. 88; Thomas, H., *The Spanish Civil War*, 3rd ed. (Harmondsworth, 1979), p. 978.

[22] *Aircraft*, Issue 95 (1994), p. 2,660; cp Thompson, J., *Italian Civil and Military Aircraft, 1930–1945* (Fallbrook, 1963), pp. 148–51.

[23] Alfocar Nassaes, loc. cit., p. 342 ff.

[24] Estimates vary between 175 and 193 killed, cp Alfocar Nassaes, loc. cit., p. 344; Pelliccia, loc. cit., p. 142.

[25] Minniti, loc. cit., p. 128.

[26] Vergnano, P., *Fiat G.50* (Turin, 1997), p. 12.

[27] This aspect is especially emphasized by Voltan, P., *Un pilota del cavallino rampante* (Battaglia Terme, 1990), p. 59.

[28] Pelliccia, loc. cit., p. 198.

[29] De Felice, R., *Mussolini l'alleato 1940–1945. I: L'Italia in guerra 1940–1943, Vol. 1: Dalla guerra 'breve' all guerra lunga* (Turin, 1990), p. 543.

[30] Cp Rocca, loc. cit., pp. 94, 122 f; Pelliccia, loc. cit., p. 181.

[31] Cp Vaccari, P. F., 'DB-601, DB-605: 'I 12 cilindri dell'Asse', in *Rivista Storica* (April 1996), p. 64; D'Avanzo, loc. cit., p. 258 f; re engine problems see also Ceva, L./Curami, A., 'Luftstreitkräfte und Luftfahrtindustrie in Italien, 1936–1943', in Bogg, H. (ed.), *Luftkriegführung im Zweiten Weltkrieg* (Herford/Bonn, 1993), pp. 122 ff.

[32] Rocca, loc. cit., p. 95.

[33] De Felice, *Mussolini l'alleato*, p. 541; Pirelli, A., *Taccuini 1922/1943* (Bologna, 1984), p. 381.

[34] Ceva/Curami, loc. cit., p. 116 f.

[35] Ciano, G., *Diario 1939–1943*, 5th ed. (Milan, 1971), pp. 101, 190.

[36] D'Avanzo, loc. cit., p. 254; Rocca, loc. cit., p. 103 f; Pelliccia, loc. cit., p. 136.

[37] Rochat, loc. cit., p. 110 f.

[38] Pelliccia, loc. cit., p. 195.

[39] Emiliani, A./Ghergo, G. F./Vigna, A., *Regia Aeronautica: periodo prebellico*, p. 116; Garello, G., *Regia Aeronautica e Armée de l'Air*, Part 2 (Rome, 1975), p. 70.

[40] Corvaja, S., 'Perché falli il nostro attacco a Gibilterra', in *Storia Illustrata*, No. 288, pp. 22–9, 32–8; Finlayson, T. J., *The Fortress Came First* (Grendon, 1991); Pesce, G., 'Spie in libertà ad Alegeciras', in *Rivista Storica*, No. 1/1996, pp. 32–9.

[41] Cp Malizia, N., 'Quei cieli amari di Gran Bretagna', in *Ala Tricolore*, No. 9/1985, p. 3; Ricci, C., *Il Corpo Aereo Italiano (CAI) sul fronte della Manica (1940–1941)* (Rome, 1994), p. 10.

[42] Ricci, loc. cit., p. 62.

[43] Today this plane (MM 5701) is in the RAF Museum in London-Hendon.

[44] Colville, J., *Downing Street Tagebücher 1939–1945* (Berlin, 1991), p. 211.

[45] Ricci, loc. cit., p. 163 f; other authors credit CAI with 15 aerial victories, cp Licheri, S., *L'arma aerea italiana nella seconda guerra mondiale* (Milan, 1976), p. 39; Pelliccia, loc. cit., p. 216, but these claims are not confirmed by the British.

[46] Curami, A., 'Appunti sulla Regia Aeronautica nei Balcani 1940–41', in *Annali della Fondazione 'Luigi Micheletti', L'Italia in guerra 1940–1943* (Brescia, 1990–1), p. 151; slightly divergent data is given by Licheri, loc. cit., p. 70 f.

[47] Borgiotti, A./Gori, C., *Gli Stuka della R. Aeronautica 1940–1945* (Modena, 1976), p. 14.

[48] Curami, loc. cit., pp. 145 f, 152; divergent figures in Licheri, loc. cit., p. 71.

[49] Buckley, C., *Greece and Crete 1941* (Athens, 1984), pp. 21, 45.

[50] Re numerical data cp Pelliccia, loc. cit., p.236; Rocca, loc. cit., p. 169; Licheri, loc. cit., p. 75.

[51] Shores, C., *Dust Clouds in the Middle East* (London, 1996), p. 11; Emiliani, A./Ghergo, G. F./Vigna, A., *Regia Aeronautica: I fronti africani* (Parma, 1979), p. 60 f.

[52] Shores, loc. cit., p. 60.

[53] Cp Patience, K., 'The Italian Raid on Bahrain', in *After the Battle*, Issue 56 (1987), pp. 18–21; D'Avanzo, G., *Morte a Fregene* (Rome, 1993), pp. 167 ff, 181 f; Neulen, H. W., 'Orangen auf New York', in *Jet & Prop*, 4/1997, p. 15; Traversari, B., 'Dal raid su Tokyo al progetto New York', in *Storia Illustrata*, No. 318 (May 1984), p. 36.

[54] Shores, loc. cit., p. 91.

[55] Ibid. p. 104; Licheri, loc. cit., p. 122 f.

[56] Differing data about the size of the SAS aircraft park are made in the literature: 101, 132 or 183 aircraft, cp Garello, G., 'La militarisation de l'Aviation Civile Italienne durant la Seconde Guerre Mondiale', Part 1, in *Avions*, No. 43 (October 1996), p. 2; Traversari, loc. cit., p. 34; Neulen, 'Orangen auf New York', p. 15; Emiliani, A./Ghergo, G. F./Vigna, A., *Regia Aeronautica: periodo prebellico*, p. 108

[57] Shores, loc. cit., p. 139 f; Bragadin, M. A., *Il dramma della marina italiana 1940–1945* (Milan, 1982), p. 112 f.

[58] Pagliano, F., *Aviatori italiani* (Milan, 1970), pp. 35–42; Neulen 'Orangen auf New York', p. 16; Traversari, loc. cit., p. 37.

[59] Cp Pagliano, loc. cit., pp. 177–185; Traversari, loc. cit., p. 37.

[60] Licheri, loc. cit., p. 44.

[61] Pedriali, F., 'Biplani d'assalto in Africa Settentrionale', in *Rivista Storica*, No. 10/1995, p. 14 f.

[62] Licheri, loc. cit., p. 57; Pelliccia, loc. cit., p. 238; Rocca, loc. cit., p. 156.

[63] Ring, H./Girbig, W., *Jagdgeschwader 27*, 6th ed. (Stuttgart, 1979), p. 83.

[64] Re Luigi Gorrini cp Neulen, H. W., 'Der letzte der "wütenden Wespen"', in *Jet & Prop*, 4/1996, pp. 13–17; Pagliano, loc. cit., pp. 195–202; Gibertini, G, 'Luigi Gorrini MOVM', in *Aerei*, No 12/1989, pp. 46–52.

65 Borgiotti/Gori, loc. cit., p. 58; Emiliani/Ghergo/Vigna, *Regia Aeronautica: I fronti africani*, p. 91.

66 Attard, J., *The Battle of Malta* (Valletta, 1988), p. 55.

67 Pelliccia, loc. cit., p. 235.

68 Re the SM.79 cp 'Savoia Marchetti S.M.79', in *Aircraft*, Issue 195 (1996), pp. 5,440–451; Spaggiari, L./D'Agostino, C., *SM-79 il gobbo maledotto* (Milan, 1979); Rovelli, M., 'S.79 "Sparviero"', in *Storia Illustrata*, No. 318 (May 1984), pp. 117–21; Gentilli, R., *Savoia Marchetti S.79 in Action* (Carrollton/Texas, 1986).

69 Emiliani, A./Ghergo, G. F./Vigna, A., *Regia Aeronautica: Il settore mediterraneo* (Milan, 1976), p. 43.

70 Attard, loc. cit., p. 133.

71 Attard, loc. cit., p. 187 f; cp also Reuth, R. G., *Entscheidung im Mittelmeer* (Koblenz, 1985), p. 186.

72 Pelliccia, loc. cit., p. 263; Licheri, loc. cit., p. 157.

73 Cp Apostolo, G., *Reggiane Re 2001* (Turin, 1996).

74 This success was achieved by Martino Aichner, but the sinking was acknowledged only years after the war; Aichner finally received the highest Italian award for bravery, the Medaglia d'Oro al Valor Militare, after a 47-year delay on 28 March 1989.

75 Rocca, loc. cit., p. 230 f; Bonvicini, G., *Carlo Faggioni e gli aerosiluranti italiani* (Milan, 1987), p. 68 f.

76 Pelliccia, loc. cit., p. 264; Licheri, loc. cit., p. 181.

77 Reuth, loc. cit., p. 202

78 Pelliccia, loc. cit., p. 268; cp also Licheri, loc. cit., p. 136 f.

79 Cp Pelliccia, loc. cit., p. 270; Pedriali, *Biplani d'assalto*, p. 23 f.

80 Flaccominio, S., *I falchi del deserto*, 3rd ed. (Milan, 1965), p. 137

81 Cp Bonvicini, loc. cit., pp. 91–100; Boschesi, B. P./Rovelli, M., 'I mitici "Gobbi" all'attaco disperato di Bougie', in *Storia Illustrata*, No. 318 (May 1984), pp. 106–116; Aichner, M., *Il gruppo Buscaglia* (Milan, 1991), pp. 119–131.

82 The remains of the six crew members were transported to Italy with full military honours in January 1984.

83 Chiocci, G., *Gli affondatori del cielo* (Rome, 1972), p. 153.

84 Licheri, loc. cit., p. 201 f; cp also Pelliccia, loc. cit., p. 281.

85 Rocca, loc. cit., p. 262; cp also Garello, La militarisation, part 2, p. 5; Traversari, loc. cit., p. 40.

86 Malizia, N., *Ali sulla steppa* (Rome, 1987), p. 211.

87 Ibid., p. 97.

88 Pagliano, loc. cit., p. 195; D'Amico, F./Valentini, G., *The Messerschmitt 109 in Italian Service 1943–1945* (Boylston, 1985), p. 44 Note 5.

89 Malizia, *Ali sulla steppa*, p. 137.

90 Ibid., pp. 162, 174, 187, 208; the article 'Macchi MC.200, 202 and 205' in *Aircraft*, Issue 181 (1996), p. 5,057 mentions only 12 MC.202s transferred to the Eastern Front; Gentilli, R./Gorena, L., *Macchi C.202 in Action*, new ed. (Carrollton, 1995), p. 27 mentions a total of 14 MC.202s with 21° Gruppo C.T.

91 Cp Messe, G., *Der Krieg im Osten* (Zürich, 1948), p. 85 f.

92 Malizia, *Ali sulla steppa*, p. 173.

93 Hentschel, G., *Die geheimen Konferenzen des Generalluftzeugmeisters* (Koblenz, 1989), p. 195.

⁹⁴   Cp Notes by the German Ambassador von Macksensen in Rome of 9 April 1943, ADAP Series E: 1941–1945, Vol. V, Document No. 285, p. 542 f; Notes re Hitler/Mussolini meeting on 19 July 1943, ADAP Series E: 1943–1945, Vol. VI, Document No. 159, pp. 267–70.

⁹⁵   De Felice, *Mussolini l'alleato*, p. 563.

⁹⁶   Pelliccia, loc. cit., p. 285.

⁹⁷   Letter from Luigi Gorrini to the author dated 20 March 1996.

⁹⁸   Garello, *Regia Aeronautica e Armée de l'Air*, Part 3, pp. 156, 168; only 60 D.520s in Regia Aeronautica service are mentioned in the article 'Dewoitine D.520', in *Aircraft*, Issue 114 (1995), p. 3,188.

⁹⁹   Cp D'Amico/Valentini, *The Messerschmitt 109 in Italian Service*, pp. 10–45.

¹⁰⁰ Emiliani, A./Ghergo, G. F./Vigna, A., *Aviazione italiana: La guerra in Italia* (Parma, 1982), p. 23.

¹⁰¹ Cp Arena, N., *Reggiane 2005 'Sagittario'*, new ed. (Modena, 1994); Arena, N., *Macchi 205 'Veltro'*, new ed. (Modena, 1994); Arena, N., *Fiat G.55 'Centauro'*, new ed. (Modena, 1994); Arena, N., *La Regia Aeronautica 1939–1943, Vol. 4: 1943: L'anno dell'armistizio* (Naples, 1994), p. 828 f.

¹⁰² Cp Arena, *Macchi MC.205 'Veltro'*, pp. 39–42; Pagliano, loc. cit., pp. 195–201; Neulen, 'Der letzte der "wütenden Wespen"', pp. 15, 17; Gibertini, loc. cit., p. 50 ff.

¹⁰³ Rigoli, A., *Decollo verso l'ignoto* (Trieste, 1993), p. 23.

¹⁰⁴ Cp Harvey, S., 'L'effort de guerre italien et le bombardement stratégique de l'Italie', in *Revue d'histoire de la deuxième guerre mondiale*, No. 143 (July 1986), pp. 61–77.

¹⁰⁵ Cp D'Amico, F./Valentini, G., 'Cacciatori della notte', in *JP* 4 (January 1995), pp. 74–81; Garello, G., 'La caccia notturna italiana 1940–1942', in *Aerofan*, No. 57 (April–June 1996), pp. 2–25; Grande, G., 'La caccia notturna scientifica 1942–43', in *Aerofan*, No. 58 (July–September 1996), pp. 127–140.

¹⁰⁶ Steinhoff, J., *Die Strasse von Messina* (Munich, 1973), p. 193.

¹⁰⁷ Pelliccia, loc. cit., p. 298.

¹⁰⁸ Pesce, G., '10 Juglio 1943, La guerra nel Mediterraneo al giro di boia', in Pesce, G., *L'Aeronautica Italiana all'epilogo del conflitto* (no date or place of publication), p. 23.

¹⁰⁹ Ibid., p. 12; D'Amico/Valentini, *The Messerschmitt 109 in Italian Service*, p. 32.

¹¹⁰ Arena, *Macchi MC.205 'Veltro'*, p. 22.

¹¹¹ Massimello, G., 'Un pilota del "Quarto" raconta', in *Aerofan*, No. 58 (July–September 1996), p. 125.

¹¹² Letter from Luigi Gorrini to the author dated 4 March 1996; Neulen, 'Der letzte der "wütenden Wespen"', p. 15.

¹¹³ Morris, E., *La guerra inutile*, 2nd ed. (Milan, 1994), p. 492.

¹¹⁴ Rocca, loc. cit., p. 286.

¹¹⁵ Pagliano, loc. cit., p. 246.

¹¹⁶ Pelliccia, loc. cit., p. 307; cp also Rochat, 'Le Forze Aeree Italiane dall'armistizio alla liberazione', in *Studie ricerche di storia contemporanea*, No. 43 (June 1995), p. 27; Emiliani/Ghergo/Vigna, *Aviazione italiana: La guerra in Italia*, pp. 8, 38–42; D'Avanzo, loc. cit., p. 388, mentions 877 operationally ready aircraft.

¹¹⁷ KTB OKW, Vol. IV: 1 January 1944–22 May 1945, Second Half-volume IV/8, (Herrsching 1982), p. 1,545; cp also Arena, N., *La Regia Aeronautica 1943–1946, Part 1: Dall'armistizio all cobelligeranza* (Modena, 1978), p. 16.

¹¹⁸ BA/MA RL 2III/974.

¹¹⁹ Pelliccia, loc. cit., p. 312.

[120] Cp Rigoli, loc. cit., pp. 138 f, 210.

[121] Morris, loc. cit., p. 451.

ITALY: AERONAUTICA NAZIONALE REPUBBLICANA (ANR)

[122] Alegi, G., 'La legione che nun fu mai', in *Storia contemporanea* (December 1992), p. 1,082.

[123] Letter from Luigi Gorrini to the author dated 30 January 1996; Neulen, 'Der letzte der "wütenden Wespen"', p. 16.

[124] Satta, M., 'Un pilota dell'Aeronautica Repubblicana', in *Storia Militare*, No. 14 (November 1994), p. 36.

[125] Cp D'Avanzo, *Morte a Fregene*; Mari, R., 'Una notte di cinquanti'anni fa nella pineta di Fregene', in *Storia Verità*, No. 13 (January–February 1994), pp. 12–16.

[126] Arena, N., *L'Aeronautica Nazionale Repubblicana* (Parma, 1995), p. 38.

[127] Cp Roba, J.-L./Mombeek, E., 'Les Macchis 205 au sein du II./JG 77', in *Replic*, No. 12 (July–August 1992), p. 35 ff.

[128] Pesce, G., 'Nasce nell'Italia del Nord un governo insurrezionale', in Pesce, *L'Aeronautica Italiana all'epilogo del conflitto*, p. 55; cp also D'Amico, F./Grande, G., 'GTV: Storie di piloti disarmati', in *JP* 4 (September 1994), pp. 80–6.

[129] Pesce, G., 'L'Aeronautica Nazionale Repubblicana combatte al Nord', in Pesce, *L'Aeronautica Italiana all'epilogo del conflitto*, p. 66 f, and in *Rivista Storica*, 6/1995, p. 24 ff; cp also Arena, *L'Aeronautica Nazionale Repubblicana*, pp. 321–32; it has to be pointed out that there are frequently great discrepancies between the claims of ANR pilots and the losses admitted by the Anglo-American authorities.

[130] Pesce, 'L'Aeronautica Nazionale Repubblicana combatte al Nord', p. 67, also in *Rivista Storica*, 6/1995, p. 26; Arena, *L'Aeronautica Nazionale Repubblicana*, p. 334.

[131] Satta, loc. cit., p. 43.

[132] Spaggiari/D'Agostino, loc. cit., p. 161.

[133] Beale, N./D'Amico, F./Valentini, G., *Air War Italy 1944–1945* (Shrewsbury, 1996), p. 42; cp also Arena, *L'Aeronautica Nazionale Repubblicana*, p. 279 ff. To clear up the events of the night of 4/5 June the author contacted the government of Gibraltar. He received a reply on 15 April 1994 stating that there were no records of any kind in the archives about an air raid on the Rock on that night. This reply seems rather surprising.

[134] Buscaglia, the Aerosiluranti ace, was not killed during his attack on Bougie on 12 November 1942, but was, unbeknown to anyone in Italy, captured badly wounded. After the armistice he decided to support the royal side and was released to southern Italy in June 1944, where he lost his life in a flying incident on 28 August 1944. The fact that Buscaglia had fought for the Allied side made it necessary to rename the torpedo-bomber group.

[135] Arena, *Fiat G.55 'Centauro'*, p. 31 f; Curami, A., 'Miti e realtà dell'industria bellica della RSI', in *Rivista di storia contemporanea*, No. 2–3 (April–July 1993), p. 353.

[136] Longo, L. E., *RSI Antologia per un'atmosfera* (Milan, 1995), p. 222.

[137] Alegi, loc. cit., p. 1.054 ff; cp also Beale/D'Amico/Valentini, loc. cit., p. 35.

[138] Re the events of August 1944 see Alegi, loc. cit., pp. 1,047–85; Beale/D'Amico/Valentini, loc. cit., p. 89 ff; Arena, *L'Aeronautica Nazionale Repubblicana*, loc. cit., pp. 192–207.

[139] Arena, *L'Aeronautica Nazionale Repubblica*, loc. cit., p. 204; Alegi, loc. cit., p. 1,076.

[140] In winter 1944/5 Neumann was for a while replaced by Oberst Lützow, who was 'banned from the Reich' because of his opposition to Göring.

[141] Cp *Ala Tricolore*, No. 5 (September–October 1996), p. 4.

¹⁴² Cp Viganò, M., 'Quell'aereo per la Spagna ...', in *Storia Verità*, No. 23–24 (September–December 1995), pp. 4–10; Bonino, A., *Mussolini mi ha detto* (publ. by M. Viganò, Rome, 1995), pp. 62–4; Pallottelli, V., 'Le memorie inedita del pilota del Duce', in *Storia Illustrata*, No. 332 (July 1985), p. 10 f.

¹⁴³ Likewise the author, in his article 'Bis zum bitteren Ende', in *Jet & Prop*, 5/1993, p. 43.

¹⁴⁴ Alegi, loc. cit., p. 1049.

¹⁴⁵ Ibid., p. 1,050, footnote 10.

¹⁴⁶ Piekalkewicz, J., *Schweiz 39–45*, 2nd ed. (Stuttgart, 1979), pp. 277, 349–55.

ROMANIA: FORTELE AERIENE REGALE ROMANA

¹ The best source for the production figures of the Romanian aviation industry and the deliveries of foreign aircraft is in the works of Axworthy, M., *The Third Axis, Fourth Ally* (London, 1995), pp. 239–82; 'On three fronts', in *Air Enthusiast*, No. 56 (1994), pp. 8–27; 'Flank Guard', in *Air Enthusiast*, No. 64 (July–August 1996), pp. 28–31.

² Cp Axworthy, *Third Axis, Fourth Ally*, pp. 253–66; 'On three fronts', pp. 14–20; see also Stapfer, H. H., 'Beim Rollen waren die IAR 80 Piloten blind', in *Jet & Prop*, 2/1997, p. 18–25.

³ Axworthy, *Third Axis, Fourth Ally*, p. 267; 'On three fronts', loc. cit., p. 21. On the other hand, the article 'Savoia-Marchetti S.M.79' in *Aircraft*, Issue 195 (1996), p. 5450, mentions 24 examples with Jumo 211 Da engines built in Italy; so also does Thompson, *Italian Civil and Military Aircraft*, p. 265; cp also Spaggiari/D'Agostino, loc. cit., pp. 86, 142.

⁴ Bucurescu (ed.), *Aviata Romana pe frontul de Est si in aparatea teritoriului, Vol. 1: 22 iunie 1941–31 decembrie 1942* (Bucharest, 1993), p. 11; Axworthy, 'Flank Guard', p. 28, gives slightly different figures and starts from the premise that the rearmament plan originated in 1939.

⁵ Heinkel, E./Thorwald, J., *Stürmisches Leben* (Munich, 1977), p. 292.

⁶ Cp Avram, V., 'Les Heinkel He 122 roumains', in *Avions*, No. 38 (May 1996), pp. 40–6.

⁷ Cp to that extent the correspondence between the Romanian Undersecretary for Aviation and the German Air Attaché of 14/22 January 1943, BA/MA RL 2III/674.

⁸ BA/MA RL 2III/674.

⁹ Bucurescu, loc. cit., Vol. 4, p. 14.

¹⁰ Penetelescu, A./Dobre, F., Craciunoiu, C., *Grupareà Aeriana de Lupta 11.09–16.10.1941* (Bucharest, 1995), p. LVII.

¹¹ Roba, J.-L./Craciunoiu, C., *Seaplanes over the Black Sea* (Bucharest, 1995), p. 11; Axworthy, *Third Axis, Fourth Ally*, p. 285.

¹² Schreier, H., *JG 52. Das erfolgreichste Jagdgeschwader des Zweiten Weltkrieges* (Berg am See, 1990), p. 54 f.

¹³ Pentelescu/Dobre/Craciunoiu, loc. cit., p. 16.

¹⁴ Pentelescu/Dobre/Craciunoiu, loc. cit., p. 14.

¹⁵ Axworthy, *Third Axis, Fourth Ally*, p. 288; 'Flank Guard', loc. cit., p. 35; cp also Pentelescu/Dobre/Craciunoiu, loc. cit., p. 16.

¹⁶ Letter from the Undersecretary for Aviation to the German Air Attaché dated 14 January 1943, BA/MA RL 2III/674.

¹⁷ Notes about the conversation between Reichsmarschall Göring and Marshal Antonescu at Karinhall on 13 February 1942, ADAP, Series E: 1941–1945, Vol. 1, Document Nr. 241, p. 440.

¹⁸ Axworthy, *Third Axis, Fourth Ally*, p. 291; 'Flank Guard', loc. cit., p. 37.

[19] Facon, P, 'Les forces aériennes roumaines pendant la Seconde Guerra Mondiale: 1939–1945', in *Moniteur de l'Aéronautique*, No. 44, p.24.

[20] Bucurescu, loc. cit., Vol. 1, p. 102 f; Axworthy, *Third Axis, Fourth Ally*, p. 292.

[21] Gosztony, P., *Hitlers fremde Heere* (Düsseldorf/Vienna, 1976), pp. 291–4.

[22] KTB OKW, Vol. II: I January 1942–31 December 1942, 2nd Half-volume II/4 (Herrsching, 1982), p. 1,019.

[23] Herhudt von Rohden, H.-D., *Die Luftwaffe ringt um Stalingrad* (Berlin, 1993), p. 17.

[24] KTB OKW, Vol. II: 1 January 1942–31 December 1942, 1st Half-volume, II/3 (Herrsching, 1982), p. 93.

[25] Gosztony, *Hitlers fremde Heere*, p. 328.

[26] Axworthy, *Third Axis, Fourth Ally*, p. 295 f, 'Flank Guard', Part 2, in *Air Enthusiast*, No. 65 (September–October 1996), p. 72.

[27] Letter from Undersecretary of State for the Luftwaffe to the German Air Attaché dated 14 January 1943, BA/MA RL 2III/674.

[28] Axworthy, *Third Axis, Fourth Ally*, p. 298.

[29] Cp Roba/Craciunoiu, 'La chasse de nuit germano-roumaine', loc. cit.; according to other information the night fighter unit involved was supposedly the 68th Squadron.

[30] *Die Wehrmachtberichte 1939–1945, Vol. 2: 1 January 1942 to 31 December 1943* (Munich, 1985), p. 521.

[31] Vlad, D., 'Uncle Sam's Baksheesh', in *Air International* (October 1994), p. 246 f; Storck, R., 'Endstation USA', in *Flugzeug* 5/1994, p. 17 gives the name of the pilot as Teodor Nikolai.

[32] Cp Avram, V., *Aviatia de Asalt* (Bucharest, 1994); Avram, V., 'L'aviation d'assault roumaine de 1943 à 1945', Part 1, in *Le Fana de l'Aviation*, No. 325 (December 1996), pp. 16–26; Part 2, in *Le Fana de l'Aviation*, No. 326 (January 1997), pp. 48–60.

[33] Cp 'Henschel Hs 129', in *Aircraft*, Issue 167 (1996), pp. 4667–73.

[34] Axworthy, *Third Axis, Fourth Ally*, p. 302.

[35] Ibid., p. 304.

[36] Re Ionescu cp Bucurescu, I. (ed.), *Aviatia Romana in Lupta pe frontul de est si in aparatea teritoriului, Vol. 2: 1 ianuarie 1943–23 august 1944* (Bucharest, 1994), p. 400 ff.

[37] Emilian, I. V., *Der phantastische Ritt* (Preussisch Oldendorf, 1977), p. 347 ff

[38] KTB OKW Vol. IV: 1 January 1944–22 May 1945, 1st Half-volume IV/7 (Herrsching, 1982), p. 801.

[39] Cp Bucurescu, loc. cit., Vol. 2, p. 295 f; Roba, J.-L./Mombeek, E., *La chasse de jour allemande en Roumanie* (Bucharest, 1994), p. 22 ff; Axworthy, *Third Axis, Fourth Ally*, p. 311.

[40] Cp telegram from the German ambassador in Bucharest to the Foreign Ministry dated 14 September 1942, and the notes of Ambassador Schmidt of 26 September 1942, ADAP, Series E: 1941–1945, Vol. III, Document No. 288, p. 429 f, Document No. 312, p. 551 f.

[41] Newby, L. W., *Into the Guns of Ploesti* (Osceola, 1991), p. 99; cp also Axworthy, *Third Axis, Fourth Ally*, p. 311; Roba/Mombeek, *La chasse de jour allemande*, pp. 28–31.

[42] Notes of senior civil servant Clodius of 13 August 1943, ADAP, Series E: 1941–1945, Vol. VI, Document No. 223, p. 393.

[43] Notes of senior civil servant Clodius of 17 February 1944, ADAP, Series E: 1941–1945, Vol. VII, Document No. 222, p. 424 f.

[44] Roba/Mombeek, *La chasse de jour allemande*, p. 38.

[45] Axworthy, *Third Axis, Fourth Ally*, p. 313.

[46] Neumann, E., 'Jafü Balkan – Jafü Rumänien', MSS, p. 1

[47] Vizanty, D., 'Die Rumänen flogen keine Fw 190', in *Jägerblatt*, 5/1983, p. 34.

348

48   Axworthy, *Third Axis, Fourth Ally*, p. 314

49   Neumann, loc. cit., p. 2

50   KTB OKW, Vol. IV, 1st Half-volume, p. 785.

51   Axworthy, *Third Axis, Fourth Ally*, p. 315.

52   KTB OKW, Vol. IV, 1st Half-volume, p. 784.

53   Vizanty, 'Die Rumänen flogen keine Fw 190', p. 35.

54   Re the number of shot-down aircraft cp Newby, loc. cit., p. 151; Roba/Mombeek, *La chasse de jour allemande*, p. 63; Axworthy, *Third Axis, Fourth Ally*, p. 315; Bernád/Mujzer/Hangya, loc. cit., p. 100.

55   Notes by Ambassador Schmidt of 7 August 1944, ADAP, Series E: 1941–1945, Vol. VIII, Document No. 150, p. 303.

56   Roba/Mombeek, *La chasse de jour allemande*, p. 83 f.

57   Telegram from the German ambassador in Bucharest to the Foreign Ministry dated 19 August 1944, ADAP, Series E: 1941–1945, Document No. 165, p. 331.

58   Re the loss figures cp Axworthy, *Third Axis, Fourth Ally*, p. 314; Newby loc. cit., p. 180.

59   Rotaru, J./König, C./Dutu, A., *Romanian Army in World War II* (Bucharest, 1995), p. 100.

60   Neumann, loc. cit., p. 1; the frequently quoted conversation between Neumann and Dan Vizanty – cp Vizanty, D., 'Un grand nom de l'aviation: le Prince Cantacuzène-Bizu', in *Pionniers*, No. 81 (July 1984), p. 30, and Vizanty, D., 'Wie aus Waffenbrüder Kriegsgegner wurden', in *Jägerblatt*, No. 6/1988, p. 12 – never took place, at least not in this form; cp letter from E. Neumann to the author dated 6 December 1995.

61   Vizanty, 'Un grand nom de l'aviation', p. 32.

62   Roba/Craciunoiu, *La chasse de nuit germano-roumaine*, pp. 86, 89, 98.

63   Neumann, loc. cit., p. 3.

64   Stapfer, H.-H., 'Aus Freund wurde Feind', in *Jet & Prop*, 2/1992, p. 51; far too high figures are quoted by Rotaru/König/Dutu, loc. cit., p. 126.

65   Avram, *L'aviation d'assault roumaine de 1943 à 1945*, Part 2, p. 58.

66   Cp Bucurescu, loc. cit., Vol. 2, p. 397 ff.

HUNGARY: MAGYAR KIRÁLYI HONVÉD LÉGIERÖ

1   Sárhidai, G./Punka, G./Kozlik, V., *Hungarian Eagles* (Aldershot, 1996), p. 4.

2   Ibid., p. 8.

3   See the chapter about Slovakia.

4   Sárhidai/Punka/Kozlik, loc. cit. p. 10; cp also Punka, G., *Hungarian Air Force* (Carrollton, 1994), p. 2.

5   Apostolo, G., *Fiat CR.42* (Turin, 1995), p. 42.

6   Gaal, J. R., 'Bombers at large', in *Air Combat* (November 1977), p. 83.

7   *Aircraft*, Issue 57 (1993), p. 1,592.

8   Pelliccia, loc. cit., p. 181; cp also Rocca, loc. cit., p. 94.

9   Korbuly, D., 'Ungarns Eintritt in den Zweiten Weltkrieg', in *Der Donauraum*, No. 1/1971, p. 23 f.

10   Re the unusual numbering system of the MKHL cp Gaal, J. R., 'The Hungarian Air Force in World War II', in *Air Pictorial* (May 1964), p. 148. For example, 2/3 Squadron indicated the 3rd Squadron of the 2nd Wing. The numbers indicating groups were given in Roman numerals, as in the German Luftwaffe.

NOTES

[11] Sárhidai/Punka/Kozlik, loc. cit., p. 16; Punka, *Hungarian Air Force*, p. 6, does not mention the 1/2 Fighter squadron.

[12] Nebelin, M., '"Barbarossa" and Ungarn', in *Militärgeschictliche Mitteilungen*, 53 (1994), p. 109 f; cp also Korbuly, loc. cit., p. 24.

[13] There is no agreement about the composition of this formation in the literature; cp Sárhidai/Punka/Kozlik, loc. cit., p. 18; Punka, *Hungarian Air Force*, p. 7; Gaal, *The Hungarian Air Force*, p. 145 f; Gaal, J. R., 'The Bridge over the River Bug', in *Air Combat* (March 1978), p. 80; Gosztony, *Hitlers fremde Heere*, p. 156.

[14] This attack on the bridge is described in detail by Gaal in 'The Bridge over the River Bug', pp. 80–7.

[15] Sárhidai/Punka/Kozlik, loc. cit., p. 19; Gosztony, *Hitlers fremde Heere*, p. 161 give the Hungarian aircraft losses as 30 planes.

[16] Gosztony, *Hitlers fremde Heere*, p. 210 f; Sárhidai/Punka/Kozlik, loc. cit., p. 21 says only 50 bombers took part.

[17] Vasari, E., *Ein Königsdrama im Schatten Hitlers* (Vienna/Munich, 1968), p. 175 ff; Sárhidai/Punka/Kozlik, loc. cit., p. 24.

[18] Sárhidai/Punka/Kozlik, loc. cit., p. 31; according to Punka, *Hungarian Air Force*, p. 38, the retraining did not take place till the end of 1943.

[19] ADAP, Series E: 1941–1945, Vol. V, Document No. 274, p. 522.

[20] ADAP, Series E: 1941–1945, Vol. V, Document No. 315, p. 639 f.

[21] Punka, G., *'Messer', the Messerschmitt 109 in the Royal Hungarian 'Honvéd' Air Force* (Budapest, 1995), p. 10.

[22] Cp Punka, *'Messer'*, p. 19; Sárhidai/Punka/Kozlik, loc. cit., p. 26.

[23] Re Heppes cp Musciano, loc. cit., pp. 161–5.

[24] Cp Gosztony, *Hitlers fremde Heere*, p. 339 f; Punka, *'Messer'*, p. 23 f; Sárhidai/Punka/Kozlik, loc. cit., p. 27.

[25] Cited according to Gosztony, *Hitlers fremde Heere*, p. 278.

[26] Sárhidai/Punka/Kozlik, loc. cit., p. 33.

[27] The Hungarian squadrons frequently changed their numbers. The figure 102 often quoted in text indicates that the squadron belonged to the 102. Aviation brigade; cp Gaal, *The Hungarian Air Force*, p. 148.

[28] Cooper, loc. cit., p. 315.

[29] Sárhidai/Punka/Kozlik, loc. cit., p. 30.

[30] The actual date of redesignation is disputed; cp Sárhidai/Punka/Kozlik, loc. cit., p. 30 (October 1943), and Punka, *'Messer'*, p. 113 (April 1944).

[31] Punka, *'Messer'*, p. 10; Mujzer, P., 'Les Messerschmitt Me 210Ca hongrois', Part 1, in *Avions*, No. 46 (January 1997), p. 11.

[32] Cooper, loc. cit.; Irving, D., *Die Tragödie der deutschen Luftwaffe* (Frankfurt/Berlin, 1990), p. 222.

[33] Mujzer, 'Les Messerschmitt Me 210Ca hongrois', Part 1, p. 14; cp also 'Messerschmitt Me 410 – der letzte Zerstörertyp', in *Aircraft*, Issue 19 (1993), p. 523 f.

[34] Re the history of the Hungarian He 112 cp Mujzer, P., 'Les Heinkel He 112 hongrois', in *Avions*, No. 37 (April 1996), pp. 39–42.

[35] Cp Gosztony, P., 'Ungarns militärische Rolle im Zweiten Weltkrieg', Part 3, in *Wehrwissenschaftliche Rundschau*, No. 6/1981, pp. 39–42.

[36] Mujzer, 'Les Messerschmitt Me 210Ca hongrois', Part 3, in *Avions*, No. 48 (March 1997), p. 22 f.

37 Sárhidai/Punka/Kozlik, loc. cit., p. 35.
38 Cp Mujzer, 'Les Messerschmitt Me 210Ca hongrois', Part 2, in *Avions*, No. 47 (February 1997), p. 14 f; Tobak, T., *Les Pumas Rouges* (no place of publication, 1996), p. 126 f.
39 Tobak, loc. cit., p. 126.
40 Punka, *'Messer'*, p. 53.
41 Ibid., p. 55.
42 Re Debrödy cp Musciano, loc. cit., p. 165 f; Hefty, U., 'Hungarian Ace', in *RAF Flying Review*, Vol. XVII, No. 3, pp 33f, 44.
43 Cp Hefty, loc. cit., p. 34; Musciano, loc. cit., p. 165; Tobak, loc. cit., p. 82 ff; Punka, 'Messer', p. 110 f.
44 Punka, 'Messer', p. 58; Tobak, loc. cit., pp. 161, 405.
45 Tobak, loc. cit., p. 178.
46 Cooper, loc. cit., p. 249.
47 Blake, S., 'Ambush over Hungary', in *Aerial Combat*, No. 14 (1984), pp. 12–20; Punka, *'Messer'*, p. 62.
48 Punka, *'Messer'*, p. 68; according to Mujzer, 'Les Messerschmitt Me 210Ca hongrois', Part 3, p. 26, this attack took place on 27 August; cp Punka, *Hungarian Air Force*, p. 16.
49 Herrmann, H., *Bewegtes Leben* (Munich, 1993), p. 369.
50 Tobak, loc. cit., p. 224.
51 Ibid., p. 374.
52 Beale/D'Amico/Valentini, loc. cit., pp. 133 f, 165.
53 Cp Punka, G., 'Einsätzflüge im Dunkel der Nacht', in *Jet & Prop*, 4/1992, p. 54 ff.
54 Punka, *'Messer'*, p. 72; Sárhidai/Punka/Kozlik, loc. cit., p. 41.
55 Punka, *'Messer'*, p. 117; Punka, *Hungarian Air Force*, p. 49.
56 Gosztony, P., *Endkampf an der Donau 1944/45* (Vienna/Munich, 1978), pp. 304–5.
57 Dierich, W., *Die Verbände der Luftwaffe 1935–1945* (Stuttgart, 1976), p. 58.
58 Cp Punka, *'Messer'*, p. 116; on p. 84, on the other hand, he mentions the operational service of several Hungarian pilots during the Ardennes offensive.
59 Tobak, loc. cit., p. 323.
60 Ibid., p. 319.
61 For a more detailed report on this aircraft model see the articles 'Lavotchkin La-5/7', in *Aircraft*, Issue 78 (1994), pp. 2162–8.
62 Punka, *'Messer'*, p. 103; cp also Tobak, loc. cit., pp. 358–60.

BULGARIA: VOZDUSHNI VOISKI

1 New edition (London, 1995).
2 These three handbooks were slightly reworked by V. Madej and republished in 1982 in Allentown/Pennsylvania under the title *Southeastern Europe Axis Armies Handbook*.
3 These figures include only Allied aircraft that actually crashed in Bulgaria. We can be certain that numerous other aircraft attacked by Bulgarian fighter pilots were lost due to combat damage in other parts of Europe.
4 Walkow, T., 'Die Geschichte der bulgarischen Luftstreitkräfte bis zum 9.9.1944', MSS, Appx. 1.
5 Re the history of the Bulgarian air force in the First World War cp ibid., *Part I: 1892–1919*, pp. 4–8.
6 According to Walkow, ibid. *Part II: 1919–1944*, p. 1, seven aircraft could have been hidden. The article '"Balkan Interlude", The Bulgarian Air Arm in World War II', in *Air*

NOTES

Enthusiast, No. 39 (May–August 1989), p. 60, on the other hand, states that 20 planes evaded the destruction order.

⁷ Walkow, *Die Geschichte der bulgarischen Luftstreitkräfte*, Part II, p. 1.

⁸ Re Winter's activities cp Petrov, B., 'Die bulgarischen Flugzeuge des deutschen Professors Winter', in *Jet & Prop*, 6/1993, pp. 36 f, 42 f; 1/1994, p. 44 ff; 'Balkan Interlude', p. 60; Ivanov, C./Dicev, N./Liège, F., 'Bulgarian Aircraft Industry 1924–1945', in *Skyways*, Issue 33 (January 1995), p. 18 ff.

⁹ Walkow, *Die Geschichte der bulgarischen Luftstreitkräfte*, Part II, p. 2.

¹⁰ 'Balkan Interlude', p. 63.

¹¹ In this case too the data differs in the literature of aviation history as far as the actual number of aircraft is concerned; cp Walkow, *Die Geschichte der bulgarischen Luftstreitkräfte*, Part II, p. 3; 'Balkan Interlude', p. 65; Bateson, R. P., 'Bulgaria at War', Part 1, in *Air Pictorial* (March 1972), p. 91 f.

¹² Re the training of Bulgarian pilots in Germany cp Walkow, *Die Geschichte der bulgarischen Luftstreitkräfte*, Part II, p. 3 ff; Kowatschew, A., 'Als bulgarische Jagdflieger in Werneuchen waren', in *Jägerblatt*, Issue 4/1996, p. 20 ff.

¹³ In this case too the aviation literature does not agree about the number of delivered aircraft; cp Walkow, *Die Geschichte der bulgarischen Luftstreitkräfte*, Part II, p. 6; 'Balkan Interlude', p. 66; Bateson, Part 1, p. 94.

¹⁴ Hoppe, H.-J., *Bulgarien, Hitlers eigenwilliger Verbündeter* (Stuttgart, 1979), p. 124.

¹⁵ Walkow, *Die Geschichte der bulgarischen Luftstreitkräfte*, Part II, p. 8.

¹⁶ Green, W., *Augsburg Eagle* (Harvest Hill, 1987), p. 81, states that Germany delivered 19 Bf 109Es in 1942 in two phases (ten plus nine).

¹⁷ The estimate by Bateson, 'Bulgaria at War', Part 2, in *Air Pictorial* (April 1972), p. 141, that Bulgaria received only four German aircraft during the first nine months of 1942 seems far too low.

¹⁸ ADAP, Series E: 1941–1945, Vol. V, Document No. 18, p. 32.

¹⁹ KTB OKW, Vol. III, 1 January 1943–31 December 1943, 2nd Half-volume III/6 (Herrsching, 1982), p. 1411 ff.

²⁰ Garello, *Regia Aeronautica e Armée de l'Air*, part 3, p. 127.

²¹ 'Balkan Interlude', p. 70; Bateson, Part 2, p. 143; cp also Roba, J.-L./Botquin, G., 'Les avions français dans la Luftwaffe', Part 2, in *Avions*, No. 30 (September 1995), p. 32.

²² 'Balkan Interlude', p. 58; cp also Newby, loc. cit., pp. 92, 95; Cony, C, 'L'Avia B-534, Part 8: B-534 bulgares contre B-24 Liberator', in *Avions*, No. 45 (December 1996), p. 39 f.

²³ 'Balkan Interlude', p. 59; Bateson, Part 2, p. 142; Walkow, *Die Geschichte der bulgarischen Luftstreitkräfte*, Part II, p. 10 f.

²⁴ Cp 'Balkan Interlude', p. 71; Walkow, *Die Geschichte der bulgarischen Luftstreitkräfte*, Part II, p. 12 f.

²⁵ According to the figures in 'Balkan Interlude', p. 71, and as mentioned by Bateson, Part 2, p. 143; Walkow, *Die Geschichte der bulgarischen Luftstreitkräfte*, Part II, p. 13, gives the number of attacking B-24 bombers as 60, escorted by 60 P-38s.

²⁶ ADAP, Series E: 1941–1945, Vol. VII, Document No. 141, p. 271.

²⁷ KTB OKW, Vol. III, 2nd Half-volume, III/6, p. 1349.

²⁸ Two or even three Bf 109G-6s were lost due to accidents during the ferry flights.

²⁹ Walkow, *Die Geschichte der bulgarischen Luftstreitkräfte*, Appendix 1

³⁰ Walkow, *Die Geschichte der bulgarischen Luftstreitkräfte*, Part II, p. 14; Hoppe, loc. cit., pp. 153, 157.

[31]   ADAP, Series E: 1941–1945, Vol. VII, Document No. 181, p. 349.

[32]   Walkow, *Die Geschichte der bulgarischen Luftstreitkräfte*, Vol. II, p. 16; cp also 'Balkan Interlude', p. 72.

[33]   Hénard, J., Die Stätten der Qual und des Unrechts werden freigelegt. Keine Schonzeit mehr für kommunistische Mythen: Bulgarien entdeckt die historische Wahrheit (The places of torment and injustice are revealed. No more 'close season' for Communist myths: Bulgaria discovers the historical truth), in Frankfurter Allgemeine Zeitung, 10 May 1990.

[34]   Walkow, T., 'Kurze Biographie des Obersten Walkow', MSS, p. 1.

CROATIA: ZRAKOPLOVSTVO NDH

[1]   Frka, D., 'Croatian Air Force in WW 2', Part 1, in *Scale Models International* (May 1993), p. 28; Frka, D., 'Les Potez 25 de l'aviation croate 1941–1945', in *Potez 25*, published by the magazine *Avions* (Boulogne sur Mer, 1996), p. 199.

[2]   D'Amico, F./Valentini, G., 'La Legione croata in guerra', in *JP* 4 (April 1993), p. 58; the operations of Croat airmen with KG 3 were evaluated from the propaganda point of view by the war reporter Gerhard Rauchwetter in *'U' über der Ostfront* (Zagreb, 1943).

[3]   The Croat squadron was initially listed as 10./KG 3, later probably as 15. (kroat.)/KG 3. This arrangement was finally adapted for the Croats serving with KG 53 and JG 52, cp. D'Amico/Valentini, 'La Legione croata in guerra', p. 58; Rosch, B. C., *Luftwaffe Codes, Markings & Units* (Atglen, 1995), p. 236.

[4]   *Die Wehrmachtberichte 1939–1945, Vol. 2: January 1942 to December 1943* (Munich, 1985), p. 4; cp Rauchwetter, p. 69.

[5]   Cp Kiehl, H., *Kampfgeschwader 'Legion Condor' 53*, 2nd ed. (Stuttgart, 1996), pp. 295 f, 348.

[6]   Up to now the best, if rather rambling, story of the Croat fighter pilots serving with JG 52 is by Savic, D./Micerevski, M., 'Ustaska Lovačka Legija na istonočnom Frontu', in *Aerosvet* (October–November 1991), p. 40 f.

[7]   Fast, N., *Das Jagdgeschwader 52*, Vol. II (Bergisch Gladbach, 1988), p. 305.

[8]   *Die Wehrmachtberichte 1939–1945*, Vol. 2, p. 176.

[9]   Fast, N., *Das Jagdgeschwader 52*, Vol. III, 2nd ed. (Bergisch Gladbach, 1992), p. 112.

[10]   Cp the monthly aerial victory reports of JG 52 for March, April and May 1943, copies in author's possession.

[11]   Green, loc. cit., p. 118.

[12]   Fast, N., *Das Jagdeschwader 52*, Vol. I, 3rd ed. (Bergisch Gladbach, 1990), p. 237; Schreier, loc. cit., p. 191; the figure of 300-plus confirmed victories is mentioned by Saviô/Micevski, loc. cit., p. 41, and Pebal, H. von, Hravtska Krila: *Die kroatischen Flieger im 2. Weltkrieg* (Graz, no date of publication), pp. 66 ff, 72.

[13]   Frka, 'Croatian Air Force in WW II', Part 1, p. 29.

[14]   Frka, 'Les Potez 25', pp. 198–201.

[15]   D'Amico/Valentini, 'La Legiona croata in guerra', p. 61; cp also Liège, F., Croatian Air Force 1941–1945, Part 1, in SAFO, Vol. 17, No. 4 (68), December 1993, p. 115.

[16]   Frka, 'Croatian Air Force in WW II', Part 2, in *Scale Models International* (June 1993), p. 32; *Insignia* (Winter 1995), p. 15.

[17]   Cp Lucchini, C., Croati sul G.50, in *JP* 4 (February 1994), pp. 80–6; Vergnano, P., *Fiat G.50* (Turin, 1997), p. 33.

[18]   'Dorniers fliegender Bleistift', in *Aircraft*, Issue 139 (1995), p. 3,884.

[19]   Frka, 'Croatian Air Force in WW II', Part 2, p. 28.

NOTES

20 Piekalkiewicz, J., *Krieg auf dem Balkan 1940–1945* (Munich, 1984), p. 207.
21 Omrčanin, J., *The pro-allied putsch in Croatia in 1944 and the massacre of the Croatians by Tito communists in 1945* (Philadelphia, 1975), p. 22.
22 ADAP, Series E: 1941–1945, Vol. VII, Document No. 155, pp. 302, 304.
23 Rosch, loc. cit., p. 279 f.
24 Dierich, loc. cit., p. 269.
25 Ibid., p. 175.
26 Green, loc. cit., p. 118; there is some evidence that the Croats listed these two squadrons as 11. and 12. Jato of the 4. Skupina 'Legionarska'; see Frka, 'Croatian Air Force in WW II', Part 2, p. 30; cp also D'Amico/Valentini, 'La Legiona croata in guerra', p. 60.
27 D'Amico/Valentini, 'La Legiona croata in guerra', p. 61; Liège, 'Croatian Air Force 1941–1945', Part 2, p. 116.
28 Beale/D'Amico/Valentini, loc. cit., pp. 67 f, 72, 74, 86 f, 103, 193, 205.
29 Cp Völkl, E., 'Abrechnungsfuror in Kroatien', in Henke, K.-D./Woller, H. (eds.), *Politische Säuberung in Europa* (Munich, 1991), pp. 358–94.
30 Cp 'Das Schicksal unserer kroatischen kamaraden', in *Jägerblatt*, No. 1/1963, p. 4 f.

SLOVAKIA: SLOVENSKÉ VZDUŠNE ZBRANĚ

1 Rajlich, J./Sehnal, J., *Slovak Airmen 1939–1945* (Kutná Hora, 1991), p. 2; Rajlich, J./Sehnal, J., '"Tatra Eagles", The Slovak Air Force in combat', in *Air Enthusiast*, No. 56 (1994), p. 63.
2 Vraný, J., *Avia B-534* (Prague, 1994), p. 44 f.
3 Re Luftwaffe actions on 23/24 March 1939 Cp Rajlich/Sehnal, *Slovak Airmen*, p. 3 f; Rajlich/Sehnal, 'Tatra Eagles', p. 64 f; Rajninec, J./Sanders, J. V., 'Conflict over the Carpathians', in *Air Enthusiast* (September 1971), pp. 180–3; Mujzer, P., 'Hungarian Royal Air Force 1938/39', Part 2, in SAFO, Vol. 18, No. 3 (71), September 1974, pp. 87–91.
4 Jelinek, Y., *The Parish Republic: Hlinka's Slovak People's Party 1939–1945* (New York/London, 1976), p. 67.
5 Rajlich/Sehnal, *Slovak Airmen*, pp. 7, 11; Thomas, N., *Foreign Volunteers of the Allied Forces 1939–45* (London, 1991), p. 7.
6 Rajlich/Sehnal, *Slovak Airmen*, p. 11
7 Förster, J., 'Die Gewinnung von Verbündeten in Südosteuropa', in *Das Deutsche Reich und der Zweite Weltkrieg*, published by Militärgeschichtlichen Forschungsamt, Vol. 4 (Stuttgart, 1983), p. 362.
8 Cp the aircraft models listed in *Aircraft*, Issue 175 (1996), p. 4900.
9 Rajlich/Sehnal, *Slovak Airmen*, p. 21; Rajlich/Sehnal, 'Tatra Eagles', p. 66; Vrany, *Avia B-534*, p. 48.
10 Rajlich/Sehnal, *Slovak Airmen*, p. 55; Rajlich/Sehnal, 'Tatra Eagles', p. 64.
11 KTB OKW, Vol. II: 1 January 1942–31 December 1942, 1st Half-volume II/3 (Herrsching, 1982), p. 32.
12 These details have been taken from the monthly reports prepared by JG 52, covering March, April and May 1943; copies in author's possession. Somewhat different figures for the number of aerial victories are given by Krajc, M., 'Messerschmitt Bf 109 in the Slovak Air Arms', in *Luftwaffe Verband* (July 1997), p. 23 f.
13 The figure for the number of aerial victories varies between 204 and 216; cp Rajlich/Sehnal, *Slovak Airmen*, p. 27; Rajlich/Sehnal, 'Tatra Eagles', p. 67; Schreier, loc. cit., p. 191; Fast, *Das Jagdgeschwader 52*, Vol. I, p. 237; Vol. II, p. 58; Krajc, loc. cit., p. 23 f.

[14] Rajlich/Sehnal, *Slovak Airmen*, pp. 28, 61; Rajlich/Sehnal, 'Tatra Eagles', p. 68; another version is furnished by Krajc, loc. cit., p. 25.

[15] ADAP Series E: 1941–1945, Vol. VIII, Document No. 220, p. 424.

II SPECIAL CASES

FINLAND: SUOMEN ILMAVOIMAT

[1] Shores, C. F., *Finnish Air Force 1918–1968* (London, 1968), unpaginated; other figures are found in Condon, R. W., *Winterkrieg Russland–Finnland* (Munich, 1980), p. 95 (96 aircraft), and in Sandström, A., *Krieg unter der Mitternachtssonne* (Graz/Stuttgart, 1996), p. 341 (200 aircraft).

[2] Written statement by Mr Hannu Valtonen, Director of the Keski-Suomen Ilmailumuseo, dated 14 May 1996.

[3] Luukkanen, *Fighter over Finland* (London, 1963), p. 31 f.

[4] Juutilainen, I., *Double Fighter Knight* (Tampere, 1996), pp. 31, 40.

[5] Juutilainen, loc. cit., pp. 14 f, 35; cp also Luukkanen, loc. cit., p. 46 ff.

[6] Keskinen, K./Stenman, K./Niska, K., *Bristol Blenheim* (Forssa, 1984), p. 95.

[7] Cp Ericson, L., *Svenska Frivilliga* (Stockholm, 1996), p. 100 ff; *Svenska frivilliga I Finland 1939–44* (Stockholm, undated), pp. 176–87; Luukkanen, loc. cit., p. 212; Keskinen, K./Stenman, K./Niska, K., *Englantilaiset Hävittäjät* (Forssa, 1985), p. 79; Shores, *Finnish Air Force* (unpaginated); Norling, S. E., *Sangre en la nieve* (Granada, 1996), pp. 63–6; Stenman, K., 'Gloster Trilogy', in *Air Enthusiast*, No. 66 (November–December 1996), pp. 29–30.

[8] Norling, loc. cit., pp. 176–8; Ritaranta, E., 'Vapaaehtoisia Vaivaksi Asti', in *Suomen Ilmailuhistoriallinen Lehti*, 1/1996, pp. 15 f, 18 f.

[9] Luukkanen, loc. cit., p. 63.

[10] Cp Luukkanen, loc. cit., p. 66; Keskinen, K./Stenman, K./Niska, K., *Finnish Fighter Aces*, 2nd ed. (Forssa, 1994), p. 151 f; Stenman, 'Gloster Trilogy', p. 28.

[11] Luukkanen, loc. cit., p. 192; Shores, *Finnish Air Force* (unpaginated).

[12] Sandström, loc. cit., p. 136.

[13] Sandström, loc. cit., p. 341; Shores, *Finnish Air Force* (unpaginated).

[14] Juutilainen, loc. cit., p. 50.

[15] Botquin, G., 'L'epopée du Morane Saulnier 406', Part 9, in *Le Fana de l'Aviation*, No. 108 (November 1978), p. 23; Luukkanen, loc. cit., pp. 214–7.

[16] Shores, *Finnish Air Force* (unpaginated); an overview of the different estimates of the numerical strength of the Finnish air force in mid-1941 is provided by Förster, G. R., 'Die Einbeziehung Skandinaviens in die Planung 'Barbarossa'', in *Das Deutsche Reich und der Zweite Weltkrieg*, Vol. 4, p. 396.

[17] Written statement by Mr Hannu Valtonen, Director of the Keski-Suomen Ilmailumuseo, dated 1 March 1996.

[18] Juutilainen, loc. cit., pp. 56–9, 68–71.

[19] Written statement by Mr 'Joppe' Karhunen, dated 22 May 1996, addressed to the author.

[20] Erfurth, W., *Der finnische Krieg 1941–1944* (Munich, 1978), p. 88.

[21] Juutilainen, loc. cit., p. 121; cp also Keskinen/Stenman/Niska, *Finnish Fighter Aces*, p. 152.

[22] Cp Botquin, loc. cit., p. 26 f.

[23] Cp Keskinen, K./Stenman, K./Niska, K., *Suomalaiset Hävittäjät* (Kangasala, 1990).

[24] Stenman, K., 'Finland's Frontline. The Bf 109 in Finnish service', in *Air Enthusiast*, No. 50 (May–July 1993), p. 52.

[25] Juutilainen, loc. cit., p. 132.

[26] Luukkanen, loc. cit., p. 150.

[27] Luukkanen, loc. cit., p. 160.

[28] Re the story of the Finnish Ju 88 cp Stenman, K., 'Short, but gallant. The career of the Finnish Junkers Ju 88s', in *Air Enthusiast*, No. 60 (November–December 1995), pp. 35–9.

[29] Sandström, loc. cit., p. 286 ff.

[30] Re the story of SB-2 operations with LeLv 6 cp Stenman, K., 'The Anti-Soviet Tupolevs', in *Air Enthusiast*, No. 27, pp. 9–20; Keskinen, K./Stenman, K./Niska, K., *Venäläiset Pommittajat* (Forssa, 1982), p. 94 f.

[31] Stenman, 'Short, but gallant', p. 37; Keskinen/Stenman/Niska, *Bristol Blenheim*, p. 94 f.

[32] Juutilainen, loc. cit., p. 164 f.

[33] ADAP, Series E: 1941–1945, Vol. VII, Document No. 315, p. 601 f.

[34] ADAP, Series E: 1941–1945, Vol. VII, Document No. 351, p. 657 f; Erfurth, loc. cit., p. 168 ff; Sandström, loc. cit., p. 294.

[35] Stenman, 'Finland's Frontline', p. 55.

[36] Juutilainen, loc. cit., p. 186.

[37] Stenman, 'Finland's Frontline', p. 52; Musciano, loc. cit., p. 63; 159 delivered Bf 109Gs are quoted by Keskinen, K./Stenman, K./Niska, K., *Messerschmitt Bf109G* (Forssa, 1991), p. 138; cp also Green, loc. cit., p. 116.

[38] Luukkanen, loc. cit., p. 181.

[39] Juutilainen, loc. cit., p. 198.

[40] Cp Stenman, K., 'Battle Unit Kuhlmey', in *Air Enthusiast*, No. 34 (September–December 1987), pp. 1–6.

[41] With thanks to the 'Gefechtsverband Kuhlmey', in *Jägerblatt*, No. 1/1995, p. 15.

[42] Stenman, 'Finland's Frontline', p. 58.

[43] Statement by Mr Hannu Valtonen, Director of the Keski-Suomen Ilmailumuseo, dated 14 May 1996.

[44] Stenman, 'Finland's Frontline', p. 59; Juutilainen, loc. cit., pp. 9, 13.

[45] Juutilainen, loc. cit., p. 13; Keskinen, K./Stenman, K./Niska, K., *Brewster Model 239*, 4th ed. (Forssa, 1995), p. 94 f.

VICHY-FRANCE: L'ARMÉE DE L'AIR DE L'ARMISTICE

[1] Garello, G., *Regia Aeronautica e Armée de l'Air*, Part 2, p. 78.

[2] Ehrengardt, C. J./Shores, C. F., *L'Aviation de Vichy au combat, Vol. 1: Les campagnes oubliées, 3 juillet 1940–27 novembre 1942* (Paris, 1985), p. 12.

[3] Auphan, P., *Histoire élémentaire de Vichy* (Paris, 1971), pp. 43, 48; Jäckel, E., *Frankreich in Hitlers Europa* (Stuttgart, 1966), p. 41.

[4] Auphan, loc. cit., p. 246.

[5] Ehrengardt/Shores, loc. cit., Vol. 1, p. 49; Airdoc (Publ.), *L'Aviation Militaire Française d'Armistice 1940–1942* (Salon-de-Provence, 1993), p. 4.

[6] Cp Ehrengardt/Shores, loc. cit., Vol. 1, p. 51 f; Airdoc, loc. cit., p. 4; Finlayson, loc. cit., p. 60 f.

[7] Garello, loc. cit., Part 2, pp. 82, 85.

[8] Garello, loc. cit., Part 2, p. 84.

[9] Cp 'Dewoitine D.520', in *Aircraft*, Issue 114 (1995), pp. 3182–8.

¹⁰ Garello, loc. cit., Part 2, p. 80.
¹¹ Cp Ehrengardt/Shores, loc. cit., Vol. 1, pp. 54–61.
¹² Cp Ott, G., 1941: 'Als die Luftwaffe für den Irak flog', in *Jet & Prop*, 3/1991, pp. 23–6, 34; 4/1991, p. 50 ff.
¹³ In his description of the fighting in Syria the author has followed the excellent work by Ehrengardt, C. J./Shores, C. F., *L'Aviation de Vichy au combat, Vol. 2: La campagne de Syrie, 8 juin–14 juillet 1941* (Paris, 1987), as well as the book by Shores, C., *Dust Clouds in the Middle East*, loc. cit., pp. 198–270.
¹⁴ Baudru, R., 'Quand l'Armée de l'Air partit en Syrie, combattre la RAF', in *Le Fana de l'Aviation* (October 1983), pp. 16–25.
¹⁵ Borgogni, M., *Mussolini e la Francia di Vichy* (Siena, 1991), p. 237.
¹⁶ Cp Ehrengardt/Shores, loc. cit., Vol. 2, pp. 66, 164; Benoist-Méchin, J., *De la défaite au désastre, Vol. 1: Les occasions manquées juillet 1940–avril 1942* (Paris, 1984), pp. 184, 193.
¹⁷ Ehrengardt/Shores, loc. cit., Vol. 2, pp. 128, 136; Shores, *Dust Clouds*, p. 269; Airdoc, loc. cit., p. 6, puts the losses at 179 planes; likewise Garello, loc. cit., Part 2, p. 90.
¹⁸ Lottman, H., *L'épuration 1943–1953* (Paris, 1986), p. 302 f.
¹⁹ Garello, loc. cit., Part 2, p. 90 f.
²⁰ Re the fighting in Madagascar Cp Ehrengardt/Shores, loc. cit., Vol. 1, pp. 62–78; Shores, *Dust Clouds*, pp. 276–96.
²¹ Airdoc, loc. cit., p. 57; a detailed description of events in Indochina is in Ehrengardt/Shores, loc. cit., Vol. 1, pp. 80–95.
²² In this regard, it is rather startling to read the statement by R. Strumpf in 'Der Krieg im Mittelmeerraum 1942/43: die Operationen in Nordafrika und im Mittleren Mittelmeer', in *Das Deutsche Reich und der Zweite Weltkrieg*, published by Militärgeschichtlichen Forschungsamt, Vol. 6 (Stuttgart, 1990), p. 717: 'There was no sign of the French air force …'.
²³ Re the Allied landings in North Africa cp Ehrengardt/Shores, loc. cit., Vol. 1, pp. 112–49.
²⁴ Garello, loc. cit., Part 3, p. 126 ff; on the other hand, Ehrengardt/Shores, loc. cit., Vol. 1, p. 157 state that 1,271 French military aircraft fell into Allied hands.
²⁵ Garello, loc. cit., Part 3, p. 127; 'Dewoitine D.520', loc. cit., pp. 3184, 3188.
²⁶ Chadeau, E., *L'industrie aéronautique en France 1900–1950* (Paris, 1987), p. 357 ff; cp also Klemm, P. F., 'La production aéronautique française de 1940 à 1942', in *Revue d'histoire de la deuxième guerre mondiale*, No. 107 (July 1977), pp. 53–74; Facon, P., 'Aperçus sur la collaboration aéronautique Franco-Allemande (1940–1943)', in *Revue d'histoire de la deuxième guerre mondiale*, No. 108 (October 1977), pp. 85–102.
²⁷ Klemm, loc. cit., p. 72.

III FOREIGN FLYING PERSONNEL IN THE GERMAN LUFTWAFFE
¹ Re the overall ambiguity and problems cp Neulen, H. W., *An deutsche Seite*, 2nd ed. (Munich, 1992).
² KTB OKW, Vol. IV, January 1944–22 May 1945, 2nd Half-volume IV/8 (Herrsching, 1982), p. 1,558.
³ Cp Arráez Cerdá, J., 'Los "Viriatos del Aire"', in *Defensa*, No. 222 (October 1996), pp. 55–60; Alves, R., 'Quem foram os "Viriatos so Ar"', in *Historia*, No. 35 (September 1981), pp. 2–14; Herrera Alonso, E., 'Viriatos do Ar, Aviadores portugueses en la guerra de España',

357

NOTES

Aeroplano, No. 12/1994, pp. 126–34; Krug, A., 'Aviadores portugueses na guerra de Espanha (1938–39)', in *Mais Alto* (May 1964).
4   Cp Dos Santos, S. L., 'Egon-Albrecht – a Brazilian Ace in the Luftwaffe', in *Luftwaffe Verband*, No. 10, p. 19 f.
5   Gellermann, G. W., *Moskau ruft Heeresgruppe Mitte ...* (Koblenz, 1988), pp. 209, 311.
6   Boog, H., *Die deutsche Luftwaffenführung 1939–1945* (Stuttgart, 1981), p. 289.
7   Cooper, loc. cit., p. 362.

Norwegians

1   ADAP, Series D: 1937–1941, Vol. IX.2, Document No. 223, p. 337 ff.
2   ADAP, Series E: 1941–1945, Vol. I, Document No. 248, p. 470.
3   Ueberschär, G. R., 'Kriegführung und Politik in Nordeuropa', in *Das Deutsche Reich und der Zweite Weltkrieg*, Vol. 4, p. 880 f.
4   Cp Jansen, T. B., Dahl, F. H., *Parti og plakat NS 1933–1945* (Oslo, 1988).
5   Blindheim, S., *Nordmenn under Hitlers fane*, 2nd ed. (Norek Boklag, 1978), p. 107.
6   Copy in author's possession.
7   Thomas, *Foreign Volunteers of the Allied Forces*, p. 13 f; cp also *Jane's Fighting Aircraft of World War II*, new ed. (London, 1995), p. 50.
8   Leysen, A., *Hinter dem Spiegel. Eine Jugend in Flandern 1939–1945* (Munich, 1996), pp. 71, 109.
9   Hougen, H., 'Errinerungen', MSS p. 5 f.
10   Ibid., p. 7.
11   Ibid., p. 13.
12   Ibid., p. 13.
13   Ibid., pp. 13–14.
14   Ibid., p. 14.
15   Ibid., p. 16.
16   Ibid., p. 36.
17   Ibid., p. 42.
18   Dierich, loc. cit., p. 120; Stahl, P. W., *'Geheimgeschwader' KG 200*, 3rd ed. (Stuttgart, 1980), p. 177 ff.
19   Hougen, loc. cit., p. 48.
20   Letter from Harald Hougen to the author dated 10 February 1996.
21   The following description is based on the written communications from Alf Lie to the author, dated 16 and 29 November 1995.
22   Larsen, S. U., 'Die Ausschaltung der Quislinge in Norwegen', in Henke/Woller, loc. cit., p. 259 f.

Danes

1   The author would like to thank Jörn Junker in Risskov/Denmark and Hans Ring in Übersee for supplying important details about Danes in the Luftwaffe.
2   Norling, loc. cit., p. 176; Ritaranta, loc. cit., pp. 16, 19
3   Cp Aders, G./Held, W., *Jagdgeschwader 51 'Mölders'*, 2nd ed. (Stuttgart, 1993), p. 211.
4   Copy in the author's possession.
5   Ring/Girbig, Jagdgeschwader 27, p. 331.
6   Littlejohn, D., *Foreign Legions of the Third Reich, Vol. 1: Norway, Denmark, France* (San Jose/California, 1979), p. 112.

358

Frenchmen

1 Re Costantini cp Ory, P., *Les collaborateurs 1940–1945* (Paris, 1976), p. 96 ff.

2 Cp Lambert, P. P./Le Marec, G., *Les Français sous le casque allemand* (Paris, 1994), p. 70 f; Lambert, P. P./Le Marec, G., *Partis et Mouvements de la Collaboration* (Paris, 1993), p. 120.

3 ADAP Series D: 1937–1941, Vol. XIII.1, Document No. 78, p. 82, footnote.

4 KTB OKW, Vol. II: I January 1942–31 December 1942, 2nd Half-volume II/4 (Herrsching, 1982), pp. 1032 f, 1048.

5 Rosch, loc. cit., p. 365.

6 *Aircraft*, Issue 130 (1995), p. 3636; Garello, *Regia Aeronautica et Armée de l'Air*, Part 3, p. 138.

7 Roba, J.-L./Botquin, G., 'Les avions français dans la Luftwaffe', Part 3, in *Avions*, No. 31 (October 1995), p. 38.

8 Flugzeugbestands- und Flugbetriebsstatistic. Betriebsmonatsmeldung für März 1944. Generalquartiermeister, Chef des Nachschubwesens d.Lw.vom 29 Juni 1944; copy in the author's possession.

9 Copy in the author's possession.

10 Copy in the author's possession.

11 Lufthansa Dokumentationsdienst, No. 90–4: 'Der Flugzeugpark der Deutschen Lufthansa AG 1926–1945' (Cologne, no date), pp. 15, 18.

12 Garello, *Regia Aeronautica e Armée de l'Air*, Part 3, p. 147 f.

13 Letter from Werner Bittner, Deutsche Lufthansa AG Firmenarchiv, to the author dated 4 September 1995.

14 Note from Flugbetriebssleitung/Landflug to Director Luz dated 11 July 1944, Deutsche Lufthansa AG Firmenarchiv.

15 For most of the information on René Dubois the author would like to thank his Belgian colleagues Jean-Louis Roba and Eric Mombeek, as well as Dr Fritz Marktscheffel.

16 In the article 'Vom Denkmal zum Museumsstück … ('From monument to museum piece), in *Jet & Prop*, 5/1992, pp. 48–51, R. Baudru suggests that Roger Fargeau d'Epieds, a member of the French militia at Limoges, could possibly have flown with the Bongard Wing against the French partisans in June 1944. This is more than doubtful given Fargeau d'Epieds' age – he was born in 1909. In any case, the Bundesarchiv/Zentralnachweissstelle has no record confirming any flying activity by Fargeau d'Epieds.

17 Interrogation Report on an Me 109 pilot who deserted and landed at Santa Maria airfield on 25 July 1944 at 16.45 hours (copy); cp also Beale/D'Amico/Valentini, loc. cit., pp. 59, 72; Kitchens, J. H./Beamen, J. R., 'Wie das Rätsel um die Bf 109G-6 "weisse 2" geklärt wurde', in *Jet & Prop*, 1/1997, pp. 40–43.

18 Cp Ernst, R., *Rechenschaftbericht eines Elsässers* (Berlin, 1954); further details re Robert Ernst are in the book by Arzalier, F., *Les perdants* (Paris, 1990).

19 Ernst, loc. cit., p. 363.

20 Dierich, W., *Kampfgeschwader 55 'Greif'*, 2nd ed. (Stuttgart, 1994), p. 311.

21 Letter from Charles F. Kern to the author dated 26 September 1996.

22 Exactly 50 years after this aerial victory Charles F. Kern met two members of the bomber's crew in Belgium.

23 Letter from Charles F. Kern to the author dated 5 October 1996.

NOTES

Belgians

1   Neulen, *An deutscher Seite*, pp. 73, 85.
2   Thomas, *Foreign Volunteers of the Allied Forces*, p. 17; cp also *Jane's Fighting Aircraft of World War II*, p. 17.
3   Cp De Bruyne, E., *Dans l'étau de Degrelle* (Jalhay, 1994), p. 55 f.
4   Cp ibid., p. 190, Note 6.
5   The name has also been wrongly published as Adolphe Henier. The Airmen Card Index card at the Bundesarchiv/Zentralnachweisstelle is clearly marked 'Adolphe Renier'.
6   Cp Vincx, J., *Vlaanderen in Uniform 1940–1945*, Vol. 4 (Antwerpen, 1982), p. 266.
7   For details of Guido Rombaut's fate the author would like to thank his Belgian colleague Jean-Louis Roba.
8   Cp Leysen, *Hinter dem Spiegel*, p. 62.
9   Statement from the Bundesarchiv/Zentralnachweisstelle Az. Z-I 40-598/95 of 1 December 1995.
10   Cp Mombeek, E., *Reichsverteidigung, Die Geschichte des Jagdgeschwaders 1 'Oesau'* (Brussels, 1993), pp. 185, 187, 202.
11   Dannemark, H., '50 Jahre danach', unpublished MSS (1993), p. 7 f.
12   Written statements by Joseph Justin to the author dated 3 and 13 October 1997.

Spaniards

1   Kleinfeld, G. R./Tambs, L. A., *Hitler's Spanish Legion. The Blue Division in Russia* (London/Amsterdam, 1979), p. 4.
2   Cp Neulen, *An deutscher Seite*, pp. 116–125.
3   Hermann, F., 'Uniformbesonderheiten der spanischen "Blauen Division" und "Blauen Staffel"', in *Zeitschrift für Heereskunde*, No. 260/261 (1975), pp. 133–42; cp also Carrera, J. M., *The Blue Division and Squadron. Its Organisation and Uniforms* (Madrid, 1991), p. 45 ff.
4   Larrazábal, J. S., 'Actuación en Rusia de las Escuadrillas Expedicionarias Españolas', in *Aeroplano*, No. 2 (October 1984), p. 59; Coppel, J. F., 'Los Caidos de la Escuadrilla Azul', in *Defensa*, No. 127 (November 1988), p. 67; Thiele, H./Arráez Cerdá, J., 'Die "Blauen Staffeln" in Russland', in *Flugzeug*, 2/1995, p. 52 f.
5   Fast, *Das Jagdgeschwader 52*, Vol. I, p. 152.
6   Aders/Held, *Jagdgeschwader 51 'Mölders'*, p. 109; according to Green, *Augsburg Eagle*, pp. 81, 89, 15. (span.)/JG 52 was switched from the Bf 109E-7 to Bf 109F-4 only in October 1942.
7   Urwich-Ferry, J., *Ohne Pass durch die U.d.S.S.R.*, Vol. 1 (Munich, 1982), p. 265.
8   Cp Coppel, J. F., 'Españoles en Rusia', in *Avion*, No. 10/1991, pp. 54–7.
9   Coppel, 'Españoles en Rusia', p. 56; however, it is generally assumed that the 4th Squadron was trained at Colomiers, cp Thiele/Arráez Cerdá, loc. cit., Issue 3/1995, p. 21; Fuentes Verdu, A., 'Alas españoles en el cielo ruso', in *Defensa*, Extra No. 16 (June 1991), p. 39.
10   Copy of the speech in the author's possession.
11   Perez San Emeterio, C., 'La última lección de Indalecio Rego', in *Aeroplano*, No. 11/1993, pp. 9–18.
12   Larrazábal, loc. cit., p. 91.
13   Letter from Heinrich Heuser to the author dated 20 June 1995.
14   Larrazábal, loc. cit., p. 91; according to Thiele/Arráez Cerdá, loc. cit., Issue 3/1995, p.

24, the Spaniards achieved a total of 137 aerial victories; 170 aerial victories are mentioned by Coppel, 'Los caidos de la Escuadrilla Azul', p. 78.
[15]   Vadillo, F., Balada final de la Division Azul (Granada, 1996), p. 196.

Estonians
[1]   Jurs, A., *Estonian Freedom Fighters in World War II* (Paris/Ontario, 1990), p. 286.
[2]   Written statement by Remi Milk to the author dated 10 March 1997.
[3]   Arro, H., 'Estnische Flieger in der Luftwaffe', MSS (1997), p. 2.
[4]   Cp Geust, C. F., *Under the Red Star* (Shrewsbury, 1993), p. 143.
[5]   Cp Jurs, loc. cit., p. 287; Arro, 'Estnische Flieger', p. 3; Geust, loc. cit., p. 144; Gerdessen, F., 'Estonian Air Power, 1918–1945', in *Air Enthusiast*, No. 18 (April–July 1982), p. 74.
[6]   At least according to Gerdessen, loc. cit., p. 75; according to other information the Ar 95s were actually delivered to Chile, cp *Aircraft*, Issue 14 (1993), p. 390; Nowarra, H. J., *Die deutsche Luftrüstung 1933–1945*, Vol. 1 (Koblenz, 1993), p. 51. In any case, it is indisputable that the Estonian squadrons had planes of this type.
[7]   Arro, 'Estnische Flieger', p. 4; Arro, H., *Eesti Lendurid Lahingute Tules*, 2nd ed. (Tallinn, 1996), pp. 22–3; Vanags-Baginskis, A., 'Latvian and Estonian Units of the Luftwaffe', MSS, p. 18.
[8]   Written statement by Valdo Raag to the author dated 4 November 1996.
[9]   In fact these were Waffen-SS units.
[10]   Written statement by Dr Benno Abram to the author date 9 October 1996.
[11]   Copy in the author's possession.
[12]   Rowehr, J./Hümmelchen, G., *Chronik des Seekrieges 1939–45* (Herrsching, no date of publication), p. 356.
[13]   Jurs, loc. cit., p. 290.
[14]   Arro, 'Estnische Flieger', p. 6.
[15]   Written statement by Arvo Putmaker to the author dated 20 November 1996.
[16]   Copy of the document in the author's possession.
[17]   Copy of the document in the author's possession.
[18]   Copy of the document in the author's possession.
[19]   Arro, *Eesti Lendurid*, pp. 95, 148 f.
[20]   Arro, 'Estnische Flieger', p. 7.
[21]   Details about the last airfields used by NSGr.11 vary. The author has followed the description by Arro, 'Estnische Flieger', p. 91 f. Other assertions are made by Gerdessen, loc. cit., p. 76.
[22]   Copy of the document in the author's possession.
[23]   Cp Vanags-Baginskis, loc. cit., p. 21; Gerdessen, loc. cit., p. 76; Arro, *Eesti Lendurid*, p. 123.
[24]   From a letter by Kaljo Alaküla to the Versogungsamt Ravensburg dated 18 September 1991.

Latvians
[1]   Letter from Edvins Brūvelis dated 17 August 1999.
[2]   Ibid.
[3]   Letter from Alex Vanags-Baginskis dated 10 August 1999.
[4]   Ibid.
[5]   Interview with Indulis Ozols on 29 June 1996.

6   Vanags-Baginskis, loc. cit., p. 3; Silgailis, A., *Latvian Legion* (San Jose/California, 1986), p. 207.
7   Letter from Alex Vanags-Baginskis dated 10 August 1999.
8   Latvian Luftwaffe Veterans Association, Riga.
9   Letter from Edvins Brūvelis dated 17 August 1999.
10   Vanags-Baginskis, loc. cit., p. 6.
11   According to Geust, loc. cit., p. 148, it was supposed to have been a fighter squadron, but that seems most unlikely. A Latvian fighter squadron was formed independently of NSGr.12.
12   Letter from Alex Vanags-Baginskis dated 10 August 1999.
13   Interview with Indulis Ozols dated 29 June 1999.
14   Silgailis, loc. cit., p. 208; Stüber, H., *Die lettischen Divisionen im VI SS-Armeekorps* (Osnabrück, 1981), p. 274.
15   Copy in the author's possession.
16   Vanags-Baginskis, loc. cit., pp. 5, 7 f.
17   Letter from Artur Gärtner to the author dated 16 August 1997.
18   Mombeek, *Reichsverteidigung*, pp. 264, 285 ff.
19   Ibid., pp. 293, 303, 317; Girbig, W., *Start in Morgengrauen* (Stuttgart, 1989), p. 159; Franks, N., *Battle of the Airfields* (London, 1994), p. 89 f, 92; Geust, loc. cit., p. 149.
20   Interview with Indulis Ozols, of 29 1996; cp also Ozols, Indulis, 'Seržanta Klinta pēdējais lidojums', in *Daugavas Vanagi* (Jan–Feb 1992), pp. 18–25.
21   Letter from Arnolds Mencis to the author dated 20 July 1997.
22   Vanags-Baginskis, loc. cit., p. 8.
23   Letter from Edvins Brūvelis dated 17 August 1999.
24   Silgailis, loc. cit., p. 213.
25   Ibid., p. 214; Vanags-Baginskis, loc. cit., p. 10.
26   Vanags-Baginskis, loc. cit., p. 14.
27   Latvian Luftwaffe Veterans Association, Riga.
28   Ibid.
29   Letter from Arnolds Mencis to the author dated 20 July 1997.

Russians
1   KTB OKW, Vol. I: 1 August 1940–31 December 1941, Half-volume 1/2 (Herrsching, 1982), p. 1,108.
2   Ketley, B./Rolfe, M., *Luftwaffe Fledglings 1935–1945* (Aldershot, 1996), pp. 11, 83; cp also Botquin, G./Roba, J.-L., 'Les avions soviétiques dans la Luftwaffe', in *Avions*, No. 40 (July 1996), pp. 35–8.
3   Hoffman, J., *Die Geschichte der Wlassow-Armee* (Freiburg, 1984), p. 97 f.
4   Dierich, *Die Verbände der Luftwaffe*, p. 267.
5   Cp Hoffman, loc. cit., p. 98 ff.
6   'Wir haben bewusst mit dem Sowjetsystem gebrochen', in *Die Aktion* (April/May 1944), p. 170 f.
7   'Wir haben bewusst mit dem Sowjetsystem gebrochen', loc. cit., p. 173.
8   Fröhlich, S., *General Wlassow. Russen und Deutsche zwischen Hitler und Stalin* (Cologne, 1987), pp. 245, 248.
9   ROA = Russkaya Osvoboditelnaya Armiya; this was the collective designation of all soldiers of various Russian peoples fighting on the German side.

[10] Hoffman, loc. cit., p. 105.
[11] Ibid., p. 107 f.
[12] Warlimont, W., *Im Hauptquartier der deutschen Wehrmacht 39–45*, 3rd 3d. (Munich, 1978), p. 535.
[13] Cp the organization of the flying formations of the German Luftwaffe and the ROA in Bohemia-Moravia on 24 April 1945, in *Plastic Kits Revue* (Czech), No. 11/1992, p. 7.

Bibliography

A: Unpublished Material

Arro, Hendrik, 'Estnische Flieger in der Luftwaffe', 15pp MSS (1997)

Bundesarchiv/Zentralnachweisstelle: Copies of Airmen Card Index cards of foreign members of the Luftwaffe

Dannemark, Henri, '50 Jahre danach', 15pp MSS (1993)

Flugzeugbestands- und Flugbetriebsstatistik. Betriebsmonatsmeldungen für März 1944, Generalquartiermeister, Chef des Nachschubwesens d.Lw.Az.-52 f Nr. 23050/44 g.Kdos. (2/III B), Berlin, 29 June 1944 (copy)

Hougen, Harald, 'Erinnerungen', 48pp MSS in Norwegian, translated by Ian E. Hougen

Interrogation Report on an Me 109 pilot who deserted and landed at Santa Maria airfield on 25 July 1944 at 16.45 hours (René Darbois), copy

Jagdgeschwader 52. Monatserfolgsberichte für März, April und Mai 1944 (copy)

Ministero del Aire (Madrid): 'Campaña de Rusia 1941–1944, Escuadrillas Españoles de Caza', MSS (undated), copy

Neumann, Eduard, 'Jafü Balkan – Jafü Rumänien', 3pp MSS (1996)

Valtonen, Hannu (Keski-Suomen Ilmailumuseo), 'Output of Finnish Aviation Industries in 1921–92', 4pp MSS (1996)

Vanags-Baginskis, Alexander, 'Latvian and Estonian units of the Luftwaffe', 21pp MSS with Appendices (copy)

Walkow, Todor, 'Kurze Biographie des Obersten Wassil Walkow' (1996)
   'Die Geschichte der Bulgarischen Luftstreitkräfte bis zum 9. 9.1944, Part I: 1892–1919', 8pp MSS (1996), 'Part II: 1919–1944', 19pp MSS with Appendices (1996)

B: Written and verbal statements

Dr Benno Abram, 4 and 9 October 1996

Kaljo Alaküla, 4 October and 5 December 1996

Hendrik Arro, 7 and 25 May 1996

Henri Dannemark, 22 July 1996

Artur Gärtner, 16 August 1997

Luigi Gorrini, 30 January, 4 March and 20 March 1996

Heinrich Heuser, 20 June and 22 October 1996

Harald Hougen, 29 January, 10 February and 10 March 1996

Joseph Justin, 3 and 13 October 1996

'Joppe' Karhunen, 22 May 1996

Charles F. Kern, 26 September, 5 October and 1 November 1996

Alf Lie, 16 and 29 November 1995

Arnolds Mencis, 20 July 1996

Remi Milk, 10 and 19 March 1997

Eduard Neumann, 29 January 1996

Indulis Ozols, 29 June and 4 July 1996

Arvo Putmaker, 20 November 1996
Valdo Raag, 4 November 1996
Kalju Reitel, 4 October 1996

C: Published Sources (documents, diaries, reminiscences, stories of personal experiences, unit chronicles) and literature

ADAP – Akten zur Deutschen Auswertigen Politik, Serie D, 1937–1941 (Göttingen, 1970): Vol. XIII. 1, June to September 1941; Vol. XIII. 2, September to December 1941; Serie E, 1941–1945 (Göttingen, 1969–1979): Vol. I, December 1941 to February 1942; Vol. II, March to June 1942; Vol. III, June to September 1942; Vol. IV, October to December 1942; Vol. V., January to April 1943; Vol. VI, May to September 1943; Vol. VII, October 1943 to April 1944; Vol. VIII, May 1944 to May 1945

Aders, Gebhard/Held, Werner, *Jagdgeschwader 51 'Mölders'. Eine Chronik. Berichte – Erlebnisse – Dokumente*, 2nd ed. (Stuttgart, 1993)

Aichner, Martino, *II Gruppo Buscaglia. Aerosiluranti italiani nella seconda guerra mondiale* (Milan, 1991)

Aircraft (in German), Issues I (1992) to 216 (1997)

Airdoc (Publ.), *L'Aviation Militaire Française d'Armistice 1940–1942* (Salon-de-Provence, 1993)

Ala Tricolore (Brescia), Issues 1/1986 to 4/1997

Alegi, Gregory, 'La legione che non fu mai. L'Aeronautica Nazionale Repubblicane e la crisi dell'estate 1944', in *Storia contemporanea*, 23rd year of publication, No. 6 (December 1992), pp. 1047, 1985

Alfocar Nassaes, José Luis, *La aviación legionaria en la guerra española* (Barcelona, 1975)

Alves, Rui, 'Quem foram os "Viriatos do Ar"', in *Historia*, No. 35 (Sep 1981), pp. 2–14

Apostolo, Giorgio, *Fiat CR.42* (Ali d'Italia, 1) (Turin, 1995)

    Aer.Macchi C.202 (Ali d'Italia, 2) (Turin, 1995)

    Reggiane Re 2001 (Ali d'Italia, 3) (Turin, 1996)

    Nei cieli di guerra. La Regia Aeronautica a colori 1940–45 (Milan, 1996)

Arena, Nino, *Air War in North Italy 1943–1945* (Modena, 1975)

    La Regia Aeronautica 1943–1946, 2 vols. (Modena, 1975)

    'L'aviazione civile nella R.S.I.', in *Storia Verità*, No. 2 (June–July 1991), pp. 6–9

    '"Il primo e l'ultimo"', in *Storia Verità*, No. 6 (May–June 1992), pp. 14–16

    'L'aviazione dell'onore', in *Storia Verità*, No. 6 (May–June 1992), pp. 1–8

    Reggiane Re 2005 'Saggitario', new ed. (Modena, 1994)

    Macchi 205 'Veltro', new ed. (Modena, 1994)

    Fiat G.55 'Centauro', Fiat G.59, new ed. (Modena, 1994)

    La Regia Aeronautica 1939–1943, Vol. 4, L'anno dell'armistizio (Naples, 1994)

    L'Aeronautica Nazionale Repubblicana. La guerra aerea in Italia 1943–1945 (Parma, 1995)

Arena, Nino/Pini, Giorgio, *Schemi e colori mimetici dell'Aeronautica Militare Italiana*, new ed. (Modena, 1994)

Arráez Cerdá. Juan, 'Los "Viriatos del Aire", Aviadores Portugueses en las Guerra Civil Española', in *Defensa*, No. 222 (October 1996), pp. 55–60

Arro, Hendrik, *Eesti Lendurid Lahingute Tules*, 2nd ed. (Tallinn, 1996)

Arzalier, Francis, *Les perdants. La dérive fasciste des mouvements autonomistes et independantistes au XXe siècle* (Paris, 1990)

Assessorato alla Cultura del Comune di Treviso, *Obiettivo Venerdi Santo. Il bombardamento di Treviso del 7 aprile 1944 nei documenti dell'aeronautica militare statunitense* (Treviso, 1992)

Attard, Joseph, *The Battle of Malta. An epic true story of suffering and bravery* (Valletta, 1988)

Auphan, Paul, *Histoire élémentaire de Vichy* (Paris, 1971)

Avram, Valeriu, *Aviatia de Asalt. Documente si Memorii Grupul 8 1943–1945* (Bucharest, 1994)

 'Les Heinkel 112 roumains', in *Avions*, No. 38 (May 1996), pp. 40–46

 'L'aviation d'assault roumaine de 1943 à 1945', in *Le Fana de l'Aviation*, No. 325 (December 1996), pp. 16–26; No. 326 (January 1997), pp. 48–60

Axworthy, Mark, 'On three fronts. Romania's aircraft industry during World War II', in *Air Enthusiast*, No. 56 (1994), pp. 8–27

 Third Axis, Fourth Ally. Romanian Armed Forces in the European War 1941–1945 (London, 1995)

 'Flank Guard. Romania's Aerial Advance on Stalingrad', in *Air Enthusiast*, No. 64 (July–August 1996), pp. 28–39; No. 65 (September–October 1996), pp. 72–5

 'Balkan Interlude. The Bulgarian Air Arm in WW II', in *Air Enthusiast*, No. 39 (May–August 1989), pp. 58–74

Bateson, Richard P., 'Bulgaria at War, Part 1: Rebirth of an Air Force', in *Air Pictorial* (March 1972), pp. 82–94; 'Part 2: Into Battle', in *Air Pictorial* (April 1972), pp. 140–3; 'Part 3: Under the Allied Onslaught', in *Air Pictorial* (May 1972), pp. 177–81

Baudru, Rémi, 'Vom Denkmal zum Museumsstück', in *Jet & Prop*, 5/1992, pp. 48–51

 'Quand l'Armée de l'Air partit en Syrie combattre la RAF', in *Le Fana de l'Aviation* (October 1993), pp. 16–25

Beale, Nick/D'Amico, Ferdinando/Valentini, Gabriele, *Air War Italy 1944–1945. The Axis Air Forces from the Liberation of Rome to the Surrender* (Shrewsbury, 1996)

Beith, Richard, *The Italian South Atlantic Air Mail Service 1939–1942* (Chester, 1993)

Benoist-Méchin, Jacques, *De la défaite au désastre, Vol. 1: Les occasions manquées. Juillet 1940–avril 1942* (Paris, 1984)

Bernád, Dénes/Mujzer, Péter/Hangya, János, *Horrido. Légicsaták a Keleti Fronton* (Budapest, 1992)

Blake, Steve, 'Ambush over Hungary. A "Puma" Pilot's Revenge', in *Aerial Combat*, No. 14 (1984), pp. 12–20

Blindheim, Svein, *Nordmenn under Hitlers fane. Dei norske frontkjemparane*, 2nd ed. (Noreks Boklag, 1978)

Bonino, Antonio, *Mussolini mi ha detto. Memorie del Vicesegretario del Partito fascista Repubblicano 1944/45* (publ. by Marino Viganò, Rome, 1995)

Bonvicini, Guido, *Carlo Faggioni e gli aerosiluranti italiani* (Milan, 1987)

Boog, Horst, *Die deutsche Luftwaffenführung 1935–1945. Führungsprobleme, Spitzengliederung, Generalstabsausbildung* (Stuttgart, 1982)

 (ed.) *Luftwaffenführung im Zweiten Weltkrieg. Ein internationaler Vergleich* (Vorträge *zur Militärgeschichte*, Vol. 12) (Herford/Bonn, 1993)

Borgiotti, A./Gori, C., *Gli Stuka della R. Aeronautica 1940–1945* (Modena, 1976)

Borgogni, Massimo, *Mussolini e la Francia di Vichy. Dalla dichiarazione di guerra al fallimento del riavvicinamento italo-francese (giugno 1940–aprile 1942)* (Siena, 1991)

Boschesi, B. Palmiro/Rovelli, Mario, 'I mitici "Gobbi" all'attaco disperato di Bougie', in *Storia Illustrata*, No. 318 (May 1984), pp. 106–16

Botquin, Gaston, 'L'epopée du Morane Saulnier 406, Part 9: Dans le ciel de la "brave petite Finlande", le 406 a sa dernière heure de gloire, in *Le Fana de l'Aviation*, No. 108 (November 1978), pp. 23–7

Botquin, Gaston/Roba, Jean-Louis, 'Les avions soviétiques dans la Luftwaffe', in *Avions*, No. 40 (July 1996), pp. 35–8

Bragadin, Marc'Antonio, *Il dramma della marina Italiana 1940–1945* (Milan, 1982)

Buckley, Christopher, *Greece and Crete 1941* (Athens, 1984)

Bucurescu, Ion, *Aviatia Romana pe frontul de est si in apararea teritoriului, Vol. 2: 1 ianuarie 1943–23 august 1944* (Bucharest, 1994)

Bucurescu, Ion/Sandachi, George-Paul, *Aviatia Romana pe frontul de est si in apararea teritoriului, Vol. 1; 22 iunie 1941–31 decembrie 1942* (Bucharest, 1993)

Caballero Jurado, Carlos, 'La Aviacion de la R.S.I. (1943–1945)', in *Defensa*, No. 134 (June 1989), pp. 58–64

Cannistraro, Philip V., *Historical Dictionary of Fascist Italy* (Westport/London, 1982)

Carrera, José Maria Bueno, *The Blue Division and Squadron. Its Organization and Uniforms* (Madrid, 1991)

Caruana, Richard J., *Air War in the Med, Part Two: Air War over Malta. The Axis* (Valletta, 1989)

The Aviazione Nazionale Repubblicana. Italian Air Forces 1943–1945 (Valletta, 1989)

Cecon, Mario, 'Le Officine Aeronautiche di Monfalcone', in *Rivista Storica*, 1/1995, pp. 66–73

Cerdá, Juan Arráez, 'Les avions italiens internés en Espagne, 1942–1945', in *Avions*, No. 29 (August 1995), pp. 32–4

Ceva, Lucio/Curami, Andrea, 'Luftstreitkräfte und Luftfahrtindustrie in Italien, 1936–1943', in Boog, Horst, *Luftkriegführung im Zweiten Weltkrieg* (Herford/Bonn, 1993), pp. 113–136

Chadeau, Emanuel, *L'industrie aéonautique en France 1900–1950. De Blériot à Dassault* (Paris, 1987)

Chiocci, Francobaldo, *Gli affondatori del cielo* (Milan, 1972)

Ciampaglia, Giuseppe, 'Il "Mistero del falco"', in *Rivista Storica*, 6/1994, pp. 36–43

Ciano, Galeazzo, *Diario 1939–43*, 5th ed. (Milan, 1971)

Cimicchi, Giuseppe, *Ali di guerra sul mediterraneo* (Rome, 1980)

Coggi, Igino, 'La caccia di Salò', in *Storia Illustrata*, No. 256 (March 1979), pp. 108–15

Colville, John, *Downing Street Tagebücher 1939–1945* (Berlin, 1991)

Condon, Richard W., *Winterkrieg Russland–Finland* (Munich, 1980)

Cony, Christophe, 'L'Avia B-534, Part 8: B-534 bulgares contre B-24 Liberator', in *Avions*, No. 45 (December 1996), pp. 39–40

Cooper, Matthew, *Die Luftwaffe 1933–1945. Eine Chronik. Versäumnisse und Fehlschläge* (Stuttgart, 1988)

Coppel, Jorge Fernandez, 'Los caidos de la Escuadrilla Azul', in *Defensa*, No. 127 (November 1988), pp. 66–78

'Españoles en Rusia', in *Avion*, 10/1991, pp. 54–7

Corvaja, Santi, 'Perché falli il nostro attacco a Gibilterra', in *Storia Illustrata*, No. 288, pp. 22–8, 32–8

'I cento giorni sulla Manica dei bombardieri italiani', in *Storia Illustrata*, No. 313 (December 1983), pp. 36–48

Coverdale, John F., *La intervención fascista en la Guerra Civil española* (Madrid, 1979)

Curami, Andrea, Appunti sulla Regia Aeronautica nei Balcani 1940–1941, in *Annali della Fondazione 'Luigi Micheletti': L'Italia in guerra 1940–3* (Brescia, 1990–1), pp. 114–53

'Miti realtà dell'industria bellica della R.S.I.', in *Rivista di storia contemporanea*, No. 2–3 (April–July 1993), pp. 309–56

D'Amico, Ferdinando/Grande, Giuseppe, CTV: 'Storie di piloti disarmati', in *JP* 4 (September 1994),pp. 80–6

D'Amico, Ferdinando/Valentini, Gabriele, *The Messerschmitt 109 in Italian Service 1943–1945* (Boylston/Massachusetts, 1985)

Regia Aeronautica, Vol. 2: Pictorial History of the Aeronautica Nazionale Repubblicana and the Italian Co-belligerent Air Force 1943–1945 (Carrollton/Texas, 1986)

'La Legione croata in guerra', in *JP* 4, (April 1993), pp. 57–60

'Cacciatori della notte', in *JP* 4 (January 1995), pp. 74–81

D'Avanzo, Giuseppe, *Ali e poltrone* (Rome, 1976)

Morte a Fregene (Rome, 1993)

De Bruyne, Eddy, *Dans l'étau de Degrelle. Le Service du Travail Obligatoire ou de l'usine à la Waffen-SS* (Jalhay, 1994)

De Felice, Renzo, *Mussolini l'alleato 1940–1945, Part 1: L'Italia in guerra 1940–1943*, 2 vols. (Turin, 1990)

Das Deutsche Reich und der Zweite Weltkrieg, publ. by Militärgeschichtichen Forschungsamt, Vol. 4 (Stuttgart, 1983), Vol. 6 (Stuttgart, 1990)

Dierich, Wolfgang (ed.), *Die Verbände der Luftwaffe 1935–1945* (Stuttgart, 1976)

Kampfgeschwader 55 'Greif'. Eine Chronik aus Dokumenten und Berichten 1937–1945, 2nd ed. (Stuttgart, 1994)

Dos Santos, Sergio Luis, 'Egon Albrecht – a Brazilian Ace in the Luftwaffe', in *Luftwaffe Verband*, No. 10, pp. 19–20

Ehrengardt, Christian, J./Shores, Christopher, F., *L'Aviation de Vichy au Combat, Vol. 1: Les campagnes oubliées, 3 juillet 1940–27 novembre 1942* (Paris, 1985); *Vol. 2: La campagne de Syrie, 8 juin–14 juillet 1941* (Paris, 1987)

Emilian, Ion Valeriu, *Der phantastische Ritt* (Preussisch Oldendorf, 1977)

Emiliani, Angelo/Ghergo, Giuseppe, F./Vigna, Achille, *Regia Aeronautica: periodo prebellico e fronti occidentali* (Milan, 1975)

Regia Aeronautica: il settore mediterraneo (Milan, 1976)

Regia Aeronautica: I fronti africani (Parma, 1979)

Aviazione Italiana: la guerra in Italia (Parma, 1982)

'Die Entstehung der kroatischen Luftwaffenlegion', in *Jägerblatt*, No. 11–12/1963, p. 22

Erfurth, Waldemar, *Der finnische Krieg 1941–1944* (Munich, 1978)

Ericson, Lars, *Svenska Frivilliga* (Stockholm, 1996)

Ernst, Robert, *Rechenschaftsbericht eines Elsässers* (Berlin, 1954)

Facon, Patrick, 'Les forces aériennes roumaines pendant la Seconde Guerre Mondiale: 1939–1945', in *Moniteur de l'Aéronautique*, No. 44, pp. 18–27

'Aperçus sur la collaboration aéronautique Franco-Allemande (1940–1943)', in *Revue d'histoire de la deuxième guerre mondiale*, No. 108 (1977), pp. 85–102

Fast, Niko, *Das Jagdgeschwader 52*, Vols. I–VI (Bergisch Gladbach, 1988–1992)

Fernandez, José, 'La Breda 65', in *Avions*, No. 30 (September 1993), pp. 22–9; No. 31 (October 1995), pp. 21–6; No. 32 (November 1995), pp. 34–7

Finlayson, T. J., *The Fortress Came First. The Story of the Civilian Population of Gibraltar during the Second World War* (Grendon, 1991)

'Finnlands Jagdflieger', in *Jägerblatt*, No. 6/1960, p. 14

Flaccominio, Sergio, *I falchi del deserto*, 3rd ed. (Milan, 1995)

Franks, Norman, *The Battle of the Airfields, 1st January 1945* (London, 1994)

Frka, Daniel, 'Croatian Air Force in WW 2', in *Scale Models International* (May 1993), pp. 26–31; June 1993, pp. 26–32

Les Potez 25 de l'aviation croate 1941–1945, publ. by the editorial staff of the magazine Avions (Boulogne sur Mer, 1996), pp. 198–201

Fröhlich, Sergej, General Wlassow. *Russen und Deutsche zwischen Hitler und Stalin*, revised by Edel von Freier (Cologne, 1987)

Fuentes Verdu, Antonio, 'Alas españoles en las cielo ruso', in *Defensa*, Extra No. 16 (June 1991), pp. 36–40

Gaal, Julius R., 'The Hungarian Air Force in World War II', in *Air Pictorial* (May 1964), pp. 144–8

'Bombers at large', in *Air Combat* (November 1977), pp. 83–9

'The Bridge over the River Bug', in *Air Combat* (March 1978), pp. 80–7

Gaiser, Gerd, *Die sterbende Jagd* (Frankfurt/Hamburg, 1957)

Garello, Giancarlo, *Regia Aeronautica e Armée de l'Air 1940–1943*, 3 vols. (Rome, 1975)

La 173a Sq. RST nella Seconda Guerra Mondiale. Gli uomini e le macchine (Milan, 1981)

'La caccia notturna italiana 1940–1942', in *Aerofan*, No. 57 (April–June 1996), pp. 2–25

'La militarisation de l'Aviation Civile Italienne durant la Seconde Guerre Mondiale', in *Avions*, No. 43 (October 1996), pp. 2–4; No. 44 (November 1996), pp. 3–7

Gatta, Bruno, *Gli uomini del Duce* (Milan, 1986)

Gellermann, Günther W., *Moskau ruft Heeresgruppe Mitte … Was nicht im Wehrmachtbericht stand. Die Einsätze des geheimen Kampfgeschwaders 200 im Zweiten Weltkrieg* (Koblenz, 1988)

Gentilli, Roberto, *Savoia Marchetti S.79 in Action* (Carrollton/Texas, 1988)

Guerra aerea sull'Etiopia 1935–1939 (Florence, 1992)

Gentilli, Roberto/Gorena, Luigi, *Macchi C.202 in Action* (Carrollton/Texas, 1980, new ed. 1995)

Geust, Carl-Fredrik, *Under the Red Star* (Shrewsbury, 1993)

Gibertini, Giorgio, 'Luigi Gorrini M.O.V.M.', in *Aerei*, No. 12 (December 1989), pp. 46–52

Girbig, Werner, *Start im Morgengrauen, Eine Chronik vom Untergang der deutschen Jagdwaffe in Westen 1944/45* (Stuttgart, 1989)

Gosztony, Peter, *Hitlers fremde Heere. Das Schicksal der nichtdeutschen Armeen im Ostfeldzug* (Düsseldorf/Vienna, 1976)

369

Endkampf an der Donau 1944/45 (Vienna/Munich, 1978)

Deutschlands Waffengefährten an der Ostfront 1941–1945 (Stuttgart, 1981)

'Ungarns militärische Rolle im Zweiten Weltkrieg', in *Wissenschaftliche Rundschau*, No. 5/1977, pp. 158–65; No. 5/1981, pp. 152–60; No. 6/1981, pp. 183–9; No. 5/1982, pp. 157–64

Stalins fremde Heere. Das Schicksal der nichtsowjetischen Truppen in Rahmen der Roten Armee 1941–1945 (Bonn, 1991)

Grande, Giuseppe, 'La caccia notturna scientifica 1942–1943', in *Aerofan*, No. 58 (July–September 1996), pp. 127–40

Green, William, *Augsburg Eagle. The Messerschmitt Bf 109* (Harvest Hill, 1987)

Griehl, Manfred/Dressel, Joachim, *Die deutschen Kampfflugzeuge im Einsatz 1936–1945* (Wölfersheim/Berstadt, 1990)

Gumbrecht, Heinz Ulrich/Kittler, Friedrich/Siegert, Bernhard (eds.), *Der Dichter als Kommandant. D'Annunzio erobert Fiume* (Munich, 1996)

Gunston, Bill, *Military Aviation Library World War II. Japanese and Italian Aircraft* (London, 1985)

Harvey, S., 'L'effort de guerre italien et le bombardement stratégique de l'Italie', in *Revue d'histoire de la deuxième guerre mondiale*, No. 143 (July 1986), pp. 61–77

Hefty, U, 'Hungarian Ace (György Debrödy)', in *RAF Flying Review*, Vol. 17, No. 3, pp. 33–4, 44

Heinkel, Ernst/Thorwald, Jürgen, *Stürmisches Leben* (Munich, 1977)

Hentschel, Georg, *Die geheimen Konferenzen des Generalluftzeugmeisters* (Koblenz, 1989)

Herhudt von Rohden, Hans-Detlef, *Die Luftwaffe ringt um Stalingrad* (Berlin, 1993)

Herrera Alonso, Emilio, 'Viriatos do Ar. Aviadores portugueses en la guerra de España', in *Aeroplano*, No. 12/1994, pp. 126–34

Herrmann, Friedrich, 'Uniformbesonderheiten des spanischen "Blauen Division" und "Blauen Staffel", in *Zeitschrift für Heereskunde*, No. 260/261 (1975), pp. 132–42

Herrmann, Hajo, *Bewegtes Leben. Kampf- und Jagdflieger 1935–1945* (Munich, 1993)

Hillgruber, Andreas/Hümmelchen, Gerhard, *Chronik des Zweiten Weltkrieges. Kalendarium militärischer und politischer Ereignisse 1939–1945* (Königstein, 1978)

Höfling, Rudolf, 'Das italienische Jagdflugzeug mit dem amerikanischen Aussehen. Reggiane Re 2000 Falco', in *Flugzeug*, No. 1/1993, pp. 23–4

Hoffmann, Joachim, *Die Geschichte der Wlassow-Armee* (Freiburg, 1984)

Hoppe, Hans-Joachim, *Bulgarien – Hitlers eigenwilliger Verbündeter* (Stuttgart, 1979)

Irving, David, *Die Tragödie der deutschen Luftwaffe, aus den Akten und Erinnerungen von Feldmarschall Erhard Milch* (Frankfurt/Berlin, 1990)

Ivanov, C./Dicev, N./Liège, F., 'Bulgarian Aircraft Industry 1924–1945', in *Skyways*, Issue 33 (January 1955), pp. 18–33

Jäckel, Eberhard, *Frankreich in Hitlers Europa. Die deutsche Frankreichpolitik im Zweiten Weltkrieg* (Stuttgart, 1996)

Jane's Fighting Aircraft of World War II, new ed. (London, 1995)

Jelinek, Yeshayahu, *The Parish Republic: Hlinka's Slovak People's Party 1939–1945* (New York/London, 1976)

Jensen, Tom B./Dahl, Hans-Fredrik, *Parti og plakat NS 1933–1945* (Oslo, 1988)

Jurs, August, *Estonian Freedom Fighters in World War II* (Ontario, 1990)

Juutilainen, Ilmari, *Double Fighter Knight* (Tampere, 1996)

Keskinen, Kalevi, *Dornier Do 17Z, Junkers Ju 88A-4* (Helsinki, 1971), Suomen Ilmavoimien Historia 2

Keskinen, Kalevi/Stenman, Kari/Niska, Klaus, *Fiat G.50* (Forssa, 1977), Suomen Ilmavoimien Historia 8

Venäläiset Pommittajat. Soviet Bombers (Forssa, 1982), Suomen Ilmavoimien Historia 9

Bristol Blenheim (Forssa, 1984), Suomen Ilmavoimien Historia 10

Englantilaiset Hävittäjät (Forssa, 1985), Suomen Ilmavoimien Historia 12

Syöksypommittajat. Dive Bombers and Liaison Aircraft (Forssa, 1989), Suomen Ilmavoimien Historia 13

Suomalaiset Hävittäjät (Kangasala, 1990), Suomen Ilmavoimien Historia 14

Messerschmitt Bf 109G (Forssa, 1991), Suomen Ilmavoimien Historia 6

Hävittäjä-Ässät. Finnish Fighter Aces, 2nd ed. (Forssa, 1994). Suomen Ilmavoimien Historia 11

Brewster Model 239, 4th ed. (Forssa, 1995), Suomen Ilmavoimien Historia 15

Meritoimintakoneet. Maritime Aircraft (Tampere, 1995), Suomen Ilmavoimien Historia 15

Ketley, Barry/Rolfe, Mark, *Luftwaffe Fledglings 1935–1945. Luftwaffe Training Units and their Aircraft* (Aldershot, 1996)

Kiehl, Heinz, *Kampfgeschwader 'Legion Condor', 53. Eine Chronik, Berichte, Erlebnisse, Dokumente 1936–1942*, 2nd ed. (Stuttgart, 1996)

Kitchens, James, H./Beaman, John R., 'Wie das Rätsel um die Bf 109G-6 "weisse 2" geklärt wurde', in *Jet & Prop*, No. 1/1997 (March–April 1997), pp. 40–4

Kleinfeld, Gerald R./Tambs, Lewis, A., *Hitler's Spanish Legion. The Blue Division in Russia* (London/Amsterdam, 1979)

Klemm, Peter F., 'La production aéonautique française de 1940 à 1942', in *Revue d'histoire de la deuxième guerre mondiale*, No. 107 (1977), pp. 53–74

Korbuly, Deszö, 'Ungarns Eintritt in den Zweiten Weltkrieg', in *Der Donauraum*, No. 1/1971, pp. 18–27

Kowatschew, Assen, 'Als bulgarische Jagdflieger in Werneuchen waren', in *Jägerblatt*, Issue 4/1996, pp. 20–3

Krajc, Milan, 'Messerschmitt Bf 109 in the Slovak Air Arms', in *Luftwaffe Verband* (July 1997), pp. 19–28

Kriegstagebuch des Oberkommandos der Wehrmacht 1939–1945, 8 vols., publ. by P. E. Schramm, (Herrsching, 1982)

Krug, Augusto, 'Aviadores portugueses na guerra de Espanha (1938–39)', in *Mais Alto* (May 1964)

Lambert, Pierre Philippe/Le Marec, Gérard, *Partis et mouvements de la collaboration. Paris 1940–1944* (Paris, 1993)

Les Français sous le casque allemand. Europe 1941–1945 (Paris, 1994)

Larrazábal, Jesus Salas, *Das Flugzeug im spanischen Bürgerkrieg 1936–1939: Flieger auf beiden Seiten* (Stuttgart, 1973)

'Actuacion en Rusia de las Escuadrillas Expedicionarias Españolas', in *Aeroplano*, No.2 (October 1984), pp. 51–96

Larsen, Stein U., 'Die Ausschaltung der Quislinge in Norwegen', in Henke, Klaus-

BIBLIOGRAPHY

Dietmar/Woller, Hans (eds.), *Politische Säuberung in Europa. Die Abrechnung mit Faschismus und Kollaboration nach dem Zweiten Weltkrieg* (Munich, 1991), pp. 241–80

Lazzati, Guilio, *Ali nella tragedia. Gli aviatori italiani dopo 1'8 settembre* (Milan, 1970)

Ledet, Michael, 'L'Arado 65. Le premier chasseur d'Hitler', Part 2, in *Avions*, No. 49 (April 1997), pp. 17–21

Lefèvre, Eric/Mabire, Jean, *La LVF 1941. Par –40° devant Moscou* (Paris, 1985)

Lévay, Gyozo, 'I proved my point', in *RAF Flying Review*, Vol. XVII, No. 8, pp. 32–3, 47

Leysen, André, *Hinter dem Spiegel. Eine Jugend in Flandern 1939–1945* (Munich, 1996)

Licheri, Sebastiano, *L'arma aerea italiana nella seconda guerra mondiale. 10 giugno 1940–8 settembre 1943* (Milan, 1976)

Liège, Frédéric, 'Croatian Air Force 1941–1945', in SAFO, Vol. 17, No. 1 (65) (January 1993), pp. 9–12; Vol. 17 (68) (December 1993), pp. 115–20; Vol. 18, No. 3 (71) (September 1994), pp. 81–5

Littlejohn, David, *Foreign Legions of the Third Reich, Vol. 1: Norway, Denmark, France* (San Jose/California, 1979)

Longo, Luigi Emilio, 'Intervista con Giuseppe Baylon, primo e ultimo capodi di S.M. dell'Aeronautica della R.S.I.', in *Storia Verità*, No. 6 (May–June 1992), pp. 14–16

R.S.I. Antologia per un'atmosfera (Milan, 1995)

Lottman, Herbert, *L'épuration 1943–1953* (Paris, 1986)

L.R., '1 luglio 1933–1 luglio 1993. Sessant'anni fa la mitica trasvolata dell centuri alata di Balbo', in *Storia Verità*, No. 12 (August–December 1993), pp. 16–21

Lucchini, Carlo, 'Croati sul G.50', in *JP* 4 (February 1994), pp. 80–6

Lufthansa Dokumentationsdienst No. 90–4: Der Flugzeugpark der Deutschen Lufthansa AG 1926–1945 (Cologne, no date)

Luukkanen, Eino, *Fighter over Finland. The Memoirs of a Fighter Pilot* (London, 1963)

Madej, Victor, *Southeastern Europe Axis Armies Handbook* (Allentown/Pennsylvania, 1982)

Malizia, Nicola, *Ali nella tragedia di Spagna (1936–1939)* (Modena, 1986)

Ali sulla steppa. La Regia Aeronautica nella campagna di Russia (Rome, 1987)

Margosein, Kim/Boshniakov, Stephen, 'A forgotten Ace', in SAFO, Vol. 19, No. 1 (73) (April 1995), p. 29

Mari, Roberto, 'Operazione "S" obiettivo Manhattan', in *Storia Verità*, No. 18 (November–December 1994), pp. 37–9

'Una notte di cinquant'anni fa nella pineta di Fregene', in *Storia Verità*, No. 13 (January–February 1994), pp. 12–16

Massimello, Giovanni, 'Un pilota del "Quarto" raconta. Ricordi del sergente maggiore pilota Amleto Monterumici della 90ª Squadriglia, 10° Gruppo, 4° Stormo Caccia Terrestre', in *Aerofan*, No. 58 (July–September 1996), pp. 115–26

'Gli assi della caccia italiana (1940–1945)', in *Storia Militare*, No. 6 (March 1994), pp. 34–7

'Ancora sugli assi italiani', in *Storia Militare*, No. 28 (January 1996), pp. 15–19

Massini, Vitaliano, '1941 – l'Irak contro l'Inghilterra', in *Storia Verità*, No. 2 (June–July 1991), pp. 21–3

Messe, Giovanni, *Der Krieg im Osten* (Zürich, 1948)

Minniti, Fortunato, 'Aspetti dell politica fascista degli armamenti dal 1935 al 1943', in De Felice, Renzo (ed.), *L'Italia fra tedeschi e alleati. La politica estera fascista e la seconda guerra mondiale* (Bologna, 1973), pp. 127–37

Mombeek, Eric, *Reichsverteidigung. Die Geschichte des Jagdgeschwaders 1 'Oesau'* (Brussels, 1993)

Morris, Eric, *La guerra inutile. La campagna d'Italia 1943–1945*, 2nd ed. (Milan, 1994)

Mujzer, Péter, 'Royal Hungarian Air Force 1938–1939', in SAFO, Vol. 18, No. 2 (70) (June 1994), pp. 41–4; Vol. 18, No. 3 (71) (September 1994), pp. 87–91

'Les Heinkel 112 hongrois', in *Avions*, No. 37 (April, 1996), pp. 39–42

'Les Messerschmitt Me 210 Ca hongrois', in *Avions*, No. 46 (January 1997), pp. 10–14; No. 47 (February 1997), pp. 14–18; No. 48 (March 1997), pp. 22–30

Musciano, Walter A., *Die berühmten Me 109 und ihre Piloten 1939–1945* (Augsburg 1994)

Nebelin, Manfred A., '"Barbarossa" und Ungarn. Aus dem Kriegstagebuch des Deutschen Generals beim Oberkommando der Königlich Ungarischen Wehrmacht 1941', in *Militärgeschichtliche Mitteilungen*, 53 (1994), pp. 101–2

Neulen, Hans Werner, *An deutscher Seite. Internationale Freiwillige von Wehrmacht und Waffen-SS*, 2nd ed. (Munich, 1992)

'Internationales fliegendes Personal der deutschen Luftwaffe 1939–1945', in *Der Tanzbödeler*, 11th year of publ. (1993), No. 43, pp. 17–23

'Bis zum bitteren Ende' (Geschichte der Aeronautica Nazionale Repubblicana), in *Jet & Prop*, 4/1993, pp. 38–44; 5/1993, pp. 40–5

'Der letzte der "wütenden Wespen"' (Luigi Gorrini), in *Jet & Prop*, 4/1996, pp. 13–17

'"Orangen auf New York". Fernkampfeinsätze der Regia Aeronautica', in *Jet & Prop* 4/1997, pp. 15–20

'David gegen Goliath. Die finnische Luftwaffe im Winterkrieg 1939/40', in *Jet & Prop*, 3/1999, pp. 16–23

'Le dernier chevalier: "Joppe" Karhunen', in *Avions*, No. 76 (July 1999), pp. 54–8

'Un as italien de la chasse et des Stukas: Ennio Tarantola', in *Avions*, No. 77 (August 1999), pp. 41–7

Newby, Leroy, W., *Into the Guns of Ploesti. The human drama of the Bomber war for Hitler's oil, 1942–1944* (Osceola/USA, 1991)

Noël, Jean/Passingham, Malcolm, 'Les avions militaires roumaines de 1910 à 1945', in *Le Fana de l'Aviation*, No. 238 (September 1989), pp. 34–40

Norling, S. Erik, *Sangre en la Nieve. Voluntarios europeos en la Ejército finlandés y la Waffen-SS en el Frente de Finlandia (1939–1945)* (Granada, 1996)

Nowarra, Heinz J., *Die deutsche Luftrüstung 1933–1945*, Vols. 1–4 (Koblenz, 1993)

Omrčanin, Ivo, *The pro-Allied putsch in Croatia in 1944 and the massacre of Croatians by Tito communists in 1945* (Philadelphia, 1975)

Ory, Pascal, *Les collaborateurs 1940–1945* (Paris, 1976)

Ott, Günther, '1941: Als die Luftwaffe für den Irak flog', in *Jet & Prop*, 3/1991, pp. 23–6, 34; 4/1991, pp. 50–2

Ozols, Indulis, 'Seržanta Klinta pēdējais lidojums', in *Daugavas Vanagi* (January–February 1992), pp. 18–25

Pagliano, Franco, 'Vita e morte di un soldate' (Adriano Visconti), in *Candido*, No. 20/1955 of 15 May 1955

Aviatori italiani (Milan, 1970)

Pallotelli, Virgilio, 'Le memorie inedita del pilota del Duce', in *Storia Illustrata*, No. 332 (July 1985), pp. 10–11

Patience, Kevin, 'The Italian Raid on Bahrain', in *After the Battle*, Issue 56 (1987), pp. 18–21

Pebal, Hans von, *Hrvatska Krila. Die kroatischen Flieger im 2. Weltkrieg* (Graz, no publication date)

Pedriali, Ferdinando, 'Disastro aereo nel Mediterraneo', in *Rivista Storica*, 3/1995, pp. 34–40

'L'Aviazione del Negus. La prima forza dell'Africa nera', in *Rivista Storica*, 9/1995, pp. 27–31

'Biplani d'assalto in Africa Settentrionale', in *Rivista Storica*, 10/1995, pp. 14–24

Pelliccia, Antonio, *La Regia Aeronautica. Dalle origini all Seconda Guerra Mondiale (1923–1943)* (Rome, 1992)

Pentelescu, Aurel/Dobre, Florica/Craciunoiu, Cristian, *Gruparea Aeriana de Lupta 22.09–16.10.1941. Liberation of Bessarabia and Conquest of Odessa* (Bucharest, 1995)

Perez San Emeterio, Carlos, 'La última lección de Indalecio Rego', in *Aeroplano*, No. 11/1993, pp. 8–18

Pesce, Giuseppe, *L'8° Gruppo Caccia in due conflitti mondiali* (Modena, 1974)

L'Aeronautica Italiana all'epilogo del conflitto, publ. by the Associazione Nazionale Ufficiali dell'Aeronautica (no date or place of publication)

'L'Aeronautica Italiana nel 43. Il dramma della suddivisione tra Nord e Sud', in *Rivista Storica*, 6/1994, pp. 72–81

'L'Aeronautica Italiana nella guerra di liberazione', in *Rivista Storica*, 3/1995, pp. 49–55

'L'Aeronautica Nazionale Repubblicana combatte al nord', in *Rivista Storica*, 6/1995, pp. 24–34

'Spie in libertà ad Algeciras. Racconto del Cap. Venanzi', in *Rivista Storica*, 1/1996, pp. 32–9

Petrov, B., 'Die bulgarischen Flugzeuge des deutschen Professors Winter', in *Jet & Prop* 6/1993, pp. 36–7, 42–3; 1/1994, pp. 44–7

Piekalkiewicz, Janusz, *Schweiz 39–45. Krieg in einem neutralen Land*, 2nd ed. (Stuttgart/Zug, 1979)

Luftkrieg 1939–1945 (Munich, 1982)

Krieg auf dem Balkan 1940–1945 (Munich, 1984)

Pirelli, Alberto, *Taccuini 1922/1943* (Bologna, 1984)

Postiglioni, Umberto/Degl'Innocenti, Andrea, *Colori e schemi mimetici dell Regia Aeronautica 1935–1945*, 2nd ed. (Trieste, 1994)

Punka, Georg, 'Einsätzflüge im Dunkel der Nacht (Ungarns Nachtschlachtflieger)', in *Jet & Prop*, 4/1992, pp. 54–6

Hungarian Air Force (Carrollton/Texas, 1994)

'*Messer*'. *The Messerschmitt 109 in the Royal Hungarian 'Honvéd' Air Force* (Budapest, 1995)

Rajlich, Jiři/Sehnal, Jiři, *Slovak Airmen 1939–1945* (Kutná Hora, 1991)

'"Tatra Eagles". The Slovak Air Force in combat, 1942–1945', in *Air Enthusiast*, No. 56 (1994), pp. 63–8

Rajlich, J./Stojczew, Z./Lalak, Z., *Sojusznicy Luftwaffe*, Part 1 (Warsaw, 1997)

Rajlich, J./Lalak, Z./Baczkowski, W./Murawski, M. J., *Sojusznicy Luftwaffe*, Part 2 (Warsaw, 1998)

Rajninec, Juraj/Sanders, James V., 'Conflict over the Carpathians', in *Air Enthusiast* (September 1971), pp. 180–3

Rauchwetter, Gerhard, *'U' über der Ostfront. Als deutscher Kriegsberichter bei einem Kampffliegerverband der Kroatischen Legion* (Zagreb, 1943)

Raunio, Jukka, 'Jörn Ulrich vapaaehtoisten valioita', in *Suomen Ilmailuhistoriallinen Lehti*, 1/1996, pp. 10–12

Reuth, Ralf Georg, *Entscheidung im Mittelmeer. Die südliche Peripherie Europas in der deutschen Strategie des Zweiten Weltkrieges 1940–1942* (Koblenz, 1985)

Ricci, Corrado, *Il Corpo Aereo Italiano (C.A.I.) sul fronte della Manica (1940–1941)* (Rome, 1994)

Rigoli, Adelmo, *1943: Decollo verso l'ignoto* (Trieste, 1993)

Ring, Hans/Girbig, Werner, *Jagdgeschwader 27*, 6th ed. (Stuttgart, 1979)

Ritaranta, Eino, 'Vapaaehtoisia Vaivaksi Asti', in *Suomen Ilmailuhistoriallinen Lehti*, 1/1996, pp. 13–19

Roba, Jean-Louis/Botquin, Gaston, 'Les avions français dans la Luftwaffe', in *Avions*, No. 29 (August 1995), pp. 28–31; No. 30 (September 1995), pp. 30–2; No. 31 (October 1995), pp. 38–41

Roba, Jean-Louis/Craciunoiu, Cristian, *Seaplanes over the Black Sea. German-Romanian operations 1941–1944* (Bucharest, 1995)

  La chasse de nuit germano-roumaine 1943–1944 (Bucharest, 1997)

Roba, Jean-Louis/Mombeek, Eric, 'Les Macchi 205 au sein du II/JG 77', in *Replic*, No. 12 (July–August 1992), pp. 35–7

  La chasse de jour allemande en Roumanie (Bucharest, 1994)

Rocca, Gianni, *I desperati. La tragedia dell'aeronautica italiana nella seconda guerra mondiale* (Milan, 1991)

Rochat, Giorgio, *Italo Balbo, aviatore e ministro dell'aeronautica 1926–1933* (Ferrara, 1979)

  'Le Forze Aeree Italiane dall'armistizio alla liberazione', in *Studi e ricerche di storia contemporanea*, No. 43 (June 1995), pp. 25–44

Rohwer, J./Hümmelchen, G., *Chronik des Seekrieges 1939–1945* (Herrsching, no date)

Rosch, Barry C., *Luftwaffe Codes, Markings & Units 1939–1945* (Atglen/USA, 1995)

Rotaru, Jipa/König, Carol/Dutu, Alesandru (eds.), *Romanian Army in World War II* (Bucharest, 1995)

Rovelli, Mario, 'S.79 "Sparviero"', in *Storia Illustrata*, No. 318 (May 1984), pp. 117–21

Sandström, Allan, *Krieg unter der Mitternachtssonne. Finnlands Freiheitskampf 1939–1945* (Graz, 1996)

Sárhidai, Gyula/Punka, Gyögy/Kozlik, Viktor, *Hungarian Eagles. The Hungarian Air Forces 1929–1945* (Aldershot, 1996)

Satta, Mario, 'Un pilota dell'Aeronautica Repubblicana. Un ricordo del tenente Vittorio Satta', in *Storia Militare*, No. 14 (November 1994), pp. 36–44

Savič, Dragan/Micevski, Milan, 'Ustaška Lovacka Legija na istočnom Frontu', in *Aerosvet* (October–November 1991), pp. 40–1

'Das Schicksal unsere kroatischen Kamaraden', in *Jägerblatt*, No. 1/1963, pp. 4–5

Schmoll, Peter, *Die Messerschmitt-Werke im Zweiten Weltkrieg. Die Flugzeugproduktion der Messerschmitt GmbH Regensburg von 1938 bis 1945* (Regensburg, 1998)

Schreier, Hans, *JG 52. Das erfolgreichste Jagdgeschwader des Zweiten Weltkrieges* (Berg am See, 1990)

Schröder, Bernd Philipp, *Irak 1941* (Freiburg, 1980)

Segrè, Claudio G., *Italo Balbo* (Bologna, 1988)

Semerdjiev, Steven/Petrov, Iwan, 'Der "fliegende Bleistift" unter fremder Flagge', in *Flugzeug* 2/1993, pp. 45–6

Sgarlato, Nico, *Italian Aircraft of World War II* (Warren/Michigan, 1979)

Shores, Christopher F., 'Finland's Air War, Part 1: The Winter War', in *Air Pictorial*, No. 6/1968, pp. 192–6; 'Part 2: Continuation War', in *Air Pictorial*, No. 7/1968, pp. 231–4
Finnish Air Force 1918–1968 (London, 1969)
Regia Aeronautica, Vol. 1: A Pictorial History of the Italian Air Force 1940–1943 (Carrollton/Texas, 1976)
Dust Clouds in the Middle East. The air war for East Africa, Iraq, Syria, Iran and Madagascar, 1940–1942 (London, 1996)

Silgailis, Arturs, *Latvian Legion* (San Jose/California, 1986)

Silvestri, Armando, 'L'ultima caduto a difesa del cielo italiano', *in Secolo d'Italia* (5.6.1986); also in *Ala Tricolore*, No. 3/1997, p. 4

Spaggiari, L./D'Agostino, C., *SM-79 il gobbo maledotto* (Milan, 1979)

Stahl, P. W., *'Geheimgeschwader' KG 200. Die Wahrheit nach über 30 Jahren*, 3rd ed. (Stuttgart, 1980)

Stapfer, Hans Heiri, 'Aus Freund wurde Feind (Rumäniens Luftwaffe im 2. Weltkrieg)', in *Jet & Prop*, 2/1992, pp. 48–53; 3/1992, pp. 40–4
'Beim Rollen waren die I.A.R. 80 Piloten blind', in *Jet & Prop*, 2/1997, pp. 18–25

Steinhoff, Johannes, *Die Strasse von Messina. Tagebuch des Kommodore* (Munich, 1973)
In letzter Stunde. Verschwörung der Jagdflieger (Bergisch Gladbach, 1977)

Stenman, Kari, 'The Anti-Soviet Tupolevs. Finland's Russian Bombers', in *Air Enthusiast*, No. 27, pp. 9–20
'Battle Unit Kuhlmey', in *Air Enthusiast*, No. 34 (September–December 1987), pp. 1–7
'Finland's Frontline. The Bf 109 in Finnish Service', in *Air Enthusiast*, No. 50 (May–July 1993), pp. 52–9
'Short, but gallant. The career of the Finnish Junkers Ju 88s', in *Air Enthusiast*, No. 60 (November–December 1995), pp. 35–40
'Gloster Trilogy. Finland's use of Gloster biplanes', in *Air Enthusiast*, No. 66 (November–December 1996), pp. 35–40

Stipdonk, Paul/Meyer, Michael, *Das Jagdgeschwader 51 (Mölders). Eine Bilddokumentation über die Jahre 1938–1945* (Zweibrücken, 1996)

Stöber, Hans, *Die lettischen Divisionen im VI.SS-Armeekorps* (Osnabrück, 1981)

Storck, Rudolf, 'Endstation USA. Wie eine Ju 88 vor fünfzig Jahren nach Amerika flog', in *Flugzeug*, 5/1994, pp. 17–21

Svenska frivilliga I Finland 1939–44 (Stockholm, no date)

Taylor, Blaine, *Fascist Eagle. Italy's Air Marshal Italo Balbo* (Missoula/Montana, 1996)

Thiele, Harold/Arráez Cerdá, Juan, 'Die "Blauen Staffeln" in Russland', in *Flugzeug*, 2/1995, pp. 50–3; 3/1995, pp. 20–4

Thomas, Hugh, *The Spanish Civil War*, 3rd ed. (Harmondsworth, 1979)

Thomas, Nigel, *Foreign Volunteers of the Allied Forces 1939–45* (London, 1991)

Thompson, Jonathan, *Italian Civil and Military Aircraft 1930–1945* (Fallbrook/California, 1963)

Tobak, Tibor, *Les Pumas Rouges, Témoignage d'un as de la chasse hongroise 1941–1945* (no place of publ., 1996)

Toliver, Raymond F./Constable, Trevor J., *Adolf Galland, General der Jagdflieger. Eine Biographie* (Munich, 1992)

Traietti, Luciano, *Gli eroi dimenticati* (Rome, 1982)

Traversari, Bruno, 'Dal raid su Tokyo al progetto New York', in *Storia Illustrata*, No. 318 (1984), pp. 33–40

Urwich-Ferry, Johann, *Ohne Pass durch de U.d.S.S.R.*, 2 vols. (Munich, 1982)

Vaccari, Pier Francesco, 'DB-601, DB-605: I 12 cilindri dell'Asse', in *Rivista Storica* (April, 1996), pp. 61–9

Vadillo, Fernando, *Balada final de la Division Azul. Los Legionarios* (Madrid, 1996)

Vasari, Emilio, *Ein Königsdrama im Schatten Hitlers. Die Versuche des Reichsverwesers Horthy zur Gründung einer Dynastie* (Vienna/Munich, 1968)

Vergnano, Piero, *Fiat G.50* (Turin, 1997), Ali d'Italia 6

Viganò, Marino, 'Quell'aereo per la Spagna ...', in *Storia Verità*, No. 23–24 (September–December 1995), pp. 4–10

Vincz, Jan, *Vlaanderen in Uniform 1940–1945*, Vol. 4 (Antwerpen, 1982)

Vizanty, Dan, 'Die Rumänen flogen keine Fw 190. Wie am 10. Juli 1944 die Gruppe Vizanty 24 Lightnings abschoss', in *Jägerblatt*, 5/1983, pp. 32–6

'Un grand nom de l'Aviation: le Prince Cantacuzène-Bizu. "Alea jacta est"', in *Pionniers, Revue Aéronautique*, No. 81 (1984), pp. 30–4; No. 82 (1984), pp. 22–32. Abbr. German text under the title 'Wie aus Waffenbrüder Kriegsgegner wurden', in *Jägerblatt*, No. 6/1988, pp. 12–19; No. 1/1989, pp. 8–12

Vlad, Danut, 'Uncle Sam's Baksheesh', in *Air Pictorial* (October 1994), pp. 246–7

Völkl, Ekkehard, 'Abrechnungsfuror in Kroatien', in Henke, K.-D./Woller, H. (eds.), *Politische Säuberung in Europa. Die Abrechnung mit Faschismus und Kollaboration nach dem Zweiten Weltkrieg* (Munich, 1991), pp. 358–94

Voltan, Paolo, *Un pilota del cavallino rampante* (Battaglia Terme, 1990)

Vrany, Jiři, *Avia B-534* (Prague, 1994)

Warlimont, Walter, *Im Hauptquartier der deutschen Wehrmacht 39–45. Grundlagen, Formen, Gestalten*, 3rd ed. (Munich, 1978)

Die Wehrmachtberichte 1939–1945, 3 vols. (Munich, 1985)

'"Wir haben bewusst mit dem Sowjetsystem gebrochen." Frühere Offiziere der Sowjet-Luftwaffe sprechen zu den Ostarbeiter', in *Die Aktion* (April/May 1944), pp. 170–4

Index of Names